CBSE Term II 2022

Science

Class X

Complete Theory Covering NCERT

Case Based Questions

Short/Long Answer Type Questions

3 Practice Papers with Explanations

Author
Physics *(Naman Jain)*
Chemistry *(Jyoti Aggarwal)*
Biology *(Anam Aarzoo)*

arihant
ARIHANT PRAKASHAN (School Division Series)

ARIHANT PRAKASHAN (School Division Series)

卐 **Administrative & Production Offices**

Regd. Office
'Ramchhaya' 4577/15, Agarwal Road, Darya Ganj, New Delhi -110002
Tele: 011- 47630600, 43518550

卐 **Head Office**
Kalindi, TP Nagar, Meerut (UP) - 250002, Tel: 0121-7156203, 7156204

卐 **Sales & Support Offices**
Agra, Ahmedabad, Bengaluru, Bareilly, Chennai, Delhi, Guwahati, Hyderabad, Jaipur, Jhansi, Kolkata, Lucknow, Nagpur & Pune.

卐 **ISBN :** 978-93-25796-62-1

PO No : TXT-XX-XXXXXXX-X-XX

Published by Arihant Publications (India) Ltd.

For further information about the books published by Arihant, log on to www.arihantbooks.com or e-mail at info@arihantbooks.com

Follow us on    

Contents

CHAPTER 01
Carbon and its Compounds   *1-17*

CHAPTER 02
Periodic Classification of Elements   *18-33*

CHAPTER 03
How do Organisms Reproduce?   *34-53*

CHAPTER 04
Heredity and Evolution   *54-69*

CHAPTER 05
Electricity   *70-90*

CHAPTER 06
Magnetic Effects of Electric Current   *91-107*

CHAPTER 07
Our Environment   *108-124*

Practice Papers (1-3)   *125-136*

Watch Free Learning Videos

Subscribe **arihant** You Tube Channel

- ☑ Video Solutions of CBSE Sample Papers
- ☑ Chapterwise Important MCQs
- ☑ CBSE Updates

Syllabus

CBSE Term II Class XII

One Paper   **Max Marks: 40**

No.	Units	Marks
I.	Chemical Substances-Nature and Behaviour: Chapter 4 and 5	10
II.	World of Living: Chapter 8 and 9	13
IV.	Effects of Current: Chapter 12 and 13	12
V.	Natural Resources: Chapter 15	05

THEME MATERIALS

UNIT - I   Chemical Substances - Nature and Behaviour

Chapter–4   Carbon and its Compounds

Carbon compounds: Covalent bonding in carbon compounds. Versatile nature of carbon.Homologous series.

Chapter–5   Periodic Classification of Elements

Periodic Classification of Elements: Need for classification, early attempts at classification of elements (Dobereiner's Triads, Newland's Law of Octaves, Mendeleev's Periodic Table), Modern periodic table, gradation in properties, valency, atomic number, metallic and non-metallic properties.

THEME THE WORLD OF THE LIVING

UNIT - II   World of Living

Chapter–8   How do Organisms Reproduce?

Reproduction: Reproduction in animals and plants (asexual and sexual) reproductive health-need and methods of family planning. Safe sex vs HIV/AIDS.Child bearing and women's health.

Chapter–9   Heredity and Evolution

Heredity: Heredity; Mendel's contribution- Laws for inheritance of traits: Sex determination: brief introduction;

THEME **NATURAL PHENOMENA**

UNIT - IV   Effects of Current

Chapter–12 Electricity

Ohm's law; Resistance, Resistivity, Factors on which the resistance of a conductor depends. Series combination of resistors, parallel combination of resistors and its applications in daily life. Heating effect of electric current and its applications in daily life. Electric power, Interrelation between P, V, I and R.

Chapter–13 Magnetic Effects of Current

Magnetic Effects of Current: Magnetic field, field lines, field due to a current carrying conductor, field due to current carrying coil or solenoid; Force on current carrying conductor, Fleming's Left Hand Rule, Electric Motor, Electromagnetic induction. Induced potential difference, Induced current. Fleming's Right Hand Rule.

THEME **NATURAL RESOURCES**

UNIT - IV   Natural Resources

Chapter–15 Our Environment

Our Environment: Eco-system, Environmental problems, Ozone depletion, waste production and their solutions. Biodegradable and non-biodegradable substances.

CBSE Circular

Acad - 51/2021, 05 July 2021

Exam Scheme Term I & II

केन्द्रीय माध्यमिक शिक्षा बोर्ड

(शिक्षा मंत्रालय, भारत सरकार के अधीन एक स्वायत संगठन)

CENTRAL BOARD OF SECONDARY EDUCATION

(An Autonomous Organisation under the Ministryof Education, Govt. of India)

Special Scheme for 2021-22

A. Academic session to be divided into 2 Terms with approximately 50% syllabus in each term:

The syllabus for the Academic session 2021-22 will be divided into 2 terms by following a systematic approach by looking into the interconnectivity of concepts and topics by the Subject Experts and the Board will conduct examinations at the end of each term on the basis of the bifurcated syllabus. This is done to increase the probability of having a Board conducted classes X and XII examinations at the end of the academic session.

B. The syllabus for the Board examination 2021-22 will be rationalized similar to that of the last academic session to be notified in July 2021. For academic transactions, however, schools will follow the curriculum and syllabus released by the Board vide Circular no. F.1001/CBSE-Acad/Curriculum/2021 dated 31 March 2021. Schools will also use alternative academic calendar and inputs from the NCERT on transacting the curriculum.

C. Efforts will be made to make Internal Assessment/ Practical/ Project work more credible and valid as per the guidelines and Moderation Policy to be announced by the Board to ensure fair distribution of marks.

Details of Curriculum Transaction

- Schools will continue teaching in distance mode till the authorities permit in-person mode of teaching in schools.

- **Classes IX-X: Internal Assessment** (throughout the year-irrespective of Term I and II) would include the *3 periodic tests, student enrichment, portfolio and practical work/ speaking listening activities/ project.*

- **Classes XI-XII: Internal Assessment** (throughout the year-irrespective of Term I and II) would include end of topic or unit tests/ exploratory activities/ practicals/ projects.

- Schools would create a student profile for all assessment undertaken over the year and retain the evidences in digital format.

- CBSE will facilitate schools to upload marks of Internal Assessment on the CBSE IT platform.

- Guidelines for Internal Assessment for all subjects will also be released along with the rationalized term wise divided syllabus for the session 2021-22.The Board would also provide additional resources like sample assessments, question banks, teacher training etc. for more reliable and valid internal assessments.

केन्द्रीय माध्यमिक शिक्षा बोर्ड

(शिक्षा मंत्रालय, भारत सरकार के अधीन एक स्वायत संगठन)

CENTRAL BOARD OF SECONDARY EDUCATION

(An Autonomous Organisation under the Ministryof Education, Govt. of India)

Term I Examinations:

- At the end of the first term, the Board will organize **Term I Examination** in a flexible schedule to be conducted between November-December 2021 with a window period of 4-8 weeks for schools situated in different parts of country and abroad. Dates for conduct of examinations will be notified subsequently.
- The Question Paper will have Multiple Choice Questions (MCQ) including case-based MCQs and MCQs on assertion-reasoning type. Duration of test will be **90 minutes** and it will cover only the rationalized syllabus of **Term I only** (i.e. approx. 50% of the entire syllabus).
- Question Papers will be sent by the CBSE to schools along with marking scheme.
- The exams will be conducted under the supervision of the External Center Superintendents and Observers appointed by CBSE.
- The responses of students will be captured on OMR sheets which, after scanning may be directly uploaded at CBSE portal or alternatively may be evaluated and marks obtained will be uploaded by the school on the very same day. The final direction in this regard will be conveyed to schools by the Examination Unit of the Board.
- Marks of the **Term I** Examination will contribute to the final overall score of students.

Term II Examination/ Year-end Examination:

- At the end of the second term, the Board would organize **Term II or Year-end Examination** based on the rationalized syllabus of Term II only (i.e. approximately 50% of the entire syllabus).
- This examination would be held around **March-April 2022** at the examination centres fixed by the Board.
- The paper will be of **2 hours duration** and have questions of different formats (case-based/ situation based, open ended- short answer/ long answer type).
- In case the situation is not conducive for normal descriptive examination **a 90 minute MCQ based exam** will be conducted at the end of the Term II also.
- Marks of the Term II Examination would contribute to the final overall score.

6. <u>**Assessment / Examination as per different situations**</u>

A. **In case the situation of the pandemic improves and students are able to come to schools or centres for taking the exams.**

Board would conduct Term I and Term II examinations at schools/centres and the theory marks will be distributed equally between the two exams.

B. **In case the situation of the pandemic forces complete closure of schools during November-December 2021, but Term II exams are held at schools or centres.**

Term I MCQ based examination would be done by students online/offline from home - in this case, the weightage of this exam for the final score would be reduced, and weightage of Term II exams will be increased for declaration of final result.

C. **In case the situation of the pandemic forces complete closure of schools during March-April 2022, but Term I exams are held at schools or centres.**

Results would be based on the performance of students on Term I MCQ based examination and internal assessments. The weightage of marks of Term I examination conducted by the Board will be increased to provide year end results of candidates.

D. **In case the situation of the pandemic forces complete closure of schools and Board conducted Term I and II exams are taken by the candidates from home in the session 2021-22.**

Results would be computed on the basis of the Internal Assessment/Practical/Project Work and Theory marks of Term-I and II exams taken by the candidate from home in Class X / XII subject to the moderation or other measures to ensure validity and reliability of the assessment.

In all the above cases, data analysis of marks of students will be undertaken to ensure the integrity of internal assessments and home based exams.

Dr. Joseph Emmanuel
Director (Academics)

CHAPTER 01

Carbon and It's Compounds

In this Chapter...

- Covalent Bonding in Carbon Compounds
- Allotropes of Carbon
- Organic Compounds
- Hydrocarbons
- Isomerism
- Functional Groups
- Homologous Series

Carbon is the third most important element after oxygen and hydrogen, for the existence of life on the Earth. The Earth crust has only 0.02% carbon which is present in the form of minerals (like carbonates, hydrogen-carbonates, coal, petroleum, etc.) and the atmosphere has 0.03% of carbon dioxide.

Fuels (like wood, kerosene, coal, LPG, CNG, petrol, etc.) clothing material (like cotton, nylon, polyester, etc.), paper, rubber, plastics, leather, drugs and dyes are all made up of carbon.

Covalent Bonding in Carbon Compounds

The bonds which are formed by the sharing of an electron pair between the atoms (either same or different atoms) are known as **covalent bonds**.

Atomic number of carbon (C) is 6.

So, its electronic configuration $= \overset{K}{2}, \overset{L}{4}$.

Thus, there are 4 electrons in its outermost shell and its octet can be completed by the following two ways

- It could gain 4 electrons and form C^{4-} anion. But for a nucleus having 6 protons, it would be difficult to hold on 10 electrons, i.e. 4 extra electrons.

- It could lose 4 electrons and form C^{4+} cation. But a large amount of energy is required to remove 4 electrons leaving behind a carbon cation with 6 protons in its nucleus holding on just two electrons together, which is not possible.

In order to overcome this problem, carbon shares its valence electrons with other atoms of carbon or with atoms of other elements.

These shared electrons belong to the outermost shells of both atoms and in this way, both atoms attain the nearest noble gas configuration. This type of bonding is called **covalent bonding**.

Compounds having covalent bonds are called **covalent compounds**, these are generally poor conductor of electricity.

Examples of Covalent Bonding

Some example depicting of covalent bonding are as follows

1. Formation of Methane (CH_4)

In the formation of a methane molecule, one carbon atom shares its 4 electrons with four hydrogen atoms (one electron of each hydrogen atom). It shows carbon is tetravalent because it possesses 4 valence electrons and hydrogen is monovalent because it has only 1 valence electron.

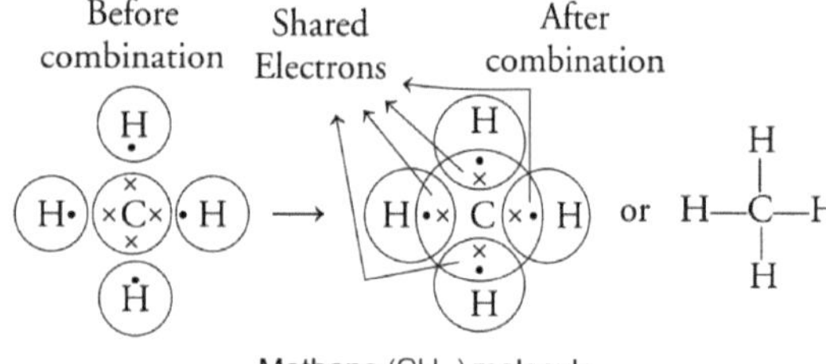

Methane (CH_4) molecule

2. Formation of Water Molecule (H_2O)

Atomic number of $O = 8$

Electronic configuration $= \overset{K}{2}, \overset{L}{6}$

Atomic number of $H = 1$

Electronic configuration $= \overset{K}{1}$

To attain the stable electronic configuration of the nearest noble gas, hydrogen needs 1 electron and oxygen needs 2 electrons. So, two hydrogen atoms share an electron pair with the oxygen atom such that hydrogen acquires a duplet configuration and oxygen an octet, resulting in the formation of two single covalent bonds.

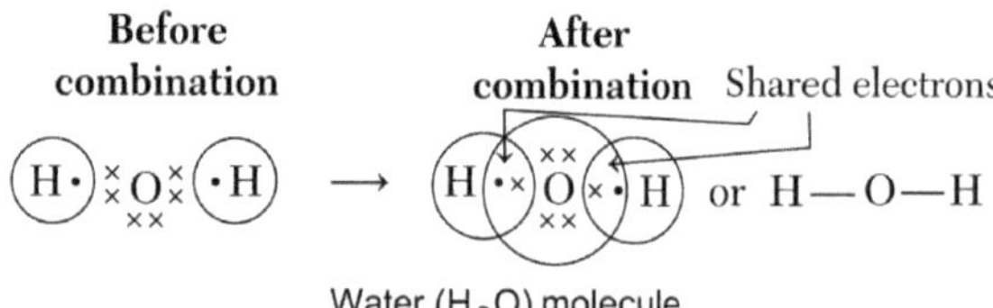

Water (H_2O) molecule

Properties of Covalent Compounds

The compounds containing covalent bonds are called **covalent compounds**. They have following properties i.e.

- Covalent compounds have low melting and boiling points due to small intermolecular forces of attraction between the atoms.
- Covalent compounds are generally poor conductors of electricity. This is because the electrons are shared between atoms and no charged particles are formed in these compounds.
- Covalent compounds are generally volatile in nature.

Allotropes of Carbon

Allotropy is the property by virtue of which an element exists in more than one form and each form has different physical properties but identical chemical properties. These different forms are called allotropes. Carbon exists in different allotropic forms; some of them are diamond, graphite and fullerene.

- Diamond is a colourless transparent substance and very hard whereas graphite is an opaque substance which have smooth surface and slippery to touch.

- Fullerenes are recently discovered allotropic forms of carbon which were prepared for the first time by HW Kroto, Smalley and Robert Curt by the action of laser beam on the vapours of graphite.

Versatile Nature of Carbon

Main factors that are responsible for the formation of large number of carbon compounds are

(i) **Catenation** The property of self linking of elements mainly C-atoms through covalent bonds to form long, straight or branched chains and rings of different sizes is called catenation. Carbon shows maximum catenation in the periodic table due to its small size and strong $C — C$ bond.

(ii) **Tetravalency of carbon** The valency of carbon is four, i.e. it is capable of bonding or pairing with four other carbon atoms or with the atoms of some other monovalent elements like hydrogen, halogen (chlorine, bromine), etc.

(iii) **Tendency to form multiple bonds** Carbon has a strong tendency to form multiple bonds due to it's small size. It shares more than one electron pair with its own atoms or with the atoms of elements like oxygen, nitrogen, sulphur, etc.

Organic Compounds

The compounds of carbon except its oxides, carbonates and hydrogen carbonate salts, are known as organic compounds.

In 1828, German chemist **Friedrich Wohler** accidently prepared urea from ammonium cyanate when he was trying to prepare ammonium cyanate by heating ammonium sulphate and potassium cyanate. Thus, synthesis of urea discarded the vital force theory.

Hydrocarbons

Organic compounds made up of carbon and hydrogen are called hydrocarbons. These are of two types, i.e.

1. Aliphatic Saturated Hydrocarbons

Saturated aliphatic hydrocarbons are called **alkane** or **paraffin**. All the carbon atoms in these are bonded through single bonds. The general formula of these compounds is $C_n H_{2n+2}$ and suffix "-ane" is used in their nomenclature.

e.g. CH_4 (methane), C_2H_6 (ethane), etc.

2. Aliphatic Unsaturated Hydrocarbons

Those compounds in which at least one double or triple bond is present between two carbon atoms are called unsaturated hdyrocarbons.

Aliphatic unsaturated hydrocarbons are of two types

(i) **Alkene** Those hydrocarbons which have at least one carbon-carbon double bond are called alkenes or olefins. The general formula of these compounds is $C_n H_{2n}$, e.g. C_2H_4 (ethene).

(ii) **Alkyne** Those hydrocarbons which must have at least one carbon-carbon triple bond are called alkynes. The general common formula of these compounds is C_nH_{2n-2}, e.g. C_2H_2 (ethyne).

Structure of Saturated and Unsaturated Compounds

Steps to draw the structure of carbon compound are

***Step* I.** First connect all the carbon atoms together with a single bond.

***Step* II.** After that use the hydrogen atoms to satisfy the remaining valencies of carbon (as carbon forms 4 bonds due to its 4 valency).

***Step* III.** If number of available H-atoms are less than what is required, satisfy the remaining valency by using double or triple bond.

1. Structure of Propane (C_3H_8)

Same rules are followed here as in case of ethane. Here, the three carbon atoms are linked together with a single bond.

C—C—C [*Step* I]

To satisfy the remaining valencies of carbon atoms, hydrogen atoms are linked with them.

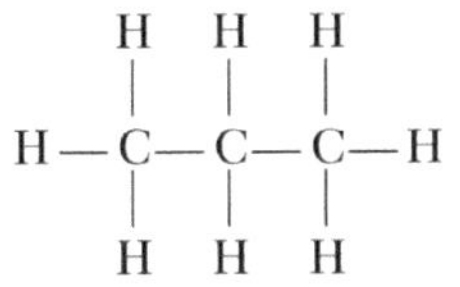

[*Step* II]

2 carbon atoms are bonded to 3 hydrogen atoms and 1 carbon atom is bonded to 2 hydrogen atoms.

Electron dot structure of propane

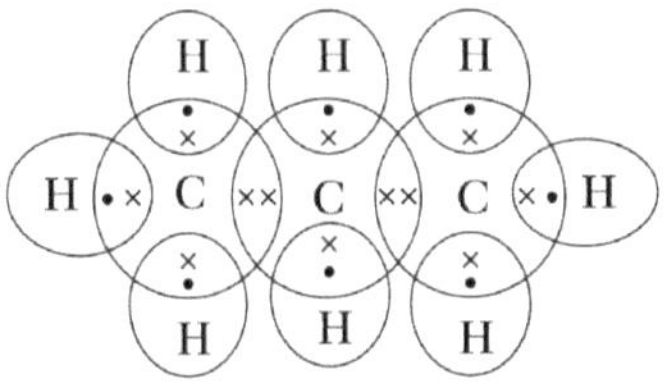

2. Structure of Ethene (C_2H_4)

Link the two carbon atoms by single bond.

C — C [*Step* I]

Link the four hydrogen atoms with carbon atom to satisfy the unsatisfied valencies of carbon.

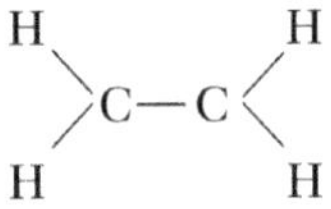

[*Step* II]

But in this case, even after linking the available hydrogen atoms with carbon atoms, still one valency of each carbon remains unsatisfy.

To satisfy it, a double bond is used between the two carbon atoms.

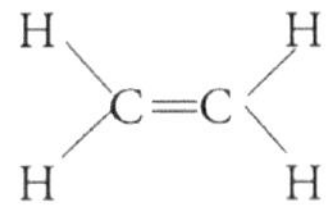

[*Step* III]

Now, all the four valencies of carbon are satisfied.

Electron dot structure of ethene

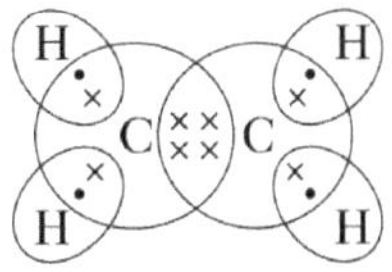

3. Structure of Ethyne (C_2H_2)

Link the two carbon atoms by single bond.

C—C [*Step* I]

Link the two hydrogen atoms with unsatisfied valencies of carbon.

H—C—C—H [*Step* II]

But in this case even after linking the available hydrogen atoms with carbon atoms, still two valencies of each carbon is unsatisfy. To satisfy it, a triple bond is used between the two carbon atoms.

H—C≡C—H [*Step* III]

In ethyne, the two carbon atoms share three pairs of electrons among themselves to form a carbon-carbon triple bond.

Each carbon atom shares one electron with each hydrogen atom to form two carbon-hydrogen single bonds.

Electron dot structure of ethyne

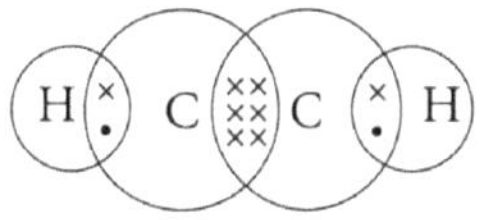

Structure of Cyclic Compounds

In some compounds, carbon atoms are arranged in the form of ring. e.g. cyclohexane (C_6H_{12}) and benzene (C_6H_6).

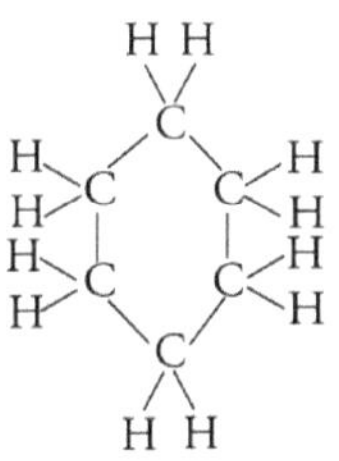

C_6H_{12} (Cyclohexane)

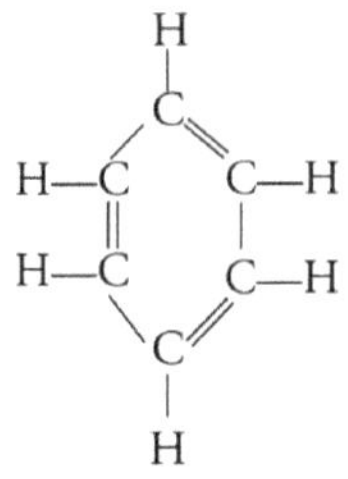

C_6H_6 (Benzene)

Isomerism

Organic compounds with same molecular formula but different chemical and physical properties are called **isomers.** This phenomenon is called **isomerism.**

The difference in properties of these compounds is due to the difference in their structures. These compounds have identical molecular formula but different structures. Hence, they are called **structural isomers** and phenomenon is called **structural isomerism.**

e.g. Two structural isomers are possible for butane $(C_4 H_{10})$.

Straight chain structure   Branched chain structure

Functional Groups

Groups which combine with a carbon chain and decide its chemical properties are called functional groups.

e.g. $-$OH in R—OH will decide the chemical properties of this compound, thus it is a functional group.

Names and Formulae of Functional Group

Name of functional group	Formula of functional group
Alcohol	$-$OH
Aldehyde	$-$CHO or $-\overset{\overset{\displaystyle O}{\|\|}}{C}-$H
Ketone	$-\overset{\overset{\displaystyle O}{\|\|}}{C}-$
Carboxylic acid	$-\overset{\overset{\displaystyle O}{\|\|}}{C}-O-$H

Thus, $-$OH in methyl alcohol (CH_3OH) and $-$COOH (carboxylic acid) in formic acid $(H \cdot COOH)$ are present as functional groups.

Homologous Series

A series of similarly constituted compounds in which the members present have the same functional group and similar chemical properties and any two successive members in a particular series differ in their molecular formula by a $-CH_2-$ unit, is called a homologous series.

e.g. CH_4, C_2H_6, C_3H_8, C_4H_{10} are the members of alkane family.

Chapter Practice

Objective Questions

• Multiple Choice Questions

1. Carbon exists in the atmosphere in the form of
(a) only carbon monoxide **(NCERT Exemplar)**
(b) carbon monoxide in traces and carbon dioxide
(c) only carbon dioxide
(d) coal

2. Which of the following will contain covalent double bond between its atoms?
(a) H_2
(b) O_2
(c) NaCl
(d) Cl_2

3. Which of the following is the correct representation of electron dot structure of nitrogen? **(NCERT Exemplar)**

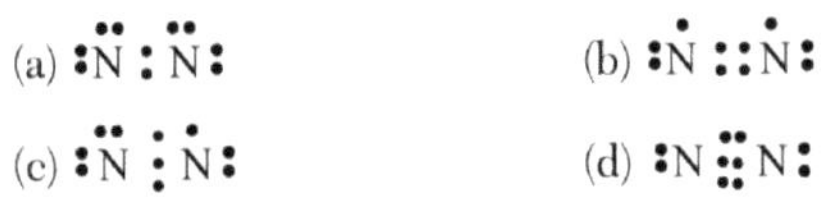

(a) $\ddot{\mathbf{:}}\text{N} : \ddot{\text{N}}\mathbf{:}$
(b) $\mathbf{:}\text{N} :: \text{N}\mathbf{:}$
(c) $\ddot{\mathbf{:}}\text{N} : \dot{\text{N}}\mathbf{:}$
(d) $\mathbf{:}\text{N} :: \text{N}\mathbf{:}$

4. Carbon can use four hydrogen atoms to form methane (CH_4), because
(a) valency of carbon is four
(b) valency of hydrogen is one
(c) Both (a) and (b)
(d) carbon gets noble gas configuration by making four covalent bonds with hydrogen

5. A molecule of ammonia (NH_3) has **(NCERT Exemplar)**
(a) only single bonds
(b) only double bonds
(c) only triple bonds
(d) two double bonds and one single bond

6. The structure of S_8 molecule is .... shaped.
(a) ring
(b) crown
(c) circle
(d) rectangle

7. Which of the following is not the use of graphite?
(a) It is used as lubricant
(b) It is used in manufacturing of lead-pencils
(c) It is used in manufacturing of artificial diamond
(d) It is used for making insulated plates

8. Which of the following elements does not show tetravalency?
(a) Ge
(b) Si
(c) C
(d) O

9. .... is the first synthesised organic compound.
(a) Alcohol
(b) Urea
(c) Vinegar
(d) Benzene

10. Pentane has the molecular formula C_5H_{12}. It has **(NCERT Exemplar)**
(a) 5 covalent bonds
(b) 12 covalent bonds
(c) 16 covalent bonds
(d) 17 covalent bonds

11. Match the following :

Column I	Column II
A. C_3H_8	(i) Cyclic compound
B. C_6H_6	(ii) Alkyne
C. C_2H_2	(iii) Alkene
D. C_4H_8	(iv) Alkane

Codes

	A	B	C	D
(a)	(iv)	(i)	(ii)	(iii)
(b)	(iii)	(iv)	(i)	(ii)
(c)	(ii)	(i)	(iv)	(iii)
(d)	(ii)	(iii)	(i)	(iv)

12. Structural formula of ethyne is **(NCERT Exemplar)**

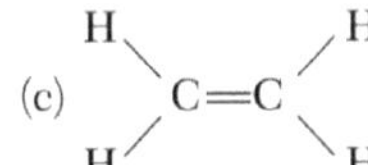

(a) $H\!-\!C \equiv C\!-\!H$
(b) $H_3C\!-\!C \equiv C\!-\!H$
(c) $\overset{H}{\underset{H}{}}C\!=\!C\overset{H}{\underset{H}{}}$
(d) 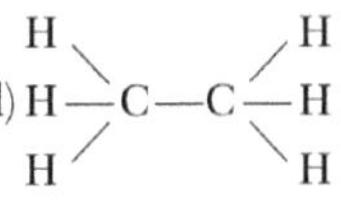 $H\!-\!C\!-\!C\!-\!H$ (with H above and below each C)

13. Which among the following are unsaturated hydrocarbons?

(i) $CH_3\!-\!CH_2\!-\!CH_3$

(ii) $CH_3\!-\!CH\!=\!CH\!-\!CH_3$

(iii) 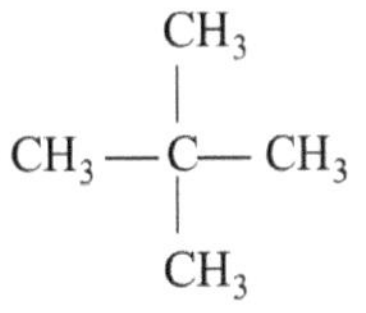 $CH_3\!-\!\underset{\underset{CH_3}{|}}{\overset{\overset{CH_3}{|}}{C}}\!-\!CH_3$

(iv) 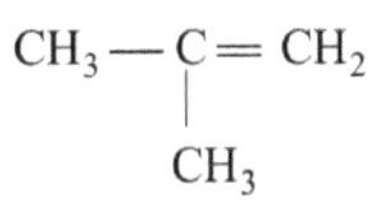 $CH_3\!-\!\underset{\underset{CH_3}{|}}{C}\!=\!CH_2$

(a) (i) and (iii)
(b) (ii) and (iii) **(NCERT Exemplar)**
(c) (ii) and (iv)
(d) (ii), (iii) and (iv)

14. Structural formula of benzene is *(NCERT Exemplar)*

(a)

(b)

(c)

(d)

15. Which of the following are correct structural isomers of butane?

(i)

(ii)

(iii)

(iv)

(NCERT Exemplar)

(a) (i) and (iii)   (b) (ii) and (iv)   (c) (i) and (ii)   (d) (iii) and (iv)

• Assertion-Reasoning MCQs

Direction (Q. Nos. 16-20) Each of these questions contains two statements Assertion (A) and Reason (R). Each of these questions also has four alternative choices, any one of which is the correct answer. You have to select one of the codes (a), (b), (c) and (d) given below.

   (a) Both A and R are true and R is the correct explanation of A.
   (b) Both A and R are true, but R is not the correct explanation of A.
   (c) A is true, but R is false.
   (d) A is false, but R is true.

16. Assertion Covalent compounds are poor conductor of electricity.

   Reason The electrons are shared between atoms and no charged particles are present.

17. Assertion Diamond does not conduct electricity.

   Reason Diamond has high refractive index.

18. Assertion Graphite is slippery to touch.

   Reason The various layers of carbon atoms in graphite are held together by weak van der Waals' forces.

19. Assertion Carbon shows maximum catenation property in the periodic table.

   Reason Carbon has small size and thus, forms strong C— C bond.

20. Assertion Following are the members of a homologous series:

     $CH_3OH, CH_3CH_2OH, CH_3CH_2CH_2OH$

   Reason A series of compounds with same functional group but differing by $—CH_2—$ unit is called a homologous series. *(CBSE 2020)*

• Case Based MCQs

21. Read the following and answer the questions from (i) to (v) given below

The bonds which are formed by the sharing of an electron pair between the atoms (either same or different atoms) are known as covalent bonds.

As neutral atom carbon has electronic configuration $K L$. To gain inert gas configuration carbon can
  $2 \ 4$
either donate 4 valence electrons (helium gas configuration) or gain 4 electrons (neon gas configuration), but it cannot do so. To acquire inert gas configuration carbon can only share its 4 valence electrons with other atoms forming covalent bonds.

The concept of covalent bonds was given by Langmuir and Lewis to explain bonding in non-ionic compounds. The covalent bonds are of three types. If each atom contributes one electron, the covalent bond formed is called a single covalent bond and is represented by a single line (—) and if each atom contributes two electrons, the covalent bond formed is called a double bond and is represented by a double line (=) and if each atom contributes three electrons, the covalent bond formed is called a triple bond and is represented by a triple line (≡).

The electrons in a covalent bond are simultaneously attracted by the two atomic nuclei. A covalent bond forms when the difference between the electronegativities of two atoms is too small for an electron transfer to occur to form ions.

 (i) Which of the following do not contain a triple bond?

    I. SO_2 II. N_2 III. HCl   IV. NH_3
   (a) I and II
   (b) I, III and IV
   (c) III and IV
   (d) I and IV

(ii) Which of the following contains a double bond?
   (a) O_2 (b) N_2
   (c) CH_4 (d) H_2O

(iii) Chlorine forms a diatomic molecule, Cl_2. The electron dot structure for this molecule is

(a) 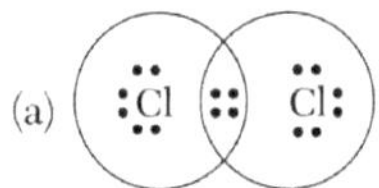 (b) 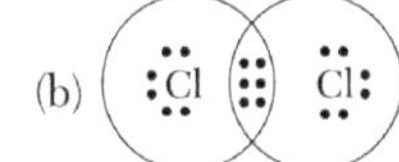

(c) 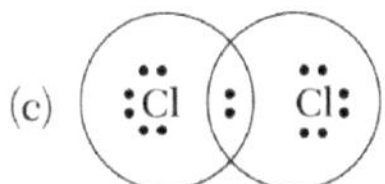 (d) 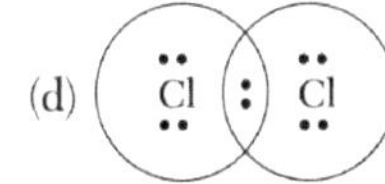

(iv) What is the covalency of nitrogen?
   (a) 1 (b) 2 (c) 3 (d) 4

(v) The shared pair of electrons is said to constitute a .... bond between two hydrogen atoms.
   (a) single (b) double
   (c) triple (d) ionic

22. Read the following and answer the questions from (i) to (v) given below

Allotropy is the property by virtue of which an element exists in more than one form and these different forms of an element are called allotropes.

Allotropes have similar chemical properties but they differ in their physical properties. Carbon exists in crystalline and amorphous forms.

In crystalline form, it occur as diamond, graphite and fullerenes. Diamond is a colourless, transparent substance having extraordinary brilliance. It is the hardest natural substance known. It is used for cutting marble, granite and glass. Graphite is a greyish-black opaque substance. It is lighter than diamond, i.e., it has lower density. It has sheet like structure having hexagonal layers.

One layer slides over the other layer which makes it soft to touch. It is the reason that graphite is used as a lubricant. The amorphous form of carbon is also known as micro-crystalline form which consists of coal, lampblack and charcoal.

(i) Substance X is a moderate conductor of electricity. Substance X has the structure shown below :

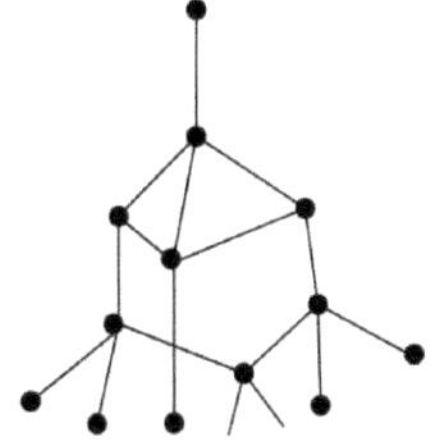

Which statements about substance X are correct?
   I. It is a covalent compound.
   II. It has a giant molecular structure.
   III. It has the same structure as graphite.
   IV. It has the same structure as diamond.
   (a) I and III (b) II and III
   (c) II and IV (d) I, II and IV

(ii) Which of the following is correct about the structure of diamond?
   (a) Carbon atoms are held together by single covalent bonds
   (b) Electrons move freely through the structure
   (c) Layers of atoms slide easily over each other
   (d) Carbon atoms conduct electricity in the molten state

(iii) Which three allotropes of carbon, do the given figures represents?

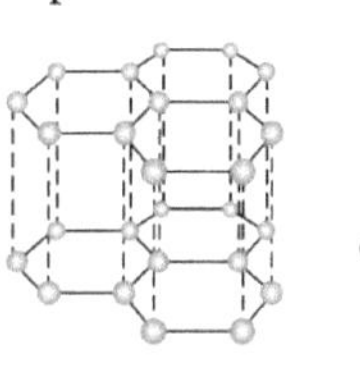 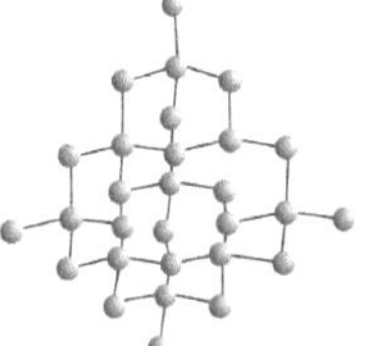 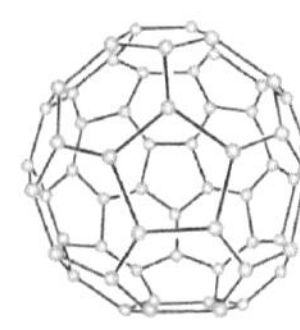

(I)   (II)   (III)

	I	II	III
(a)	Diamond	Graphite	Buckminster fullerene
(b)	Graphite	Buckminster fullerene	Diamond
(c)	Diamond	Buckminster fullerene	Graphite
(d)	Graphite	Diamond	Buckminster fullerene

(iv) Identify the incorrect statement(s).
   I. Diamond is the hardest substance known while graphite is smooth and slippery.
   II. Diamond is made up of billions of carbon atoms. Each carbon atom is bonded to four other carbon atoms in a tetrahedral manner to form a giant lattice. All carbon atoms are bonded by strong covalent bonds.
   III. Graphite is a poor conductor of electricity unlike other non-metals.
   IV. Graphite has a giant covalent structure that is made up of layers of carbon atoms. In each layer, each carbon atom is bonded to three other carbon atoms to form hexagonal rings of carbon atoms.
   (a) I and III (b) Only III
   (c) II and IV (d) I, II and IV

(v) Which of the following is an example of amorphous form of carbon ?
   (a) Wood (b) Oil
   (c) Chalk (d) Coke

PART 2
Subjective Questions

• Short Answer Type Questions

1. What do you mean by covalent bonding?

2. Explain the nature of the covalent bond using the bond formation in CH_3Cl. **(NCERT)**

3. What would be the electron dot structure of carbon dioxide which has molecular formula CO_2? **(NCERT)**

4. (i) Explain the formation of calcium chloride with the help of electron dot structure.
(Atomic numbers of Ca = 20; Cl = 17)
(ii) Why do ionic compounds not conduct electricity in solid state but conduct electricity in molten and aqueous state?

5. Carbon a group (14) element in the periodic table, is known to form compounds with many elements. Write an example of a compound formed with
(i) chlorine (group 17 of periodic table)
(ii) oxygen (group 16 of periodic table) **(NCERT Exemplar)**

6. Why covalent compounds are volatile in nature with low boiling and low melting point?

7. State the valency of each carbon atom in
(i) an alkane and   (ii) an alkyne

8. Covalent compounds are generally poor conductors of electricity. Why? **(CBSE 2020)**

9. Diamond is a poor conductor of electricity while graphite is a good conductor. Assign reason.

10. Why diamond has high melting point?

11. What are the main factors that enables carbon to form large number of compounds?

12. Select saturated hydrocarbons from the following:
C_3H_6; C_5H_{10}; C_4H_{10}; C_2H_4; C_6H_{14}

13. What will be the formula and electron dot structure of cyclopentane? **(NCERT)**

14. Answer the following
(i) Carbon is a versatile element. Give reason.
(ii) Explain the structural difference between saturated and unsaturated hydrocarbons with two examples each.
(iii) What is a functional group? Write examples of four different functional groups.

15. Write the molecular formula of the following compounds and draw their electron dot structures
(i) Ethane   (ii) Ethene   (iii) Ethyne

16. What is meant by isomers? Draw the structures of two isomers of butane, C_4H_{10}. Explain, why we cannot have isomers of first three members of alkane series?

17. Draw the possible isomers of the compound with molecular formula C_3H_6O and also give their electron dot structures. **(NCERT Exemplar)**

18. What is meant by functional group in carbon compounds? Write in tabular form the structural formula and the functional group present in the following compounds:
(i) Ethanol   (ii) Ethanoic acid

19. Describe the applications of homologous series.

20. Why is homologous series of carbon compounds so called? Write the chemical formula of two consecutive members of any homologous series and state the part of these compounds that determines their (i) physical and (ii) chemical properties.

21. Write the next higher order homologous of CH_2O, C_2H_2 and C_2H_5COOH.

• Long Answer Type Questions

22. State the reason why carbon can neither form C^{4+} cations nor C^{4-} anions, but forms covalent compound. Also state reasons to explain why covalent compounds
(i) Are bad conductors of electricity?
(ii) Have low melting and boiling point?

23. Explain the formation of oxygen (O_2) molecule and sulphur (S_8) molecule.

24. What are covalent compounds? Why are they different from ionic compounds? List their three characteristics properties.

25. Why organic compounds are called as hydrocarbons? Write the general formula for homologous series of alkanes, alkenes and alkynes and also draw the structure of the first member of each series.

26. Identify the functional group present in the following compounds

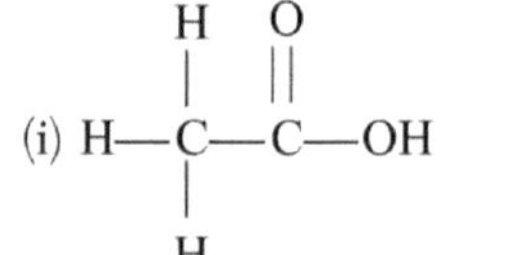

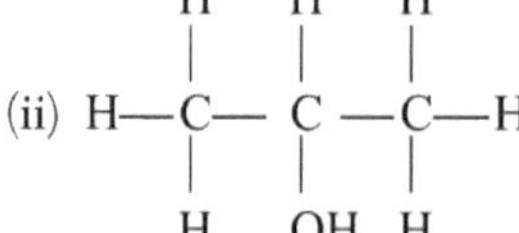

(iii) $H-\overset{\underset{|}{H}}{\underset{|}{C}}-CHO$ (iv) $H-\overset{\underset{|}{H}}{\underset{|}{C}}-\overset{\underset{|}{H}}{\underset{|}{C}}-Br$

(v) $H-\overset{\underset{|}{H}}{\underset{|}{C}}-\overset{\underset{|}{H}}{\underset{|}{C}}-\overset{\overset{O}{||}}{C}-\overset{\underset{|}{H}}{\underset{|}{C}}-H$

• Case Based Questions

27. Read the following and answer the questions from (i) to (v) given below

Compounds which contain only carbon and hydrogen are called hydrocarbon. Among these, the compounds containing all single covalent bonds are called saturated hydrocarbons while the compounds containing atleast one double or triple bond are called unsaturated hydrocarbons.

Saturated hydrocarbons after combustion give a clean flame while unsaturated hydrocarbons given a yellow sooty flame. Unsaturated hydrocarbons are more reactive than saturated hydrocarbons. Unsaturated hydrocarbons add hydrogen in the presence of catalysts such as palladium or nickel to give saturated hydrocarbons.

Study the table related to three hydrocarbons A, B, C and answer the questions that follows

Organic compound	Molecular formula
A	C_3H_8
B	C_5H_{10}
C	C_4H_6

(i) What is the name of compound B?
(ii) Write two differences between saturated and unsaturated hydrocarbons.
(iii) In unsaturated compounds, what is the minimum number of carbon atoms and why?
(iv) Among compounds A, B and C, which of the following is saturated hydrocarbon?
(v) Compound C belongs to which category of hydrocarbon and what is it's general formula ?

28. Read the following and answer the questions from (i) to (v) given below

Organic compounds with same molecular formula but different chemical and physical properties are called isomers. This phenomenon is called isomerism.

When the isomerism is due to difference in the arrangement of atoms within the molecule, without any reference to space, the phenomenon is called structural isomerism. In other words, structural isomers are compounds that have the same molecular formula but different structural formulas, i.e. they are different in the order in which different atoms are linked or they have different connectivities depending upon the order they are put together. In these compounds, carbon atoms can be linked together in the form of straight chains, branched chains or even rings.

(i) Name any set of compound that have same molecular formula but different structural formula.
(ii) Which property of carbon leads to formation of branched chains?
(iii) How many isomers of pentane are possible?
(iv) Name two compounds that contains six carbon atoms and have cyclic structure.
(v) What is the minimum number of carbon atoms required to form an isomer?

29. Read the following and answer the questions from (i) to (v) given below

Hydrocarbons are the simplest organic compounds and are regarded as parent organic compounds. All other compounds are considered to be derived from them by the replacement of one or more hydrogen atoms by other atoms or group of atoms.

Functional groups is an atom or group of atoms which makes a carbon compound (or organic compound) reactive and decide it's properties. A series of organic compounds having same functional group with similar or almost identical chemical characteristics in which all the members can be represented by the same general formula and two consecutive members of series differ by $-CH_2$ group in their molecular formula is called a homologous series.

$H-C\equiv C-\overset{\underset{|}{H}}{\underset{|}{C}}-H$, $H-\overset{\underset{|}{H}}{\underset{|}{C}}-Br$, $H-\overset{\underset{|}{H}}{\underset{|}{C}}-\overset{\underset{|}{H}}{\underset{|}{C}}-OH$,

      (P) (Q) (R)

$H-\overset{\underset{|}{H}}{\underset{|}{C}}-\overset{\underset{|}{H}}{\underset{|}{C}}-H$, $H-C\equiv C-H$, $\overset{H}{\underset{H}{>}}C=C\overset{H}{\underset{H}{<}}$

    (S) (T) (U)

(i) Which compounds belongs to same homologous series?
(ii) What is the functional group of compound R ?
(iii) Compound T belongs to which homologous series ?
(iv) Among the P, S, T and U compounds which belongs to alkane series?
(v) With respect to Q, R, S and U compounds which one is an unsaturated hydrocarbon?

EXPLANATIONS

Objective Questions

1. (c) Carbon exists in the atmosphere in the form of carbon dioxide gas (CO_2) in air (only 0.03%). Carbon also occurs in the earth's crust in the form of minerals like carbonates. It also occurs in the form of fossil fuels, organic compounds, wood, cotton and wool, etc.

2. (b) Oxygen atom has six (6) valence electrons. Thus, to complete its octet, it forms double bond with another oxygen atom to get O_2 molecule as

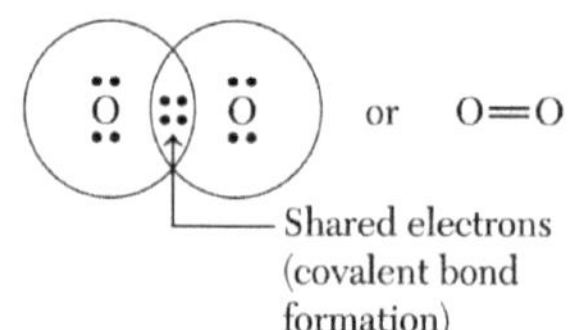

3. (d) Electronic configuration of N (atomic number 7) is $\overset{K\ L}{2\ 5}$.

Therefore, it needs three more electrons to complete its octet. Each nitrogen atom shares three electrons to form a molecule of N_2 as

4. (c) Carbon has 4 electron in its valence shell, while hydrogen has one electron in its valence shell.

To complete their octet and duplet respectively, they form covalent bonds. Carbon utilises its 4 valence electron and forms 4 covalent bonds with 4 hydrogen atoms, using one valence electron with each hydrogen atom.

5. (a) A molecule of ammonia (NH_3) has only single bonds and these are covalent bonds.

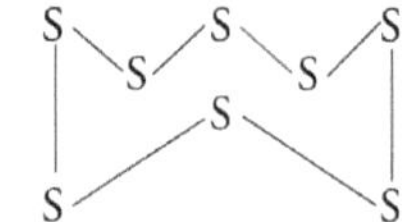

6. (b) 8 covalent bonds are formed in S molecule.

Crown shaped (S_8) molecule

7. (d) Graphite can not be used for making insulated plates, as it is a good conductor of electricity.

8. (d) C, Si and Ge belongs to group 14 and their valency is 4. But oxygen has electronic configuration 2, 6. So, its valency is 2. Hence, it does not show tetravalency.

9. (b) Friedrich Wohler accidently prepared urea from ammonium cyanate and the synthesis of urea discarded the vital force theory.

10. (c) The structural formula of pentane C_5H_{12} is

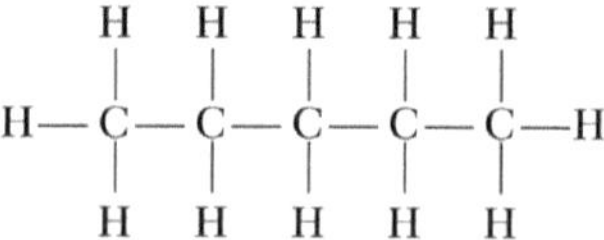

It contains 16 covalent bonds.

11. (a) C_3H_8 is an alkane because it resembles with the general formula of alkane, i.e. C_nH_{2n+2}. C_6H_6 is benzene which is a cyclic ring having double bonds in alternate carbon atoms C_2H_2 resembles with the general formula of alkyne and C_4H_8 is an alkene because number of H-atoms are double of that of carbon atoms.

12. (a) 'Eth' represents 2 carbon atoms and 'yne' shows presence of a triple bond. Thus, ethyne has the structural formula as $H—C \equiv C—H$. It is also known as acetylene.

13. (c) Unsaturated hydrocarbons have double or triple bond in their structure. Both (ii) and (iv) have double carbon-carbon bonds in their structures.

14. (c) Benzene molecule contains alternate single and double bonds. Its formula is C_6H_6.

In structure (a), double bonds are not at alternate positions. In structure (b), the formula is C_6H_{12} and in structure (d), the formula is C_6H_8.

15. (a) Structure (i) is *n*-butane.

Structure (iii) is *iso*-butane.

Since, molecular formula is same, only structures are different. So, (i) and (iii) are isomers while structure (ii) and (iv) have molecular formula C_4H_8.

16. (a) Both A and R are true and R is the correct explanation of A.

Covalent compounds consist of molecules and not ions which can transfer charge.

17. (b) Both A and R are true but R is not the correct explanation of A.

Diamond is not good conductor of electricity because of the absence of free electrons.

18. (a) Both A and R are true and R is the correct explanation of A.

A graphite crystal consists of various layers of carbon atoms in which each carbon atom is joined to three other atoms by strong covalent bonds. The various layers of carbon atoms in graphite are held together by weak van der Waals' forces making it slippery to touch.

19. (a) Both A and R are true and R is the correct explanation of A.

Catenation is the bonding of atoms of the same element into a series, called as chain.

Catenation occurs more readily with carbon, which forms strong covalent bond with other C-atoms to form long chains and structures.

20. (a) Both A and R are true and R is the correct explanation of A.

The alchohols have general formula of $C_nH_{2n+1}OH$. So, the alcohols have the series of formula from the different compounds with different between the succeeding and preceding molecules being a $—CH_2—$ unit.

21. (i) (*b*) The structures of the following given compounds are:

I. SO_2
$O = S = O$

II. N_2
$N \equiv N$

III. HCl
H—Cl

IV. NH_3
$$H—\overset{\displaystyle ..}{N}—H$$
$$|$$
$$H$$

∴ I, III and IV do not contain a triple bond. Hence, option (*b*) is correct.

(ii) (*a*) O_2 contains a double bond between it's atoms.

The structures of the given compounds are :

(a) $O_2 \Rightarrow O = O$

(b) $N_2 \Rightarrow N \equiv N$

(c) $CH_4 \Rightarrow$
$$H$$
$$|$$
$$H—C—H$$
$$|$$
$$H$$

(d) $H_2O \Rightarrow$
$$\overset{\displaystyle ..}{O}\!\!\cdot$$
$$\diagup \quad \diagdown$$
$$H \qquad H$$

(iii) (*c*) In chlorine molecule, both chlorine atoms contribute one electron and thus share single electron pair to form single covalent bond. As electrons are shared by both atoms, they acquire inert gas configuration of argon atom in valence shell.

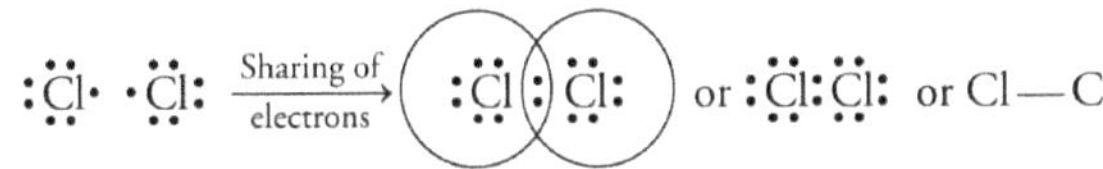

One shared electron pair

(iv) (*c*) The number of electrons shared between two atoms to complete their octet is known as the covalency of that atom. Therefore, the covalency of nitrogen is three because it needs three electrons to complete it's octet.

(v) (*a*) The shared pair of electrons constitute a single bond between the two H-atoms, which is represented by a single line between two H-atoms.

Single bond showing H_2 molecule

22. (i) (*c*) Each atom is covalently bonded to four other atoms, which in turn, are bonded to four more atoms. Thus, *X* is a giant molecule and has a structure similar to that of diamond. Substance *X* is not a compound as it consists of only one type of atoms.

(ii) (*a*) In the structure of diamond, carbon atoms are held together by single covalent bonds as this is a rigid three-dimensional network structure because each carbon atom is bonded to four other carbon atoms.

(iii) (*d*) (I) is the structure of graphite crystal which consists of layers of carbon atoms or sheets of carbon atoms.

(II) is the structure of diamond and (III) is the structure of Buckminster fullerene as their structure resembles with geodesic domes.

(iv) (*b*) In graphite, only three valence electrons are used for bond formation and hence fourth electron is free to move which makes it a good conductor of electricity.

(v) (*d*) Coke is an example of amorphous form of carbon which is obtained as a residue in destructive distillation of coal.

Subjective Questions

1. Carbon shares it's valence electrons with other atoms of carbon or with atoms of other elements in order to complete it's octet. These shared electrons belong to the outermost shells of both atoms and in this way, both atoms attain the nearest noble gas configuration. This type of bonding is called covalent bonding.

2. The bonds that are formed by sharing electrons are known as covalent bond. In covalent bonding, both atoms share the valence electrons, i.e. the shared electrons belong to the valence shells of both the atoms. CH_3Cl is called chloromethane, which contains 1 carbon atom, 3 hydrogen atoms and 1 chlorine atom.

Electronic configuration of carbon, $6 = \overset{K\ L}{2,\ 4}$

Electronic configuration of hydrogen, $1 = \overset{K}{1}$

Electronic configuration of chlorine, $17 = \overset{K\ L\ M}{2,\ 8,\ 7}$

Carbon atom has four outermost electrons, each hydrogen atom has one electron and chlorine has seven outermost electrons. Carbon shares its four outermost electrons with 3 hydrogen atoms and 1 chlorine atom to form CH_3Cl as follows

3. Atomic number of $C = 6$

Electronic configuration $= \overset{K\ L}{2,\ 4}$

Atomic number of $O = 8$

Electronic configuration $= \overset{K\ L}{2,\ 6}$

To attain the stable electronic configuration, carbon needs 4 electrons, while oxygen needs 2 electrons. So, in CO_2, each oxygen atom share two electrons from carbon. Thus, oxygen and carbon both complete their octet.

Before combination   **After combination**   Shared electrons

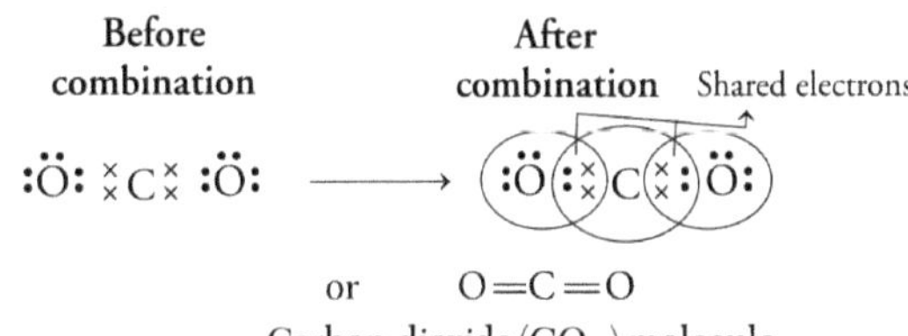

or $O = C = O$

Carbon dioxide (CO_2) molecule

4. (i) The formation of calcium chloride with the help of electron dot structure.

Element	Atomic number	Electronic configuration
Calcium (Ca)	20	2, 8, 8, 2
Chlorine (Cl)	17	2, 8, 7

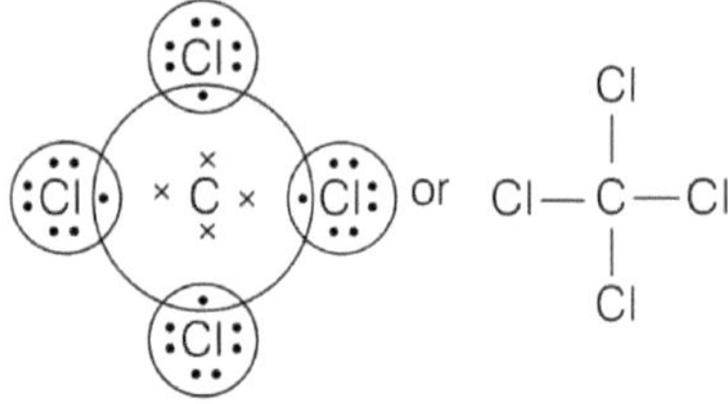

$$Ca^{2+} + 2Cl^- \longrightarrow CaCl_2$$

Two valence electrons of calcium attack the valency of two chlorine to attain the noble gas configuration.

(ii) Ionic compounds do not conduct electricity in solid state but conduct electricity in molten and aqueous state because in solid state, there is no free ion to move and pass electricity. Whereas in the molten and aqueous state, there is free ions to move and pass electricity.

5. (i) Electronic configuration of carbon, C(6) is 2, 4.

Electronic configuration of chlorine, Cl(17) is 2, 8, 7.

To attain the electronic configuration of the nearest noble gas, carbon needs 4 electron and chlorine needs 1 electron.

So, with chlorine, carbon forms carbon tetrachloride. Electron dot structure and structural formula of CCl_4 is as follows

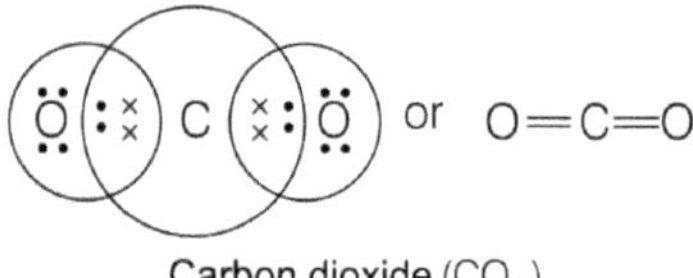

Carbon tetrachloride (CCl_4)

(ii) Electronic configuration of oxygen, O(8) is 2, 6.

With oxygen, carbon forms carbon dioxide. To attain the electronic configuration of the nearest noble gas, carbon needs 4 electrons and oxygen needs 2 electrons.

Therefore, in CO_2, each oxygen atom shares 2 electrons with carbon. Electronic configuration of carbon (6) is

2, 4

The electron dot structure and structural formula of CO_2 is as follows:

Carbon dioxide (CO_2)

6. Covalent compounds have low melting and boiling points due to small intermolecular forces of attraction between the atoms.

7. (i) Valency of each carbon atom in an alkane is four.

(ii) Valency of each carbon atom in an alkyne is four.

8. Covalent compounds are poor conductors of electricity because covalent bonds are formed by sharing of electrons between atoms.

So, they don't have a free electron that is required for electricity transfer (electricity is the flow of free electrons). Thus, they are bad conductors.

9. In the structure of diamond, all the four valence electrons of carbon are involved in the formation of covalent bonds. Thus, no free electrons are available.

Whereas, in the structure of graphite, three electrons in the valence shell of carbon are involved in covalent bond formation and the fourth electron is free to move. Therefore, graphite is a good conductor of electricity.

10. Diamond has a giant structure that consists of carbon atoms in which each carbon atom is bonded to four other carbon atoms forming a rigid three-dimensional network structure, which is responsible for it's hardness.

So, a lot of energy is required to break the network of strong covalent bonds. That's why it has high melting point.

11. The main factors that enables carbon to form large number of compounds are

(i) **Catenation** The tendency of carbon to form chains of identical atoms is known as catenation. Carbon forms long chains by combining with other carbon atoms through covalent bonds.

(ii) **Tetravalency** It has 4 valence electrons, so it can form 4 covalent bonds with four different atoms, or two double bonds or a single and a triple bond with other atoms. This tendency helps carbon to form a large number of compounds.

(iii) **Tetravalency** Carbon forms strong bonds with most of other elements like H, O, N, S, Cl etc., due to it's small size which helps it to attract more number of electrons.

12. The hydrocarbons in which all the carbon atoms are connected by only single bonds are called saturated hydrocarbons or alkanes or paraffins. The general formula of these compounds is C_nH_{2n+2}.

where, $n =$ number of carbon atoms in one molecule of a hydrocarbon.

Amongst, the given compounds, only C_4H_{10} and C_6H_{14} belongs to the formula of C_nH_{2n+2}. Therefore, C_4H_{10} and C_6H_{14} are saturated hydrocarbons.

13. General formula of cycloalkane $= C_nH_{2n}$

In cyclopentane, $n = 5$

∴ Formula of cyclopentane, $C_5H_{5 \times 2} = C_5H_{10}$

Electron dot structure of cyclopentane

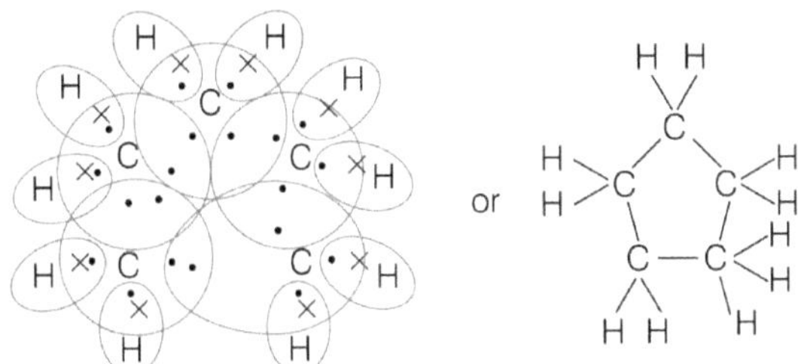

The structures of possible isomers of butane (C_4H_{10}) are

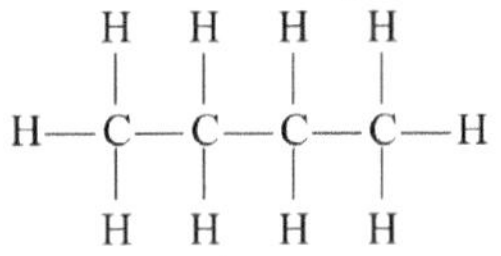

n-butane

(I)

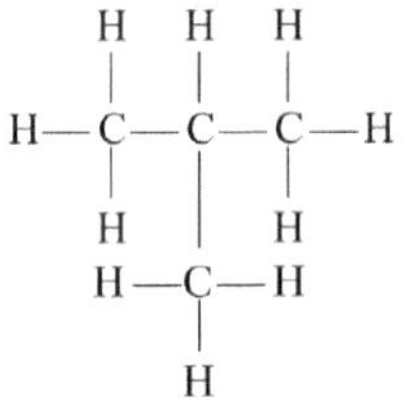

Iso-butane

(II)

14. (i) Carbon is a versatile element because of its properties. It shows the property of catenation due to which it forms a large number of compounds. Carbon is tetravalent. Due to this, it forms covalent compounds only.

(ii) Saturated hydrocarbons contain carbon-carbon single bonds. e.g. Methane (CH_4), ethane (C_2H_6). Unsaturated hydrocarbons contain atleast one carbon-carbon double or triple bond. e.g. Propene (C_3H_6), butyne (C_4H_6).

(iii) Functional group is an atom or group of atoms joined in a specific manner which is responsible for the characteristics chemical properties of the organic compounds.

Examples are alcohols $(-OH)$, aldehyde group $(-CHO)$, carboxylic group $(-COOH)$, ketone $(-CO)$ etc.

15. (i) Molecular formula of ethane is C_2H_6. Its electron dot structure is

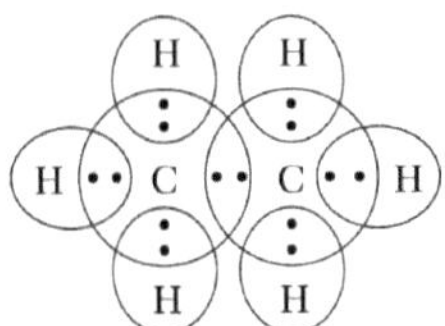

(ii) Molecular formula of ethene is C_2H_4. Its electron dot structure is

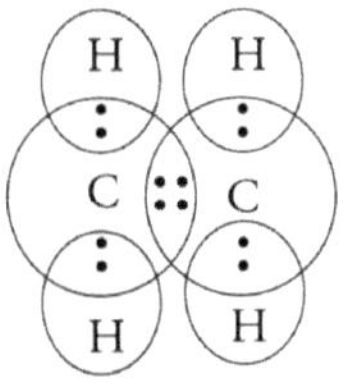

(iii) Molecular formula of ethyne is C_2H_2. Its electron dot structure is

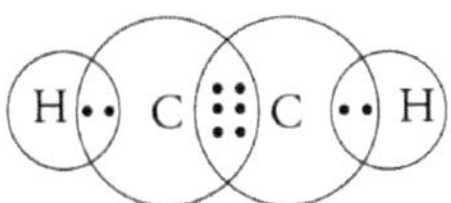

16. Isomers are those molecules which have same molecular formula but different structural formula, i.e. show different properties.

The first three members of alkane series are:

(i) CH_4 (methane)

(ii) C_2H_6 (ethane)

(iii) C_3H_8 (propane)

In the above members of alkane series, it is not possible to have different arrangements of carbon atoms, because branching is not possible from either first or last carbon. Thus, we cannot have isomers of first three members of alkane series.

17. There are four isomers possible for the molecular formula C_3H_6O. These are as follows:

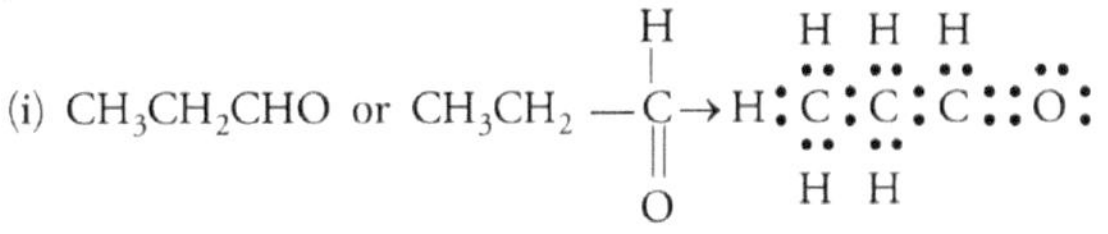

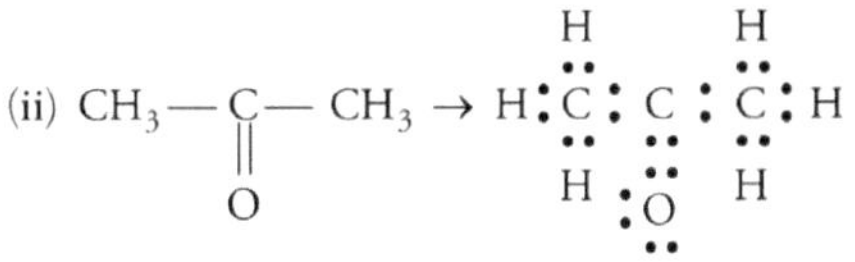

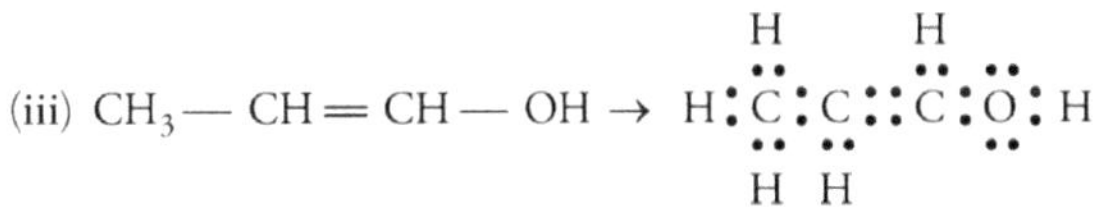

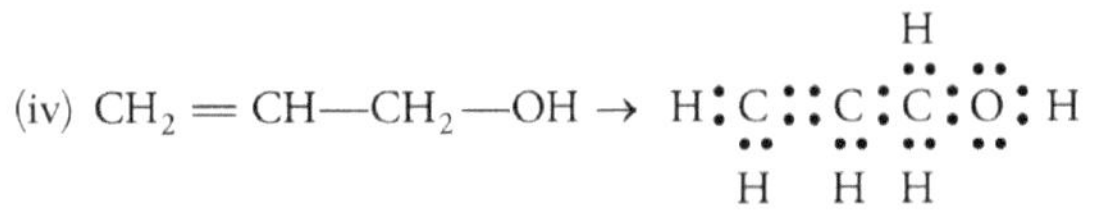

(i) CH_3CH_2CHO or $CH_3CH_2 -\overset{\displaystyle H}{\underset{\displaystyle O}{C}} \to$

(ii) $CH_3 -\overset{\displaystyle}{\underset{\displaystyle O}{C}} - CH_3 \to$

(iii) $CH_3 - CH = CH - OH \to$

(iv) $CH_2 = CH - CH_2 - OH \to$

18. An atom or a group of atoms present in a molecule which largely determines it's chemical properties is called functional group.

Compound	Structural formula	Functional group
(i) Ethanol (C_2H_5OH)	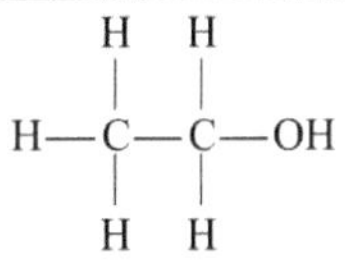	$-OH$ (Alcoholic)
(ii) Ethanoic acid (CH_3COOH)	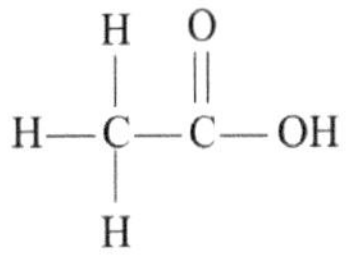	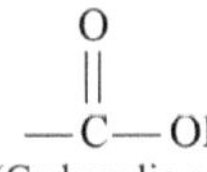 $-C-OH$ (Carboxylic acid)

19. Application of homologous series are as follows
- All members of homologous series shows similar chemical properties and generally prepared through one common method, e.g. all alkenes are prepared by dehydration of corresponding alcohols.
- The physical properties of the members change gradually, i.e. show gradation in properties as the number of carbon atom per molecule increased.

20. A homologous series is the family of organic compounds having the same functional group, similar chemical properties but the successive (adjacent) members of the series are differ by a CH_2 unit or 14 mass units.

Consecutive members of the homologous series of alcohols are

$$\left.\begin{array}{l} CH_3OH \\ C_2H_5OH \end{array}\right] \text{They differ by} -CH_2 \text{ unit.}$$

The physical properties are determined by alkyl group/hydrocarbon part/part other than the functional group.

The chemical properties are determined by functional group such as $-OH$ group.

21. Add $-CH_2$ group to each compound to obtain next homologous.

Compounds	Homologue compounds
CH_2O	$C_2H_4O, C_3H_6O, C_4H_8O...$
C_2H_2	$C_3H_4, C_4H_6, C_5H_8...$
C_2H_5COOH	$C_3H_7COOH, C_4H_9COOH, C_5H_{11}COOH...$

22. Atomic number of carbon is six. This means that it has four electrons in its outermost shell and it needs four more electrons to attain noble gas electronic configuration. It does not form C^{4+} cation, as the removal of four valence electrons will require a huge amount of energy.

The cation formed will have six protons and two electrons. This makes it highly unstable. Carbon is unable to form C^{4-} anion as its nucleus with six protons will not be able to hold ten electrons due to its small size. Thus, carbon achieves noble gas electronic configuration by sharing its four electrons either with same or different other atoms, i.e. it forms covalent compounds.

(i) Covalent compounds does not have free ions, due to this they are bad conductors of electricity in solid, molten or aqueous state.

(ii) Covalent compounds are formed by covalent bonds and it has been found that the intermolecular force of attraction in covalent compounds are weak.

Thus, low amount of energy is required to break these force of attraction. Hence, their melting and boiling points are quite low.

23. Formation of Oxygen Molecule (O_2)

The atomic number of oxygen is 8 and electronic configuration is 2, 6, i.e. has 6 electrons in it's outermost shell. So, it requires 2 electrons to complete it's octet for attaining noble gas configuration. Hence, it shares two electrons with another atom of oxygen to make a molecule of oxygen.

By doing so, both the atoms of oxygen get 8 electrons in their outermost shell. Thus, a double bond is formed between two oxygen atoms which consists of four electrons.

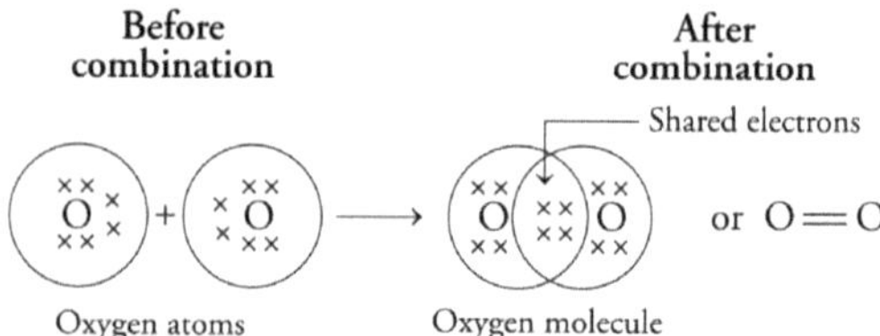

Formation of Sulphur Molecule (S_8)

The atomic number of sulphur is 16 and electronic configuration is 2, 8, 6. It also has 6 electrons in it's outermost shell and requires 2 electrons to complete it's octet state.

So, each sulphur atom shares two electrons, 1 with each adjoining sulphur atom by single covalent bonds and thus, complete it's octet.

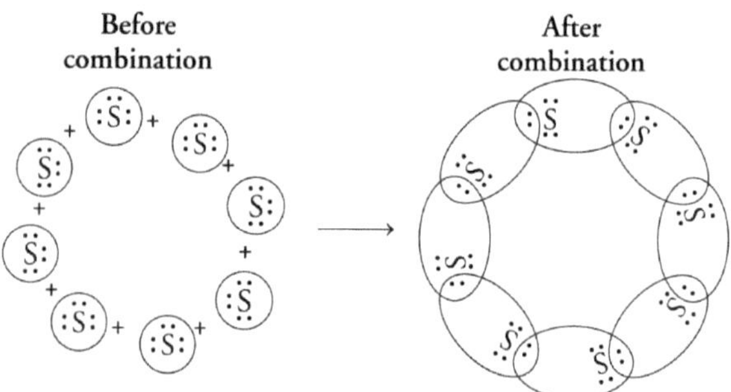

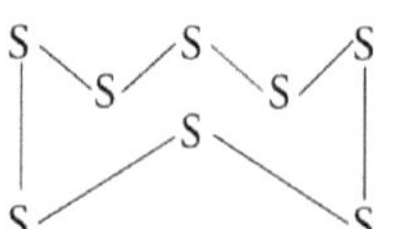
Crown shaped (S_8) molecule

Eight sulphur atoms form a puckered ring or crown structure to form an eight atom molecule.

24. Covalent compounds are those compounds which are formed by sharing of valence electrons between the atoms. e.g. Hydrogen molecule is formed by mutual sharing of electrons between two hydrogen atoms.

They are different from ionic compounds as ionic compounds are formed by the complete transfer of electrons from one atom to another, e.g. NaCl is formed when one valence electron of sodiu m gets completely transferred to outer shell of chlorine atom. The characteristic properties of covalent compounds are

(i) They are generally insoluble or less soluble in water but soluble in organic solvents.

(ii) They have low melting and boiling points.

(iii) They do not conduct electricity as they do not contain ions.

(iv) They are volatile in nature.

25. Organic compounds are called as hydrocarbons because they are made up of only the elements-carbon (C) and hydrogen (H).

General formula for the homologous series of alkanes is C_nH_{2n+2} which are classified as saturated hydrocarbons or alkanes. First member of the alkane family is "methane".

$$H—\overset{\displaystyle H}{\underset{\displaystyle H}{\overset{|}{\underset{|}{C}}}}—H$$

General formula for the homologous series of alkenes is C_nH_{2n}. which are classified in the category of unsaturated hydrocarbons. They are known as alkenes or olefins. First member of the alkene family is "ethene".

$$\overset{H}{\underset{H}{{}}}C=C\overset{H}{\underset{H}{{}}}$$

General formula for the homologous series of alkynes is C_nH_{2n-2} and they are also in the category of unsaturated hydrocarbons. First member of the alkyne family is "ethyne".

$$H—C\equiv C—H$$

26. The functional group present in the following compounds are

(i)
$$H—\overset{\displaystyle H}{\underset{\displaystyle H}{\overset{|}{\underset{|}{C}}}}—\overset{\displaystyle O}{\overset{||}{C}}—OH$$

This compound contains $—\overset{O}{\overset{||}{C}}—OH$ functional group which is the formula of carboxylic acid.

(ii)
$$H—\overset{\displaystyle H}{\underset{\displaystyle H}{\overset{|}{\underset{|}{C}}}}—\overset{\displaystyle H}{\underset{\displaystyle OH}{\overset{|}{\underset{|}{C}}}}—\overset{\displaystyle H}{\underset{\displaystyle H}{\overset{|}{\underset{|}{C}}}}—H$$

In this compound, $—OH$ functional group is present which is the formula of alcohol.

(iii)
$$H—\overset{\displaystyle H}{\underset{\displaystyle H}{\overset{|}{\underset{|}{C}}}}—CHO$$

This compound contains $—CHO$ functional group which belongs to the formula of aldehyde.

(iv)
$$H—\overset{\displaystyle H}{\underset{\displaystyle H}{\overset{|}{\underset{|}{C}}}}—\overset{\displaystyle H}{\underset{\displaystyle H}{\overset{|}{\underset{|}{C}}}}—Br$$

This compound contains halo (bromo) functional group as $—Br$.

(v)
$$H—\overset{\displaystyle H}{\underset{\displaystyle H}{\overset{|}{\underset{|}{C}}}}—\overset{\displaystyle H}{\underset{\displaystyle H}{\overset{|}{\underset{|}{C}}}}—\overset{\displaystyle O}{\overset{||}{C}}—\overset{\displaystyle H}{\underset{\displaystyle O}{\overset{|}{\underset{}{C}}}}—H$$

This compound contains $—\overset{O}{\overset{||}{C}}—$ functional group which belongs to ketone.

27. (i) Compound B has molecular formula as C_5H_{10} and contains five number of carbon atoms, i.e. $n = 5$.

It resembles with the general formula of alkene which is C_nH_{2n}.

So, the name of this compound is pent + ene = pentene. When five number of carbon atoms are present, it is named as "pent".

(ii)

Saturated hydrocarbons	Unsaturated hydrocarbons
These hydrocarbons are linked by only single covalent bond.	These hydrocarbons contains at least one double or triple bond along with single bonds. They are divided into two categories → Alkenes or Olefins → Alkynes.
General formula of these compounds is C_nH_{2n+2}.	General formula of alkene is C_nH_{2n} and general formula of alkyne is C_nH_{2n-2}.

(iii) The minimum number of carbon atoms present in an unsaturated compound is two because formation of double or triple bonds is possible only between two carbon atoms.

(iv) The molecular formula of compound A is C_3H_8, i.e. contains three number of carbon atoms and resembles with the general formula of alkanes which is C_nH_{2n+2}. So, A is saturated hydrocarbon.

While the molecular formula of compounds B and C is C_5H_{10} and C_4H_6 which resembles with the general formula of alkene and alkyne. So, B and C are unsaturated hydrocarbon.

(v) The molecular formula of compound C is C_4H_6 which resembles with alkyne because there is four number of carbon atoms and 6H-atoms, i.e. number of H-atoms are only increased by 2. So, the general formula of alkyne is C_nH_{2n-2}.

28. (i) Butane and *iso*-butane are the compounds that have same molecular formula but different structural formula.

$$\underset{\text{Butane}}{CH_3CH_2CH_2CH_3} \qquad \underset{\underset{\text{Iso-butane}}{\overset{|}{CH_3}}}{CH_3CHCH_3}$$

(ii) Due to catenation property of carbon, it forms long, straight or branched chains and rings of different sizes.

(iii) Pentane (C_5H_{12}) has three structural isomers:

$$CH_3—CH_2—CH_2—CH_2—CH_3$$
$$n\text{-pentane}$$

$$CH_3—\underset{\underset{CH_3}{|}}{CH}—CH_2—CH_3$$
$$\textit{Iso}\text{-pentane}$$

$$CH_3—\underset{\underset{CH_3}{|}}{\overset{\overset{CH_3}{|}}{C}}—CH_3$$
$$\textit{Neo}\text{-pentane}$$

(iv) Cyclohexane (C_6H_{14}) and benzene (C_6H_6) are two compounds that contain six carbon atoms and have cyclic structure.

$$C_6H_{12}$$
(Cyclohexane)

$$C_6H_6$$
(Benzene)

(v) Minimum four carbon atoms are required to show isomerism because branching is not possible with carbon-1, 2 and 3.

i.e. $\underbrace{\text{C—C—C} \qquad \underset{\underset{C}{|}}{\text{C—C}}}_{\text{Same}}$ (3-carbon atoms)

$\underbrace{\text{C—C—C—C} \qquad \underset{\underset{C}{|}}{\text{C—C—C}}}_{\text{Isomers}}$ (4-carbon atoms)

29. (i) P and T are the compounds that belongs to same homologous series. Both these compounds are alkynes and differ by $—CH_2$ unit in their molecular formula.

(ii) The functional group of compounds (R) is $—OH$ which is the formula of alcohol.

(iii) (T) is an alkyne having general formula of C_nH_{2n-2}.

(iv) Compound (S), i.e. $H—\underset{\underset{H}{|}}{\overset{\overset{H}{|}}{C}}—\underset{\underset{H}{|}}{\overset{\overset{H}{|}}{C}}—H$ belongs to an alkane series having general formula of C_nH_{2n+2}.

(v) Compound (U), i.e. $\underset{H}{\overset{H}{>}}C=C\underset{H}{\overset{H}{<}}$ is unsaturated hydrocarbon becuase it contain double bond, i.e. belongs to alkene.

Chapter Test

Multiple Choice Questions

1. Which of the following is not a property of carbon?
  (a) Carbon compounds are good conductor of heat and electricity
  (b) Carbon compounds are poor conductor of heat and electricity
  (c) Most of the carbon compounds are covalent compounds
  (d) Boiling and melting point of carbon compounds are relatively lower than those of ionic compounds

2. Which of the following is purest form of carbon?
  (a) Charcoal   (b) Coal   (c) Diamond   (d) Graphite

3. Buckminster fullerene is an allotropic form of
  (a) phosphorus (b) sulphur   (c) carbon   (d) tin

4. Which of the following is not a straight chain hydrocarbon?

  (a) $H_3C—CH_2—CH_2—CH_2—CH_2$
                                     CH_3

  (b) $H_3C—CH_2—CH_2—CH_2—CH_2—CH_3$

  (c) CH_3
          |
     $H_2C—H_2C—H_2C—CH_2$
                            |
                           CH_3

  (d) $H_3C{>}CH—CH_2—CH_2—CH_3$ (H_3C)

5. Which of the following is not the property of homologous series?
  (a) They differ by —CH_2 units
  (b) They differ by – 14 units by mass
  (c) They all contain double bond
  (d) They can be represented by a general formula

Assertion-Reasoning MCQs

Direction (Q. Nos. 6-8) Each of these questions contains two statements Assertion (A) and Reason (R). Each of these questions also has four alternative choices, any one of which is the correct answer. You have to select one of the codes (a), (b), (c) and (d) given below.
  (a) Both A and R are true and R is the correct explanation of A.
  (b) Both A and R are true, but R is not the correct explanation of A.
  (c) A is true, but R is false.
  (d) A is false, but R is true.

6. **Assertion** Carbon has a tendency to form multiple bonds.

  Reason Carbon has small size.

7. **Assertion** The only element that can form large number of compounds is carbon.

  Reason Carbon is tetravalent in nature and shows the property of catenation.

8. **Assertion** *n*-butane and *iso*-butane are examples of structural isomers.

  Reason Isomerism is possible only with hydrocarbons having 4 or more carbon atoms.

Short Answer Type Questions

9. What are the two properties of carbon which lead to the huge number of carbon compounds.

10. What is covalent bond? What type of bond exists in
  (i) CCl_4 (ii) $CaCl_2$

11. "Carbon tetrachloride is not a good conductor of electricity." Give reason to justify this statement.

12. Give answers to the following statements.
  (i) An allotrope of carbon which has a two dimensional layered structure consisting of fused benzene rings.
  (ii) An allotrope of carbon which looks like a soccer ball.
  (iii) An allotrope of carbon which contains both single and double bonds.

13. Diamond and graphite show different physical properties although they are made up of carbon. Name this relationship between diamond and graphite. Give the basis of this relationship also.

14. How diamond can be prepared artificially?

15. Catenation is the ability of an atom to form bonds with other atoms of the same element. It is exhibited by both carbon and silicon. Compare the ability of catenation of the two elements. Give reasons.

16. A compound has the formula H_2Y
  (*Y*=non-metal). State the following :
  (*i*) The outer electronic configuration of Y.
  (*ii*) The valency of Y.
  (*iii*) The bonding present in H_2Y.

Long Answer Type Questions

17. (i) What are covalent bonds ?
  (ii) How many covalent bonds are present in ethane with molecular formula C_2H_6?
  (iii) Write the formula and draw electron dot structure of carbon tetrachloride.
  (iv) In electron dot structure, the valence shell electrons are represented by crosses or dots.
  (a) The atomic number of chlorine is 17. Write its electronic configuration.
  (b) Draw the electron dot structure of chlorine molecule.

18. Write the structural formulae of all the isomers of an alkane with six C-atoms (C_6H_{14}) .

19. State five characteristics of a homologous series.

Answers

Multiple Choice Questions

  1. (*a*)   *2.* (*c*)   *3.* (*c*)   *4.* (*d*)   *5.* (*c*)

Assertion-Reasoning MCQs

  6. (*a*)   *7.* (*d*)   *8.* (*b*)

For Detailed Solutions

Scan the code

CHAPTER 02

Periodic Classification of Elements

In this Chapter...

- Earlier Attempts at the Classification of Elements
- Mendeleev's Periodic Table
- Modern Periodic Table

All substances are made up of elements. At present, there are 118 elements known, out of which 98 are naturally occurring. In order to study the properties of all these elements separately, scientists felt the necessity to group elements having similar characteristics together.

Earlier Attempts at the Classification of Elements

Several attempts have been made to classify the elements according to their properties. Later, many classifications were tried. Some important of them are discussed below

Dobereiner's Triads

He arranged three elements with similar properties into groups which are known as triads and showed that when three elements in a triad were arranged in order of increasing atomic masses, the atomic mass of middle element was roughly the average of atomic masses of other two elements. He could identify only three triads from the elements known at that time which are

Li, Na, K; Ca, Sr, Ba; Cl, Br, I

Newland's Law of Octaves

Newland arranged the known elements in order of increasing atomic masses and found that every eighth element had properties similar to that of the first. This law was applicable only upto calcium and he assumed that there were only 56 elements. To fit elements into his table, he adjusted two elements in the same slot and also put some unlike elements under the same column which have very different properties than other elements.

Mendeleev's Periodic Table

According to this, the physical and chemical properties of the elements are periodic function of their atomic masses, i.e. on arranging the elements in increasing order of their atomic masses, the similar properties were repeated after regular intervals.

He took the formulae of the hydrides and oxides formed by an element as one of the basic properties of an element for its classification. e.g. Hydride of carbon, CH_4 as RH_4 and its oxides, CO_2 as RO_2.

He then arranged 63 elements in the increasing order of their atomic masses and found that there was a periodic recurrence of elements with similar physical and chemical properties. He observed that elements with similar properties fall in the same vertical column. These vertical column are called **groups** and horizontal rows of elements are called **periods**.

Features of Mendeleev's Periodic Table

- It consists of 8 vertical columns, called **groups** and 6 horizontal rows, called periods.
- In every period, elements are arranged in increasing order of their atomic masses.

- He left gaps for the elements not discovered at that time and named such elements by prefixing a Sanskrit numeral Eka (one), *divi* (two) to the name of the preceding similar element in the same group. e.g. Eka-boron, Eka-aluminium, which after their discovery were named as scandium, gallium.
- He also predicted the atomic masses and properties of several elements that were not known at that time.

Properties of Eka-aluminium and Gallium

Property	Eka-aluminium	Gallium
Atomic mass	68	69.7
Formula of oxide	E_2O_3	Ga_2O_3
Formula of chloride	ECl_3	$GaCl_3$

- One of the strengths of Mendeleev's periodic table was that, when noble gases like helium, neon were discovered, they could be placed in a new group without disturbing the existing order.

Limitations of Mendeleev's Periodic Table

- Elements with dissimilar properties were kept in same group.
- Position of hydrogen was not fixed in periodic table.
- Elements with similar properties were kept in different groups.
- Heavier elements were kept before the lighter elements.
- Position of isotopes and isobars could not be explained.

Mendeleev's Periodic Table (Published in a German journal in 1872)

In the formula of oxides and hydrides at the top of the columns, the letter 'R' is used to represent any of the elements in the group.

Group →	I		II		III		IV		V		VI		VII		VIII
Oxide	R_2O		RO		R_2O_3		RO_2		R_2O_5		RO_3		R_2O_7		RO_4
Hydride	RH		RH_2		RH_3		RH_4		RH_3		RH_2		RH		
Periods ↓	*A*	*B*	*A*	*B*	*A*	*B*	*A*	*B*	*A*	*B*	*A*	*B*	*A*	*B*	Transition series
1	H 1.008														
2	Li 6.939		Be 9.012		B 10.81		C 12.011		N 14.007		O 15.999		F 18.998		
3	Na 22.99		Mg 24.31		Al 29.98		Si 28.09		P 30.974		S 32.06		Cl 35.453		
4 **First series**	K 39.102		Ca 40.08			Sc 44.96		Ti 47.90		V 50.94		Cr 50.20		Mn 54.94	Fe 55.85 Co 58.93 Ni 58.71
Second series		Cu 63.54		Zn 65.37	Ga 69.72		Ge 72.59		As 74.92		Se 78.96		Br 79.909		
5 **First series**	Rb 85.47		Sr 87.62			Y 88.91		Zr 91.22		Nb 92.91		Mo 95.94		Tc 99	Ru 101.07 Rh 102.91 Pd 106.4
Second series		Ag 107.87		Cd 112.40	In 114.82		Sn 118.69		Sb 121.75		Te 127.60		I 126.90		
6 **First series**	Cs 132.90		Ba 137.34			La 138.91		Hf 178.49		Ta 180.95		W 183.85			Os 190.2 Ir 192.2 Pt 195.09
Second series		Au 196.97		Hg 200.59	Tl 204.37		Pb 207.19		Bi 208.98						

Modern Periodic Table

In 1913, **Henry Moseley** showed that the atomic number of an element is a more fundamental property. On the basis of this, he modified Mendeleev's periodic law as "physical and chemical properties of the elements are a periodic function of their atomic number". This is called **modern periodic law.**

When the elements were arranged in the increasing order of their atomic number, the obtained table is called **modern periodic table**.

In this periodic table, hydrogen is kept at the top left corner because of its unique characteristics. The position of cobalt and nickel is also justified.

Modern Periodic Table

Key:
- Metals
- Metalloids
- Non-metals

The *zig-zag* line separates the metals from the non-metals.

Period	1	2	3	4	5	6	7	8	9	10	11	12	13	14	15	16	17	18
1	1 H Hydrogen 1.0																	2 He Helium 4.0
2	3 Li Lithium 6.9	4 Be Beryllium 9.0											5 B Boron 10.8	6 C Carbon 12.0	7 N Nitrogen 14.0	8 O Oxygen 16.0	9 F Fluorine 19.0	10 Ne Neon 20.2
3	11 Na Sodium 23.0	12 Mg Magnesium 24.3											13 Al Aluminium 27.0	14 Si Silicon 28.1	15 P Phosphorus 31.0	16 S Sulphur 32.1	17 Cl Chlorine 35.5	18 Ar Argon 39.9
4	19 K Potassium 39.1	20 Ca Calcium 40.1	21 Sc Scandium 45.0	22 Ti Titanium 47.8	23 V Vanadium 50.9	24 Cr Chromium 52.0	25 Mn Manganese 54.9	26 Fe Iron 55.9	27 Co Cobalt 58.9	28 Ni Nickel 58.7	29 Cu Copper 63.5	30 Zn Zinc 65.4	31 Ga Gallium 69.7	32 Ge Germanium 72.6	33 As Arsenic 74.9	34 Se Selenium 79.0	35 Br Bromine 79.9	36 Kr Krypton 83.8
5	37 Rb Rubidium 85.5	38 Sr Strontium 87.6	39 Y Yttrium 88.9	40 Zr Zirconium 91.2	41 Nb Niobium 92.9	42 Mo Molybdenum 95.9	43 Tc Technetium (99)	44 Ru Ruthenium 101.1	45 Rh Rhodium 102.3	46 Pd Palladium 106.4	47 Ag Silver 107.9	48 Cd Cadmium 112.4	49 In Indium 114.8	50 Sn Tin 118.7	51 Sb Antimony 121.8	52 Te Tellurium 127.6	53 I Iodine 126.9	54 Xe Xenon 131.3
6	55 Cs Caesium 132.9	56 Ba Barium 137.3	57 La* Lanthanum 138.9	72 Hf Hafnium 178.5	73 Ta Tantalum 181.0	74 W Tungsten 183.9	75 Re Rhenium 186.2	76 Os Osmium 190.2	77 Ir Iridium 192.2	78 Pt Platinum 195.1	79 Au Gold 197.0	80 Hg Mercury 200.6	81 Tl Thallium 204.4	82 Pb Lead 207.2	83 Bi Bismuth 209.0	84 Po Polonium (210)	85 At Astatine (210)	86 Rn Radon (222)
7	87 Fr Francium (223)	88 Ra Radium (226)	89 Ac** Actinium (227)	104 Rf Rutherfordium (267)	105 Db Dubnium (268)	106 Sg Seaborgium (271)	107 Bh Bohrium (272)	108 Hs Hassium (277)	109 Mt Meitnerium (276)	110 Ds Darmstadtium (281)	111 Rg Roentgenium (280)	112 Cn Copernicium (285)	113 Nh Nihonium (286)	114 Fl Flerovium (289)	115 Mc Moscovium (290)	116 Lv Livermorium (291)	117 Ts Tennessine (294)	118 Og Oganesson (294)

f-block or inner-transition elements

*** Lanthanoids**

58 Ce Cerium 140.1	59 Pr Praseodymium 140.9	60 Nd Neodymium 144.2	61 Pm Promethium (145)	62 Sm Samarium 150.4	63 Eu Europium 152.0	64 Gd Gadolinium 157.3	65 Tb Terbium 158.9	66 Dy Dysprosium 162.5	67 Ho Holmium 164.9	68 Er Erbium 167.3	69 Tm Thulium 168.9	70 Yb Ytterbium 173.0	71 Lu Lutetium 175.5

**** Actinoids**

90 Th Thorium 232.0	91 Pa Protactinium (231)	92 U Uranium 238.1	93 Np Neptunium (237)	94 Pu Plutonium (242)	95 Am Americium (243)	96 Cm Curium (247)	97 Bk Berkelium (245)	98 Cf Californium (251)	99 Es Einsteinium (254)	100 Fm Formium (253)	101 Md Mendelevium (256)	102 No Nobelium (254)	103 Lr Lawrencium (257)

Features of Modern Periodic Table

This table has 18 vertical columns, known as **groups** and 7 horizontal rows, known as **periods.**

A few important features of the elements present in groups and periods are as follows

- The groups are not divided into sub-groups.
- The elements present in a group have the same number of valence electrons and valency.
- The number of shells increases as we go down the group.
- The elements present in a group have identical chemical properties and their physical properties like density, melting point vary gradually.
- Elements of a period have the same number of shells but they do not contain the same number of valence electrons. So, their chemical properties are also different.
- The number of valence shell electrons increases by one unit as the atomic number increases by one unit on moving from left to right in a period.
- In this table, elements of group 13, 14, 15, 16 and 17 are called normal elements which includes metals, non-metals and metalloids and elements of group 3, 4, 5, 6, 7, 8, 9, 10, 11 and 12 are called transition elements.
- In this periodic table, elements from atomic number 58 to 71 called as lanthanides and elements from 91 to 103 called as actinoids are kept out of the table.

Position of Elements in the Modern Periodic Table

For this, first of all write electronic configuration of the given element. Number of shells present in the electronic configuration shows the period number of that element. Number of valence electrons present in the electronic configuration show the group number of the element.

e.g. Electronic configuration of the element with atomic number 19 is 2, 8, 8, 1, since it has four shells, thus it is element of fourth period. Due to presence of one electron in the last shell, its group number is 1. After donating one electron, it acquires a stable configuration, hence its valency is also 1.

Trends in Modern Periodic Table

(i) **Valency** In a period, it increases with respect to hydrogen from 1 to 4 after that it decreases. On the other hand with respect to oxygen, valency increases from 1 to 7. In a group, valency remains same as outer electronic configuration is same.

(ii) **Atomic size** Atomic size decreases on moving from left to right in a period due to increase in nuclear charge. It increases down the group as new shells are being added.

(iii) **Metallic and non-metallic properties** Effective nuclear charge acting on the valence shell electrons increases across a period and decreases down the group. Therefore, metallic character decreases across a period and increases down a group. Non-metallic character, however increases across a period and decreases down a group.

Metals like Na, Mg are present on left side of periodic table, whereas non-metals like S, Cl are present on right side of periodic table.

There are some metals which exhibits both the properties of metal and non-metals. These are called metalloids like Po, Te, Sb, etc.

(iv) **Electronegativity** The electronegativity of the elements increases along a period, since the non-metallic character increases. Similarly, it decreases down the group, since the non-metallic character decreases.

(v) **Nature of oxides** On moving from left to right in a period, due to increase in non-metallic character, basic nature of oxides decreases while acidic nature increases.

$$\underset{\text{Strongly basic}}{\underbrace{Na_2O \quad MgO}} \; , \; \underset{\text{Amphoteric}}{Al_2O_3} \; , \; \underset{\substack{\text{Weakly} \\ \text{acidic}}}{SiO_2} , \; \underset{\text{Acidic}}{\underbrace{P_2O_5 \quad SO_2}} , \; \underset{\substack{\text{Strongly} \\ \text{acidic}}}{Cl_2O_7}$$

On going down the group, the order is reversed.

Chapter Practice

Objective Questions

- **Multiple Choice Questions**

1. Dobereiner could identify how many triads from the elements known at that time ?
(a) One (b) Two (c) Three (d) Four

2. Upto which element, the law of octaves was found to be applicable? **(NCERT Exemplar)**
(a) Oxygen (b) Calcium (c) Cobalt (d) Potassium

3. What type of oxide would Eka-aluminium form? **(NCERT Exemplar)**
(a) EO_3 (b) E_3O_2 (c) E_2O_3 (d) EO

4. Which one of the following elements exhibit maximum number of valence electrons? **(NCERT Exemplar)**
(a) Na (b) Al (c) Si (d) P

5. Choose the correct statement.
(a) Valency and valence electrons are always equal
(b) Valency is determined by using the number of valence electrons
(c) Valence electrons are always equal to 8-valency
(d) Valency is always equal to 8-valence electrons

6. Elements with code letters Q and R occupy the positions shown in the outline of the periodic table.

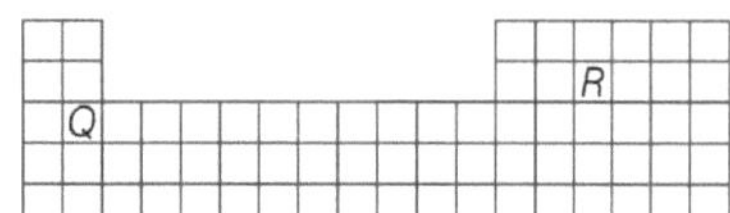

What is the formula of the compound formed between them?
(a) QR_2 (b) Q_2R (c) Q_2R_3 (d) Q_3R_2

7. Which of the following statements is incorrect for atomic size ?
(a) Atomic size of B > Be (b) Atomic size of Be > B
(c) Atomic size of N > O (d) Atomic size of C > N

8. Which of the following gives the correct increasing order of the atomic radii of O, F and N?
(NCERT Exemplar)
(a) O, F, N (b) N, F, O (c) O, N, F (d) F, O, N

9. Which of the following statements is not a correct statement about the trends when going from left to right across the periods of periodic table? **(NCERT)**
(a) The elements become less metallic in nature
(b) The number of valence electrons increases
(c) The atoms lose their electrons more easily
(d) The oxides become more acidic

10. Match the following columns :

	Column I (Elements)	Column II (Groups)
A.	Be	(i) Group 17
B.	F	(ii) Group 15
C.	P	(iii) Group 2
D.	Ar	(iv) Group 18

Codes

	A	B	C	D			A	B	C	D
(a)	(iii)	(i)	(ii)	(iv)		(b)	(i)	(ii)	(iii)	(iv)
(c)	(ii)	(iv)	(iii)	(i)		(d)	(iv)	(ii)	(i)	(iii)

11. Which metal is among the first ten elements in modern periodic table?
(a) Lithium (Li) (b) Boron (B)
(c) Carbon (C) (d) Potassium (K)

12. An element X is forming an acidic oxide. Its position in modern periodic table will be **(CBSE 2020)**
(a) group 1 and period 3 (b) group 2 and period 3
(c) group 13 and period 3 (d) group 16 and period 3

13. An oxide of a metal shows no action with blue-litmus but turns red-litmus to blue in its aqueous solution. The possible formula of the metal oxide can be
(a) MgO (b) CO_2 (c) SO_2 (d) H_2O

14. The position of four elements A, B, C and D in the modern periodic table are shown below. The element which is most likely to form a basic oxide is

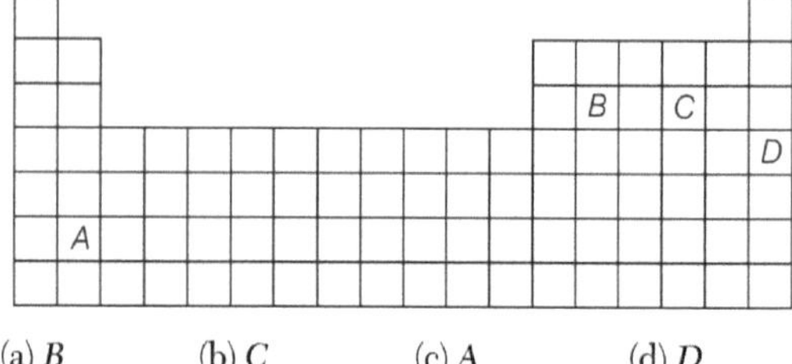

(a) B (b) C (c) A (d) D

15. Consider the part of periodic table given below:

Group/Period	1	2	13	14	15	16	17	18
I	a							j
II	b	e				g	h	k
III	c			f			i	l
IV	d							

The most electropositive element is

(a) c (b) d (c) l (d) k

• Assertion-Reasoning MCQs

Direction (Q. Nos. 16-20) *Each of these questions contains two statements Assertion (A) and Reason (R). Each of these questions also has four alternative choices, any one of which is the correct answer. You have to select one of the codes (a), (b), (c) and (d) given below.*

(a) Both A and R are true and R is the correct explanation of A.
(b) Both A and R are true, but R is not the correct explanation of A.
(c) A is true, but R is false.
(d) A is false, but R is true.

16. Assertion Be, Mg and Ca can be classified as Dobereiner's triads.
Reason Atomic mass of Mg is approximately the average of the sum of atomic masses of Be and Ca.

17. Assertion Sodium is an element of group 1 of the modern periodic table.
Reason All the elements of group 1 of the modern periodic table contain two electrons in their outermost shell.

18. Assertion Noble gases are also called inert gases.
Reason Noble gases have a complete octet.

19. Assertion Atomic size increases on going down the group in the modern periodic table.
Reason New shells are being added as we go down the group in the modern periodic table.

20. Assertion Electronegativity of flourine is greater than that of oxygen.
Reason The electronegativity of the elements increases along a period since the metallic character increases.

• Case Based MCQs

21. Read the following and answer the questions from (i) to (v) given below

The modern periodic table is based on the increasing order of atomic radius. The atomic size increases down the group. This is because new shell are being added as we go down the group. The atomic radius decreases in moving from left to right along a period.

Modern periodic law states that "the physical and chemical properties of all the elements are the periodic function of their atomic radius.

The atomic radii of group 1 and group 2 elements are given in the table.

Group 1	Atomic radii (nm)	Group 2	Atomic radii (nm)
Li	0.152	Be	0.112
Na	0.186	Mg	0.160
k	0.231	Ca	0.197
Rb	0.244	Sr	0.215
Cs	0.262	Ba	0.217
Fr	0.270	Ra	0.220

(i) Who discovered modern periodic table?
(a) Henry Moseley
(b) Johann Wolfgang Dobereiner
(c) John Newlands
(d) Dmitri Ivanovich Mendeleev

(ii) Along the period 3, which atom can loose electron easily?
(a) Li   (b) Na   (c) Be   (d) Mg

(iii) Which metal has the highest metallic character in group 1?
(a) Li   (b) Na   (c) K   (d) Rb

(iv) Which of the following properties increases down the group?
(a) Electronegativity
(b) Electropositive nature of element
(c) Non-metallic character
(d) Acidic oxide character

(v) Which atom is most electronegative along the period 4?
(a) K   (b) Rb   (c) Sr   (d) Ca

22. Read the following and answer the questions from (i) to (v) given below

The noble gases make up a class of chemical elements with similar properties under standard conditions, they are all odourless, colourless, monoatomic gases with very low chemical reactivity. These gases are also called as inert gases or aerogens. The properties of the noble gases can be well explained by modern theories of atomic structure. Their outer shell of valence electrons is considered to be full, giving them little tendency to participate in chemical reactions.

The linkage formed from one electrostatic attraction between oppositely charged ions in a chemical compound is called ionic or electrocovalent bond. Such a bond forms when the valence electrons of one atom are transferred permanently to another atom.

The table given below refers to the elements of the periodic table with atomic number from 3 to 18. These elements are shown by letters.

(Not by the usual symbols of the elements).

3	4	5	6	7	8	9	10
A	B	C	D	E	F	G	H
11	12	13	14	15	16	17	18
I	J	K	L	M	N	O	P

(i) Which of the following are noble gases ?
   (a) H and P　　　　　　(b) G and O
   (c) D and L　　　　　　(d) A and I

(ii) Which are halogens ?
   (a) H and L　　　　　　(b) C and M
   (c) G and O　　　　　　(d) E and P

(iii) Which of the following elements have valency 4 ?
   (a) F and N　　　　　　(b) C and K
   (c) D and L　　　　　　(d) H and P

(iv) Which of the following can form ionic bond?
   (a) B and H　　　　　　(b) J and P
   (c) E and P　　　　　　(d) A and G

(v) Which of the following elements have 2 valence electrons?
   (a) D and L　(b) B and J　(c) A and I　(d) C and K

PART 2
Subjective Questions

• Short Answer Type Questions

1. What were the limitations of Dobereiner's classification?　　　　　　　　**(NCERT)**

2. Can the following groups of elements be classified as Dobereiner's triad?
   (i) Na, Si, Cl　　　　　　(ii) Be, Mg, Ca
   Atomic mass of Be-9; Na-23; Mg-24; Si-28; Cl-35; Ca-40
   Justify your answer in each case.　　**(CBSE 2019)**

3. Did Dobereiner's triads also exist in the columns of Newlands' octaves? Compare and find out.　　**(NCERT)**

4. Elements have been arranged in the following sequence on the basis of their increasing atomic masses. F, Na, Mg, Al, Si, P, S, Cl, Ar, K.
   (i) Pick two sets of elements which have similar properties.
   (ii) The given sequence represents which law of classification of elements?

5. What were the limitations of Newlands' law of octaves?　　　　　　　　**(NCERT)**

6. What were the criteria used by Mendeleev in creating his periodic table?　　**(NCERT)**

7. In Mendeleev's periodic table, the elements were arranged in the increasing order of their atomic masses. However, cobalt with atomic mass of 58.93 amu was placed before nickel having an atomic mass of 58.71 amu. Give reason for the same.　　**(NCERT Exemplar)**

8. Write the formulae of chlorides of Eka-silicon and Eka-aluminium, the elements predicted by Mendeleev.

9. Write two main characteristics of Mendeleev's periodic table and write name of elements of second period.

10. How it can be proved that the basic structure of the 'modern periodic table' is based on the electronic configuration of atoms of different elements?　　**(CBSE 2019)**

11. 'Hydrogen occupies a unique position in modern periodic table'. Justify the statement. **(NCERT Exemplar)**

12. (i) List any two distinguishing features between Mendeleev's periodic table and the modern periodic table.
   (ii) With the help of an example, explain Dobereiner's Triads.
   (iii) State modern periodic law.　　**(CBSE 2020)**

13. Write the formula of the product formed when the element A (atomic number 19) combines with the element B (atomic number 17). Draw its electronic dot structure. What is the nature of the bond formed?　　**(NCERT Exemplar)**

14. Compare the radii of two species X and Y. Give reasons for your answer.
   (a) X has 12 protons and 12 electrons, (b) Y has 12 protons and 10 electrons　　**(NCERT Exemplar)**

15. Arrange the following elements in increasing order of their atomic radii.
   (i) Li, Be, F and N　　　　(ii) Cl, At, Br and I
   　　　　　　　　　　　　　　(NCERT Exemplar)

16. An element X of group 15 exists as diatomic molecule and combines with hydrogen at 773 K in presence of the catalyst to form a compound, ammonia which has a characteristic pungent smell.
   (i) Identify the element X. How many valence electrons does it have?
   (ii) Draw the electron dot structure of the diatomic molecule of X. What type of bond is formed in it?
   (iii) Draw the electron dot structure for ammonia and what type of bond is formed in it?

17. A salt when dissolved in water dissociates into cations and anions as follows:

$$AB \underset{-H_2O}{\overset{+H_2O}{\rightleftharpoons}} A^+ + B^-$$

If both the ions consist same number of electrons and the molecular weight of salt is 74.5, then identify the position of A and B in the periodic table.

18. Three elements A, B and C have 3, 4 and 2 electrons respectively in their outermost shell. Give the group number to which they belong in the modern periodic table. Also, give their valencies. **(NCERT Exemplar)**

19. Based on the group valency of elements, write the molecular formula of the following compounds giving justification for each.
  (i) Oxide of first group elements
  (ii) Halide of the elements of group thirteen
  (iii) Compound formed when an element A of group 2 combines with an element, B of group seventeen. **(CBSE 2019)**

20. From the elements Li, K, Mg, C, Al, S identify the
  (i) elements belonging to the same group. **(CBSE 2020)**
  (ii) element which has the tendency to lose two electrons.
  (iii) element which prefers sharing of electrons to complete its octet.
  (iv) most metallic element.
  (v) element that forms acidic oxide.
  (vi) element that belongs to group 13.

21. The following table shows the position of five elements A, B, C, D and E in the modern periodic table.

Group →	1	2	3 to 12	13	14	15	16	17	18
Period ↓									
2	A							B	C
3		D				E			

Answer the following giving reasons:
  (i) Which element is a metal with valency two?
  (ii) Which element is least reactive?
  (iii) Out of D and E which element has a smaller atomic radius? **(CBSE Sample Paper)**

22. (i) What term can be used for the elements separating metal from non-metals and why?
  (ii) Give the names of the metalloids in the periodic table along with their atomic number.
  (iii) In which groups of the periodic table are they located?

23. A group of elements in the periodic table are given below (boron is the first member of the group and thallium is the last).
Boron, aluminium, gallium, indium, thallium

Answer the following question in relation to the above group of elements.
  (i) Which element has the most metallic character?
  (ii) Which element would be expected to have the highest electronegativity?
  (iii) Will the elements in the group to the right of this boron group be more metallic or less metallic in character? Justify your answer.

• Long Answer Type Questions

24. Use Mendeleev's periodic table to predict the formulae for the oxides of the following elements. K, C, Al, Si and Ba. **(NCERT)**

25. Compare and constrast the arrangement of element in Mendeleev's periodic table and the modern periodic table. **(NCERT)**

26. An element is placed in 2nd group and 3rd period of the periodic table, burns in presence of oxygen to form a basic oxide. **(NCERT Exemplar)**
  (i) Identify the element.
  (ii) Write the electronic configuration.
  (iii) Write a balanced equation when it burns in the presence of air.
  (iv) Write a balanced equation when this oxide is dissolved in water.
  (v) Draw the electron dot structure for the formation of this oxide.

27. Which elements has
  (i) two shells, both of which are completely filled with electrons?
  (ii) the electronic configuration 2, 8, 2?
  (iii) a total of three shells, with four electrons in its valence shell?
  (iv) a total of two shells, with three electrons in its valence shell?
  (v) twice as many electrons in its second shell as in its first shell? **(NCERT)**

28. An element X (atomic number $= 17$) reacts with an element Y (atomic number $= 20$) to form a divalent halide.
  (i) Where in the periodic table are elements X and Y placed?
  (ii) Classify X and Y as metal(s), non-metal(s) or metalloid(s).
  (iii) What will be the nature of oxide of element Y? Identify the nature of bonding in the compound formed.
  (iv) Draw the electron dot structure of the divalent halide. **(NCERT Exemplar)**

29. (i) Using the part of the periodic table given below answer the questions that follows:

Groups →	1	2	13	14	15	16	17	18
Periods ↓								
1	H							He
2	Li	Be	B	C	N	O	F	Ne
3	Na	Mg	Al	Si	P	S	Cl	Ar
4	K	Ca						

    (a) Na has physical and chemical properties similar to which element(s).

    (b) Write the electronic configuration of N and P. Which one of these will be more electronegative and why?

    (c) State a chemical property common to fluorine and chlorine.

(ii) The neutral atom of an element E consists 12 electrons in its atoms.

    (a) In which period and group is E placed?

    (b) Name the element E.

    (c) How many electrons it needs to lose or gain to achieve noble gas configuration ?

    (d) What will be the nature of oxide (acidic/basic) of E? Justify your answer.

    (e) Write the formulae of chloride of E.

• Case Based Questions

30. Read the following and answer the questions from (i) to (v) given below

Modern periodic law states that the physical and chemical properties of the elements are periodic function of their atomic radius. When these elements were arranged in the increasing order of their atomic number, the obtained table is called modern periodic table.

Numerous forms of the periodic table have been devised form time to time. A new version, which is most convinient and widely used is the modern periodic table. This table consist of 18 vertical columns called **groups** and 7 horizontal rows, known as **periods**. The first period consists of two elements.

The subsequent period consist of 8, 8, 18, 18 and 32 elements respectively. The seventh period is incomplete and like the sixth period would have maximum of 32 electrons.

(i) An element belongs to group 17. It is present in third period and its atomic number is 17. What is the atomic number of the element belonging to same group and present in fifth period ?

(ii) Name the elements present in the first period of the modern periodic table.

(iii) Atoms of different elements with same number of shells are placed in the same period. Explain.

(iv) What is the electronic configuration of the element present in third period and belongs to group 15 ?

(v) How many elements are present in mdoern periodic table ?

31. Read the following and answer the questions from (i) to (v) given below

Valency is the combining capacity of an atom of an element to acquire noble gas configuration. If depends upon the number of valence electrons present in outermost shell of its atom. For the elements of group 1, 2, 13 and 14 valency = numbers of valency electrons(s), whereas for the elements of group 15 onwards valency = 8 − valence electrons.

The concept of valency is simple and rationalise the atomic composition of a large number of compounds. Yet, in many chemistry courses, it is sidelined in favour of electronic theories of bonding, which are more difficult. When the theory of valency was devised, chemists thought that all compounds were molecular. We now known that many are non-molecular, i.e. they comprise a large number of atoms bound together in a continuous framework. The theory can however be adapted to include non-molecular compounds.

The atomic number and valence of element A, B, C, D and E are given in below table.

Elements	Atomic number	Number of valence electron
A	3	1
B	9	7
C	17	7
D	20	2
E	36	0

(i) What is the valency of element B ?

(ii) If element C reacts with an element D, which type of compound they will form.

(iii) What is the name of element E ?

(iv) Element A belongs to which period in the modern periodic table ?

(v) Among A, C, D and E, which element belongs to group 17 ?

EXPLANATIONS

Objective Questions

1. (c) Dobereiner could identify only three triads from the elements known at that time. These are

Li, Na, K; Ca, Sr, Ba; Cl, Br, I

2. (b) Newlands' law of octaves was applicable only to lighter elements having atomic masses upto 40 u, i.e. upto calcium. After calcium, every eighth element did not possess properties similar to that of the first element.

3. (c) Gallium has a valency of 3. Hence, it forms an oxide having molecular formula E_2O_3. In other options, valency of E is not 3.

4. (d) Na (group 1) has one, Al (group 13) has three (13-10), Si (group 14) has four (14-10) and P (group 15) has five (15-10) valence electrons. Therefore, P has maximum number of valence electrons, i.e. 5 (maximum among the given).

5. (b) The number of electrons present in the outermost orbit of the element are known as valence electrons, while number of electrons used by any element in any chemical reaction is called its valency.

Both are co-related as follows

  (i) For first four elements in any period,

     Valence electrons = Valency

  (ii) For last four elements in any period,

     Valency = 8 – valence electrons

6. (d) Q belongs to group II, so its valency is +2. R belongs to 15 or VA group, so its valency is −3 (as it requires 3 electrons to complete its octet).

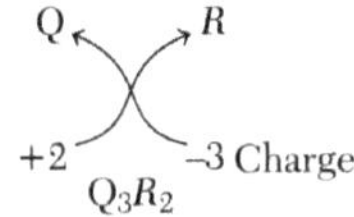

7. (a) In long form of periodic table, atomic size decreases along the period due to increase in effective nuclear charge. Thus, atomic size of B is less than of Be.

8. (d) Because along the period, atomic radii decreases as the atomic number increases. Thus, the correct increasing order is F < O < N.

9. (c) On moving from left to right, the atomic number increases and hence, the nuclear charge increases. With the increase of nuclear charge, the force binding the electron increases, so the atom lose the electrons with more difficulty and not easily.

10. (a) The correct match for the given item is

    A-(iii), B-(i), C-(ii), D-(iv).

- Be belongs to group 2 because it contains 2 valence electrons.
- F belongs to group 17 because it contains 7 valence electrons.
- P contains 5 electrons in it's outermost shell, so it belongs to group 15.
- Ar belongs to group 18 because it has full-filled electronic configuration.

11. (a) Lithium is the metal among the first ten elements as boron is a metalloid, carbon is a non-metal and potassium is not in first ten elements because it's atomic number is 19.

12. (d) Oxides of metals are of basic in nature while those of non-metals are acidic.

Group 1 and group 2 consists of metals. Therefore, all the elements of these groups form basic oxides. The element present in group 13 and period 3 is aluminium, whose oxides is amphoteric in nature.

Group 16 consists of non-metals. Therefore, all the elements of this group forms acidic oxide. Thus, an element X which form an acidic oxides belongs to group 16 and period 3.

13. (a) ∵ The oxide turns the red-litmus to blue but shows no effect on blue litmus. Also, the oxide is a metal oxide, thus one of its component must be a metal. Hence, it is MgO.

14. (c) The element A will form a basic oxide while B, C and D will form an acidic oxide. This is because on moving along a period, the acidic character of the oxide increases.

15. (b) The most electropositive element is 'd' as electropositive character increases down the group and decreases along a period.

16. (a) Both A and R are true and R is the correct explanation of A. According to the Dobereiner's triads, the three elements in a traid were arranged in the order of increasing atomic masses, the atomic mass of middle element was roughly the average of the atomic masses of the other two elements. So, taking Be, Mg and Ca as a triad.

Elements	Be	Mg	Ca
Atomic mass	9	24	40

Average atomic mass of first and third element

$$\frac{9+40}{2} = 24.5$$

17. (c) A is true but R is false. All the elements of group I contains one valence electron and valency as the electronic configuration of Li = 2, 1, Na = 2, 8, 1 and K = 2, 8, 8, 1. All the elements contain only one valence electron.

18. (a) Both A and R are true and R is the correct explanation of A. Noble gases are also called inert gases because they don't need to react with other elements to fill their outer shell octet, as they already posses full valence shell.

19. (a) Both A and R are true and R is the correct explanation of A.

20. (c) A is true but R is false. Electronegativity of fluorine is greater than that of oxygen, since the non-metallic character increases along a period from left to right in the modern periodic table.

21. (i) (a) In 1913, Henry Moseley discovered the modern periodic table by modifying Mendeleev's periodic law.

    (ii) (b) Along the period 3, (Na) sodium can loose electron easily because moving from left to right along a period, atomic radius decreases due to increase in effective nuclear charge which tends to pull the valence electrons closer to the nucleus and hence, tendency to lose the electrons decreases.

(iii) (*d*) Rb has the highest metallic character because down the group, the effective nuclear charge decreases as the atomic radius increases. So, the outermost electrons are farther away from nucleus which can be lost easily. Hence, metallic character increases down the group.

(iv) (*b*) Electropositive nature increases down the group due to increase in atomic size.

(v) (*d*) Along the period 4, Ca is the most electronegative atom because along a period, non-metallic character increases and so electronegativity also increases.

22. (i) (*a*) *H* and *P* have complete octet. So, they are noble gases.

(ii) (*c*) *G* and *O* have 7 electrons in their outermost shell. So, they belongs to halogen group.

(iii) (*c*) *D* has 6 electrons. So, its electronic configuration is 2, 4.

L has 14 electrons. So, its electronic configuration is 2, 8, 4.

∴ Both have 4 valency.

(iv) (*d*) *A* has one valence electron. So, its valency is 1. It can form A^+ ion.

G has seven valence electron. It needs one electron to complete its octet. So, *A* can make ionic bond with *G* and form stable compound, *AG*.

(v) (*b*) *B* has 4 electrons. So, its electronic configuration is 2, 2 and hence, have 2 valence electrons.

J has 12 electrons. So, it's electronic configuration is 2, 8, 2 so, it also contains 2 valence electrons.

∴ Both *B* and *J* contains 2 valence electrons.

Subjective Questions

1. All the elements discovered at that time could not be classified into triads, only a limited number of elements could be arranged in such triads.

e.g. The three elements nitrogen (N), phosphorus (P) and arsenic (As) have similar properties. Therefore, they should be regarded to form a triad.

However, the actual mass of the middle element P(31.04) is much lower than the average (44.454) of the atomic masses of nitrogen (14.4) and arsenic (74.94). Therefore, these three elements do not constitute a Dobereiner's triad inspite of their similar chemical properties.

2. (i) Na, Si and Cl have different properties, therefore, they do not form Dobereiner's triad even though the atomic mass of the middle atom (Si) is approximately the average of the atomic masses of Na and Cl, i.e.

Na (23); Si (28); Cl (35)

$$\text{Atomic mass of Si} = \frac{23 + 35}{2} = \frac{58}{2} = 29$$

(ii) Be, Mg and Ca have many similar properties and also the atomic mass of the middle element Mg is approximately the average of the atomic masses of Be and Ca, i.e.

Be (9); Mg (24); Ca (40)

$$\text{Atomic mass of Mg} = \frac{9 + 40}{2} = \frac{49}{2} = 24.5$$

Therefore, they form Dobereiner's triad.

3. Yes, Dobereiner's triads also exist in the columns of Newlands' octaves, e.g. lithium (Li), sodium (Na) and potassium (K) constitute a Dobereiner's triads. Now, if we consider Li as the first element, then the eighth element from it is Na and if we consider Na as the first element, then the eight element from it is K.

Similarly, Dobereiner's triad consisting of the elements beryllium (Be), magnesium (Mg) and calcium (Ca) is also included in the column of Newlands' octaves.

Thus, Dobereiner's triads are included in the columns of Newlands' octaves.

4. (i) Here, the elements are arranged in the order of increasing atomic masses, so according to Newlands' law of octaves there is a repetition of every eighth element as compared to the given element. The two sets of elements which have similar properties are

Set I → F, Cl

Set II → Na, K

F and Cl are first and eighth element in the above sequence, therefore, they have similar properties. Although Na and K have similar properties but they are not related as first and eighth element in the above sequence.

(ii) The given sequence is according to Newlands' law of octaves represented as

F Na Mg Al Si P S Cl Ar K

5. • This law was applicable only upto calcium. After calcium, every eighth element did not possess the same properties similar to that of the first.

• Newland assumed that there were only 56 elements existed in nature and no more elements would be discovered in the future. But, later on, several new elements were discovered, whose properties did not fit into the law of octaves.

• In order to fit elements into his table, Newlands' adjusted two elements in the same slot and also put some unlike elements under the same column.

e.g. Cobalt and nickel are in the same slot and these are placed in the same column as fluorine, chlorine and bromine which have very different properties than these elements. Iron, which resembles cobalt and nickel in properties, has been placed far away from these elements. Hence, Newlands' law of octaves worked well with lighter elements only.

6. The criteria used by Mendeleev were:

(i) The arrangement of elements in increasing order of atomic masses.

(ii) Similarity in chemical properties of the elements.

7. In Mendeleev's periodic table, cobalt (Co) with a higher atomic mass of 58.93 u is placed before nickel (Ni) due to the following reasons :

(i) The properties of cobalt are similar to those of rhodium (Rh) and iridium (Ir) (same group) and

(ii) The properties of nickel are similar to those of palladium (Pd) and platinum (Pt) (same group).

8. Eka-silicon is germanium (Ge). It lies in group 4 of the Mendeleev's periodic table and thus, has a valency of 4.

∴ The formula of its chloride is $GeCl_4$.

Eka-aluminium is gallium (Ga). It lies in group 3 of the Mendeleev's periodic table and thus, has a valency of 3.

$\therefore$ The formula of its chloride is $GaCl_3$.

9. Two main characteristics of Mendeleev's periodic table are :

  (i) It consists of 8 vertical columns, called groups and 6 horizontal rows, called period.

  (ii) In every period, elements are arranged in increasing order of their atomic masses.

Name of elements of second period are lithium, beryllium, boron, carbon, nitrogen, oxygen, fluorine.

10. Electronic configuration of an element decides its position in modern periodic table.

If we take an example of sodium (Na), which has atomic number $= 11$, i.e. it's electronic configuration $= 2, 8, 1$

As Na contains 1 electron in its outermost shell, this means that it belongs to group 1 and sodium contains 3 shells so, it belongs to period number 3.

$\therefore$ We can conclude that,

Group number = Number of valence electrons

                     (When valence electrons are 1 and 2)

and group number = 10 + valence electrons

                     (When valence electrons are 3 and above)

Period number = Number of shells in which electrons are filled.

11. Hydrogen occupies a unique position in the modern periodic table due to the following reasons

  (i) Both hydrogen and alkali metals have similar outer electronic configuration as both have one electron in the valence shell. Therefore, some of the properties of hydrogen are similar to those of alkali metals and hence, it can be placed in group 1 alongwith alkali metals.

  (ii) Both hydrogen and halogens have similar outer electronic configuration (both have one electron less than the nearest inert gas configuration). Therefore, some of the properties of hydrogen are similar to those of halogens and hence, it can be placed in group 17 alongwith halogens.

  (iii) In some properties, it differs from both hydrogen and halogens, e.g. the oxide of hydrogen, i.e. H_2O is neutral but the oxides of alkali metals (i.e. Na_2O, K_2O etc.) are basic while those of halogens (i.e. Cl_2O_7, Br_2O_5, I_2O_5 etc.) are acidic.

12. (i)

Mendeleev's periodic table	Modern periodic table
In the Mendeleev's periodic table, the elements were arranged in increasing order of their atomic masses.	In modern periodic table, the elements are arranged in the increasing order of their atomic number.
This table consists of 8 groups and 6 periods.	This contains 18 groups and 7 periods.

  (ii) Dobereiner arrange the elements with similar properties into groups having three elements each and named these groups as triads.

He showed that when the three elements in a triad were arranged in the order of increasing atomic masses, the atomic mass of the middle element was roughly the average of the atomic masses of other two elements, e.g.

Elements	Cl	Br	I
Atomic mass	35.5	80	127
Average atomic mass of first and that elements	$\dfrac{35.5 + 127}{2} = 81.25$		

  (iii) **Modern periodic law** The physical and chemical properties are a periodic function of their atomic number.

13. Atomic number of $A = 19$

Electronic configuration is 2, 8, 8, 1.

Hence, element A is metal potassium (K) and

Atomic number of $B = 17$.

Electronic configuration is 2, 8, 7.

It is a non-metal, chlorine (Cl).

So, the electron dot structure of KCl is

$$K^{\bullet} \quad + \quad \times\overset{\times\times}{\underset{\times\times}{Cl}}\times \longrightarrow K^+ \quad \left[\times\overset{\times\times}{\underset{\times\times}{Cl}}\times\right]^-$$

2, 8, 8, 1   2, 8, 7   2, 8, 8 2, 8, 8

Potassium   Chlorine   Potassium chloride

The bond formed between K^+ and Cl^- is ionic bond and formula of the product formed $K^+ Cl^-$ or KCl.

14. Since, species X has 12 protons and 12 electrons, it is electrically neutral. Since, species Y has 12 protons and 10 electrons, therefore, it has two units positive charge.

The electronic configuration of the two species are

Species X			Species Y	
K	L	M	K	L
2	8	2	2	8

Since, species X has three shells while species Y has two shells, therefore, species Y has smaller radius than species X.

15. (i) Atomic radii decreases along a period from left to right due to increase in nuclear charge. Li, Be, F and N belong to same period. Thus, the atomic radii of Li, Be, F and N increases in the order:

$$F < N < Be < Li$$

  (ii) Atomic radii increase in a group from top to bottom due to the corresponding increase in the number of filled electronic shells. Cl, At, Br, I belong to same group. Thus, atomic radii of Cl, At, Br and I increase in the order:

$$Cl < Br < I < At$$

16. Since, the element 'X' of group 15 exists as a diatomic molecule and combines with hydrogen at 773 K in presence of a catalyst to form ammonia which has a characteristic smell, therefore, the element 'X' is nitrogen (N).

$$\underset{\substack{\text{Nitrogen}\\ \text{(diatomic molecule)}}}{N_2} \quad + \quad \underset{\text{Hydrogen}}{3H_2} \quad \xrightarrow[\text{Catalyst}]{773\ K} \quad \underset{\substack{\text{Ammonia}\\ \text{(pungent smell)}}}{2NH_3}$$

  (i) The atomic number of nitrogen is 7. So, its electronic configuration is 2, 5. Thus, it has five valence electrons.

  (ii) Nitrogen has 5 valence electrons. Therefore, it needs 3 more electrons to complete its octet.

To do so, it shares three of its electrons with three electrons of the other nitrogen atom to form a diatomic molecule of N_2 gas.

Thus, three **covalent bonds** are formed between two nitrogen atoms and each nitrogen atom is left with one lone pair of electrons.

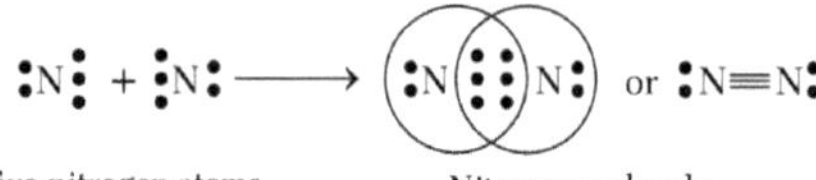

(iii) Electron dot structure for ammonia is as follows :

In NH_3 molecule, there are three N—H single covalent bonds and one lone pair of electrons on the nitrogen atom.

17. Since, both the ions consists of same number of electrons and has +1 and −1 charges, hence the ions should belong to group 1A (cation, i.e. A^+) and group VII A (anion, i.e. B^-).

Same number of electrons indicates that their electronic configuration is same as that of a noble gas whose atomic number lie between that of the two elements A and B.

Dividing the molecular weight (which is sum of atomic masses of A and B), we get the rough idea about the atomic mass of the noble gas which is $\dfrac{74.5}{2} = 37.25$, i.e. nearest to argon (Ar - 40).

Hence, A is K (group IA, 4th period) and element B is Cl (group VII A, 3rd period).

18. (i) Element A has 3 valence electrons, therefore, its valency is 3 and thus belongs to group 13 $(3 + 10)$. As such, it could be any one of the following elements : B, Al, Ga, In or Tl.

(ii) Element B has 4 valence electrons, therefore, its valency is 4 and it belongs to group 14 $(4 + 10)$. The element B could be any one of the following : C, Si, Ge, Sn or Pb.

(iii) Element C has two valence electrons, therefore, its valency is 2 and it belongs to group 2. The element C could be any one of the following : Be, Mg, Ca, Sr, Ba or Ra.

19. (i) The valency of the group 1 elements is 1 and that of oxygen is 2.

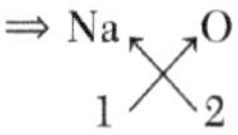

∴ Molecular formula of oxide $= Na_2O$

(ii) The valency of group 13 element is 3 and that of halide is 1.

$$\Rightarrow Al_{\;3} \times Cl_{\;1}$$

∴ Molecular formula of halide $= AlCl_3$

(iii) Molecular formula of compound formed $= AB_2$

($\because$ Valency of group 2 element (A) is 2 and that of group 17 element (B) is 1).

∴

$$A_{\;2} \times B_{\;1}$$

$\Rightarrow AB_2$

20. The electronic configurations of the given elements are as follows

$$_3Li \rightarrow 2, 1$$
$$_{19}K \rightarrow 2, 8, 8, 1$$
$$_{12}Mg \rightarrow 2, 8, 2$$
$$_6C \rightarrow 2, 4$$
$$_{13}Al \rightarrow 2, 8, 3$$
$$_{16}S \rightarrow 2, 8, 6$$

(i) Element belong to same group are Li and K as they both contain one electron in their outermost shell.

(ii) Element which has tendency lose two electrons is magnesium as it cantains 2 electrons its outermost shell.

(iii) Element which prefer sharing of electron to complete its octet is carbon due to its small size and strong C— C bond.

(iv) Most metallic element is potassium. Elements of group 1 are metallic in nature as they readily loose their one valence electron.

(v) Non-metals form acidic oxides. Among the given elements, S is a non-metal. Thus, it forms most acidic oxide.

(vi) Aluminium belongs to group 13 as it contains 3 elements in its outermost shell.

21. (i) Element 'D' is a metal with valency two.

Because, the group number of an element having upto two valence electrons is equal to the number of valence electrons.

(ii) 'C' is the least reactive element. Because, it belongs to group 18. Group 18 (Noble gases) are least reactive due zero valency of group 18 elements.

(iii) 'E' has a smaller atomic radius than 'D' because 'E' is on the right side of the modern periodic table.

Across the period, atomic size/radius decreases on moving left to right. This is due to an increase in nuclear charge which tends to pull the valence electrons closer to the nucleus and reduces the size of the atoms.

22. (i) Metalloids as these elements show the properties of both the metals and non-metals.

(ii) The list of metalloids alongwith their atomic number is as follows:

B (5), Si(14), Ge (32), As (33), Sb (51), Te (52) and Po (84).

(iii) These elements are located in groups 13, 14, 15 and 16.

23. (i) Thallium has the most metallic character. Metallic character increases down in a group.

(ii) Boron has the highest electronegativity because electronegativity decreases down a group.

(iii) Less metallic in character, because on moving across a period, metallic nature decreases.

24. Oxygen is a member of group VI A in Mendeleev's periodic table. Its valency is 2. Similarly, the valencies of all the elements given can be predicted from their respective group.

This can help in writing the formula of their oxides.

(i) Potassium (K) is a member of group IA. Its valency is 1. Therefore, the formula of its oxide is K_2O.

(ii) Carbon (C) is a member of group IVA. Its valency is 4. Therefore, the formula of its oxide is C_2O_4 or CO_2.

(iii) Aluminium (Al) belongs to group IIIA and its valency is 3. Therefore, the formula of its oxide is Al_2O_3.

(iv) Silicon (Si) is present in group IVA after carbon. Its valency is also 4. Therefore, the formula of its oxide is Si_2O_4 or SiO_2.

(v) Barium (Ba) belongs to group IIA and its valency is 2. Therefore, the formula of its oxide is Ba_2O_2 or BaO.

25.

Mendeleev's periodic table	Modern periodic table
The properties of elements are the periodic functions of their atomic mass.	The properties of elements are the periodic functions of their atomic number.
It has 8 groups.	It has 18 groups.
There is no place for isotopes of an element.	Isotopes of an element are assigned the same place with their respective elements as they have the same atomic number.
No fixed position was given to hydrogen in this periodic table.	Hydrogen is given a special position in modern periodic table.
Inert gases were not known at the time of Mendeleev.	Inert gases have been placed at the end of period in group 18.

26. (i) Since, the element lies in group 2, it must be an alkaline earth metal. Since, it lies in the third period, it must be magnesium (Mg).

(ii) Atomic number of Mg is 12, therefore, its electronic configuration is $\overset{K\ \ L\ \ M}{2,\ 8,\ 2}$.

(iii) When Mg burns in the presence of air, it forms a basic oxide, MgO.

$$\underset{\text{Magnesium}}{2Mg\ (s)} + \underset{\text{Oxygen}}{O_2(g)} \xrightarrow{\text{Heat}} \underset{\text{Magnesium oxide}}{2MgO\ (s)}$$

(iv) When MgO is dissolved in water, it forms magnesium hydroxide.

$$\underset{\text{Magnesium oxide}}{2MgO\ (s)} + \underset{\text{Water}}{2H_2O\ (l)} \longrightarrow \underset{\text{Magnesium hydroxide}}{2Mg(OH)_2(aq)}$$

(v) Mg has 2 valence electrons [as electronic configuration of $_{12}Mg = [2, 8, 2]$. Oxygen has 6 valence electrons [as electronic configuration of $_8O = [2, 6]$. Electron dot structure for the formation of magnesium oxide.

27. (i) Noble gases are the elements which have completely filled shells. The noble gas with two shells (K, L) is Ne having atomic number 10 and electronic configuration $\overset{K\ L}{2\ 8}$ both of the shells are completely filled.

(ii) Electronic configuration 2, 8, 2 suggests that atomic number is 12 (2 + 8 + 2). Magnesium (Mg) has atomic number 12.

(iii) The element with three shells and four electrons in the valence shell will have electronic configuration $\overset{K\ L\ M}{2\ 8\ 4}$. The atomic number of this element is 14 (2+8+4) so it will belong to group 14. Hence, it is silicon (Si).

(iv) Element with two shells and 3 electrons in the valence shell will exist in second period and will have the electronic configuration $\overset{K\ L}{2\ 3}$.

The atomic number of this element will be 5 (2, 3). So, it will be boron (B).

(v) The element has two shells. We know that first shell can have only 2 electrons, so according to the question there will be 4 electrons (double the number of electrons in the first shell) in the valence shell. The electronic configuration will be $\overset{K\ L}{2\ 4}$, so the atomic number is 6. Hence, the element is carbon (C).

28. (i) The electronic configuration of element X with atomic number 17 is 2, 8, 7. Since, it has 7 valence electrons. Therefore, it lies in group 17 (10 + 7). Further, since in element X, third shell is being filled, it lies in third period. In other words, X is chlorine.

The electronic configuration of element Y with atomic number 20 is 2, 8, 8, 2. Since, it has 2 valence electrons, it lies in group 2. Further, since in element Y, fourth shell is being filled, it lies in 4th period. In other words, Y is calcium.

(ii) Since, element X (i.e. Cl) has seven electrons in the valence shell and needs one more electron to complete its octet. Therefore, it is a non-metal. Further, the element Y has two electrons in the valence shell that can be easily lost to achieve the stable electronic configuration of the nearest inert gas, therefore, it is a metal.

(iii) Since, element Y (i.e. Ca) is a metal, therefore, its oxide (i.e. CaO) must be basic in nature. Further, metals and non-metals form ionic compounds, therefore, the nature of bonding in calcium oxide is ionic.

(iv) Electronic configuration of $_{20}Ca = 2, 8, 8, 2$ [valence electrons = 2], electronic configuration of $_{17}Cl = 2, 8, 7$ [valence electrons = 7]. The electron dot structure of divalent metal halide,

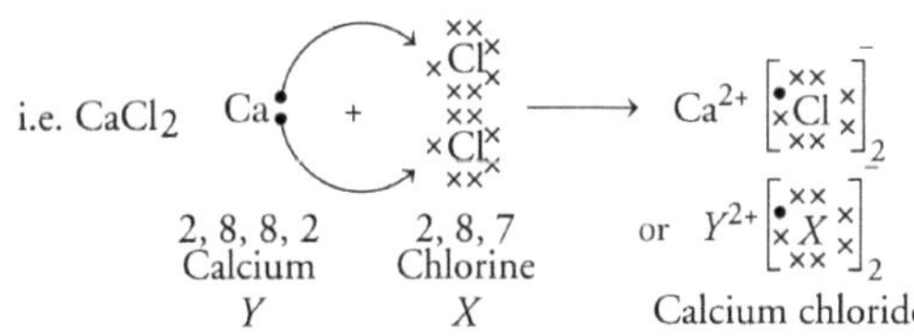

29. (i) (a) Lithium and potassium, due to presence of same number of valence electrons.

(b) $N \rightarrow 2, 5$ $P \rightarrow 2, 8, 5$

N is more electronegative element as electronegativity decrease on moving down the group.

(c) Both fluorine and chlorine form their hydrides on reacting with hydrogen.

$$H_2 + F_2 \longrightarrow 2HF$$
$$H_2 + Cl_2 \longrightarrow 2HCl$$

(ii) (a) The electronic configuration of $E = \begin{matrix} K & L & M \\ 2, & 8, & 2 \end{matrix}$

Hence, it should be placed in 3rd period and group II A.

(b) The element E is magnesium (Mg).

(c) Mg loses 2 electrons to form noble gas (Ne) with configuration as $\begin{matrix} K & L \\ 2, & 8 \end{matrix}$.

(d) Since, Mg is electropositive, it will form basic oxide.

(e) The formula of chloride is ECl_2 or $MgCl_2$.

30. (i) The element whose atomic number is 17 and belongs to third period is chlorine. If we go down the group, i.e. in fifth period, number of shells increases as $18e^-$ are increased in consecutive periods.

Therefore, the atomic number of the element belonging to same group and present in fifth period is $17 + 18 + 18 = 53$.

(ii) Hydrogen (H) and helium (He).

(iii) The number of valence shell electrons increases by one unit as the atomic number increases by one unit on moving from left to right in a period. Therefore, the atoms of different elements with same number of shells are placed in the same period.

(iv) As the element belongs to group-15, i.e., it's valence electrons are 5 and valency is 3, so it has the electronic configuration $= 2, 8, 5$.

(v) At present, 118 elements are known to us. All these have different properties. Out of these 118 elements, only 94 are naturally occurring.

31. (i) The atomic number of element B is 9 and number of valence electrons are 7, i.e. it belongs to group 17.

Valency $= 8 -$ valence electrons
$$= 8 - 7 = 1$$

Hence, the valency of B is 1.

(ii) Electronic configuration of element C is 2, 8, 7, i.e. it has 7 valence electrons and valency is -1 (as it requires 1 electron to complete it's octet) and electronic configuration of element D is 2, 8, 8, 2, i.e. it has 2 valence electrons and valency.

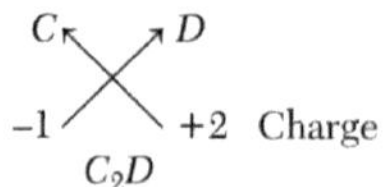

This forms a divalent compound (C_2D).

(iii) The atomic number of element E is 36, so the electronic configuration is $[Ar]3d^{10}4s^2 4p^6$. Therefore, this element belongs to 4th period as last electron goes in 4th shell and have zero number of valence electrons.

Hence, the element is krypton.

(iv) The atomic number of element A is 3 and electronic configuration is $1s^2 2s^1$. As last electron enters in 2nd shell, so, it belongs to period 2.

(v) The element that belongs to group 17 is 'C' because this group contain those elements which have 7 electrons in their outermost shell and element C also contains 7 valence electrons. Therefore, option (b) is correct.

Chapter Test

Multiple Choice Questions

1. Dobereiner grouped the elements into .... and Newlands' gave the ....
   (a) periods, triads
   (b) triads, law of octaves
   (c) octaves, periods
   (d) triads, periodic law

2. In Mendeleev's periodic table, gaps were left for the elements to be discovered later. Which of the following elements found a place in the periodic table later?
   (a) Germanium
   (b) Chlorine
   (c) Oxygen
   (d) Silicon

3. An element which is an essential constituent of all organic compounds belongs to
   (a) group 1
   (b) group 14
   (c) group 15
   (d) group 16

4. Which of the following is the outermost shell for elements of period 2?
   (a) K-shell
   (b) L-shell
   (c) M-shell
   (d) N-shell

5. Which group of element will form an acidic oxide?
   (a) Group 2
   (b) Group 13
   (c) Group 15
   (d) Group 18

Assertion-Reasoning MCQs

Direction (Q. Nos. 6-8) Each of these questions contains two statements Assertion (A) and Reason (R). Each of these questions also has four alternative choices, any one of which is the correct answer. You have to select one of the codes (a), (b), (c) and (d) given below.

   (a) Both A and R are true and R is the correct explanation of A.
   (b) Both A and R are true, but R is not the correct explanation of A.
   (c) A is true, but R is false.
   (d) A is false, but R is true.

6. Assertion According to Mendeleev, periodic properties of elements are functions of their atomic number.

   Reason Atomic number is equal to the number of protons.

7. Assertion The elements of the same group have similar chemical properties.

   Reason The elements of the same group have the different number of valence electrons.

8. Assertion Silicon, germanium and arsenic are the metalloids in the modern periodic table.

   Reason Silicon, germanium and arsenic has properties of metal as well as non-metals.

Short Answer Type Questions

9. Give an account of the process adopted by Mendeleev for the classification of elements. How did he arrive at "periodic law"?

10. What are valence electrons ? Does the number of valence electrons increase or decrease on moving from left to right in a period ? How does valency of elements very in the period ?

11. (i) How is the valency of an element determine if its electronic configuration is known? Determine the valency of an element of atomic number 9.
   (ii) Which one of the above elements belonging to the fourth period has bigger atomic radius and why?

12. Name
   (i) three elements that have a single electron in their outermost shells.
   (ii) two elements that have two electrons in their outermost shells.
   (iii) three elements with filled outermost shells.

13. Identify and name the metals out of the following elements whose electronic configurations are given below.
   (a) 2, 8, 2   (b) 2, 8, 1   (c) 2, 8, 7   (d) 2, 1

14. (i) What property do all elements in the same column of the periodic table as boron have in common?
   (ii) What property do all elements in the same column of the periodic table as fluorine have in common?

15. Arrange the following elements in the increasing order of their metallic character Mg, Ca, K, Ge, Ga.

Long Answer Type Questions

16. What are the limitations of Mendeleev's periodic table?

17. (i) The modern periodic table has been evolved through the early attempts of Dobereiner, Newland and Mendeleev. List one advantage and one limitation of all the three attempts.
   (ii) Name the scientist who first of all showed that atomic number of an element is a more fundamental property than its atomic mass.
   (iii) State modern periodic law.

18. (i) List two criteria Mendeleev's used in his periodic table to classify the elements. State Mendeleev's periodic law and explain why no fixed position was assigned to hydrogen in Mendeleev's periodic table ?
   (ii) How and why does the atomic size of elements vary as we move
   (a) from left to right in a period, and
   (b) down a group in the modern periodic

19. Write five main characteristics of group in modern periodic table.

Answers

Multiple Choice Questions

1. (b)   *2. (a)*   *3. (b)*   *4. (b)*   *5. (c)*

Assertion-Reasoning MCQs

6. (d)   *7. (c)*   *8. (b)*

For Detailed Solutions
Scan the code

How do Organisms Reproduce ?

In this Chapter...

- The Fundamentals of Reproduction
- Types of Reproduction
- Human Reproductive System
- Fertilisation and Post-fertilisation Changes
- Menstruation
- Reproductive Health
- Sexually Transmitted Diseases

The process by which living organisms produce its own kind of individuals to maintain the continuity of species is called reproduction. Like other essential life processes, reproduction is not essential to maintain life of an individual. But is a fundamental feature of all known life, each individual organism exists as the result of reproduction.

The Fundamentals of Reproduction

The process of reproduction involves the formation of DNA copy and other cellular apparatus required by the cells of an individual. DNA is the blueprint of all the basic design of organisms. It is present in the nucleus of a cell as a condensed structure called **chromosome**. It acts as the information source and helps in making different proteins and cellular machinery of cell, which makes up the different body designs.

Variations

DNA copying during cell division always causes some or other type of variations in newly formed cell. This brings the differences found in the morphological and physiological features of an organism.

Since no biochemical reaction is absolutely reliable, DNA copies generated are similar, but not absolutely identical. Variations lead to evolution by increasing the chances of survival of some individuals. Hence, important for the survival of species.

Types of Reproduction

Reproduction is mainly of two types, i.e. asexual reproduction and sexual reproduction.

- **Asexual Reproduction** It is a rapid mode of multiplication in which one parent (either male or female) is involved. The new individuals produced are identical to their parents.
- **Sexual Reproduction** In this process, the gametes from parents of opposite sex (male and female) fuse together to form a zygote. This zygote develops further and gives rise to new offspring. The individual produced by this method exhibits variation.

I. Modes of Asexual Reproduction

Asexual reproduction occurs in unicellular organisms by fission, budding, spore formation, fragmentation, regeneration (in animals) and vegetative propagation (in plants). It occurs in multicellular organisms by budding and regeneration.

These are as follows

(i) **Fission** The process where a unicellular organism splits itself into two or more daughter cells. It is of two types, i.e.

   (a) **Binary Fission** In this process, parent cell divides into two identical daughter cells, e.g. *Amoeba*, *Leishmania*.

In this process, nuclear division is followed by cytoplasmic division.

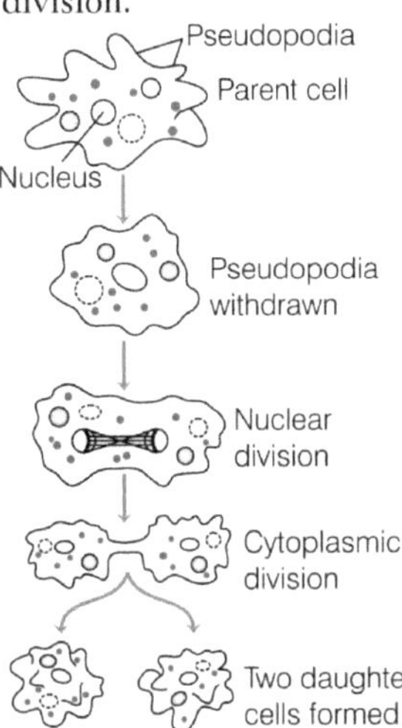

Binary fission in *Amoeba*

(b) **Multiple Fission** In this process, parent cell divides into many identical daughter organisms simultaneously, e.g. *Plasmodium*.

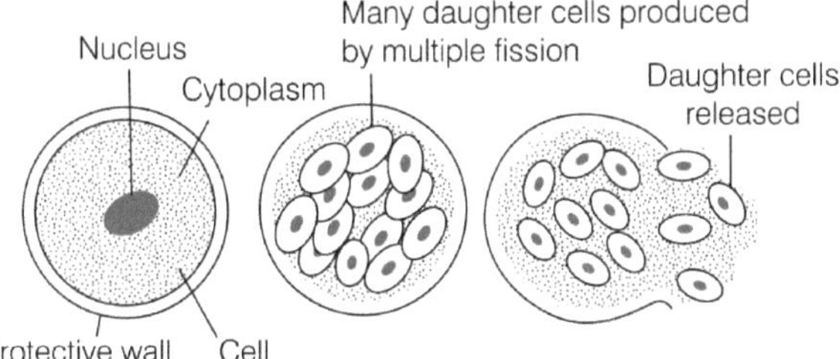

Multiple fission in *Plasmodium*

(ii) **Fragmentation** The parent body on maturation breaks up into two or more small fragments, which later grow into a complete new organism, e.g. *Spirogyra*.

(iii) **Regeneration** In this process, all fragments or parts that are separated from the body develop in new animals, e.g. sponge, *Planaria*, *Hydra*, etc.

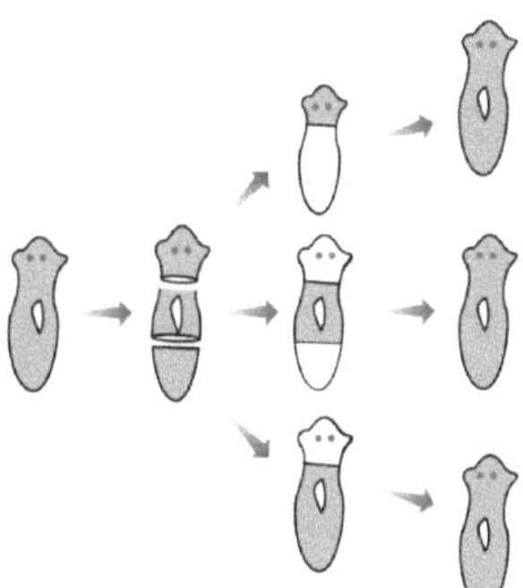

Regeneration in *Planaria*

(iv) **Budding** A daughter organism is formed from a small projection known as bud. It develops as an outgrowth due to repeated cell divisions of the parent body. When fully grown, it detaches to grow into a new independent individual, e.g. *Hydra*.

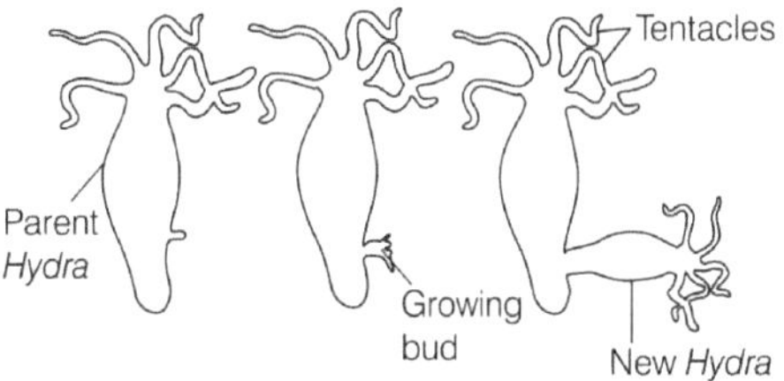

Budding in *Hydra*

(v) **Vegetative Propagation** The process of obtaining complete plant from any vegetative part of plant is called vegetative propagation. This is mainly of two types

(a) **Natural Vegetative Propagation** The vegetative propagation that occurs automatically in plants is called natural vegetative propagation. It can be achieved by root, stem, leaf, etc, e.g. *Bryophyllum*.

Leaf of *Bryophyllum* with buds

(b) **Artificial Vegetative Propagation** The artificially made vegetative propagules in plants by humans, is called artificial vegetative reproduction, e.g. cutting, layering, grafting, etc.

- **Grafting** A small part of stem from one plant without roots (scion) is attached to the part with root (stock) of another plant.
- **Layering** The development of roots on a stem, while the stem is still attached to the parent plant is called layering.
- **Tissue culture** It is a technique used for growing new plants using living tissues (like flower buds, stems, growing tips, leaves, etc.) *in vitro* in an artificial culture medium.
- Using this technique, large number of plants can be developed from a single parent.

(vi) **Spore Formation** It is a type of asexual reproduction where blob-like structures called sporangia are involved. These cells or spores have the ability to germinate under favourable conditions forming new plants, e.g. *Rhizopus*.

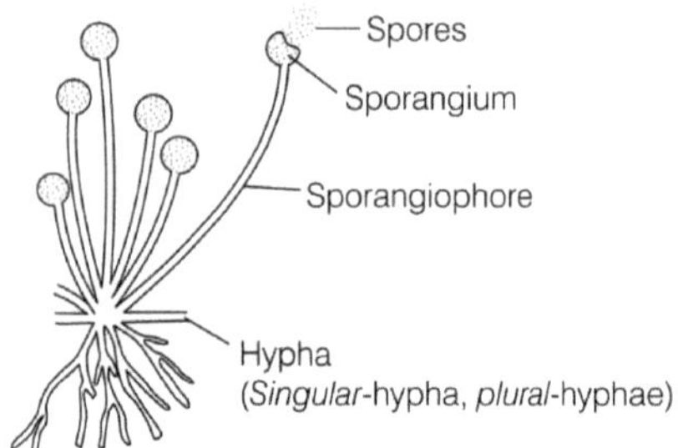

Spore formation in *Rhizopus*

II. Modes of Sexual Reproduction

In this type of reproduction, both sexes, i.e. male and female are involved. Sex cell or gamete of one parent (male) fuses with the sex cell or gamete of another parent (female). This results in production of a new cell called zygote.

Thus, the sexual mode of reproduction involves two major processes

(i) Formation of gametes by meiosis
(ii) Fusion of gametes

1. Sexual Reproduction in Flowering Plants

Angiosperms bear the reproductive parts within the flower and their seeds are enclosed in a fruit. Most plants have both male and female reproductive organs in the same flower and are known as **bisexual flowers**. While others have either male or female reproductive parts in a flower known as **unisexual flowers**.

A flower comprises of four main parts, i.e. sepals, petals, stamens and carpels. Stamens and carpels are the reproductive parts of a flower.

(i) **Stamen** It is the male reproductive part of the flower.

(ii) **Anther** It is a bilobed structure containing two pollen sacs present at tip of stamen. These produce pollen grains that are yellowish in colour.

(iii) **Carpel** (Pistil) It is the female reproductive part, which is present in the centre of the flower. It comprises of three parts

 • **Stigma** It is the terminal part of carpel which may be sticky. It helps in receiving the pollen grains during pollination.

 • **Style** It is the middle elongated part of carpel. It helps in the attachment of stigma to the ovary.

 • **Ovary** It is the swollen bottom part of carpel. It contains ovules having an egg cell (female gamete).

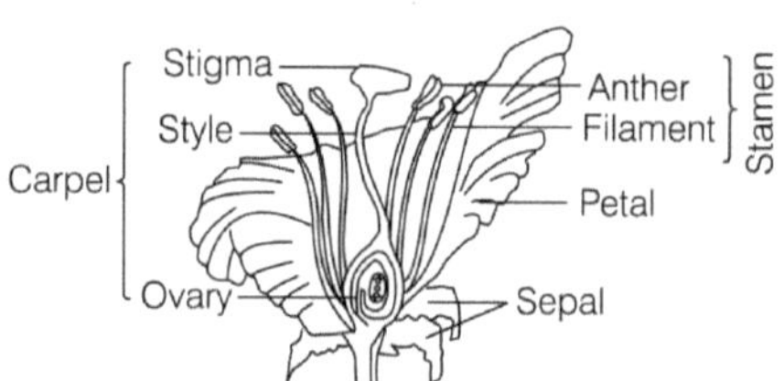

Longitudinal section of flower

Pollination

The transfer of pollen grains from the anther of the stamen to the stigma of a flower is termed as **pollination.** The pollen grains can be transferred by various agents like wind, water, insects and animals.

Pollination usually occurs in two ways

(i) **Self-pollination** The pollen from the stamen of a flower is transferred to the stigma of the same flower or another flower of same plant.

(ii) **Cross-pollination** The pollen from the stamen of a flower is transferred to the stigma of another flower of different plant of the same species.

Fertilisation

It is the process of fusion of male and female gametes. It gives rise to a **zygote**. As soon as the pollen lands on suitable stigma, it reaches the female germ cells in ovary. This occurs *via* pollen tube. The pollen tube grows out of the pollen grain, travels through the style and finally reaches the ovary.

After fertilisation, ovule develops a rough coat around itself and gets converted to seeds and ovary ripens as fruit.

The seed contains future embryo that grows under suitable conditions (germination). The fertilisation in the flowering plant is shown in the given figure.

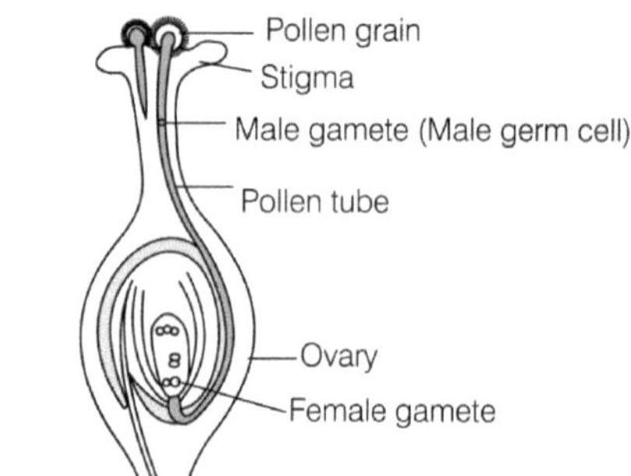

Germination of pollen grain on stigma

2. Sexual Reproduction in Human Beings

Human beings can reproduce sexually after attaining puberty. It represents period of adolescence when reproductive organs start developing and sexual maturity is attained. Some changes during puberty are common in males and females such as hair growth in armpits and genitals, oily skin, acne, etc.

Specific changes in boys include facial hair growth, hoarse voice, etc. In girls, these changes are enlargement of breast size, begining of menstruation, etc.

Human Reproductive System

The system of organs required by males and females for the process of sexual reproduction is called reproductive system.

(i) **Male Reproductive System** It includes parts which produce the germ cells and those which deliver these cells at the site of fertilisation.

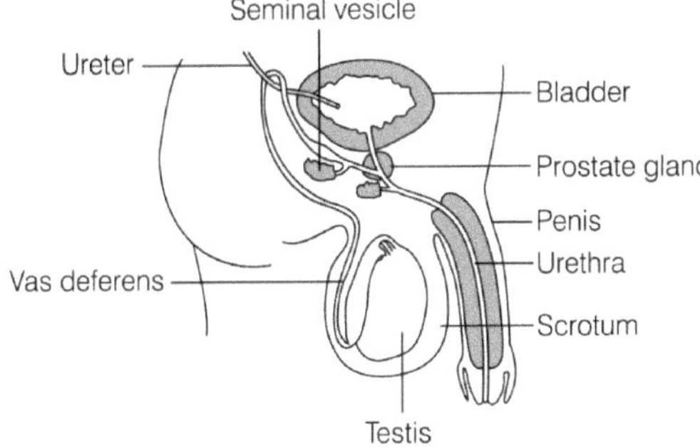

Male reproductive system

Parts and Details of the Male Reproductive System

Parts	Details
Testes	• Paired, oval-shaped male sex organs. • Consist of seminiferous tubules, where the sperms are produced. • Produce a male sex hormone called **testosterone**, which brings about changes in appearance of boys at puberty.
Scrotum	• Small pouch that contains testis. • Present outside the abdominal cavity. As sperms are formed here, this requires a lower temperature than the normal body temperature.
Vas deferens	• Tube-like structure which connects testis to the urethra in order to allow the passage of semen.
Urethra	• Common passage for both the sperms and urine. It never carries both of them at the same time.
Prostate gland and seminal vesicles	• Secretes seminal fluid and nutrients. • Fluid and nutrients combine with sperm to form **semen**. Milky, viscous fluid contains fructose, proteins and other chemicals for nourishing and stimulating sperms.
Penis	• External male genital organ. • Transfers sperms into the vagina of the female during copulation.
Sperms	• Tiny and motile bodies that use their long tail to move through the female reproductive tract.

(ii) **Female Reproductive System** It includes internal and external sex organs that function in reproduction of new offspring. In human, female reproductive system is immature at birth and develops to maturity at puberty to be able to produce gametes, and to carry a foetus.

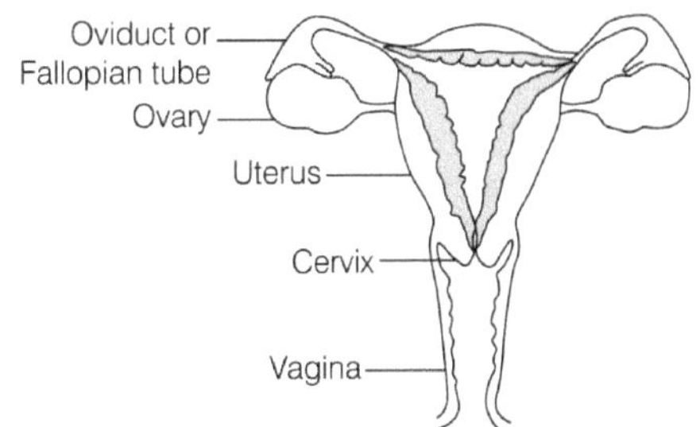

Female reproductive system

Parts and Details of the Female Reproductive System

Parts	Details
Ovaries	• Paired, oval-shaped organs located in the abdominal cavity near the kidney. • Produce thousands of ova or egg cells. • Secrete female sex hormones like **oestrogen** and **progesterone**.
Oviduct (Fallopian tube)	• It has a funnel-shaped opening near the ovary. • Carries ova or egg from ovary to the uterus. • It is the site of fertilisation. • These open into the **uterus** from both the sides.
Uterus (womb)	• Hollow, pear-shaped, bag-like structure. • The growth and development of foetus takes place.
Cervix	• It is the lower and the narrower portion of uterus which opens into the vagina.
Vagina	• Receives the sperms from the male partner. • Serves as a birth canal.

Fertilisation and Post-Fertilisation Changes

• Fusion of sperm with ovum is called **fertilisation**. It results in the formation of diploid zygote. This process takes place in the **oviduct** or **Fallopian tube**. The formation of embryo is the result of cleavage and growth in **zygote**.

• The embryo sinks downward, reaches into the soft uterine lining and gets embedded. This process is known as **implantation**.

• A disc-like structure called **placenta** grows between the uterine wall and embryo. It has finger-like projections called villi, which provide surface area for the exchange of nutrients, oxygen and waste products between the embryo and the mother.

- Childbirth (after a gestation period of approximately 9 months) occurs by strong rhythmic contractions of uterine muscles.

Menstruation

In the absence of fertilisation, the uterine lining which becomes thick and spongy to receive a fertilised egg, is no longer required. It sheds out as blood and mucus which lasts for about 2-8 days and occurs every month. This phase is known as menstruation.

Reproductive Health

It can be defined as the state of physical, mental and social fitness to lead a healthy reproductive life. Good reproductive health provides both male and female with

- the fertility control methods.
- awareness about how to limit their family size.
- protection from infection and sexually transmitted diseases.

Sex Ratio

The ratio of the number of females to the number of males in a population is known as sex ratio. A balanced female-male sex ratio is necessary for a healthy society.

Population Size

The rates of birth and death in a given population determine its size. The population size increases if the birth rate is higher than the death rate and *vice-versa*.

Methods of Family Planning

The sexual act always carries the risk of potential pregnancy. In order to avoid unplanned pregnancies, many ways have been devised, which are called **contraception** or **birth control methods**.

Methods of Family Planning

Methods	Examples	Details
Barrier	Condom	• Rubber sheath worn over the penis to stop sperm from entering the vagina. • Prevents transmission of Sexually Transmitted Diseases (STDs) and has no side effect.
	Diaphragm	• Rubber cup that is placed in the vagina over the cervix.
	Intra-Uterine Contraceptive Device (IUCD)	• Copper-T placed in uterus by doctor. • Used to prevent pregnancy. • Can cause side effects due to the irritation of uterus.
Hormonal	Oral contraceptive pills	• Contain hormones, which prevent release of ovum, so that fertilisation cannot occur. These disturb the hormonal balance (levels of FSH and LH) of the body. • Can cause side effects also.
Chemical	Spermicide	• Applied in vagina. • Kills sperms. • Can only be used with condoms or diaphragm.
Surgical	Vasectomy	• Small portion of the sperm duct is cut or tied properly. Therefore, the sperm transfer will be prevented. • Prevents sperms from coming out of urethra. • An irreversible process.
	Tubectomy	• Small portion of oviduct is cut or tied properly. The Fallopian tube in the female gets blocked. The egg will not be able to reach the uterus and thus, fertilisation will not take place. • Prevents the egg from meeting the sperms. • An irreversible process.

Female Foeticide

The killing of unborn girl child is called female foeticide. It is happening because of misuse of ultrasound technique by which people get to know the sex of the child. If it is female, they get it removed by surgery.

Sexually Transmitted Diseases (STDs)

Sexually Transmitted Diseases (STDs) are caused by different pathogens transmitted by an intimate contact between healthy person and an infected person.

Some Common STDs

Infections	Examples	Causative Organisms	Comments
Bacterial infections	Gonorrhoea	*Neisseria gonorrhoeae*	• Contracted on during unprotected sexual intercourse with an infected person. • Also passed by an infected mother to the developing foetus. • Infects ureter in men and cervix in women. • Treatment with antibiotics is effective. **Symptoms of gonorrhoea** • Discharge of pus from penis and vagina. • Burning sensation on urinating.
	Syphilis	*Treponema pallidum*	• Syphilis is transmitted from person to person by direct contact with syphilis sores These occur mainly on the external genitals, vagina, anus or in the rectum, can also occur on lips and mouth. • Syphilis can be transmitted during vaginal, anal or oral sexual contact. • Pregnant women with the disease can pass it to their unborn children. • Can be cured by antibiotics. **Symptoms of syphilis** • Appearance of sores on body parts. • Fever, ulcers, bone pain, liver disease and anaemia. These symptoms slow up during the tertiary stage of syphilis.
Viral infections	AIDS (Acquired Immuno Deficiency Syndrome)	HIV (Human Immunodeficiency Virus)	Incurable and fatal as it suppresses the immune system of the body. It can be transferred in following ways, • during unprotected sexual intercourse with an infected person. • sharing needles and transfusion of HIV unscreened blood. • from the mother to the child *via* placenta during pregnancy.
	Genital warts	HPV (Human Papilloma Virus)	• Causes warts over external genitalia and perianal area. • *Podophyllum* preparations are effective in treatment.

Chapter Practice

Objective Questions

• Multiple Choice Questions

1. Which of the following statement is correct regarding DNA copying?

I. It is a basic event in reproduction.

II. Two copies of DNA are produced in a reproducing cell.

III. Copies generated are always identical.

IV. It is accompanied by the creation of an additional cellular apparatus.

Codes

(a) I, II and IV   (b) I, II and III

(c) I and II   (d) II and IV

2. The diagram given below shows

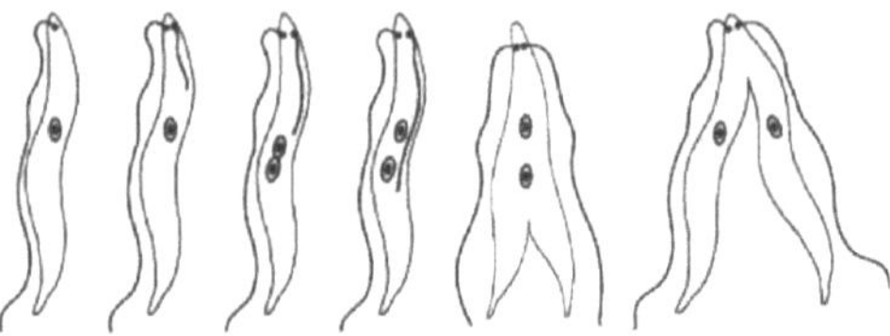

(a) binary fission in *Amoeba*

(b) multiple fission in *Plasmodium*

(c) budding in *Hydra*

(d) binary fission in *Leishmania*

3. Asexual reproduction takes place through budding in   **(NCERT)**

(a) *Amoeba*   (b) *Yeast*

(c) *Plasmodium*   (d) *Leishmania*

4. An organism which can completely regenerate from its cut body parts is

(a) *Paramecium*   (b) *Amoeba*

(c) *Planaria*   (d) *Rhizopus*

5. A *Planaria* worm is cut horizontally from the middle into two halves *P* and *Q*. Another *Planaria* worm is cut vertically into two halves *R* and *S*. Which of the cut pieces of the two *Planaria* worms could regenerate to form the complete worm ?

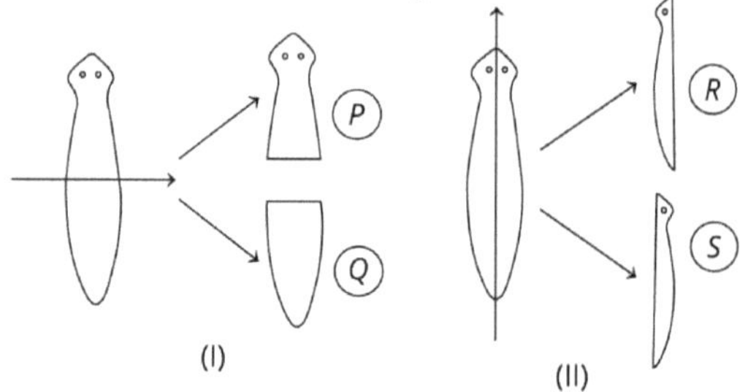

(a) Only *P*

(b) *R* and S

(c) *P* and *Q*

(d) *P*, *Q*, *R* and S

6. Identify the organisms *A* and *B* and mode of asexual reproduction exhibited by them.

(a) *A*—*Bryophyllum*, Vegetative propagation

    B—*Plasmodium*, Multiple fission

(b) *A*—*Plasmodium*, Multiple fission

    B—*Bryophyllum*, Vegetative propagation

(c) *A*—*Planaria*, Budding

    B—*Plasmodium*, Binary fission

(d) *A*—*Hydra*, Budding

    B—*Rhizopus*, Spore formation

7. Observe the diagram of pistil of a flower.

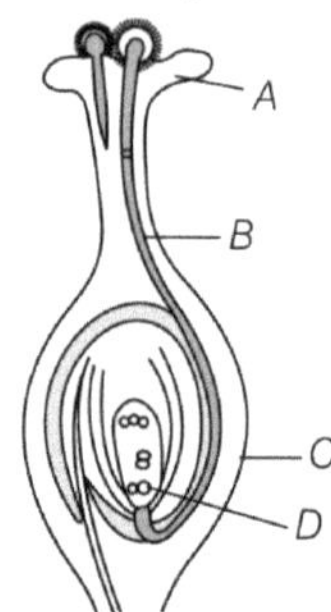

Match the labelling referred in Column I and correlate with the function in Column II.

Column I		Column II
A	1.	Female germ cell.
B	2.	Receptor of pollen grains.
C	3.	Pollen grain travels through it.
D	4.	It ripens as fruit.

Codes

	A	B	C	D
(a)	2	3	4	1
(b)	3	4	1	2
(c)	1	2	3	4
(d)	4	1	2	3

8. Carefully study the diagram of flower with labels *A* to *D*. Select the option which gives correct identification and main function and/or characteristic.

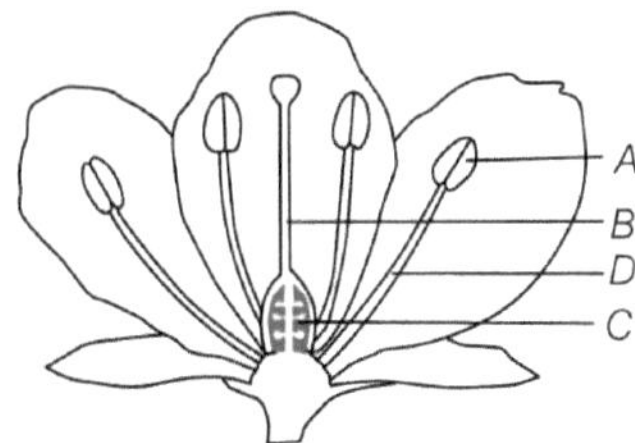

(a) *A*—Anther–Formation of ovules
(b) *B*—Stigma–Receives pollen grains
(c) *C*—Ovary–Contains pollens which develop into seeds
(d) *D*—Filament–Lifts anther to disperse pollen grains

9. In a flower, the parts that produce male and female gametes (germ cells) are   (**NCERT Exemplar**)
(a) stamen and anther
(b) filament and stigma
(c) anther and ovary
(d) stamen and style

10. Which of the following is not a secondary reproductive organ?
(a) Fallopian tube   (b) Uterus
(c) Ovary   (d) Vagina

11. The figure given below shows a female reproductive system in humans with labels *A* to *D*.

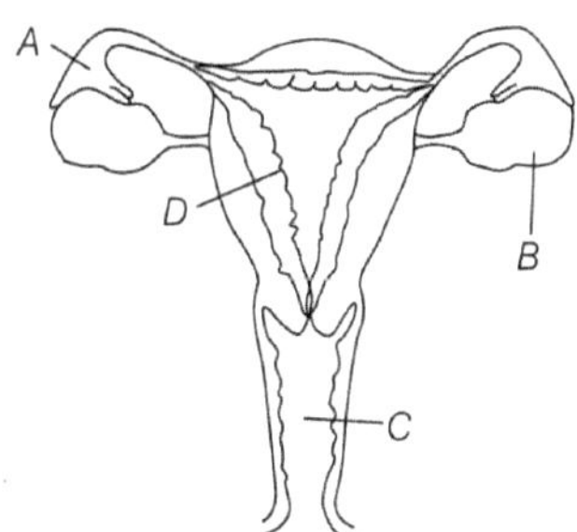

Match the labelling referred in Column I and correlate with the function in Column II.

Column I	Column II
A	1. Produce ovum
B	2. Site of fertilisation
C	3. Site of implantation
D	4. Blood and mucus comes out

Codes

	A	B	C	D			A	B	C	D
(a)	1	3	2	4	(b)		2	1	4	3
(c)	2	4	1	3	(d)		2	1	3	4

12.

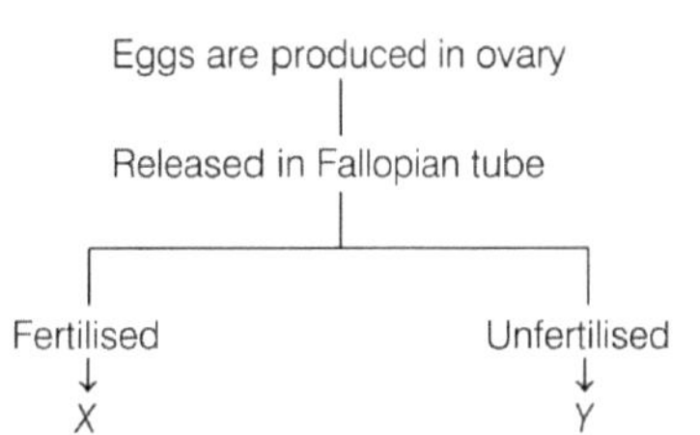

Identify the correct option from the given table which represents the correct fate of egg occurring at *X* and *Y*, respectively.

	Pregnancy	Menstruation
(a)	✓	✗
(b)	✗	✓
(c)	✓	✓
(d)	✗	✗

13. The figure given below shows male reproductive system with labels (*i*) to (*iv*).

Identify the correct label with its functions.

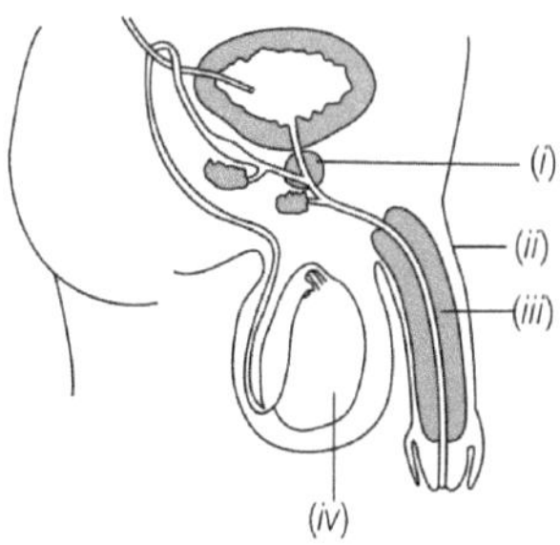

(a) (*i*) Bladder–It is essential for the mobility of sperms
(b) (*ii*) Scrotum–It transfers sperm into the vagina of female
(c) (*iii*) Urethra–It is a common passage for both the sperm and urine
(d) (*iv*) Testis–Its secretion form 20-30% of semen

14. Which of the following option contains male reproductive organs of humans?
(a) Seminal vesicle, uterus and penis
(b) Prostate gland, penis and vas deferens
(c) Vagina, testis and penis
(d) Cervix, scrotum and seminal vesicle

15. Which of the following is not the function of testosterone?
(a) Regulation of characters of puberty in boys
(b) Regulation of production of sperms
(c) Development of bones and muscles
(d) Regulation of metabolism for body growth

16. What happens to a man, when the labelled part X is cut?

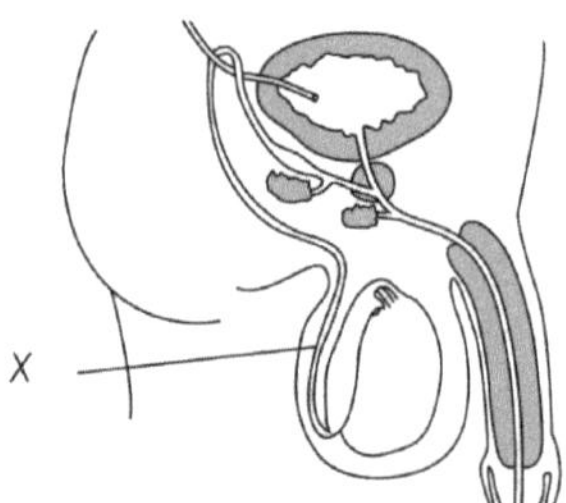

(a) Sperm ejaculation stops
(b) Testosterone production stops
(c) Urine formation stops
(d) Semen formation stops

17. Which among the following diseases is not sexual transmitted?   (**NCERT Exemplar**)
(a) Syphilis
(b) Hepatitis
(c) HIV-AIDS
(d) Gonorrhoea

• Assertion-Reasoning MCQs

Direction (Q. Nos. 18-22) For given questions, two statements are given, one labelled Assertion (A) and the other labelled Reason (R). Select the correct answer to these questions from the codes (a), (b), (c) and (d) as given below.
(a) Both A and R are true and R is the correct explanation of A
(b) Both A and R are true, but R is not the correct explanation of A
(c) A is true, but R is false
(d) A is false, but R is true

18. Assertion Individuals produced by asexual reproduction are known as clones.

Reason They are known as clones because they are genetically identical.

19. Assertion Ureter forms the common passage for both the sperms and urine.

Reason It never carries both of them at the same time.

20. Assertion Vagina is also called as birth canal.

Reason During birth, the baby passes through the vagina.

21. Assertion The uterus prepares itself every month to receive a fertilised egg.

Reason The ovary releases one egg every month.

22. Assertion AIDS is an incurable and a fatal bacterial infection.

Reason It suppresses the immune system of the body.

• Case Based MCQs

23. Read the following and answer the questions from (i) to (v) given below

Farmers, gardeners and horticulturists have developed various artificial methods of vegetative propagation for growing plants in gardens and nurseries. A very simple method of propagation involves a piece of the parent plants stem with nodes and internodes is placed in moist soil.

This grows into a new plant. In grafting, the cutting of a plants are attached to the stem of a rooted plant.

The attached cutting becomes a part of the rooted plant, draws nutrition from it and grows roots at the joint. Now if it is separated, it grows into a new plant.

In layering, one or more branches of the parent plant are bent close to the ground and covered with moist soil. The covered portions grow roots and develop into new plants.

(i) Which part of plant is more suitable for vegetative propagation?
(a) Stem   (b) Leaves
(c) Root   (d) Bulbils

(ii) Choose the odd one out.
(a) Potato   (b) Sugarcane
(c) *Bryophyllum*   (d) Wheat

(iii) In which type of artificial propagation, stock and scion are involved?
(a) Tissue culture
(b) Cuttings
(c) Grafting
(d) Layering

(iv) Which of the following statement is correct about artificial vegetative propagation of plants?
(a) We get seedless plants by this method
(b) The new plants produced by this method are similar to the parent plants
(c) Many plants can be grown from just one parent plant
(d) All of the above

(v) Which of the following method is suitable for combining the desirable characters of two plants together in a single plant?
(a) Layering   (b) Cutting
(c) Grafting   (d) All of these

24. Read the following and answer the questions from (i) to (v) given below

The uterus or womb is a hollow, pear-shaped organ in a women's lower stomach between the bladder and rectum. It sheds the lining each month during menstruation. A fertilised egg becomes implanted in the uterus and the foetus develops.

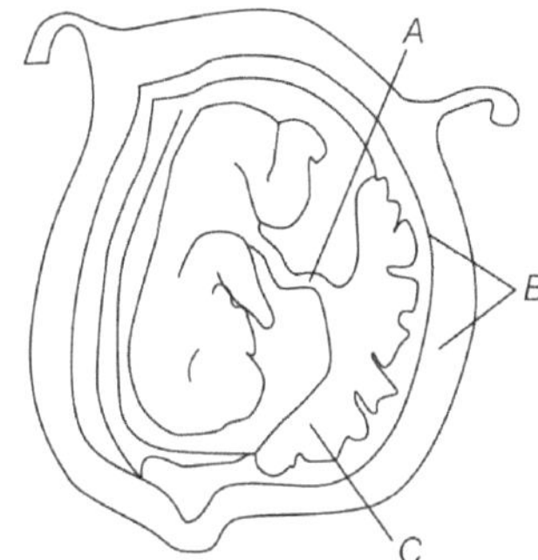

(i) Name the parts labelled as *A* and *C*.
   (a) Umbilical cord and placenta
   (b) Umbilical cord and uterine wall
   (c) Fallopian tube and ovum
   (d) Cytoplasm and umbilical cord

(ii) What determines the sex of a child?
   (a) Chromosome content of the ovum
   (b) Chromosome content of the sperm
   (c) Number of days between ovulation and fertilisation
   (d) Number of days between fertilisation and implantation

(iii) Which of the following is embedded in the uterine wall ?
   (a) Zygote   (b) Embryo's head
   (c) Placenta   (d) Eggs

(iv) Which of the following is a temporary method of family planning ?
   (a) Vasectomy   (b) Tubectomy
   (c) Copper-T   (d) Both (a) and (b)

(v) Union of male and female gametes take places in
   (a) uterus   (b) ovary
   (c) vagina   (d) oviduct

PART 2
Subjective Questions

• Short Answer Type Questions

1. What is the importance of DNA copying in reproduction? **(NCERT)**

2. Why is variation beneficial to the species, but not necessary for the individual?

3. What is a clone? Why do offspring formed by asexual reproduction exhibit remarkable similarity? **(NCERT Exemplar)**

4. Colonies of yeast fail to multiply in water, but multiply in sugar solution. Give one reason for this. **(NCERT Exemplar)**

5. Illustrate with example, the division and fragmentation method of reproduction in living organisms.

6. List two advantages of vegetative propagation over other modes of reproduction.

7. Name a plant in which layering produces a new plant.

8. Write one main difference between asexual and sexual mode of reproduction. Which species is likely to have comparatively better chances of survival, the one reproducing asexually or the one reproducing sexually? Give reason to justify your answer. **(CBSE 2018)**

9. In tobacco plant, the male gametes have twenty four chromosomes. What is the number of chromosomes in the female gamete? What is the number of chromosomes in the zygote? **(NCERT Exemplar)**

10. Differentiate between self-pollination and cross-pollination.

11. In a bisexual flower inspite of the young stamens being removed artificially, the flower produces fruit. Provide a suitable explanation for the above situation. **(NCERT Exemplar)**

12. Differentiate between unisexual and bisexual flowers and give one example of each.

13. (i) List two reasons for the appearance of variations among the progeny formed by sexual reproduction.
  (ii)

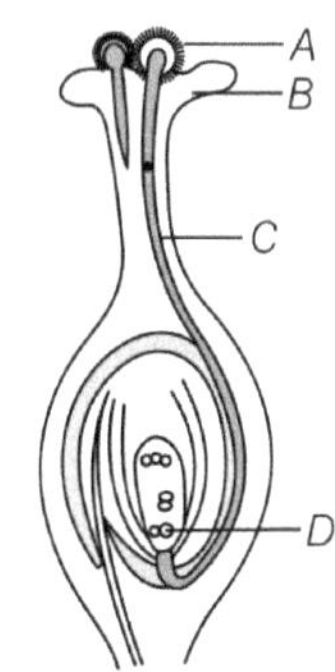

                (CBSE 2016)

(a) Name the part marked as *A* in the diagram.
(b) How does *A* reach part *B*?
(c) State the importance of the part *C*.
(d) What happens to the part marked as *D* after fertilisation is over?

14. (i) Draw a diagram showing germination of pollen on stigma of a flower and mark on it the following organs/parts   **(CBSE 2020)**
    (a) Pollen grain   (b) Pollen tube
    (c) Stigma   (d) Female germ cell
  (ii) State the significance of pollen tube.
 (iii) Name the parts of flower that develop after fertilisation into
    (a) Seed   (b) Fruit

15. Why cannot fertilisation take place in flowers if pollination does not occur?   **(NCERT Exemplar)**

16. How are general growth and sexual maturation different from each other?   **(NCERT Exemplar)**

17. Draw the human female reproductive system and label the following parts
  (i) Which organ produces ovum?
  (ii) Where does fertilisation take place?
 (iii) Where does implantation of embryo take place?
                        (CBSE 2015, 2019)

18. List two functions of ovary of female reproductive system.   **(CBSE 2016)**

19. A newly married couple wants to conceive as quickly as possible. What is the first sign of pregnancy shown by the woman ?

20. What changes are observed in the uterus if fertilisation does not occur?   **(NCERT Exemplar)**

21. How does the embryo get nourishment inside the mother's body?   **(NCERT, CBSE 2015)**

22. What is the function of the umbilical cord ?

23. Why are testes located outside the abdominal cavity?

24. Trace the path of sperm during ejaculation and mention the glands associated with the male reproductive system and their functions.   **(NCERT Exemplar)**

25. What would be the ratio of chromosome number between an egg and its zygote? How is the sperm genetically different from the egg?

26. State any two methods of contracting an STD other than the sexual contact.

27. How can people practice safe sex to avoid contracting an STD ?

28. If a woman is using a copper-T, will it help in protecting her from sexually transmitted diseases ?   **(NCERT)**

29. Write a short note on family planning.

30. (i) 'Use of a condom is beneficial for both the sexes involved in a sexual act.' Justify this statement giving two reasons.
  (ii) How do oral contraceptives help in avoiding pregnancies?
 (iii) What is sex selective abortion? How does it affect a healthy society? (State any one consequence).   **(CBSE 2020)**

31. What are the various ways to avoid pregnancy? Elaborate any one method.   **(NCERT Exemplar)**

• Long Answer Type Questions

32. Reproduction is essentially a phenomenon that is not for the survival of an individual, but for the stability of a species. Justify.   **(NCERT Exemplar)**

33. 'Reproduction helps in providing stability to population of a species'. Justify this statement.

34. (i) Name the mode of reproduction of the following organisms and state the important feature of each mode
    (a) *Planaria*   (b) *Hydra*
    (c) *Rhizopus*
  (ii) We can develop new plants from the leaves of *Bryophyllum*. Comment.

35. Explain the fertilisation process in plant with the help of a labelled diagram of a longitudinal section of a flower.

36. Define pollination. Explain the different types of pollination. List two agents of pollination. How does suitable pollination lead of fertilisation? **(CBSE 2019)**

37. Distinguish between pollination and fertilisation. Mention the site and product, of fertilisation in a flower. Draw a neat, labelled diagram of a pistil showing pollen tube growth and its entry into the ovule.   **(NCERT Exemplar)**

38. Trace the change that takes place in a flower from gamete formation to fruit formation.   **(CBSE 2020)**

39. Based on the given diagram answer the questions given below.

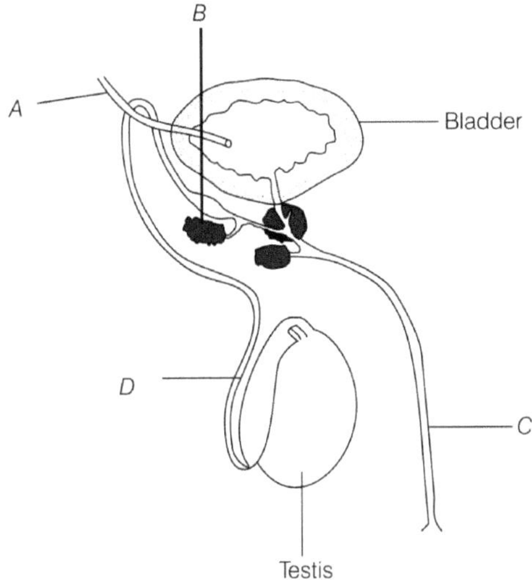

(i) Label the parts A, B, C and D.

(ii) Name the hormone secreted by testis and mention its role.

(iii) State the functions of B and C in the process of reproduction.   **(CBSE 2020)**

40. (i) Identify the given diagram. Name the parts labelled as A to E.   **(CBSE 2019)**

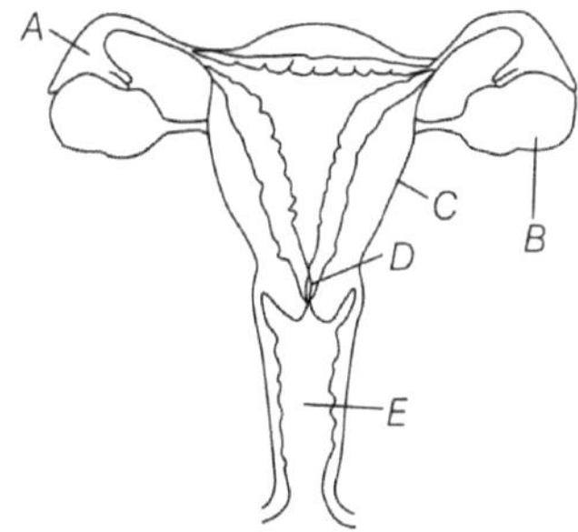

(ii) What is contraception? List three advantages of adopting contraceptive measures.

41. (i) Write the function of following parts in human female reproductive system.

(a) Ovary   (b) Oviduct   (c) Uterus

(ii) Describe in brief the structure and function of placenta.   **(CBSE 2018)**

42. Trace out the movement and fate of egg in female body.

43. Give reasons.

(i) Placenta is extremely essential for foetal development.

(ii) Blocking of vas deferens prevents pregnancy.

(iii) Wind acts as a pollinating agent.

(iv) Use of condoms prevents pregnancy.

(v) Blocking of Fallopian tubes prevents pregnancy.

44. List four points of significance of reproductive health in a society. Name any two areas related to the reproductive health which have improved over the past 50 years in our country.

• Case Based Questions

45. Read the following and answer the questions from (i) to (v) given below

Salman soaked a few seeds of Bengal gram (chana) and kept them overnight. Next morning, he drained the excess water and covered the seeds with a wet cloth. He then left the seeds for a day.

After one day, he opened the seeds into two parts and carefully observe the different parts.

(i) Which part of the flower develops into seed?

(ii) Where do the energy required for germination of seeds come from?

(iii) Which part of the seed emerges out the first?

(iv) Define germination.

(v) What are the necessary conditions for seed germination?

46. Read the following and answer the questions from (i) to (v) given below

As soon as boys and girls reach adolescent age, certain changes start happening in their bodies under the influence of sex hormones produced in their bodies. These changes are mostly related to height, size, voice pitch, physical attributes, etc.

The table below shows the average height of boys and girls upto the age of 18 years.

Age/Years	Average Height / cm	
	Boys	Girls
0 (at birth)	52	51
1	76	75
2	88	88
3	97	97
4	103	103
5	110	110
6	118	117
7	125	122
8	131	128
9	135	133
10	141	140
11	145	146
12	150	153
13	156	158
14	164	161
15	169	162
16	172	162
17	174	162
18	175	162

(i) State the changes happening in adolescent boys and girls.

(ii) When does the most rapid growth take place?

(iii) The increase in height in girls almost ceases at what age?

(iv) Significant spurt in increase of height of boys occurs at what the age?

(v) What are the changes that are common in both boys and girls at the age of adolescence?

47. Read the following and answer the questions from (i) to (v) given below.

The male has reproductive organs or genitals that are both inside and outside the pelvis. The male genitals include the testicles, the duct system, accessory glands and the penis.

In male who has reached sexual maturity, the two oval-shaped testicles make and store millions of tiny sperm cells.

Testicles are also part of the endocrine system.

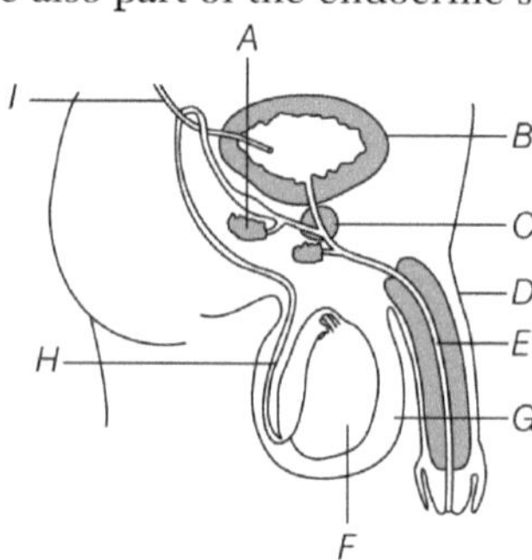

(i) Name the organ that acts as both endocrine and exocrine gland?

(ii) How is the sperm genetically different from the egg?

(iii) What is semen?

(iv) A man wants a surgical operation for family planning. Which part of his reproductive system needs to be operate?

(v) What would be the ratio of chromosome number between an egg and its zygote?

48. Read the following and answer the questions from (i) to (v) given below

The term Sexually Transmitted Disease (STD) refers to a condition passed from one person to another through sexual contact. However, it is not the only way STDs can be transmitted.

An STD develops without any symptoms early on, or if any symptoms appear they are often dismissed as regular infections.

At present, there are several type of STDs known which are caused by different type of pathogens.

Some of these STDs are curable, while other are not. The only full proof way of avoiding an STD is to practice safe sex.

(i) Give two examples of STDs.

(ii) Do you think like viruses, bacteria can also cause an STD? Give an example.

(iii) Name a method of contraception which protects us from acquiring sexually transmitted diseases?

(iv) What are IUCD? Given one example.

(v) Emergency contraceptives may prevent pregnancy if used within 72 hrs of …, … .

EXPLANATIONS

Objective Questions

1. (*a*) Statements I, II and IV are correct, whereas statement III is incorrect. Incorrect statement can be corrected as

The process of copying of DNA will have some variations each time. As a result, the DNA copies generated will be similar, but may not be identical to the original.

2. (*d*) The given diagram shows how *Leishmania* reproduces through binary fission to produce two daughter cells.

3. (*b*) Asexual reproduction in *Hydra* and yeast, takes place by budding.

4. (*c*) *Planaria* is a flatworm which possesses high regeneration ability. If its body somehow gets cut into pieces, then each piece can regenerate into a complete organism by growing the missing parts.

5. (*d*) The *Planaria* reproduces through regeneration method, therefore all the cut parts (i.e. *P, Q, R* and *S*) of the *Planaria* will regenerate to form complete worms.

6. (*a*) *A* is *Bryophyllum*, it reproduces by vegetative propagation.

B is *Plasmodium*, it reproduces by multiple fission.

7. (*a*) The given diagram shows various parts of pistil.

- *A* is stigma, it helps in receiving the pollen grains during pollination.
- *B* is style, the pollen tube grows out of the pollen grain and travels through the style.
- *C* is ovary, it ripens as fruit after the process of fertilisation.
- *D* is ovule, it is the female gamete or female germ-cell of the flower.

8. (*d*) Option (d) is correct labelled part with its functions/characteristics.

D is filament, it lifts anther to disperse pollen grains. Other options are incorrect labelled parts with their functions characteristics and can be corrected as

A is anther, it is a site of pollen formation.
B is style, it lifts stigma to receive pollen.
C is ovary, it contains ovule which develops into seeds while ovary forms the fruit.

9. (*c*) The stamen (male part) contains a swollen topmost part called anther which contains male gametes, i.e. pollen grains. Ovary (female part) makes ovules (female gametes) and stores them.

10. (*c*) The primary reproductive organs or gonads consist of the ovaries and testes. All other organs, ducts and glands in the reproductive system are considered as secondary or accessory reproductive organs. So, ovary is not a secondary reproductive organ.

11. (*b*) The correct matches are as follows

    A Oviduct or Fallopian tubes are the site of fertilisation.
    B Ovary releases one mature egg (ovum) every month.
    C Vagina, in absence of fertilisation, the lining of uterus slowly breaks and comes out through the vagina as blood and mucus.
    D. Lining of uterus is site for implantation of embryo.

Thus, option (b) is correct.

12. (*c*) The given flow chart shows the movement and fate of egg in female body.

When egg gets fertilised it forms zygote which develops into embryo. Early embryo gets implanted leading to pregnancy (*X*).

When egg does not get fertilised, it degenerates and passes out as menstrual discharge through vagina therefore leads to menstruation (*Y*).

13. (*c*) Option (c) is correct labelled part with its function.
- (*iii*) is urethra, it is a common passage for both the sperm and urine.

  Other options are incorrect labelled parts with their functions and can be corrected as
  - (*i*) is prostate gland, its secretion form 20-30% of semen which is essential for the mobility of sperms.
  - (*ii*) is penis, it transfers sperm into the vagina of female during copulation.
  - (*iv*) is testis, it produces sperms and a male sex hormone called testosterone.

14. (*b*) Option (b) contains male reproductive organs of humans.

The male human reproductive system consists of seminal vesicle, prostate gland, testis, vas deferens, urethra, penis, scrotum, etc., whereas uterus, vagina and cervix are parts of female reproductive system.

15. (*d*) Regulation of metabolism for body growth is not a function of testosterone (but by thyroid hormones).

16. (*a*) Vasectomy is a minor surgery to block sperm from reaching the semen that is ejaculated from the penis.

The labelled part *X* in the given diagram is vas deferens. Once vas deferens are cut, sperms cannot get into the semen or out of the body. Hence, ejaculation of sperms stops.

17. (*b*) The diseases which are spread by sexual contact with an infected person are called Sexually Transmitted Diseases or STDs, e.g. gonorrhoea, syphilis and AIDS. Hepatitis is a water-borne viral disease which affects liver. It is not a sexual transmitted disease.

18. (*a*) Both A and R are true and R is the correct explanation of A. The new individuals produced by asexual reproduction are always genetically identical to each other and their parents, hence are known as clones.

19. (*d*) A is false, but R is true because
In males, urethra forms the common passage for both the sperms and urine. whereas ureters are tubes that propel urine from the kidneys to the urinary bladder. It never carries sperms.

20. (*a*) Both A and R are true and R is the correct explanation of A. Vagina is called as birth canal, because the fully matured baby passes through the vagina during birth.

21. (*a*) Both A and R are true and R is the correct explanation of A. Since, the ovary releases one egg every month, the uterus also prepares itself every month to receive a fertilised egg. Its lining become thick and spongy to nourish the developing embryo.

22. (*d*) A is false, but R is true because

AIDS (Acquired Immuno Deficiency Syndrome) is caused by HIV (Human Immunodeficiency Virus), so it is a viral disease. The virus attacks the body's immune system and suppresses it.

23. (i) (a) Stems are more suitable for vegetative propagation due to the presence of nodes in them.

(ii) (*d*) Some plants undergo vegetative propagation such as potato (through nodes), sugarcane (through stem), *Bryophyllum* (through leaves). Wheat plant does not undergo vegetative propagation and is grown by sowing seeds.

(iii) (*c*) In grafting, the cut stem of a rooted plant is called stock and the cut stem of another plant without roots is called scion.

(iv) (d) The process of growing many plants from one plant by man-made methods is called artificial vegetative propagation of plants. The new plants produced by this method have similar characterstics as their parent plant. Many seedless plants can grow by this method. Hence, all the given statements are correct about artificial vegetative propagation.

Thus, option (d) is correct.

(v) (c) Grafting is a most suitable method of artificial propagation for combining the desirable characters of two plants together in a single plant.

24. (i) (*a*) A is umbilical cord, it is a narrow tube-like structure that connects the developing baby to the placenta.

C is placenta, it is an organ attached to the lining of the womb that delivers oxygen and nutrients to the growing baby.

(ii) (*b*) Sex of a child is always determined by the type of sex-chromosomes received by the father. Male produces two types of sperms, either having X-chromosome or Y-chromosome.

(iii) (*c*) Placenta is embedded in the uterine wall.

(iv) (*c*) Copper-T is an IUD (Intrauterine Device). It releases copper ions which are toxic to the egg and sperms. It stops sperm from fertilising the egg. Therefore, it prevents pregnancy for upto 10 years.

(v) (*d*) Oviduct also known as Fallopian tube, is the site of fertilisation, where male and female gametes fuse to form zygote. So, union of male and female takes place in oviducts.

Subjective Questions

1. The importance of DNA copying during reproduction are

(i) It is responsible for the transmission of parental characteristics to the offsprings.

(ii) During DNA copying in reproduction, the changes occur due to the inheritance of traits from both the parents. This leads to certain genetic variations, which are useful for the evolution of species over a period of time.

2. Variations allow organisms to exist in diverse habitats or niches. In its absence, a species may remain restricted to a particular area. If this area gets drastically altered due to various natural or man-made causes, the species may be wiped out.

However, if some variations are present in few individuals, it would help them to colonise other habitats and survive. But, if variations are present in a single organism, there would be a very little chance for it to survive and species is lost forever.

Hence, variation is beneficial to the species, but not necessary for the individuals.

3. Clones are the offsprings produced by one parent through asexual reproduction. These are genetically identical to the parent. The clones possess exact copies of the DNA of their parent and hence show remarkable similarity to the parent and to one another.

4. When the colony of yeast is in water, it does not get nutrition. Sugar solution, on the contrary provides nutrition. As the yeast gets nutrition and thus energy, it grows and begins to produce buds. This is why colonies of yeast fail to multiply in water, but multiply in sugar solution.

5. Multicellular organisms like filamentous algae (*Spirogyra*) and sea animal called sea anemone on maturation breakup into two or more small fragments or pieces. Each fragment subsequently grows to form a complete new organism. This type of asexual reproduction is known as fragmentation.

6. Two advantages of vegetative propagation are as follows

(i) Vegetative reproduction is easier and faster methods of reproduction.

(ii) It is useful in those plants/animals, which cannot reproduce sexually.

7. Layering is a type of vegetative propagation, e.g. lemon, rose, jasmine, strawberry, etc., can produce new plant by the process of layering.

8. The main difference between sexual and asexual reproduction involves the production and union of gametes in the process of fertilisation in sexually reproducing organisms which do not occur in asexual mode of reproduction.

Sexual reproduction is considered to be superior over asexual reproduction as it leads to variations, while asexual reproduction does not induce variations among progeny individuals.

Advantages of variations in individuals are

(i) It brings adaptation in individuals.

(ii) It helps in the survival of species.

(iii) It is the basis of evolution.

Hence, the species that reproduce through sexual reproduction have better chances of survival.

9. The number of chromosome in the female gamete would be same as that in the male gamete, *i.e.* it will have 24 chromosomes. The number of chromosome in the zygote would be double the number present in the gamete and hence, it would be 48.

10. Pollination is transfer of pollen grains from anther to the stigma of a flower. It is of two types

(i) **Self-pollination** Transfer of pollen from the stamens of a flower to the stigma of the same flower or on the stigma of other flower of the same plant.

(ii) **Cross-pollination** Transfer of pollen from the stamens of a flower to the stigma of different flower of different plant of same species.

11. A bisexual flower has the male as well as female reproductive organs. If the young stamen (i.e. male unit) is removed artificially, the flower still has its pistil (i.e. female unit) intact. Therefore, cross-pollination can occur.

    When the pollen grains from the anther of another flower are transferred to the stigma of this flower with the help of pollinating agents such as insects, bees, wind and water, it causes cross-pollination. After the pollen grains fall on stigma, the next step is fertilisation, followed by formation of fruits and seeds.

12. Stamens and carpels (pistils) are the reproductive organs of a flower, i.e. organs by which sexual reproduction in floral plants takes place.

    Most plants have both male and female reproductive organs in the same flower and are known as **bisexual flowers**, e.g. lily, rose, etc., while others have either male or female reproductive parts in a flower known as **unisexual flowers**, e.g. papaya, watermelon, etc.

13. (i) Variations appear among the progeny formed by sexual reproduction due to the following reasons

    (a) Sexual reproduction results in new combinations of genes that are brought together during the formation of gametes by meiotic divisions (I and II).

    (b) The combination of two sets of chromosomes, one between the homologous chromosome arms set from each parent during zygote formation, leads to variation within a species.

    (ii) (a) *A*–Pollen grain

    (b) Pollen grain reaches part *B*, i.e. stigma by pollinating agents such as insects, wind, water, etc. This process is known as pollination.

    (c) Part *C* is pollen tube. It allows the passage for the male gametes to reach the ovary having female gamete for fertilisation.

    (d) Part *D*, i.e. female gamete or egg cell that forms zygote after fertilisation.

14. (i)

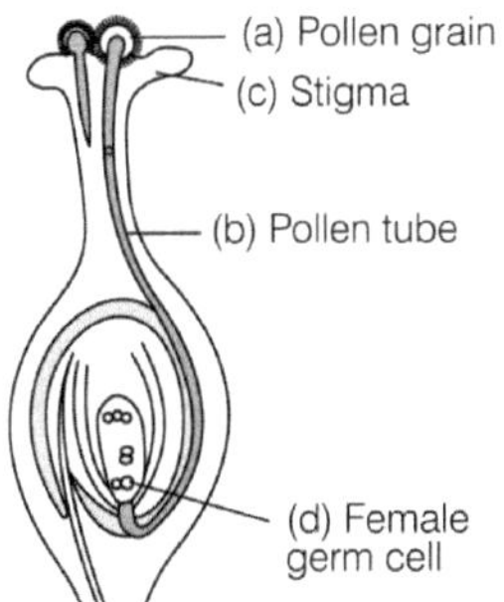

    (ii) The pollen tube takes its origin from intine of pollen grains. It grows through the style and reaches the micropyle of ovule. It carries male nuclei to the ovule for fertilisation.

    (iii) (a) Ovule develops into seed.

    (b) Mature ovary develops into fruit.

15. In a flower, fertilisation requires both male and female gametes. So, it is necessary that the male gamete reaches the female gamete. This can happen when the pollen grains are transferred to the stigma through any means of pollination.

Hence, fertilisation cannot take place in flowers if pollination does not occur due to the absence of pollen tube (i.e. the male gamete).

16. General growth refers to different types of developmental process in the body like increase in height, weight gain, changes in shape and size of the body. During this phase, the reproductive organs develop at a slower rate.

    During sexual maturation, the changes that occur prepare the body for sexual reproduction. These are specific changes reflected at puberty like cracking of voice, new hair patterns, development of breast in female, etc.

17.

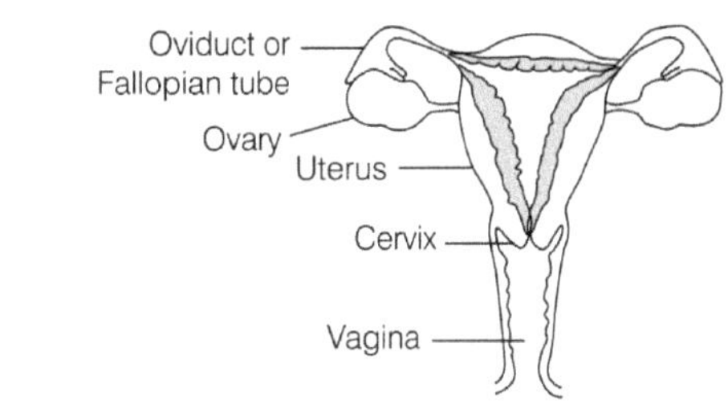

Female reproductive system

    (i) Ovum is produced by ovaries which are paired, oval-shaped organs.

    (ii) Oviduct or Fallopian tubes are the site of fertilisation. They have funnel-shaped opening near ovary and carry ova or egg from ovary to uterus.

    (iii) Implantation refers to embedding of the embryo in the thick lining of uterus.

18. Ovary in females is responsible for the production of female gametes (ova) and also produces female sex hormones, i.e. oestrogen and progesterone.

19. The absence of menstrual cycle may be the first indication of pregnancy in a woman.

20. If the egg is not fertilised, it lives for about one day. Since, the ovary releases one egg every month, the uterus also prepares itself every month to receive a fertilised egg. Its lining becomes thick and spongy, which is required for nourishing the embryo. If fertilisation, however, does not take place this lining is not needed in the absence of fertilisation and it slowly breaks and comes out through the vagina as blood and mucus. This cycle takes place roughly every month and is known as menstruation cycle and usually lasts for about 2-8 days.

21. The embryo gets nutrition from the mother's blood with the help of a special tissue called placenta. This is a disc-like tissue which develops between the uterine wall and embryo. As mother eats, the food passes through the digestive system where it breaks down into small particles. These nutrients travel through the mother's bloodstream and get exchanged with the bloodstream of foetus through placenta.

22. The umbilical cord contains blood vessels which supply blood between the foetus and the placenta.

23. Testes are located outside the abdominal cavity because sperm formation requires a lower temperature than the normal body temperature.

24. **Path of sperm during ejaculation** Formation of sperms take place in testis. Sperms come out from testis into the vas deferens. It then unites with another tube called urethra

coming from the urinary bladder. Along the path of vas deferens, glands like the prostate and the seminal vesicle add their secretion, so that sperms are in fluid medium to make their transport easier. This fluid also provides nutrition. Glands associated with male reproductive system are

(i) **Testis** It secretes the male sex hormone, testosterone.

(ii) **Prostate Gland** It makes the semen medium alkaline.

(iii) **Cowper's Gland** It secretion of this gland lubricates the urethra before ejaculation.

(iv) **Seminal Vesicle** It adds fluid content to semen.

25. The ratio of chromosome number between egg and its zygote is 1 : 2. An egg is a female gamete and it has haploid number of chromosomes. During fertilisation, it fuses with male gamete (also having haploid number of chromosomes) to form a zygote which now has diploid number of chromosomes.

Sperms and eggs are genetically different in terms of nature of sex chromosome. The sperm contains either X or Y-chromosome, whereas an egg will always have an X-chromosome.

26. Two methods of contracting an STD other than the sexual contact are as follows

(i) Sharing needles with an infected person.

(ii) Transfusion of STD unscreened blood.

27. People can practice safe sex by using condoms as it acts as barrier method of contraception and does not allow entry of semen into vagina. Therefore, prevent STDs and avoid chances of pregnancy.

28. No, copper-T does not prevent the transmission of sexually transmitted diseases. Copper-T only prevents implantation. The only safe method that can be used to prevent the transmission of sexually transmitted diseases is condoms.

29. Family planning refers to the regulation of conception by the use of contraceptive methods or devices to limit the number of offspring.

The methods used to prevent the occurrence of pregnancy are called contraceptive methods. These can be barrier, hormonal, chemical and surgical methods.

30. (i) Use of a condom is beneficial for both the sexes involved in a sexual act. It is because of the following facts

(a) It prevents pregnancy which is not desired by a couple.

(b) It saves both the partners from sexually transmitted diseases like AIDS, etc.

(ii) Oral contraceptives are the hormonal pills which are taken by the females after their menstruation ends up. It is taken for 21 days daily. It changes the cyclic events of ovulation, etc. So, mature ovum is not available for fertilisation.

(iii) Sex selective abortion means if the foetus is female, it is killed and extracted. This creates an imbalanced in the society by disturbing the sex ratio.

31. Ways to avoid pregnancy are called contraceptive methods. It includes a number of ways such as

(i) Mechanical barrier, e.g. condom.

(ii) Drugs (oral pills for females).

(iii) IUCD, e.g. copper-T.

(iv) Surgical method for permanent contraception.

Mechanical Barrier There are a number of methods that create barrier between sperm and egg

Some of them are as follows

Condom It is a fine rubber balloon-like structure worn over the penis during sexual intercourse. Semen is collected in it and not discharged into the vagina. This method also prevents the spread of STDs like AIDS, syphilis, etc.

Diaphragms or Caps It can be fitted in the cervix of a woman to prevent semen from reaching the Fallopian tube.

32. All the living organisms need energy for their survival and growth. This energy is obtained from various life processes such as nutrition, excretion and respiration.
Thus, these phenomena are essential for the survival of an individual. Compared to these life processes, reproduction is not essential for survival of an individual.

It is basically important for continuity of the generation of an organism or species as DNA copying during reproduction helps to produce similar individuals as their parents to maintain stability of a species.

33. A species occupies a well-defined niche in an ecosystem, using its ability to reproduce. During reproduction, copies of DNA pass from one generation to the next. This copying of DNA takes place with consistency in reproducing organisms and this is important for the maintenance of body design features (physiological as well as structural) which allows the organism to use that particular niche. Reproduction is therefore, linked to the stability of population of a species.

34. (i) (a) *Planaria*—Regeneration

(b) *Hydra*—Budding

(c) *Rhizopus*—Sporulation

(ii) The leaves of *Bryophyllum* bear vegetative adventitious buds which on separation can give rise to new plants.

35. Stamens and carpels are the reproductive parts of a flower.

* **Stamen** is the male reproductive part of the flower.

* **Anther** is a bilobed structure containing two pollen sacs present at tip of stamen. These produce pollen grains that are yellowish in colour.

* **Carpel** (Pistil) is the female reproductive part, which is present in the centre of the flower.
It comprises of three parts

(i) **Stigma** It is the terminal part of carpel which may be sticky. It helps in receiving the pollen grains during pollination.

(ii) **Style** It is the middle elongated part of carpel. It helps in the attachment of stigma to the ovary.

(iii) **Ovary** It is the swollen bottom part of carpel. It contains ovules having an egg cell (female gamete).

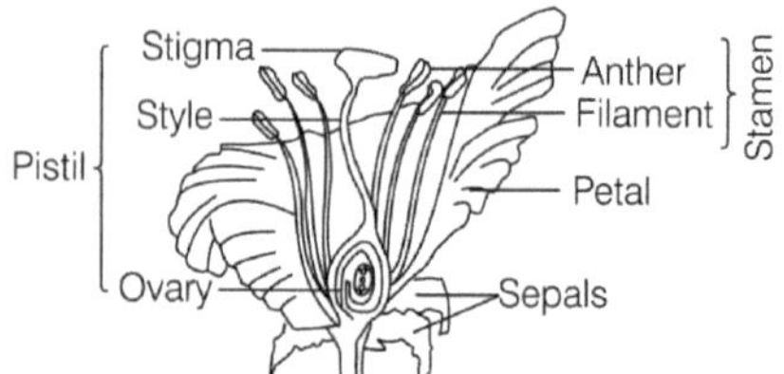

Longitudinal section of flower

Fertilisation is the process of fusion of male germ cells with the female gametes. It gives rise to a zygote. As soon as the pollen lands on suitable stigma, it reaches the female germ cells in ovary. This occurs *via* pollen tube. The pollen tube grows out of the pollen grain, travels through the style and finally reaches the ovary.

36. The transfer of pollen grains from the anther of the stamen to the stigma of a flower is termed as pollination. There are two types of pollination

   (i) **Self-pollination** The pollen from the stamen of a flower is transferred to the stigma of the same flower or another flower on the same plant.

   (ii) **Cross-pollination** The pollen from the stamen of a flower is transferred to the stigma of another flower of different individual of the same species.

The pollen grains can be transferred by various agents like wind, water, insects and animals. As soon as the pollen lands on suitable stigma, it reaches the female germ cells in ovary. This occurs *via* pollen tube.

The pollen tube grows out of the pollen grain, travels through the style and finally reaches the ovary where it fuses with female gamete (ovule) to give rise to zygote. Hence, pollination is followed by fertilisation in plants.

37. Distinguishes between pollination and fertilisation are as follows

Pollination	Fertilisation
It is the transfer of pollen grains from anther to the stigma.	It is the fusion of male and female gametes.
It is a physical process.	It is a biological process.

The site of fertilisation is ovule in the ovary.

The product of fertilisation is a zygote.

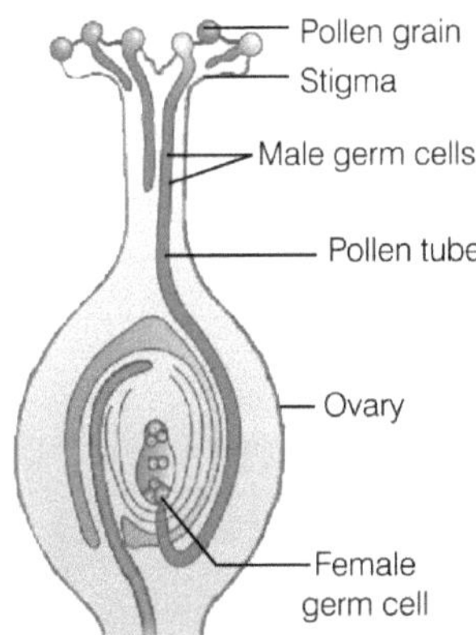

Pistil showing pollen tube growth and its entry into ovule

38. Stamen is the male reproductive part and it produces pollen grains. The ovary contains ovules and each ovule has egg cell.

The pollen grain is transferred from the stamen to the stigma. It is transferred of pollen occurs in the same flower, it is referred to as self-pollination.

On the other hand, if the pollen is transferred from one flower to another, it is known as cross-pollination. After the pollen lands on a suitable stigma, it has to reach the female germ cells which are present in the ovary.

For thus, a tube grows out of the pollen grain and travels through the style to reach the ovary.

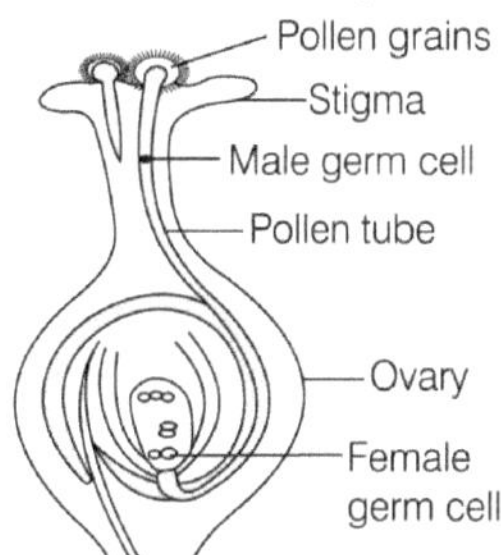

Germination of pollen on stigma The male germ cell produced by pollen grain fuses with the female gamete precut in the ovule. This fusion of germ cells is called fertilisation and gives rise to the zygote.

After the fertilisation, the zygote divides several times to form an embryo within the ovule. The ovule develops a hard coat and is gradually converted into a seed. The ovary grows rapidly and ripens to form fruit. Meanwhile the petals, sepals, stamens, style and stigma may shrivel and fall off.

39. (i) A–Ureter   B–Seminal vesicle
           C–Urethra   D–Vas deferens

   (ii) Testosterone hormone is secreted by testis. It controls spermatogenesis (formation of sperm) and secondary sexual characters in male adolescents.

   (iii) Seminal vesicle *B* temporarily stores sperms.

   Urethra (C) It transports and releases urine and sperms outside the body.

40. (i) The given figure represents the female reproductive system. The parts labelled as *A-E* are

   A. Oviduct or Fallopian tube B. Ovary
   C. Uterus   D. Cervix   E. Vagina

   (ii) The prevention of pregnancies by using artificial method is called as contraception.

   Advantages of using contraceptive measures are

   (a) To control family size, population rise or birth rate. This is done by creating awareness about small families using contraceptive measures.

   (b) To prevent chances of meeting female egg and male sperm, thus preventing future unwanted pregnancies.

   (c) Use of barrier methods of contraception protects both the partners from contracting sexually transmitted diseases like AIDS.

41. (i)

Parts of female reproductive system	Functions
(a) **Ovaries**	Produce thousands of ova or egg cells. Secrete female sex hormones like oestrogen and progesterone.
(b) **Oviduct** (Fallopian tube)	Carries ova or egg from ovary to the uterus. It is the site of fertilisation.
(c) **Uterus** (Womb)	Here, the growth and development of foetus (embryo) take place. Rhythmic contractions of the muscles in the uterus cause labour pain and childbirth.

(ii) **Structure of Placenta** It is a disc between uterine wall and embryo which is embedded in the uterine wall. It contains villi on the embryo's side of the tissue. On the mother's side, blood spaces are present, which surrounded the villi.

Functions of Placenta It provides a large surface area for glucose and oxygen to pass from the mother to the embryo. It also removes the waste generated by embryo, transferring it to mother's blood.

42. Movement and fate of egg in female body

Eggs are produced in ovary
↓
Released in Fallopian tube
↓
If fertilised, form zygote → Early embryo gets implanted leading to pregnancy and foetus starts to develop

If unfertilised, degenerate → Passes out as menstrual discharge

43. (i) Placenta is extremely essential for foetal development because it helps in nutrition, respiration, excretion, etc., of the foetus through the maternal supply.

(ii) Blocking of vas deferens prevents passage of sperms, hence, there is no fertilisation so it prevents pregnancy.

(iii) Wind acts as a pollinating agent because it helps in transfer of light weighted pollen grains from anther to stigma of a flower.

(iv) Condoms prevent entry of sperms into vagina, hence prevents pregnancy.

(v) If Fallopian tube is blocked, sperm and egg do not meet or fuse and fertilisation does not take place.

44. Reproductive health is a state of physical, emotional, mental and social well-being in relation to sexuality.

Significance of reproductive health in a society

(i) It prevents the spread of various Sexually Transmitted Diseases (STDs).

(ii) Proper medication and checkups will help in the production of healthy children.

(iii) Better sex education and awareness help in maintaining the population and prevent the population explosion.

(iv) Unwanted pregnancies are avoided.

The reproductive health in India has improved tremendously over the past 50 years. The areas in which reproductive health has improved includes

(i) Prevention of unwanted pregnancies by using contraceptives have shown the development of health in women.

(ii) Awareness of advantages of small families by using contraceptives has led to economic growth of the family.

45. (i) The ovules present in ovary of a flower develops into seeds.

(ii) Cotyledons of seed store food which fulfil the energy requirement for seed germination.

(iii) Radicle or future root of the plant emerges out the first from the germinating seed.

(iv) The process of developing seed into a seedling under appropriate conditions is known as germination.

(v) All seeds need water, oxygen and proper temperature in order to germinate.

46. (i) The changes happening in adolescent boys and girls are
The moustach starts appearing in boys and their voice becomes hoarse. There is onset of menstrual cycle in girls and their mammary glands starts developing.

(ii) Most rapid growth takes place within one year after the birth of a baby.

(iii) The increase in height of girls ceases at the age of 15 years.

(iv) In boys, significant spurt in height occurs at the age of 11-12 yrs.

(v) Both boys and girls grow body hair in their pubic area, as well as under the arms and on the legs at the age of adolescence.

47. (i) The two main functions of the testes (F) are to produce sperm and to produce the male sex hormones (testosterone). This makes the testis both an endocrine and exocrine gland.

(ii) The sperm and eggs are genetically different terms of nature of sex chromosome. The sperm contains either X or Y-chromosome whereas an egg will always have an X-chromosome.

(iii) Semen is a fluid which contains sperm cells and secretion of accessory glands. It is a milky, viscous fluid contains fructose, proteins and other chemicals for nourishing sperms.

(iv) Vasectomy is a form of male birth control that cuts the supply of sperm to semen. It is done by cutting and sealing the tubes that carry sperm, i.e. vas deferens (H).

(v) Fusion of a sperm and an egg lead to the formation of a zygote. Therefore, a zygote is diploid in nature, i.e. $2n$, whereas a sperm and an egg are haploid in nature, i.e. n. Hence, the ratio of chromosome number between an egg and its zygote is $1 : 2$.

48. (i) (a) AIDS (Acquired Immuno Deficiency Syndrome)
(b) Genital warts

(ii) Yes, bacteria are also known to cause STDs.
For example, Syphilis is an STD caused by bacteria, *Treponema, pallidum*.

(iii) Condoms protect us from acquiring STDs. It also helps in avoiding pregnancy.

(iv) IUCD stands for Intra-Uterine Contraceptive Device. It is used to prevent pregnancy, e.g. Copper-T

(v) Emergency contraceptives may prevent pregnancy if used within 72 hrs of coitus/intercourse.

Chapter Test

Multiple Choice Questions

1. Exchange of genetic material takes place in
   (a) vegetative reproduction
   (b) asexual reproduction
   (c) sexual reproduction
   (d) budding

2. Identify the option that indicates the correct function or purpose served by A, B and C.

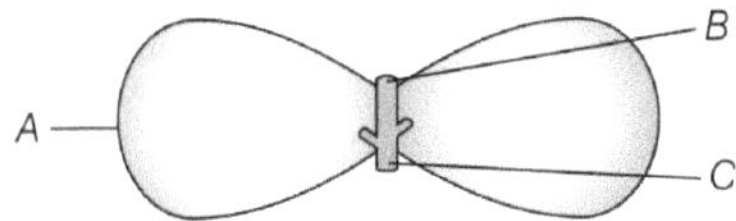

   (a) *A*-Future shoot, *B*-Future root, *C*-Store food
   (b) *A*-Future root, *B*-Future shoot, *C*-Store food
   (c) *A*-Store food, *B*-Future shoot, *C*-Future root
   (d) *A*-Future root, *B*-Store food, *C*-Future shoot

3. Which of the following option shows the correct arrangement of events in logical sequence in the life cycle of a human?
   (a) Menarche → Gestation → Menopause → Parturition → Insemination
   (b) Parturition → Gestation → Insemination → Menarche → Menopause
   (c) Menarche → Insemination → Gestation → Parturition → Menopause
   (d) Menarche → Insemination → Parturition → Gestation → Menopause

4. Select the barrier methods of contraception among the following.
   (a) Oral pill
   (b) Femidom
   (c) Copper-T
   (d) Vasectomy

5. Identify the disease which is caused by a virus.

   I. Syphilis
   II. Genital warts
   III. Gonorrhoea
   IV. AIDS

   Codes
   (a) I and II
   (b) II and III
   (c) II and IV
   (d) I and III

Assertion-Reasoning MCQs

Direction (Q. Nos. 6-7) Each of these questions contains two statements, Assertion (A) and Reason (R). Each of these questions also has four alternative choices, any one of which is the correct answer. You have to select one of the codes (a), (b), (c) and (d) given below.

   (a) Both A and R are true and R is the correct explanation of A
   (b) Both A and R are true, but R is not the correct explanation of A
   (c) A is true, but R is false
   (d) A is false, but R is true

6. **Assertion** Pollen grains from the carpel stick to the stigma of stamen.
   Reason The fertilised egg cells grow inside the ovary and become seeds.

7. **Assertion** Menstruation is the regular discharge of blood from the thick uterine lining.
   Reason It occurs when egg is fertilised by sperm.

8. **Assertion** HIV-AIDS is a bacterial disease.
   Reason It spreads through sharing of infected needles.

Short Answer Type Questions

9. List out the basic features of reproduction.

10. List two advantages of vegetative reproduction practiced in case of an orange.

11. Mention any one disadvantage of producing new plants by vegetative propagation.

12. Write the name of gamete producing parts of a flower.

13. When does pollen tube develop in a flower?

14. Write the dual purposes served by urethra in males.

15. What is placenta? Describe its structure. State its functions in case of pregnant human female.

16. What do you understand by reproductive health and sex ratio?

Long Answer Type Questions

17. Given below is the diagram of a reproductive system.

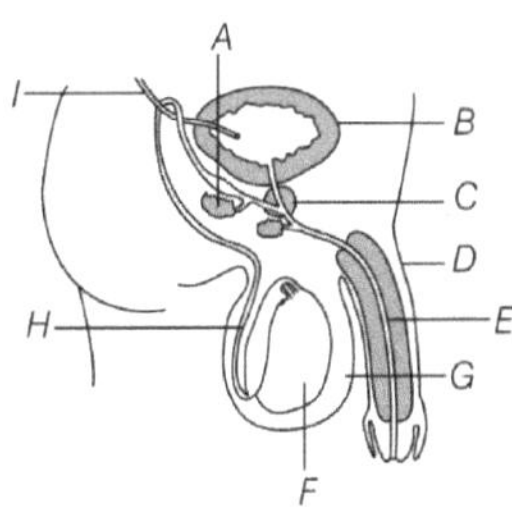

   (i) Name the system.
   (ii) Name the parts labelled as *A-I*.
   (iii) Describe the functions of parts *C, D, E* and *F*.

18. What are the different methods of contraception?

Answers

Multiple Choice Questions
   1. (c)   *2.* (c)   *3.* (c)   *4.* (b)   *5.* (c)

Assertion-Reasoning MCQs
   6. (d)   *7.* (c)   *8.* (d)

For Detailed Solutions
Scan the code

CHAPTER 04

Heredity and Evolution

In this Chapter...

- Accumulation of Variations During Reproduction
- Heredity (Inheritance of Traits)
- Mendel's Contribution towards the Inheritance of Traits
- Experiment Conducted by Mendel
- Sex-Determination

Through the process of reproduction individuals give rise to new individuals that are similar (not same) to the parents. This similarity in progeny or offspring or child is due to transmission of characters or traits from parents to their progeny.

The transfer of characters from parents to offspring is known as **heredity** and the process through which characters or traits pass from one generation to another is called **inheritance**.

Accumulation of Variations During Reproduction

The difference in the characters among the individuals of a species is termed as **variations**. These variations are accumulated by the process of **sexual reproduction**.

Depending upon the nature of variations, different individuals would have different advantages, the most important advantage of variation to a species is that it increases the chances of its survival in a changing environment.

Heredity (Inheritance of Traits)

Traits or characteristics, which are passed on from parents to their offspring (generation to generation) are controlled by genes.

A gene is a unit of DNA which governs the synthesis of one protein that constants a specific character of an organism. e.g. Inheritance of free or attached earlobes.

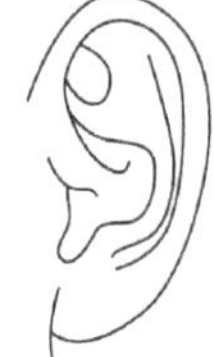

(a) Free earlobe   (b) Attached earlobe

Rules for inheritance of traits Inheritance of a trait is related to the fact that both father and mother contribute equally towards the genetic makeup of their offspring, i.e. for each trait two versions are available in the child.

Some Important Terms and Definitions Used in Heredity

Terms	Definitions
Chromosome	A long thread-like structure in the nucleus. It appears during cell division and carries genes.
Gene	A functional unit of heredity. It is present on chromosome. It is a piece of DNA that codes for one protein that inturn determines a particular character (phenotype).
Character	The feature or characteristic of an individual like height, colour, shape, etc.
Trait	An inherited character, i.e. feature, which is normally inherited and has its detectable variant too, e.g. tall and dwarf are traits of a character, i.e. height.
Allele	One of the different forms of a particular gene, occupying the same position on a chromosome.
Hybrid	An individual having two different alleles for the same trait.
Dominant allele	An allele, whose phenotype will be expressed even in the presence of another allele of that gene. It is represented by a capital letter, e.g. T.
Recessive allele	An allele, which gets masked in the presence of a dominant allele and can only affect the phenotype in the absence of a dominant gene. It is represented by a small letter, e.g. t.
Genotype	Genetic composition of an individual.
Phenotype	The expression of the genotype, which is an observable or measurable characteristic.
Back cross	Crossing F_1 hybrid with one of its parents, e.g. Tt × tt or Tt × TT.
Monohybrid cross	A hybridisation cross in which inheritance of only one pair of contrasting characters is studied.
Dihybrid cross	A cross in which inheritance of two pairs of contrasting characters is simultaneously studied.
Homozygous	A condition in which an individual possesses a pair of identical alleles controlling a given character and will breed true for this character (e.g. occurrence of two identical alleles for tallness in a P_1 tall pea plant).
Heterozygous	A condition in which an individual has a pair of contrasting alleles for any one character and will not breed true for this character (e.g. simultaneous existence of dominant and recessive alleles in F_1-hybrid tall pea plant).
Gametes	Reproductive cells containing only one set (haploid) of dissimilar chromosome.
Test cross	Crossing F_1 heterozygote with homozygous recessive parent, e.g. F_1 hybrid tall plant (Tt) with pure dwarf plant (tt).

Mendel's Contribution towards the Inheritance of Traits

The Austrian monk, **Gregor Johann Mendel** is known as **Father of Genetics**. He performed many experiments on pea (*Pisum sativum*) plant related to hybridisation.

He studied seven pairs of contrasting characters in pea plants and only one character at a time.

Experiments Conducted By Mendel

More than a century ago, Mendel worked out the main rules for inheritance. He performed following two experiments

1. Monohybrid Cross : Inheritance of Traits for One Contrasting Character

- Mendel took pea plants with different characteristics such as height (tall and short plants).
- The progeny produced from them (F_1-generation plants) were all tall. Mendel then allowed F_1 progeny plants to undergo self-pollination.
- In the F_2-generation, he found that all plants were not tall, three quarter were tall and one quarter of them were short. This observation indicated that both the traits of shortness and tallness were inherited in F_1-generation. But, only the tallness trait was expressed in F_1-generation.
- Two copies of the traits are inherited in each sexually reproducing organism.

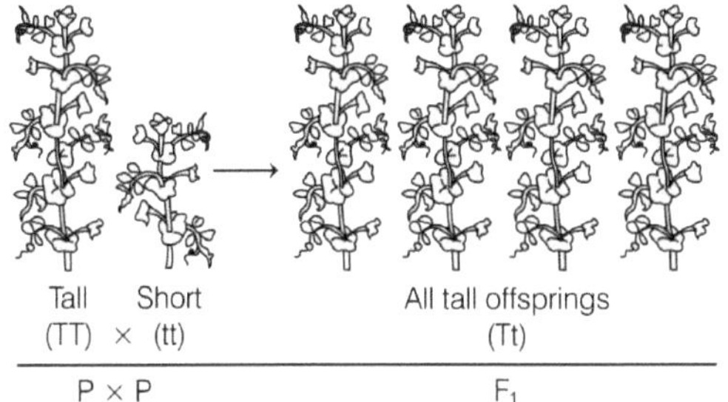

Mendel's experiment showing law of dominance

- TT and Tt are phenotypically tall plants, whereas tt is a short plant. For a plant to be tall, the single copy of 'T' is enough. Therefore, in traits Tt, 'T' is a dominant trait, while 't' is a recessive trait.

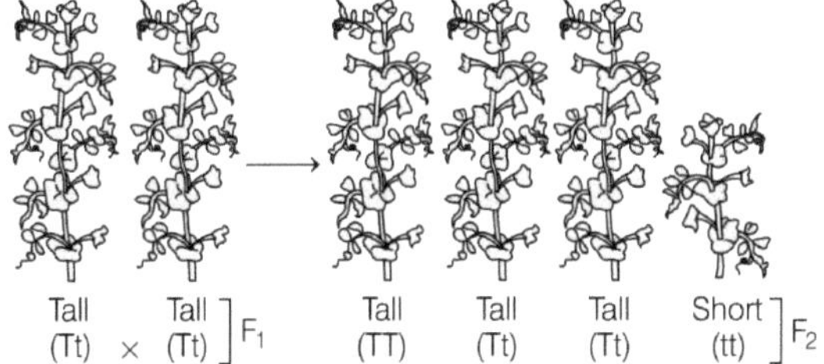

Mendel's experiment showing law of segregation

- In F_2-generation, both the characters are recovered, though one of these is not seen in F_1 stage. During gamete formation, the factor or allele of a pair segregate from each other.

Thus, the phenotypic ratio is 3 : 1 and the genotypic ratio is 1 : 2 : 1 for the inheritance of traits for one contrasting character, i.e. monohybrid cross.

2. Dihybrid Cross : Inheritance of Traits for Two Visible Contrasting Characters

- Mendel took pea plants with two contrasting characters, i.e. one with a green round seed and the other one with a yellow wrinkled seed.
- When the F_1 progeny was obtained, they had round and yellow seeds, thus establishing that round and yellow are dominant traits.
- Mendel then allowed the F_1 progeny to be self-crossed (self-pollination) to obtain F_2 progeny. He found that seeds were round yellow, round green, wrinkled yellow and some were wrinkled green.
- The ratio of plants with above characteristics was $9:3:3:1$, respectively (Mendel observed that two new combinations had appeared in F_2).

In F_2-generation, all the four characters were assorted out independent of the others. Therefore, he said that a pair of alternating or contrasting characters behaves independently of the other pair. For example, seed colour is independent of seed coat. The independent inheritance of two separate traits shape and colour of seeds is schematically shown below

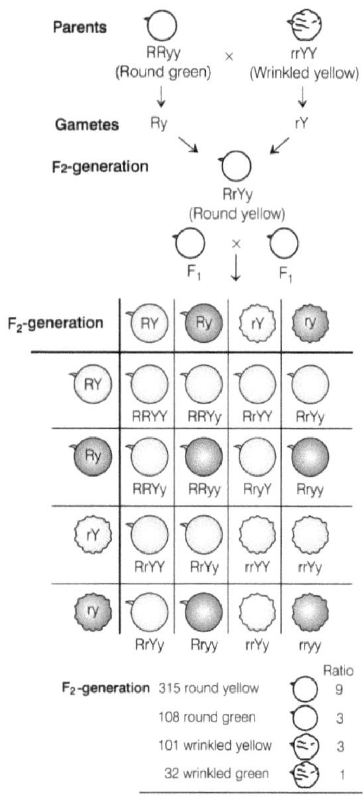

Expression of Traits

Cellular DNA is the source of information for making proteins in the cell. A section of DNA that provides information for one particular protein is called a **gene** for that protein. Expression of trait in body depends on the functioning of a gene. If the gene is working normally, sufficient protein will be produced for normal body functions. If the gene for a specific protein is altered, the protein will be less efficient or will not be functional at all.

Mechanism of Inheritance

- Both the parents contribute a copy of the same gene to their progeny. Each germ cell thus, has one set of gene, present as chromosome. Each cell of the body will have two copies of each chromosome, one inherited from each parent.
- When two germ cells combine, they restore the normal number of chromosomes in the progeny. This ensures the stability of the DNA of species. Such mechanism of inheritance explains the result of Mendel's experiments. It is used by all sexually and asexually reproducing organisms.

Sex-Determination

It is the process by which sex of a newborn individual is determined. Different strategies can determine sex in different species. For example, in reptiles environment factors such as temperature at which fertilised eggs are kept determine sex of the offspring. The determination of sex occurs largely by genetic control in **human beings**. In human beings, there are 23 pairs of chromosomes, out of which 22 pairs are **autosomes** and one pair is **sex-chromosomes**.

Females have a perfect pair of sex chromosome (homogametic), but males have a mismatched pair (heterogametic) in which one is X (normal sized) and the other is Y-chromosome (short in size).

Hence, an egg fertilised by X-chromosome carrying sperm results in a zygote with XX, which becomes a female and if an egg is fertilised by Y-chromosome carrying sperm, it results in a XY zygote that becomes male.

Thus, the sex of the children will be determined by what they inherit from their father. A child who inherits an X-chromosome will be a girl and one who inherits a Y-chromosome will be a boy. The inheritance of sex in humans is diagrammatically shown below

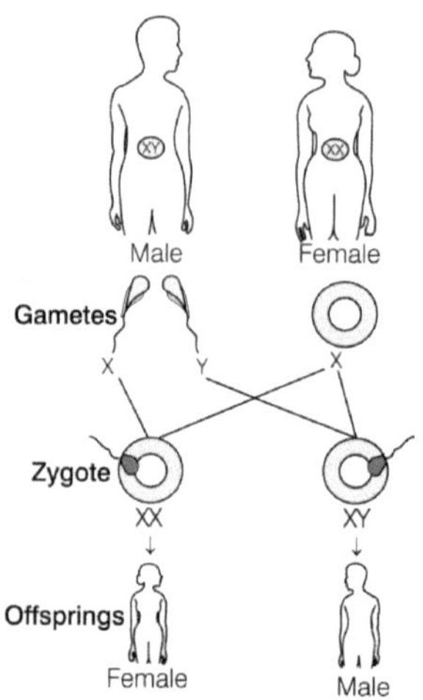

Sex-determination in human beings

Chapter Practice

Objective Questions

• Multiple Choice Questions

1. The process through which characters pass from one generation to another is called

(a) inheritance   (b) heredity
(c) variation   (d) evolution

2. Which of the following statements is not true with respect to variation?

(a) All variations in a species have equal chance of survival
(b) Change in genetic composition results in variation
(c) Selection of variants by environment factors forms the basis of evolutionary processes.
(d) Variation is minimum in asexual reproduction.

3. Free earlobes are ...(i)... traits and attached earlobes are ...(ii)... traits.

(a) (i) recessive, (ii) dominant
(b) (i) dominant, (ii) recessive
(c) (i) inherited, (ii) dominant
(d) None of the above

4. A trait in an organism is influenced by   **(NCERT Exemplar)**

(a) paternal DNA only
(b) maternal DNA only
(c) both maternal and paternal DNA
(d) neither by paternal nor by maternal DNA

5. Which amongst the listed tools was used to study the law of inheritance in pea plant by Gregor J Mendel?

(a) Family tree   (b) Pedigree chart
(c) Punnett square   (d) Herbarium sheet

6. A cross between a tall plant (TT) and short pea plant (tt) resulted in progeny that were all tall plants because   **(NCERT Exemplar)**

(a) tallness is the dominant trait
(b) shortness is the dominant trait
(c) tallness is the recessive trait
(d) height of pea plant is not governed by gene 'T' or 't'

7. If a pea plant with round green seed (RRyy) is crossed pea plant with wrinkled yellow seed (rrYY), the seeds produced in F_1-generation are

(a) wrinkled and green   (b) wrinkled and yellow
(c) round and yellow   (d) round and green

8. The genotype of the height of an organism is written as Tt. What conclusion may be drawn?

(a) The allele for height has at least two different genes
(b) There are atleast two different alleles for the gene for height
(c) There are two different genes for height, each having a single allele
(d) There is one allele for height with two different forms

9. The first generation cross of pure tall and short pea plant gives tall pea plants. F_2-generation will give

(a) dwarf pea plant   (b) tall pea plant
(c) Both tall and dwarf plants   (d) None of these

10. A cross between a pure-breed pea plant A and B is shown below.

Parents plants : A × B

F_1-generation : A

F_2-generation : A, A, A, B

Choose the correct option for A and B.

(a) A are tall and B are round
(b) A are tall and B are dwarf
(c) A are dwarf and B are tall
(d) A are round and B are tall

11. If pea plants having round green seeds and wrinkled yellow seeds are crossed, what phenotypic ratio will be obtained in F_2 progeny plants?

(a) $1:2:1$ (b) $3:1$ (c) $9:3:3:1$ (d) $9:3:4$

12. The result of a dihybrid cross between two individuals is recorded as

Phenotypes of progeny	Numbers of seeds obtained
Round, A	315
Round, B	108
C, Yellow	101
Wrinkled, D	32

Choose the correct option for A, B, C and D.

	A	B	C	D
(a)	Green	Yellow	Round	Yellow
(b)	Yellow	Green	Wrinkled	Green
(c)	Yellow	Yellow	Wrinkled	Green
(d)	Green	Green	Round	Yellow

13. Carefully study the cross shown below with labels (i), (ii) and (iii). Identify the option that indicates the correct labellings.

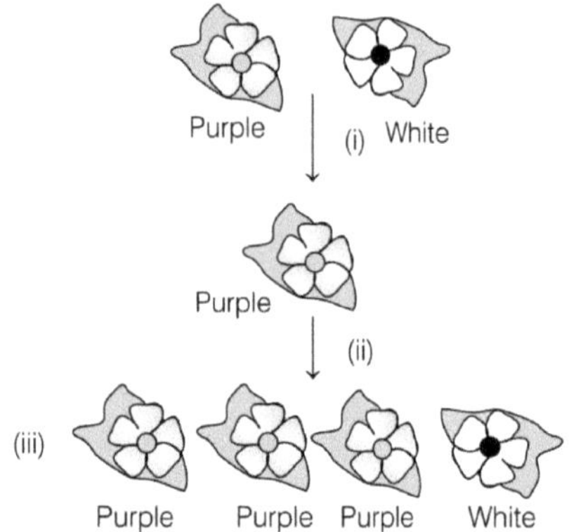

(a) (i) Cross-fertilisation, (ii) Self-fertilisation, (iii) F_1-generation
(b) (i) Self-fertilisation, (ii) Cross-fertilisation, (iii) F_2-generation
(c) (i) Cross-fertilisation, (ii) Self-fertilisation, (iii) F_2-generation
(d) (i) Self-fertilisation, (ii) F_2-generation (iii) Cross-fertilisation

14. Observe the diagram given below.

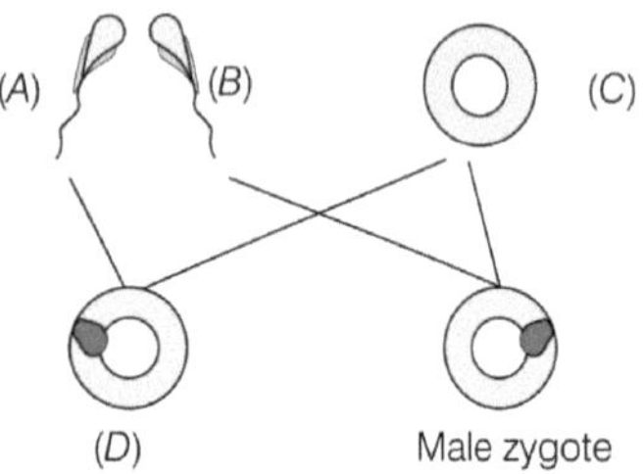

Match the labelling referred in Column I and correlate with Column II.

	Column I		Column II
	A.	1.	Y sperm
	B.	2.	Ovum
	C.	3.	X sperm
	D.	4.	Female zygote

Codes

	A	B	C	D
(a)	3	1	2	4
(b)	2	3	1	4
(c)	2	1	3	4
(d)	1	2	4	3

15. Choose the correct statement from the following.
I. Variation in plants are much lesser than human beings.
II. Each trait in child is influenced by only paternal DNA.
III. An individual having two different alleles for the same trait is called hybrid.
IV. Traits that are passed on from parents to their offspring are controlled by genes.

Codes
(a) I, II and III   (b) I, III and IV
(c) II, III and IV   (d) I, II and IV

● **Assertion-Reasoning MCQs**

Direction (Q. Nos. 16-20) Each of these questions contains two statements, Assertion (A) and Reason (R). Each of these questions also has four alternative choices, any one of which is the correct answer. You have to select one of the codes (a), (b), (c) and (d) given below.
(a) Both A and R are true and R is the correct explanation of A
(b) Both A and R are true, but R is not the correct explanation of A
(c) A is true, but R is false
(d) A is false, but R is true

16. **Assertion** Dominant allele is an allele whose phenotype expresses even in the presence of another allele of that gene.

Reason It is represented by a capital letter, e.g. T.

17. **Assertion** Mendel self-crossed F_1 progeny to obtain F_2-generation.

Reason F_1 progeny of a tall plant with round seeds and a dwarf plant with wrinkled seeds are all dwarf plants having wrinkled seeds.

18. **Assertion** The ratio of F_2 plants when Mendel took pea plants with two contrasting characters was $9 : 3 : 3 : 1$.

Reason The ratio of F_2 plants when Mendel took pea plants with one contrasting character was $1 : 1$.

19. **Assertion** All the human female gemetes will have only X-chromosome.

Reason Females are homogametic with two X-chromosomes.

20. **Assertion** The sex of a child will be determined by chromosome received from the father.

Reason A human male has one X and one Y-chromosome.

• Case Based MCQs

21. Read the following and answer the questions from (i) to (v) given below

Mendel's experiment on sweet pea plants having axial flowers with round seeds (AARR) and terminal flowers with wrinkled seeds (aarr) is shown below.

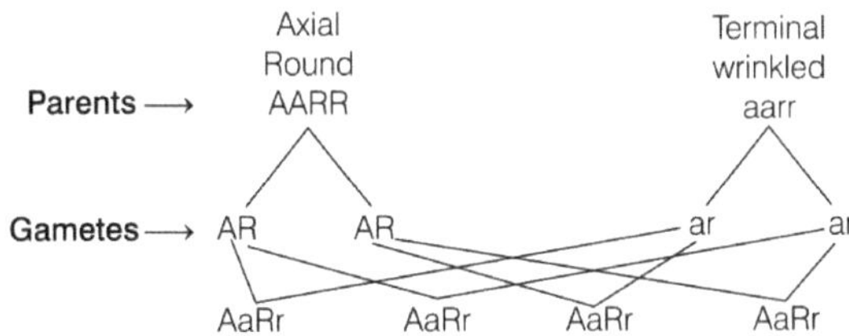

(i) Phenotype of F_1 progeny
(a) axial round
(b) axial wrinkled
(c) terminal wrinked
(d) terminal round

(ii) Phenotype of F_2 progeny produced upon by the self-pollination of F_1 progeny
(a) axial round and axial winkled
(b) terminal round
(c) terminal wrinkled
(d) All of the above

(iii) The phenotypic ratio of the F_2-generation will be
(a) 3 : 1   (b) 9 : 3 : 3 : 1
(c) 1 : 2 : 1   (d) 1 : 3

(iv) A cross between two individuals results in 9 : 3 : 3 : 1 for four possible phenotypes of progeny. This is an example of a
(a) dihybrid cross   (b) F_1-generation
(c) monohyorid cross   (d) test cross

(v) Which of the following law is mainly explained by the given cross?
(a) Law of dominance
(b) Law of segregation
(c) Law of independent assortment
(d) None of the above

23. Read the following and answer the questions from (i) to (v) given below

Gregor Johann Mendel is known as a 'Father of Modern Genetics' for his work in the field of the genetics. He worked out the main rules for inheritance patterns. The heredity in most of the living organisms is found to be regulated by certain definite principles.

Mendel opted for garden pea (*Pisum sativum*) to conduct his experiments. He performed self-pollination and cross-pollination to understand the inheritance patterns of traits.

His experiments with garden pea along with the inferences drawn together constitute, the foundation of modern genetics.

Mendel's contributions were unique because of the use of distinct variables and application of mathematics to the problem. He kept the record of each generation separately and studied the inheritance of only one pair of characters at a time.

(i) Mendel took .... contrasting characteristics of pea plants.
(a) eight   (b) seven
(c) six   (d) five

(ii) After cross pollination of true-breeding tall and dwarf plants, the F_1-generation was self-fertilised. The resultant plants have genotype in the ratio
(a) 1 : 2 : 1 (homozygous tall : heterozygous tall : homozygous dwarf)
(b) 1 : 2 : 1 (homozygous tall : dwarf : heterozygous tall)
(c) 3 : 1 (tall : dwarf)
(d) 3 : 1 (dwarf : tall)

(iii) Which Mendelian law states that inheritance of one character is always independent to the inheritance of other character within the same individual?
(a) Law of dominance
(b) Law of segregation
(c) Law of independent assortment
(d) Both (b) and (c)

(iv) Which one is the possible progeny in F_2-generation of pure breed tall plant with round seed and short plant with wrinkled seed?
(a) Tall plant with round seed
(b) Tall plant with wrinkled seed
(c) Short plant with round seed
(d) All of the above

(v) Round and yellow seed is
(a) recessive   (b) dominant
(c) hybrid   (d) incomplete dominance

PART 2
Subjective Questions

• Short Answer Type Questions

1. What do you mean by heredity? Who is its founder?
(CBSE 2020)

2. If a trait 'A' exists in 10% of the population of an asexually reproducing species and a trait 'B' exists in 60% of the same population, which trait is likely to have arisen earlier?

3. How does the creation of variations in a species promote survival?

4. In any population, no two individuals are absolutely similar. Why?

5. A child questioned his teacher that why do organisms resemble their parents more as compared to grandparents. In which way, will the teacher explain to the child? **(CBSE 2015)**

6. Why did Mendel choose pea plant for his experiments?

7. How do Mendel's experiments show that traits may dominant or recessive? **(CBSE 2016)**

8. What do you mean by dominant and recessive characteristics?

9. Explain difference between phenotype and genotype.

10. In a pea plant, find the contrasting trait if
    (i) the position of flower is terminal
    (ii) the flower is white in colour
    (iii) shape of pod is constricted **(CBSE 2015)**

11. How do Mendel's experiments show that traits are inherited independently? **(CBSE 2016)**

12. In a certain species of animal black fur (B) is dominant over brown fur (b). Predict a genotype and phenotype of the offspring when both parents are Bb or have heterozygous black fur.

13. A man with blood group A married a woman with blood group O and their daughter has blood group O. Is this information enough to tell you which of the traits blood group A or O is dominant? Why or why not? **(NCERT)**

14. Write the phenotypic ratio of progeny of F_2-generation of a dihybrid cross. **(2018, 15)**

15. Consider the cross between two parents with contrasting characteristics given below.

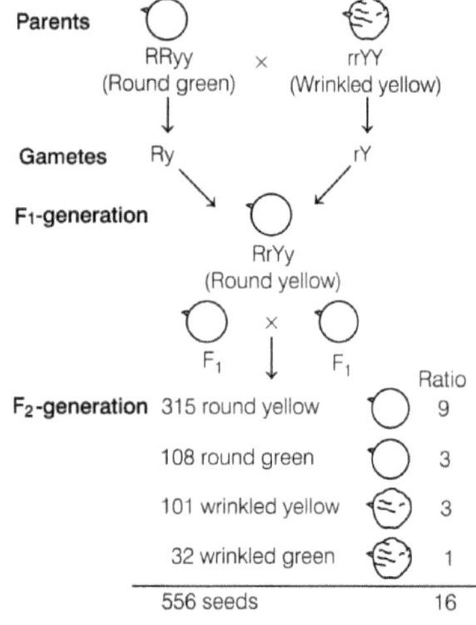

Recompile the above observations and explain the law of inheritance associated with them.

16. Name the plant Mendel used for his experiments. What type of progeny was obtained by Mendel in F_1 and F_2-generations when he crossed the tall and short plants? Write the ratio he obtained in F_2-generation plants. **(CBSE Delhi 2019)**

17. Study the following cross showing self-pollination in F_1 progeny. Fill in the blank and answer the questions that follows.

RRyy	× rrYY	Parents
(Round green)	(Wrinkled yellow)	
RrYy	×	F_1-generation
(Round yellow)		

    (i) In above question, what is the combination of characters in the F_2 progeny? What are the ratios?
    (ii) Give reasons for the appearance of new combination of characters in the F_1 progeny. **(NCERT Exemplar)**

18. How is the sex of a child determined in human beings?

19. Does genetic combination of mother play a significant role in determining the sex of a newborn? **(NCERT Exemplar)**

• Long Answer Type Questions

20. 'A trait may be inherited, but may not be expressed'. Justify this statement with the help of a suitable example.

21. Discuss Mendelian laws with examples.

22. What do you understand by Mendel's dihybrid cross? When pea plants having round and yellow seeds were crossed with plants having wrinkled and green seeds and then all the plants of F_1-generation had round and yellow seeds. Find out the phenotypic ratio of F_2-generation.

23. After self-pollination in pea plants with round, yellow seeds, following types of seeds were obtained by Mendel

Seeds	Numbers
Round, yellow	630
Round, green	216
Wrinkled, yellow	202
Wrinkled, green	64

Analyse the result and describe the mechanism of inheritance which explains these results. **(CBSE 2020)**

24. 'In humans, there is a 50% probability of the birth of a boy and 50% probability that a girl will be born'. Justify the statement on the basis of the mechanism of sex-determination in human beings. **(CBSE 2020)**

• Case Based Questions

25. Read the following and answer the questions from (i) to (v) given below

Inheritance from the previous generation provides both, a common body design and subtle changes in it, for the next generation. Now, when the new generation reproduces, the second generation produced will have variations that they inherit from the first generation, as well as newly created differences.]

For example, if one bacterium divides and gives rise to two individuals each of them will divided again and give rise to two other individuals in the next generation.

The four individual bacteria generated would be very similar with minor differences that occurred due to small inaccuracies to copying of DNA.

However, in sexual reproduction, even greater diversity will be generated. Depending upon the nature of variations, different individuals would have different advantages, the most important advantage of variation to a species is that it increases the chance of its survival in a changing environment.

  (i) What do you understand by the term 'gene' ?
 (ii) In which type of reproduction exchange of genetic material takes place ?
(iii) What is the cause of variation in asexual reproducing organisms ?
(iv) Differentiate between genotype and phenotype of an organism.
 (v) What is the chemical composition of chromosome ?

26. Read the following and answer the questions from (i) to (v) given below

A person first crossed pure-breed pea plants having round-yellow seeds with pure-breed pea plants having wrinkled-green seeds and found that only A-B type of seeds were produced in the F_1-generation.

When F_1-generation pea plants having A-B type of seeds were cross-breed by self-pollination, then in addition to the original round yellow and

wrinkled-green seeds, two new varieties A-D and C-B types of seeds were also obtained.

  (i) What are A-B type of seeds?
 (ii) State whether A and B are dominant traits or recessive traits.
(iii) What are A-D type of seeds?
(iv) What are C-B type of seeds?
 (v) Out of A-B and A-D types of seeds, which one will be produced in (*a*) minimum number and (*b*) maximum number in the F_2-generation?

27. Read the following and answer the questions from (i) to (v) given below

Mendel selected garden pea for his experiments because he discovered for the first time the occurrence of two types of seeds in pea plants growing in the garden of his monastery. Mendel then used a number of contrasting visible characters of garden peas like.

	Characters	Dominant	Recessive
1.	Plant height	Tall	Dwarf
2.	Flower position	Axial	Terminal
3.	Pod colour	Green	Yellow
4.	Pod shape	Full	Constricted
5.	Flower colour	Violet	White
6.	Seed shape	Round	Wrinkled
7.	Seed colour	Yellow	Green

Mendel's experiments were performed in three stages in selection of pure or true breeding parents, hybridisation and obtaining of F_1-generation of plants and self-pollination of hybrid plants and raising of subsequent generations like F_2, F_3, F_4, etc.

  (i) How many contrasting traits were taken by Mendel in his monohybrid crosses?
 (ii) Give a monohybrid cross to explain the F_1-generation formed by a plant with green pod colour and yellow pod colour.
(iii) State the first law of Mendel.
(iv) What do understand by homozygous tall plant and heterozygous tall plant?
 (v) A Mendelian experiment consisted of breeding pea plant bearing violet flowers with pea plants bearing while flowers. What will be the results in F_1 progeny?

28. Read the following and answer the questions from (i) to (v) given below

Observe the following cross between tall plants having round seeds and dwarf plants having wrinkled seeds.

The individuals obtained in the F_1-generation were thereafter self-crossed.

$$\text{TTRR} \quad \times \quad \text{ttrr}$$
(Tall, Round)   (Dwarf, Wrinkled)

$$\text{TtRr} \quad \times \quad \text{TtRr} \quad (F_1\text{-generation self-crossed})$$
(Tall, Round)   (Tall, Round)

(i) What would be the phenotypes of the individuals obtained in the F_2-generation? Give their ratios.

(ii) Why do you think all the individuals of the F_1-generation were tall with round seeds?

(iii) What will be the number of progeny obtained in F_2-generation in a dihybrid cross with pure dominant traits?

(iv) What would be the phenotype of the individual obtained in F_1-generation?

(v) According to you, what is responsible for the inheritance of traits?

29. Read the following and answer the questions from (i) to (v) given below

A person crossed pure-breed tall pea plants with pure-breed dwarf pea plants and obtained pea plants of F_1-generation. He then performed two types of experiments.

In the first, he self-crossed the plants of F_1-generation (experiment A) and in the second, he crossed the plants of F_1-generation with the pure-breed dwarf parent plants (experiment B).

Experiment A : F_1 progeny $\times F_1$ progeny

Experiment B : F_1 progeny $\times$ Homozygous dwarf plant

(i) What would be the phenotype of plants in the F_1-generation?

(ii) What would be the phenotype and genotype ratio of F_2-generation in experiment 'A'?

(iii) How would the genotypic ratio in F_2 generation different in experiment 'B'?

(iv) How do we describe the phenotypic character that is experssed in F_1-generation? What is the term given to the contrasting character?

(v) Name the type of cross shown in experiment B.

EXPLANATIONS

Objective Questions

1. (*a*) The process through which characters or traits pass from one generation to another is called inheritance.

2. (*a*) Statement in option (a) is not true with respect to variation because

All variations in a species do not have equal chances of survival. Some of the variations may be so drastic that the new DNA copy cannot work with cellular apparatus it inherits. Such, a newborn cell dies soon.

3. (*b*) Free earlobes are dominant (i) traits and attached earlobes are recessive (ii) traits.

4. (*c*) A trait in an organism is influenced by both maternal and paternal DNA.

5. (*c*) Punnett square was used by Gregor J Mendel to determine the law of inheritance in his experiments with pea plant.

6. (*a*) In F_1-generation, the cross between TT and tt will result into all tall plants, because tallness is the dominant trait.

7. (*c*)

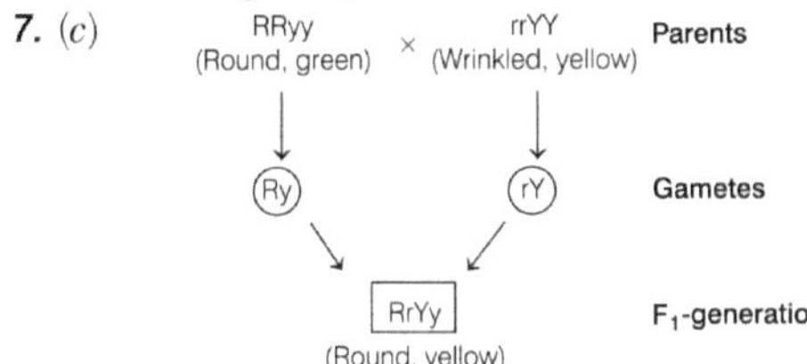

8. (*b*) An allele is a variant form of a gene, which are located at the same position on a chromosomes. The heterozygous organism (Tt) shows that it has two different alleles (T-tall and t-dwarf) for the gene of the height.

9. (*c*) When a pure tall (TT) plant is hybridised with dwarf plant (tt), it will always give tall plants in F_1-generation.

But, when they are self-pollinated, it will give both tall and dwarf plants in F_2-generation.

10. (*b*) When pure breed pea plant A is crossed with pure breed pea plant B. It is found that the plants which look like B do not appear in F_1-generation but re-emerge in F_2-generation, which means A is dominant over B trait and both of them are contrasting traits. (i.e. A are tall and B are dwarf).

11. (*c*) If pea plants having round green seeds and wrinkled yellow seeds are crossed, phenotypic ratio of $9 : 3 : 3 : 1$ will be obtained in F_2 progeny.

12. (*b*) The dihybrid cross between round green plant and wrinkled yellow plant is shown as

Parents	RRyy (Round, green)	×	rrYY (Wrinkled, yellow)	
Gametes	Ry		rY	
F_1-generation		(RrYy) (Round, yellow)		
Selfing	F_1	×	F_1	
		↓		**Ratio**
F_2-generation	315 round, yellow (*A*)			9
	108 round, green (*B*)			3
	101 wrinkled (*C*), yellow			3
	32 wrinkled, green (*D*)			1
	556 seeds			16

13. (*c*) In the given cross, a purple flowered plant (dominant) is cross fertilised with white flowered plant (recessive). The F_1-progeny obtained contain all plants with purple flowers. The progeny of F_1-generation is self-fertilised to give rise to F_2-generation having plants with purple flowers and white flowers in ratio $3 : 1$.

Hence, (i) represent cross-fertilisation, (ii) represent self-fertilisation and (iii) represent F_2-generation.

14. (*a*) The given diagram shows sex-determination in human. There are two types of sperms in male. Sperms having X-chromosome (A) and sperms having Y-chromosome (B), whereas the female ovum contains only one type of chromosome (C), i.e. X.

When X sperm fuses with ovum, the female zygote (D) is formed, whereas when Y sperm fuses with ovum, the male zygote is formed. Thus, option (a) is correct.

15. (*b*) Statements I, III and IV are correct, whereas statement II is incorrect and can be corrected as

Each trait in child is influenced by both paternal as well as maternal DNA.

16. (*b*) Both A and R are true, but R is not the correct explanation of A.

Dominant allele is an allele whose phenotype will be expressed even in the presence of another allele of that gene. It is represented by a capital letter, e.g. T. It can be expressed itself in both homozygous and heterozygous conditions.

17. (*c*) A is true, but R is false because

When Mendel self-crossed F_1-generation to obtain F_2-generation. F_1 progeny of a tall plant with round seeds and a dwarf plant with wrinkled seeds are all tall plants with round seeds. This is because tallness and round shape are both dominant traits, while dwarfness and wrinkled shapes of seeds are recessive traits.

18. (*c*) A is true, but R is false.

The ratio of F_2 plants when Mendel took pea plant with one contrasting characters, i.e. monohybrid cross was $3 : 1$.

19. (*a*) Both A and R are true and R is the correct explanation of A. Females are homogametic with two X-chromosomes. That is why, all human female gametes will have only X-chromosomes.

20. (*a*) Both A and R are true and R is the correct explanation of A. A human male has one X and one Y-chromosome. When a child inherits X-chromosome from the father, it will be a girl and one who inherits a Y-chromosome will be a boy.

21. (i) (*a*) Axial round seed is the phenotype of F_1-generation.

(ii) (*d*) Phenotype of F_2 progeny produced upon by the self-pollination of F_1 progeny will be axial round, axial-wrinkled, terminal round and terminal wrinkled plants.

Thus, option (d) is correct.

(iii) (*b*) The phenotypic ratio of the F_2-generation will be $9 : 3 : 3 : 1$.

(iv) (*a*) A cross between two individuals results in $9 : 3 : 3 : 1$ for four possible phenotypes of progeny. This is an example of a dihybrid cross.

(v) (*c*) The given cross mainly explains the law of independent assortment.

22. (i) (*b*) Mendel studied seven pairs of contrasting characteristics of pea plants.

(ii) (*a*) After cross pollination of true breeding tall and dwarf plants, the F_1-generation was self-fertilised.
The resultant plants have genotype in the ratio 1 : 2 : 1 (homozygous tall : heterozygous tall : homozygous dwarf)

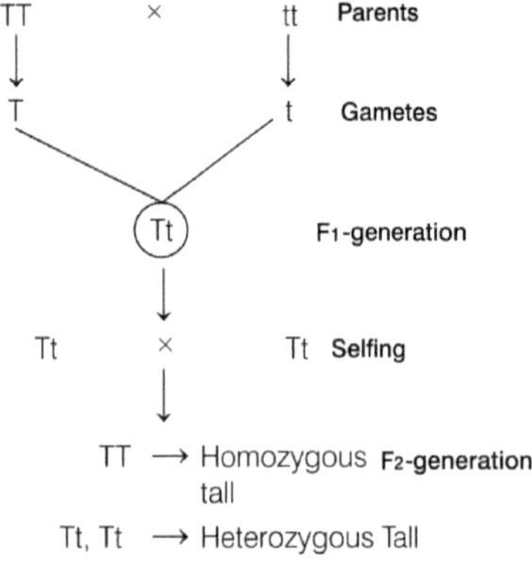

Hence, the genotypic ratio is 1 : 2 : 1.

(iii) (*c*) Law of independent assortment states that inheritance of one character is always independent to the inheritance of other characters within a same individual.

(iv) (*d*) In F_2-generation of pure breed tall plant with round seeds and short plant with wrinkled seed, the possible progeny will be observed are tall plant with round seeds, tall plants with wrinkled seeds, short plant with round seeds and short plant with wrinkled seeds.

Thus, option (d) is correct.

(v) (*b*) Round and yellow seeds show dominant character.

Subjective Questions

1. The transmission of characters from the parents to their offspring is called heredity. Heredity was discovered by Gregor Mendel through his work on pea plant.

2. In a population of asexually reproducing species, the chances of appearance of new traits due to variations are very low and the trait which is already present in the population is likely to be in higher percentage and would have been arisen earlier.
Therefore, the trait B present in 60% of the population is the trait which have arisen earlier.

3. During reproduction, copying of DNA takes place, which is not 100% accurate, thereby causing variations. If these variations are favourable, they help the individuals to survive and pass these variations to their progeny.

Depending upon the nature of variations, different individuals have different advantages, which promotes their survival like bacteria which can withstand heat will survive better in a heat wave.

4. Variations occur in the genes of the organisms produced due to the mutations, reshuffling of genes and inheritance of acquired traits during the evolutionary process which make all individuals different from one another. Thus, in any population, no two individuals are absolutely similar.

5. The two parents involved in sexual reproduction produce gametes which fuse together forming a zygote. It gradually develops into a young child showing certain similarities with the parents. Since, a child inherits its characters from both the parents the resemblance with them is very close. The grandparents and the child resemble less closely because a gap of gene pool is created by the parents of the child

Variations of two generations mixing together and addition of new variations from parents, increases the difference between them to a greater extent. Hence, a child resembles more closely to its parents than the grandparents.

6. Reasons for selecting pea plant for experiment by Mendel are as follows
- Pea is an annual plant with short life cycle. So, several generations can be studied in short period.
- It produces bisexual flowers, which are mainly self-pollinating.
- It can be cross-pollinated.
- A number of contrasting characters were available in it.

7. Mendel crossed a pure tall pea plant (TT) with pure dwarf pea plant (tt) and observed that all the progeny were hybrid tall (Tt), i.e. only one of the traits was able to express itself in the F_1-generation, which is the dominant trait.

The other trait is called the recessive trait which remains suppressed.

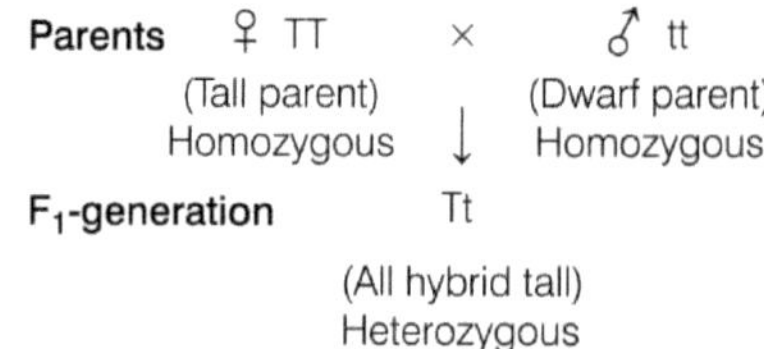

However, when he self-crossed plants of F_1-generation, he observed that one-fourth of the plants were dwarf and three-fourth were tall.

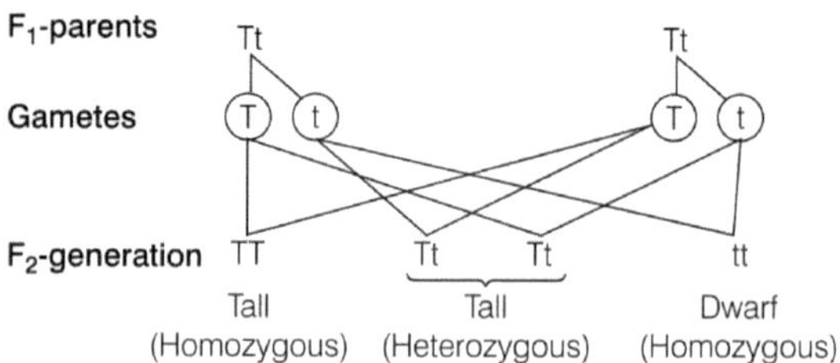

The expressed trait T for the tallness is dominant trait, while the trait 't' of dwarfness is recessive. Thus, Mendel's experiments show that trait may be dominant or recessive.

8. Dominant character The character which will express in F_1-generation in both homozygous and heterozygous conditions are dominant characters.

e.g. Tallness of plant, purple flower colour, etc.

Recessive character The character which will express only in homozygous condition, but not in heterozygous conditions or in F_1-generation is known as recessive character.
e.g. Dwarfness, white flower colour, etc.

9.

Phenotype	Genotype
It represents the external morphology of an organism for a particular character,	It is the genetic makeup of an individual for a character.
Same phenotype may or may not belong to same genotype.	Same genotype produces same phenotype.

10. Contrasting traits of pea plant were used by Mendel and were classified as dominant or recessive.

	Characters	Given traits	Contrasting traits
(i)	Position of flower	Terminal	Axial
(ii)	Colour of flower	White	Violet
(iii)	Shape of pod	Constricted	Full

11. Mendel performed a dihybrid cross between pure pea plants to show that traits are inherited independently. He selected a pea plant with round green (RRyy) and wrinkled yellow (rrYY) seeds.

In the F_1 progeny, it was found that all plants were round yellow. But in F_2 progeny, some plants were round green and some were wrinkled yellow.

However, there were plants which showed new combinations. Some of them were round with yellow seeds, while others were wrinkled with green seeds. Thus, the round/wrinkled trait and green/yellow seed traits are independently inherited.

12.

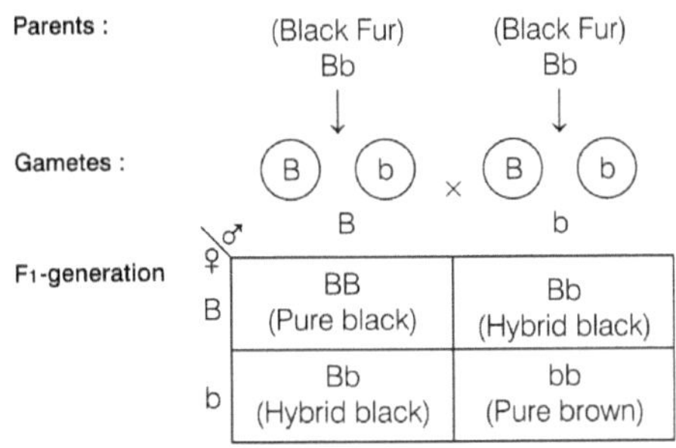

Phenotype   3 : 1
      Black   Brown

Genotype   1 : 2 : 1
      Pure   Hybrid   Pure brown
      black   black

Therefore, the phenotypic ratio of black fur and brown fur offspring is 3 : 1. The genotypic ratio of offspring is 1 : 2 : 1.

13. The information is insufficient to tell whether the trait 'A' or 'O' is dominant. It can find out by assuming the following cases.

In case I Let assume that trait 'A' is dominant. Father that have $I^A I^O$ and mother having $I^O I^O$ type of gene for blood group. In this case 50% of the progeny will have blood group 'A' and 50% of the progenies will have blood group 'O', when father's blood group is $I^A I^O$ and mother is $I^O I^O$.

Whereas, in case of father having $I^A I^A$ type of gene and mother having $I^O I^O$ type of gene, all of the progeny (100%) will have blood group A.

In case II Let assume that 'O' is dominant. In this case, the child may have blood group 'O'. Since in both the assumptions, the child can have blood group 'O', so it cannot infer which trait is dominant.

14. When pea plants with two contrasting characters, i.e. one with a green round seeds and the other with a yellow wrinkled seeds are crossed, all the F_1 progeny obtained had round and yellow seeds.

When the F_1 progeny is self-crossed to obtain F_2 progeny, four types of seeds were obtained as round yellow, round green, wrinkled yellow and wrinkled green in ratio 9 : 3 : 3 : 1 respectively.

Hence, the phenotypic ratio of F_2 progeny is 9 : 3 : 3 : 1.

15. Mendel took pea plants with two contrasting characters, i.e. one with a green round seeds and the other with a yellow wrinkled seeds. When the F_1 progeny was obtained, they had round and yellow seeds. Mendel then allowed the F_1 progeny to be self-crossed to obtain F_2 progeny.

He found that seeds were round yellow, round green, wrinkled yellow and some were wrinkled green. The ratio of plants with above characteristics was 9 : 3 : 3 : 1, respectively.

In F_1-generation, all the characters were asserted out independently of each other. Therefore, he stated that a pair of contrasting or alternating characters behave independently of the other pair.

16. Mendel used the pea plant for his experiments. He took pea plants with different characteristics such as height (tall and short plants). The progeny produced from them (F_1-generation) plants were all tall.

Mendel then allowed F_1 progeny plants to undergo self-pollination. In the F_2-generation, he found that all plants were not tall, three quarter were tall and one quarter of them were short. The ratio he obtained in F_2-generation plants is 9 : 3 : 3 : 1.

17.

RRyy (Round green)	× rrYY (Wrinkled yellow)	Parents
RrYy (Round yellow)	× **RrYy** (Round yellow)	F_1-generation

(i) In F_2-generation, the combination of characters is
Round yellow = 9, Round green = 3
Wrinkled yellow = 3, Wrinkled green = 1
Thus, the ratio is 9 : 3 : 3 : 1

(ii) In F_1-generation, the production of all round yellow (RrYy) seeds explains that the round shape and yellow colour of the seeds were dominant traits over the wrinkled shape and green colour of the seeds which segregated during F_2-generation.

18. A male gamete carries either one X or one Y-chromosome, while a female gamete carries only X-chromosomes. Therefore, sex of the child depends upon what happens during fertilisation.

(i) If a sperm carrying X-chromosome fertilises the egg, the child born will be a female (XX).

(ii) If a sperm carrying Y-chromosome fertilises the egg, the child born will be a male (XY).

Thus, the sperm (the male gamete) determines the sex of the child.

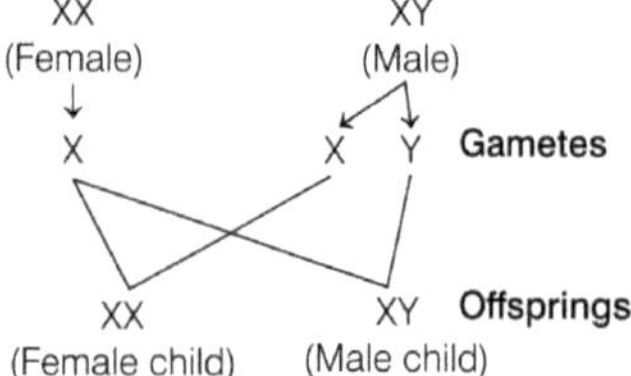

19. No, the genetic combination of mother does not play any significant role in determining the sex of a newborn. This is because the female cell carries two X-chromosomes (XX). While, the male cell carries one X and one Y-chromosome.

The fusion of X-chromosome bearing sperm (of male cell) with X-chromosome of female egg produces a female child, while the fusion of Y-chromosome bearing sperm (of male cell) with X-chromosome of female egg produces a male child. Therefore, it is the contribution of father which determines the sex of a newborn.

20. 'A trait may be inherited, but may not be expressed'. Mendel crossed tall pea plants with dwarf pea plants.

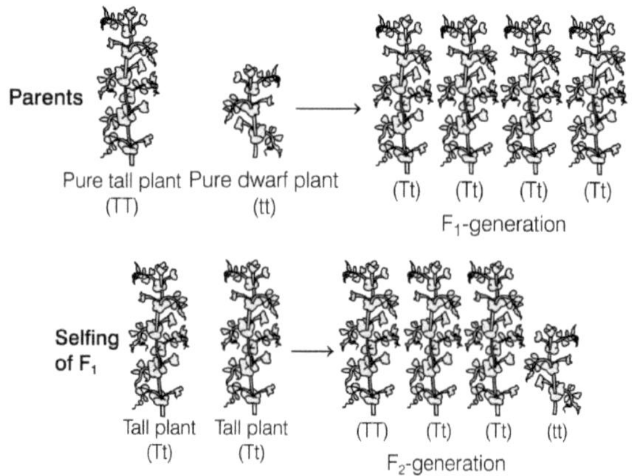

Mendel's observation F_1-generation contained all tall plants with genotype Tt, where 'T' represents a dominant trait and 't' represents a recessive trait. This means when F_1-generation underwent selfing, the trait that was unexpressed in F_1 (dwarf) was observed in some F_2-progeny. Thus, both traits, tall and dwarf, were expressed in F_2-generation in the ratio of 3 : 1.

21. The three major laws of inheritance proposed by Mendel are as follows

(i) **Law of Dominance** (First Law) According to this law, when two homozygous individuals with one or more contrasting characters are crossed, the F_1 hybrid have both the contrasting alleles of a pair, but only one (i.e. dominant trait) allele expresses and it does not allow the other one (recessive trait) to appear.

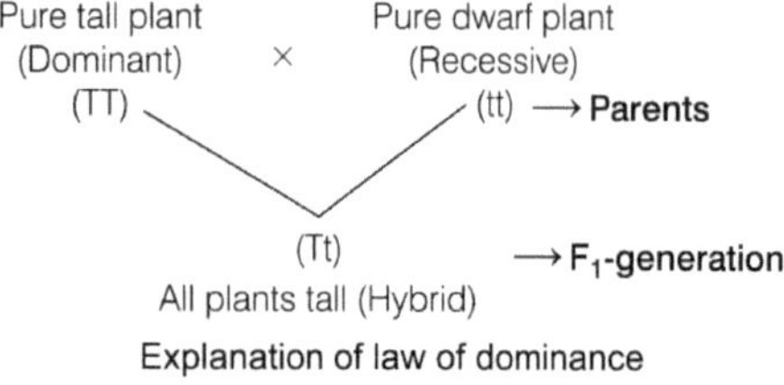

(ii) **Law of Segregation or Law of Purity of Gametes** (Second Law) This law states that the factors or alleles of a pair segregate from each other during gamete formation such that a gamete receives only one of the two factors. They do not show any blending.

e.g. The reappearance of wrinkled seed character in F_2-generation, which was suppressed in F_1-generation by the round seed character.

This law is also be proven by monohybrid cross.

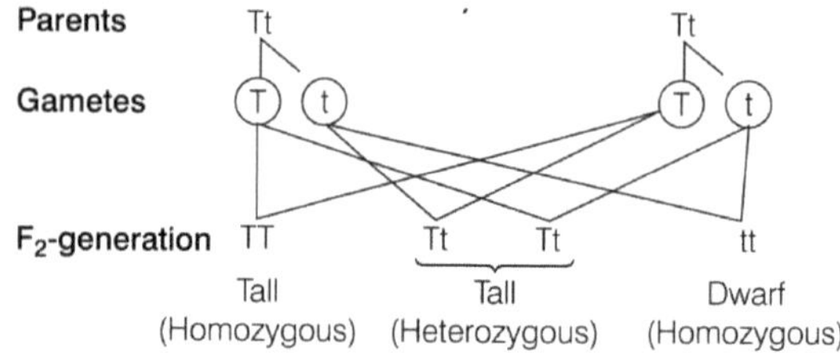

(iii) **Law of Independent Assortment** (Third Law) This law states that two factors of each character assort or separate out independent of the factors of other characters at the time of gamete formation and get randomly rearranged in the offspring.

e.g. In dihybrid cross, between pure round and yellow seed pea plants with plants having wrinkled and green seeds, the F_2-generation produced two parental and two hybrid combinations.

This law can be proven by dihybrid cross

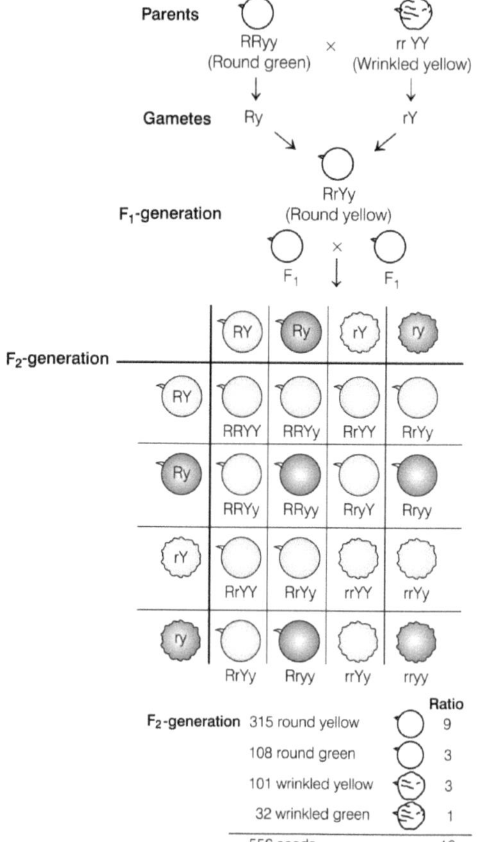

22. Dihybrid Cross When cross between two varieties having two contrasting characters takes place, then it is called dihybrid cross.

In F_1-generation, on the basis of law of dominance, only dominant characters appear. During gamete formation, genes of contrasting characters separate and only one gene enters each gamete.

On self-fertilisation, the F_1-generation develops F_2-generation in which $9 : 3 : 3 : 1$ phenotypic ratio appears. In F_2-generation, new combination also develops.

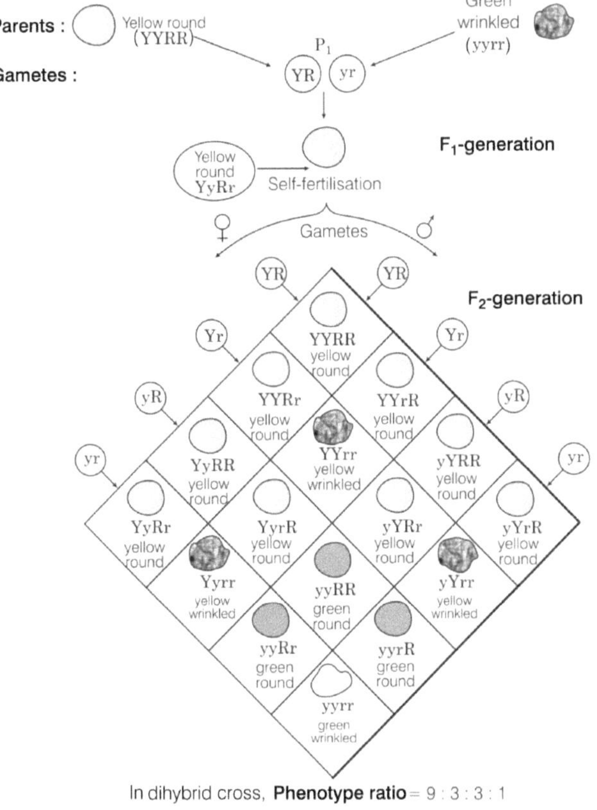

In dihybrid cross, **Phenotype ratio** $= 9 : 3 : 3 : 1$

Yellow round : Yellow wrinkled : Green round : Green wrinkled
$\quad 9 \quad : \quad 3 \quad : \quad 3 \quad : \quad 1$

23. In dihybrid cross, the ratio of phenotype of F_2-generation obtained by selfing of F_1-generation is $9 : 3 : 3 : 1$, in which parental as well as new combination are observed. This shows law of independent assortment in which two characters under consideration assort in an independent manner to give rise to different combination.

It means that the genes of all the characters are independent from each other and combined to make new varieties.

24. Humans have 23 pairs of chromosome. Both male and female carry two sets of sex chromosome.

Male (XY) has one X and one Y sex chromosome. Female (XX) has both X sex chromosome.

All children will inherit an X-chromosome from their mother regardless of whether they are boys or girls.

Thus, the sex of the children will be determined by what they inherit from their father. A child who inherits an X-chromosome from her father will be a girl and one who inherits a Y-chromosome from him will be a boy.

25. (i) A gene is a unit of DNA which governs the synthesis of one protein that provides a specific character of the organisms.

(ii) Exchange of genetic material takes place in sexual reproduction.

(iii) Environmental factors and mutations cause variation in asexual reproducing organisms.

(iv) The genetic constitution of an organisms is called genotype, whereas the phenotype is the physical appearance or characteristics of the organism.

(v) The chemical composition of a chromosome is DNA and histone proteins.

26. (i) A-B type of seeds are round in shape and yellow in colour as round and yellow both constitute the dominant character, hence expressed in F_1-generation.

(ii) A(round) and B(yellow) are dominant traits.

(iii) Round-green (A-D).

(iv) Wrinkled-yellow (C-B).

(v) (a) A-D in minimum number.
(b) A-B in maximum number.

27. (i) One contrasting trait, i.e. tall and dwarf plants were taken by Mendel in his monohybrid crosses.

(ii)
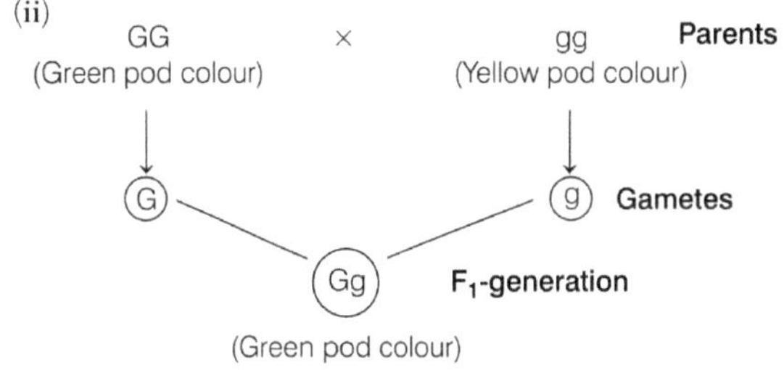

(iii) The first law of Mendel is law of dominance, which states that the when two alleles of an inherited pair is heterozygous, then the allele that is expressed is dominant, whereas the allele that is not expressed is recessive.

(iv) Homozygous tall plant will have two identical copies of single gene, i.e. TT.

Heterozygous tall plant will have two different copies of single gene, i.e. Tt.

(v) Heterozygous pea plants with violet flowers will result in F_1-progeny.

28. (i) In F_2-generation, the phenotypes of the individuals obtained would be

Tall and round $= 9$; Tall and wrinkled $= 3$;

Dwarf and round $= 3$; Dwarf and wrinkled $= 1$

Thus, the ratio is $9 : 3 : 3 : 1$.

(ii) The appearance of all tall plants with round seeds shows that the tallness and round-shaped seeds are dominant traits over the dwarfness and wrinkled shape of the seeds.

(iii) The number of progeny obtained in F_2-generation in a dihybrid cross with pure dominant traits, i.e. TTRR will be 1 which is formed by the fertilisation of gametes TR and TR.

(iv) In F_1-generation₁, all tall and round plants will be obtained.

(v) Gene is the carrier that leads to the inheritance of traits. It is the part of a chromosome that controls the appearance of a set of hereditary characteristics.

29. (i) The phenotype of all the plants in the F_1-generation would be tall.

(ii) In experiment 'A', the phenotypic ratio of tall and dwarf plants would be 3 : 1 : : Tall : Dwarf, whereas the genotypic ratio would be 1 : 2 : 1 for TT, Tt, tt genotype.

(iii) When crossed with homozygous recessive parent the genotypic ratio would be 1 : 1 for Tt, tt genotype.

(iv) The phenotypic character that a capable of expressing in the F_1-generation is described as 'dominant'. The contrasting character, i.e. dwarfness is the recessive character.

(v) In experiment B, test cross is done between the F_1 heterozygote with homozygous recessive parent.

Chapter Test

Multiple Choice Questions

1. The number of pair(s) of sex chromosomes in the zygote of humans is

(a) one   (b) two   (c) three   (d) four

2. The following results were obtained by a scientist who crossed the F_1-generation of pure breeding parents for round and wrinkled seeds.

Dominants trait	Recessive trait	Number of F_2 offspring
Round seeds	Wrinkled seeds	7524

From these results, it can be concluded that the actual number of round seeds he obtained was

(a) 1881   (b) 22572
(c) 2508   (d) 5643

3. A recessive homozygote is crossed with a heterozygote of the same gene. What will be the phenotype of the F_1-generation?

(a) All dominant
(b) 75% dominant, 25% recessive
(c) 50% dominant, 50% recessive
(d) 25% dominant, 50% heterozygous, 25% recessive

4. Identify the genotype of parent plants by observing the result of the cross given below.

F_1-generation	Aa	Aa
	Aa	Aa

(a) Both parents are homozygous
(b) Both parents are heterozygous
(c) One parent is homozygous and other parent is heterozygous
(d) Cannot say

5. Choose the correctly matched pair.

(a) X and Y-chromosomes—Autosomes
(b) Father of Genetics—Gregor Johann Mendel
(c) Monohybrid cross—Two pairs of contrasting characters
(d) Dihybrid cross—One pair of contrasting characters

Assertion-Reasoning MCQs

Direction (Q. Nos. 6-8) Each of these questions contains two statements, Assertion (A) and Reason (R). Each of these questions also has four alternative choices, any one of which is the correct answer. You have to select one of the codes (a), (b), (c) and (d) given below.

(a) Both A and R are true and R is the correct explanation of A
(b) Both A and R are true, but R is not the correct explanation of A
(c) A is true, but R is false
(d) A is false, but R is true

6. Assertion Genes present in every cell of an organism control the traits of the organisms.

Reason Gene is specific segment of DNA occupying specific position on chromosome.

7. Assertion Traits like tallness and dwarfness in pea plant are inherited independently.

Reason When a homozygous tall pea plant is crossed with dwarf pea plant, medium-sized pea plant is obtained in F_1-generation.

8. Assertion In human females, all the chromosomes are perfectly paired except sex chromosomes.

Reason X and Y are sex chromosomes in males.

Short Answer Type Questions

9. 'Only variations that confer an advantage to an individual organisms will survive in a population'. Do you agree with this statement? Why or why not?

10. Differentiate between homozygote and heterozygote.

11. Outline a project which aims to find the dominant coat colour in dogs.

12. If we cross pure breed tall (dominant) pea plants with pure breed dwarf (recessive) pea plants, we get pea plants of F_1-generation. If we now self-cross the pea plant of F_1-generation, then we obtain pea plants of F_2-generation.

(i) What do the plants of F_1-generation look like?
(ii) What is the ratio of tall plants to dwarf plants in F_2-generation?
(iii) State the type of plants not found in F_1-generation, but appeared in F_2-generation mentioning the reason for the same.

13. How is the equal genetic contribution of male and female parents ensured in the progeny?

Long Answer Type Questions

14. Ovum and sperm are both female and male gametes, respectively. But, what is so intricate in sperm which makes it solely responsible for determining the sex of the child? Explain.

15. In the following crosses, write the characteristics of the progeny obtained.

(i) RRYY   ×   RRYY
   (Round yellow) (Round yellow)
(ii) RrYy   ×   RrYy
   (Round yellow) (Round yellow)
(iii) rryy   ×   rryy
   (Wrinkled green) (Wrinkled green)
(iv) RRYY   ×   rryy
   (Round yellow)   (Wrinkled green)

Answers

Multiple Choice Questions

1. (a)   *2.* (d)   *3.* (c)   *4.* (a)   *5.* (b)

Assertion-Reasoning MCQs

6. (b)   *7.* (c)   *8.* (d)

For Detailed Solutions
Scan the code

CHAPTER 05

Electricity

In this Chapter...

- Ohm's Law
- Resistance
- Combination of Resistors
- Heating Effect of Electric Current
- Electric Power

Electricity is one of the most convenient and widely used forms of energy in today's world. It is a controllable and convenient form of energy.

Ohm's Law

It gives a relationship between **current** I, flowing in a metallic wire and **potential difference** V, across its terminals.

According to this law, the electric current flowing through a conductor is directly proportional to the potential difference applied across its ends, providing the physical conditions (such as temperature) remain unchanged.

If V is the potential difference applied across the ends of a conductor through which current I flows, then according to Ohm's law,

$$V \propto I \qquad \text{[at constant temperature]}$$

or

$$V = IR$$

or

$$I = \frac{V}{R}$$

where, R is the constant of proportionality called **resistance of the conductor** at a given temperature.

The conductors which obey Ohm's law are called **ohmic conductors** while the conductors which do not obey Ohm's law are called **non-ohmic conductors**.

V-I Graph

The graph between the potential difference V and the corresponding current I is found to be a straight line passing through the origin for ohmic (metallic) conductors.

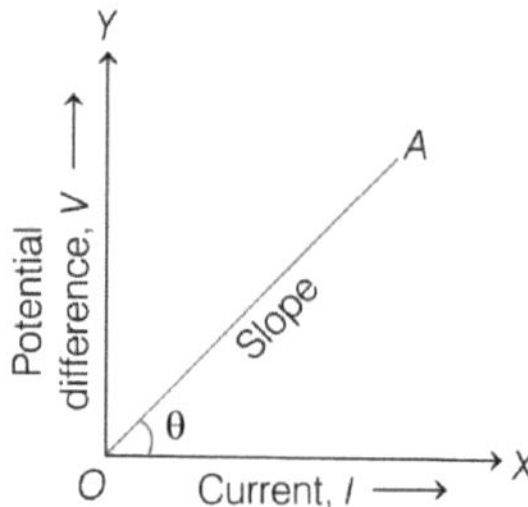

V-I graph for metallic conductor

Resistance

It is that property of a conductor by virtue of which it opposes/resists the flow of charges/current through it. Its SI unit is **ohm** and it is represented by Ω.

Resistance of a conductor is given by, $R = \dfrac{V}{I}$.

It is said to be 1 ohm, if a potential difference of 1 volt across the ends of the conductor makes a current of 1 ampere to flow through it.

i.e. $$1 \text{ ohm} = \frac{1 \text{ volt}}{1 \text{ ampere}}$$

$$\Rightarrow \qquad 1\,\Omega = \frac{1\ \text{V}}{1\ \text{A}} = 1\ \text{VA}^{-1}$$

Factors on which the Resistance of a Conductor Depends

The electrical resistance of a conductor depends on the following factors

(i) **Length of the Conductor** The resistance of a conductor R is directly proportional to its length l.

i.e. $\qquad R \propto l \qquad\qquad$ ...(i)

(ii) **Area of Cross-section of the Conductor** The resistance of a conductor R is inversely proportional to its area of cross-section A.

i.e. $\qquad R \propto \dfrac{1}{A} \qquad\qquad$ ...(ii)

(iii) **Nature of the Material of the Conductor** The resistance of a conductor depends on the nature of the material of which it is made. Some materials have low resistance, whereas others have high resistance.

Therefore, from Eqs. (i) and (ii), we can write

$$R \propto \frac{l}{A} \quad \text{or} \quad R = \rho\,\frac{l}{A}$$

where, ρ is the constant of proportionality and is called **electric resistivity** or **specific resistance** of the material of the conductor.

Resistivity

It is defined as the resistance of a conductor of unit length and unit area of cross-section. Its SI unit is **ohm-metre** (Ω-m).

- The resistivity of a material does not depend on its length or thickness but depends on the nature of the substance and temperature. It is a characteristic property of the material of the conductor and varies only, if its temperature changes.
- Insulators such as glass, rubber, ebonite, etc., have a very high resistivity (10^{12} to $10^{17}\,\Omega$-m), while conductors have a very low resistivity (10^{-8} to $10^{-6}\,\Omega$-m).
- Alloys have higher resistivity than that of their constituent metals. They do not oxidise easily at high temperatures, this is why they are used to make heating elements of devices such as electric iron, heaters, etc.
- Tungsten is almost used exclusively for filaments of electric bulbs, whereas copper and aluminium are generally used for electrical transmission lines.

Combination of Resistors

There are two methods of joining the resistors together which are as given below.

1. Series Combination

When two or more resistors are connected end to end to each other, then they are said to be **connected in series**.

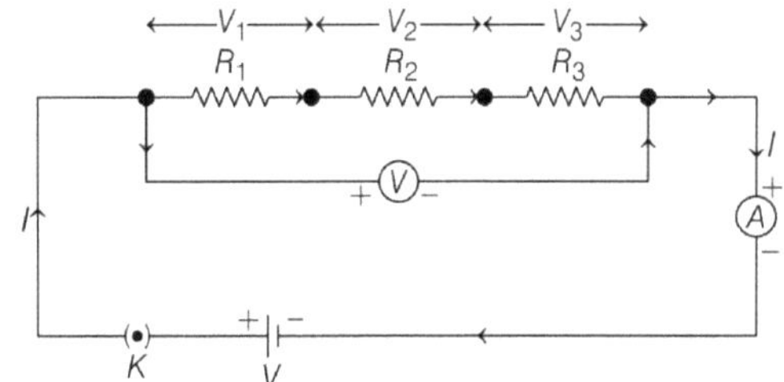

The **equivalent resistance** is equal to the sum of the all individual resistances.

i.e., $$R = R_1 + R_2 + R_3$$

The equivalent resistance is thus greater than the resistances of either resistor. This is also known as **maximum effective resistance**.

The current through each resistor is same. The potential difference across each resistor is different.

2. Parallel Combination

When two or more resistors are connected simultaneously between two points to each other, then they are said to be connected in parallel combination.

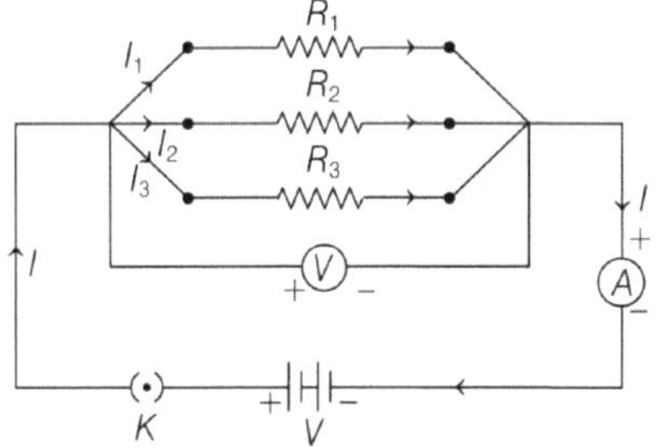

The reciprocal of equivalent resistance is equal to the sum of the reciprocal of individual resistances.

i.e. $$\frac{1}{R} = \frac{1}{R_1} + \frac{1}{R_2} + \frac{1}{R_3}$$

The equivalent resistance is less than the resistance of either resistor. This is also known as **minimum effective resistance**.

The current from the source is greater than the current through either resistor. The potential difference across each resistor is same.

Heating Effect of Electric Current

When an electric current is passed through a high resistance wire like nichrome wire, then the wire becomes very hot and produces heat.

In purely resistive circuits, the source of energy continuously gets dissipated entirely in the form of heat. This is called the heating effect of current.

This is obtained by the transformation of electrical energy into heat energy. e.g. electric heater, electric iron, etc.

Heat produced is expressed as, $H = I^2 \times R \times t$

It is known as **Joule's law of heating**.

This law implies that heat produced in a resistor is

 (i) directly proportional to the square of current for a given resistance.

 (ii) directly proportional to the resistance for a given current.

 (iii) directly proportional to the time for which the current flows through the resistor.

Practical Applications of Heating Effect of Electric Current

There are two applications of heating effect of electric current which are given below

1. Electric Bulb

It has a filament made of tungsten. So, most of the power consumed by this, is **dissipated** in the form of heat and some part is converted into light because it has high resistivity and high melting point.

The filament is thermally isolated and the bulb is filled with chemically inactive nitrogen and argon gas to prolong the life of filament.

2. Electric Fuse

It is used as a safety device in household circuits. It protects the circuits, by stopping the flow of any unduly high electric current. It is connected in series with the mains supply. It consists of an alloy of **lead** and **tin** which has appropriate melting point.

When the current flowing through the circuit exceeds the safe limit, then the fuse wire melts and breaks the circuit. This helps to protect the other circuit elements from heavy current. Fuses are always rated for different current values such as 1 A, 2 A, 5 A, 10 A, 15 A, etc.

Electric Power

It is defined as the amount of electric energy consumed in a circuit per unit time.

Electric power is expressed as, $P = VI$

or
$$P = \frac{V^2}{R}$$

The SI unit of electric power is **watt** (W).

It is said to be 1 watt, if 1 ampere current flows through a circuit having 1 volt potential difference.

i.e. $\qquad$ 1 watt $= 1$ volt $\times 1$ ampere $= 1$ VA

Commercial unit of electrical energy is **kilowatt-hour**.
$$1 \text{ kWh} = 3.6 \times 10^6 \text{ J}$$

Solved Examples

Example 1. The potential difference between the terminals of an electric heater is 75 V when it draws a current of 5 A from the source. What current will the heater draw, if the potential difference is increased to 150 V?

Sol. Given, potential difference, $V = 75$ V

Current, $\qquad I = 5$ A

We know that, $R = \dfrac{V}{I}$

$\Rightarrow \quad R = \dfrac{75}{5} = 15\ \Omega$

When potential difference is increased to 150 V, then current is

$$I' = \dfrac{V'}{R} = \dfrac{150}{15} = 10\ \text{A}$$

So, the current through the heater becomes 10 A.

Example 2. A wire of given material having length l and area of cross-section A has a resistance of 10 Ω. What would be the resistance of another wire of the same material having length $l/4$ and area of cross-section 2.5 A?

Sol. For first wire, length $= l$, area of cross-section $= A$

and resistance, $R_1 = 10\ \Omega$,

i.e. $\qquad R_1 = \dfrac{\rho l}{A} = 10\ \Omega$

$\Rightarrow \qquad \rho = \dfrac{10A}{l} \qquad\qquad \ldots\text{(i)}$

For second wire, length $= l/4$, area of cross-section $= 2.5\ A$

$\therefore$ Resistance, $R_2 = \rho \dfrac{l/4}{2.5\,A} = \dfrac{10A}{l} \cdot \dfrac{l}{4 \times 2.5\,A}$ [from Eq. (i)]

$\qquad\qquad = 1\Omega$

So, the resistance of that wire is 1 Ω.

Example 3. Resistance of a metal wire of length 2 m is 30 Ω at temperature 25°C. If the diameter of the wire is 0.6 mm, then what will be the resistivity of the metal at that temperature?

Sol. Given, length of wire, $l = 2$ m

Resistance, $R = 30\ \Omega$, Temperature, $T = 25\,°C$

Diameter of wire, $d = 0.6$ mm $= 6 \times 10^{-4}$ m

Resistivity of the wire, $\rho = ?$

We know that, $\rho = \dfrac{RA}{l} = \dfrac{R\pi d^2}{4l} \qquad \left[\because A = \dfrac{\pi d^2}{4}\right]$

$\qquad = \dfrac{30 \times \pi \times (6 \times 10^{-4})^2}{4 \times 2}$

$\qquad = 4.24 \times 10^{-6}\ \Omega\text{-m}$

The resistivity of the metal at 25°C is $4.24 \times 10^{-6}\ \Omega$-m.

Example 4. Three resistors of 5 Ω, 10 Ω and 15 Ω are connected in series with a 12 V power supply. Calculate their combined resistance, the current that flows in the circuit and in each resistor and the potential difference across each resistor.

Sol. Given, $R_1 = 5\ \Omega$, $R_2 = 10\ \Omega$, $R_3 = 15\ \Omega$, $V = 12$ V,

$\qquad R = ?,\ I = ?$ and $V_1, V_2, V_3 = ?$

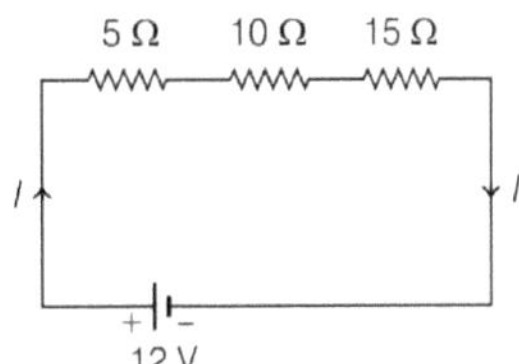

According to question, the three resistors are connected in series combination, then equivalent resistance,

$$R = R_1 + R_2 + R_3$$
$$= 5 + 10 + 15 = 30\ \Omega$$

$\therefore$ The current flowing through the circuit (I)

$$= \dfrac{\text{Potential of power supply }(V)}{\text{Total resistance of the circuit }(R)}$$

$$= \dfrac{12}{30}$$

$$= \dfrac{2}{5} = 0.4\ \text{A}$$

In series combination, the current flowing through each resistor is equal to total current flowing through the circuit. Therefore, current flowing through each resistor is 0.4 A.

$\therefore$ Potential difference across first resistor,

$$V_1 = IR_1 = 0.4 \times 5 = 2\ \text{V}$$

Potential difference across second resistor,

$$V_2 = IR_2 = 0.4 \times 10 = 4\ \text{V}$$

and potential difference across third resistor,

$$V_3 = IR_3 = 0.4 \times 15 = 6\ \text{V}$$

Example 5. Study the following electric circuit. Find the readings of (i) the ammeter and (ii) the voltmeter.

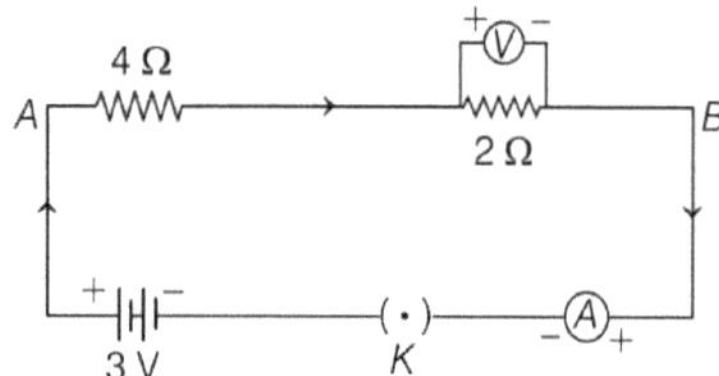

Sol. In the given circuit, the resistance of $4\,\Omega$ and bulb resistance of $2\,\Omega$ are connected in series, so equivalent resistance of the circuit,

$$R = R_1 + R_2 = 4\,\Omega + 2\,\Omega = 6\,\Omega$$

(i) Total current flowing in the circuit, (I)

$$= \frac{\text{Potential difference } (V)}{\text{Total resistance } (R)} = \frac{3}{6} = 0.5\,\text{A}$$

In series combination, current flowing through each component of the circuit is same and is equal to the total current flowing in the circuit. So, 0.5 A current will flow through the ammeter, so its reading will be 0.5 A.

(ii) Reading of voltmeter = Potential difference across $2\,\Omega$ bulb

$$\therefore \qquad V = IR = 0.5 \times 2 = 1\,\text{V}$$

$$[\because \text{ current flowing through the bulb is 0.5 A}]$$

Example 6. Two $40\,\Omega$ resistors and a $20\,\Omega$ resistor are all connected in parallel with a 12 V power supply. Calculate their effective resistance and the current through each resistor. What is the current flowing through the supply?

Sol. Given, $R_1 = 40\,\Omega$, $R_2 = 40\,\Omega$, $R_3 = 20\,\Omega$,

$$V = 12\,\text{V}, R = ?, \ I, \ I_1, \ I_2, \ I_3 = ?$$

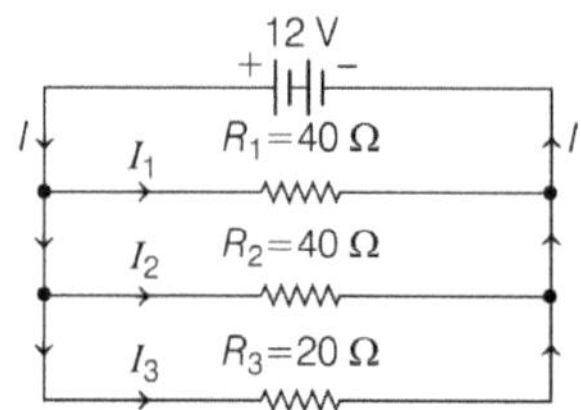

According to circuit, the three resistors are connected in parallel combination, then effective resistance,

$$\frac{1}{R} = \frac{1}{R_1} + \frac{1}{R_2} + \frac{1}{R_3}$$

$$= \frac{1}{40} + \frac{1}{40} + \frac{1}{20}$$

$$= \frac{1+1+2}{40} = \frac{4}{40} = \frac{1}{10}$$

$$\Rightarrow \qquad R = 10\,\Omega$$

So, the three resistors together have an effective resistance of $10\,\Omega$. Each resistor has a potential difference of 12 V across it.

Because in parallel combination, the potential difference across each resistance is equal to the total potential difference applied on the combination.

We know that,

$$\text{Current } (I) = \frac{\text{Potential difference } (V)}{\text{Resistance } (R)}$$

We get the following results for the current

Current through $40\,\Omega$ resistor, $I_1 = \dfrac{12}{40} = 0.3\,\text{A}$

Also, $I_2 = 0.3\,\text{A}$

Current through $20\,\Omega$ resistor, $I_3 = \dfrac{12}{20} = 0.6\,\text{A}$

$\therefore$ Current, $I = I_1 + I_2 + I_3 = 0.3\,\text{A} + 0.3\,\text{A} + 0.6\,\text{A}$

$$= 1.2\,\text{A}$$

Example 7. In the given figure, $R_1 = 5\,\Omega$, $R_2 = 10\,\Omega$, $R_3 = 15\,\Omega$, $R_4 = 20\,\Omega$, $R_5 = 25\,\Omega$ and a 15 V battery is connected to the arrangement. Calculate

(i) the total resistance in the circuit, and
(ii) the total current flowing in the circuit.

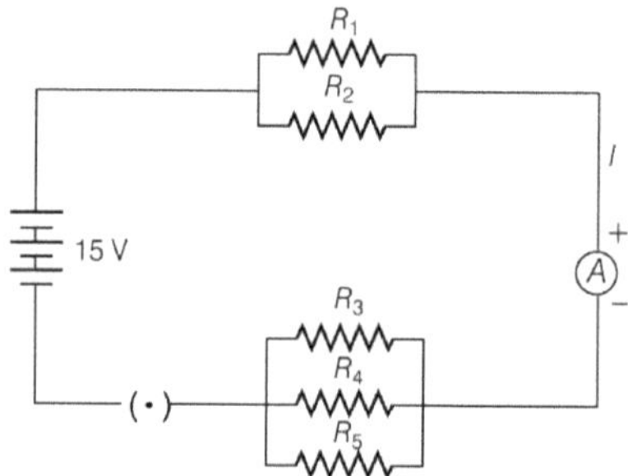

Sol. Resistors R_1 and R_2 are in parallel.

So, $\dfrac{1}{R'} = \dfrac{1}{R_1} + \dfrac{1}{R_2} \Rightarrow \dfrac{1}{R'} = \dfrac{1}{5} + \dfrac{1}{10} \Rightarrow R' = \dfrac{10}{3}\,\Omega$

Similarly, R_3, R_4 and R_5 are in parallel

$$\Rightarrow \frac{1}{R''} = \frac{1}{R_3} + \frac{1}{R_4} + \frac{1}{R_5} = \frac{1}{15} + \frac{1}{20} + \frac{1}{25}$$

$$\frac{1}{R''} = \frac{20 + 15 + 12}{300} \Rightarrow R'' = \frac{300}{47}$$

Thus, the total resistance,

$$R = R' + R'' = \frac{10}{3} + \frac{300}{47} = 3.33 + 6.38 = 9.71\,\Omega$$

The total current, $I = \dfrac{V}{R} = \dfrac{15}{9.71} = 1.54\,\text{A}$

Example 8. Find the equivalent resistance of the following circuit. Also, find the current and potential at each resistor.

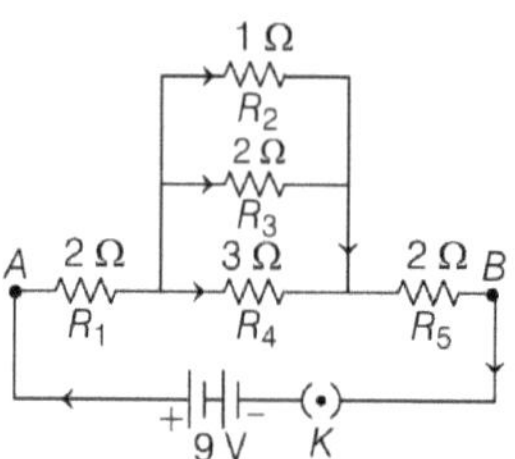

Sol. In the given circuit, R_2, R_3 and R_4 are in parallel combination. As, currents through R_2, R_3 and R_4 are different. So, their equivalent resistance R is

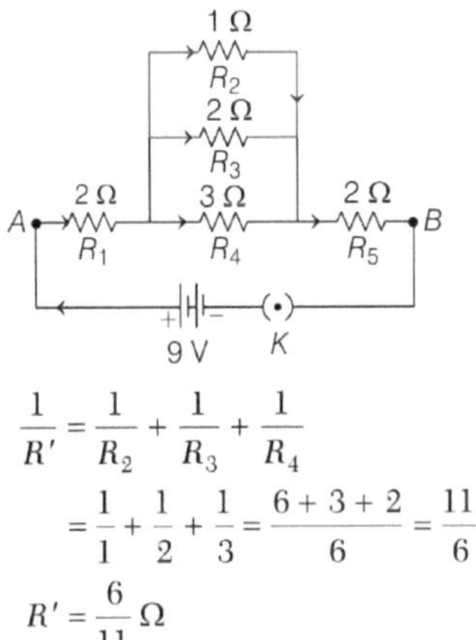

$$\frac{1}{R'} = \frac{1}{R_2} + \frac{1}{R_3} + \frac{1}{R_4}$$

$$= \frac{1}{1} + \frac{1}{2} + \frac{1}{3} = \frac{6+3+2}{6} = \frac{11}{6}$$

$$\Rightarrow \qquad R' = \frac{6}{11}\,\Omega$$

Now, the given circuit can be redrawn as shown below

Now, R_1, R' and R_5 are in series combination. As, current through R_1, R' and R_5 is same.

So, equivalent resistance of the whole circuit is

$$R = R_1 + R' + R_5 = 2 + \frac{6}{11} + 2$$

$$= \frac{22 + 6 + 22}{11} = \frac{50}{11}\,\Omega$$

Now, total current flowing through the circuit,

$$I = \frac{V}{R} = \frac{9}{50/11} = \frac{99}{50} \approx 2\,A$$

Current through R_1 and R_5 will be same as these are in series combination and will be equal to the total current flowing through the circuit.

$$\therefore \qquad I = I_1 = I_5 = 2\,A$$

Potential drop at R_1, $V_1 = I_1 R_1 = 2 \times 2 = 4\,V$

Potential drop at R_5, $V_5 = I_5 R_5 = 2 \times 2 = 4\,V$

Now, potential drop at R', V' can be calculated as

$$V = V_1 + V_5 + V'$$

$$\Rightarrow \qquad 9 = 4 + 4 + V'$$

$$\Rightarrow \qquad V' = 1\,V$$

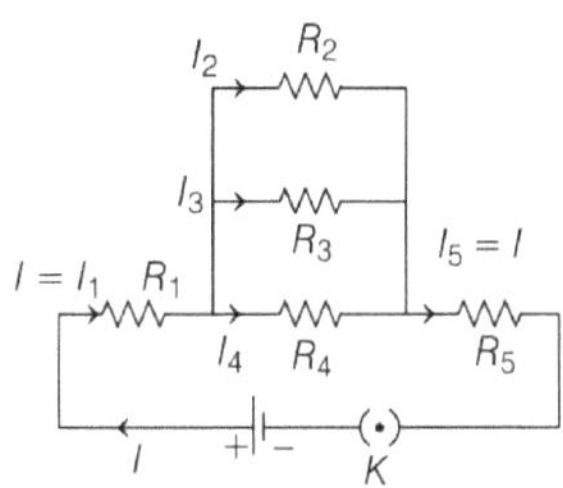

As R_2, R_3 and R_4 are in parallel combination, so potential drop at all resistances will be same as 1 V.

$$V_2 = V_3 = V_4 = V' = 1\,V$$

Current through R_2, $\quad I_2 = \frac{V_2}{R_2} = \frac{V'}{R_2} = \frac{1}{1} = 1\,A$

Similarly, $\quad I_3 = \frac{V_3}{R_3} = \frac{V'}{R_3} = \frac{1}{2} = 0.5\,A$

and $\quad I_4 = \frac{V_4}{R_4} = \frac{V'}{R_4} = \frac{1}{3} = 0.33\,A$

Example 9. An electric iron consumes energy at a rate of 880 W, when heating is at the maximum rate and 340 W, when the heating is at the minimum, the voltage is 220 V. What are the current and the resistance in each case?

Sol. Power, $P = VI$, Current, $I = P/V$

(i) When heating is at the maximum rate, $I = \dfrac{880}{220} = 4A$

Resistance of the electric iron, $R = \dfrac{V}{I} = \dfrac{220}{4} = 55\,\Omega$

(ii) When heating is at the minimum rate, $I = \dfrac{340}{220} = 1.54A$

Resistance of the electric iron, $R = \dfrac{V}{I} = \dfrac{220}{1.54} = 142.85\,\Omega$

Example 10. An electric heater of resistance $500\,\Omega$ is connected to a mains supply for 30 min. If 15 A current flows through the filament of the heater, then calculate the heat energy produced in the heater.

Sol. Given, resistance of the filament, $R = 500\,\Omega$

Current, $I = 15\,A$

Time, $t = 30\,min = 30 \times 60 = 1800\,s$

Heat produced, $H = I^2 Rt$

$$= 15^2 \times 500 \times 1800$$

$$= 2025 \times 10^5\,J = 20.25 \times 10^7\,J$$

Chapter Practice

Objective Questions

• Multiple Choice Questions

1. Which one of the following is the correct set-up for studying the dependence of the current on the potential difference across a resistor? **(CBSE 2019)**

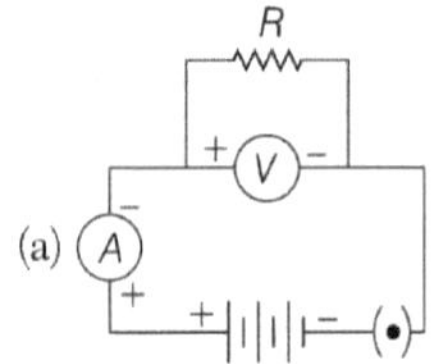 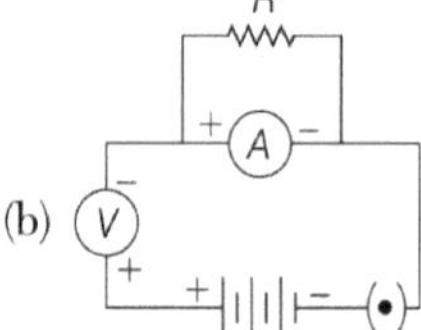

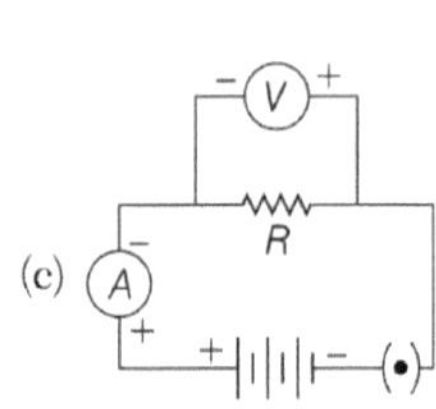 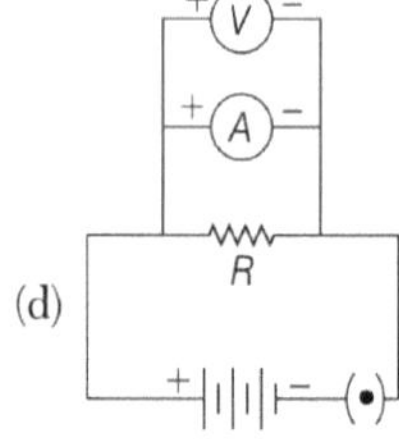

2. A student carries out an experiment and plots the V-I graph of three samples of nichrome wire with resistances R_1, R_2 and R_3 respectively. Which of the following is true?

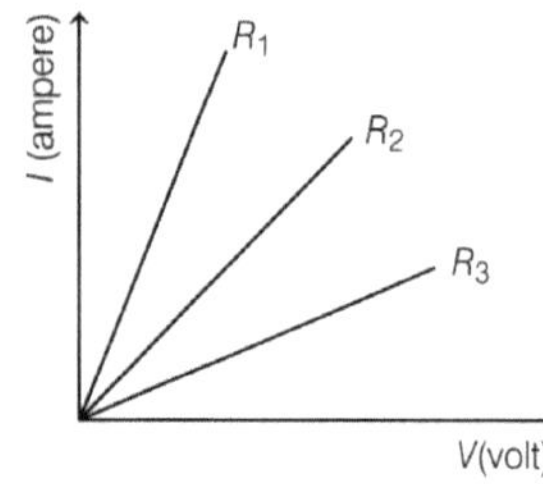

(a) $R_1 = R_2 = R_3$ (b) $R_1 > R_2 > R_3$
(c) $R_3 > R_2 > R_1$ (d) $R_2 > R_3 > R_1$

3. The resistivity does not change, if   **(NCERT Exemplar)**
(a) the material is changed
(b) the temperature is changed
(c) the shape of the resistor is changed
(d) Both material and temperature are changed

4. Specific resistance of a conductor increases on increasing its temperature.
(a) True   (b) False
(c) Can't say
(d) Information insufficient

5. A cylindrical conductor of length l and uniform area of cross-section A has resistance R. Another conductor of length $2l$ and resistance R of the same material has area of cross-section   **(CBSE 2020)**
(a) $A / 2$ (b) $3A / 2$
(c) $2A$ (d) $3A$

6. The substance which have a higher value of resistance and small number of free electrons in it, is called
(a) resistor   (b) poor conductor
(c) good conductor   (d) insulator

7. What is the maximum resistance which can be made using four resistors each of $\frac{1}{2}\Omega$?   **(CBSE 2020)**
(a) $2\,\Omega$ (b) $1\,\Omega$
(c) $2.5\,\Omega$ (d) $8\,\Omega$

8. Three $2\,\Omega$ resistances are connected so as to make a triangle. The resistance between any two vertices is
(a) $6\,\Omega$ (b) $2\,\Omega$
(c) $\frac{3}{4}\,\Omega$ (d) $\frac{4}{3}\,\Omega$

9. Determine the equivalent resistance between points X and Y in the following circuit.

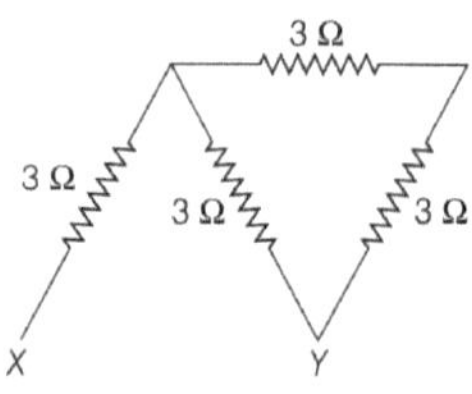

(a) $5\,\Omega$ (b) $12\,\Omega$
(c) $9\,\Omega$ (d) $6\,\Omega$

10. The filament of bulb is made up of
(a) copper   (b) tungsten
(c) tin   (d) lead

11. The current flowing through a wire of resistance $2\,\Omega$ varies with time as shown in the given figure. The amount of heat produced (in J) in 3 s would be

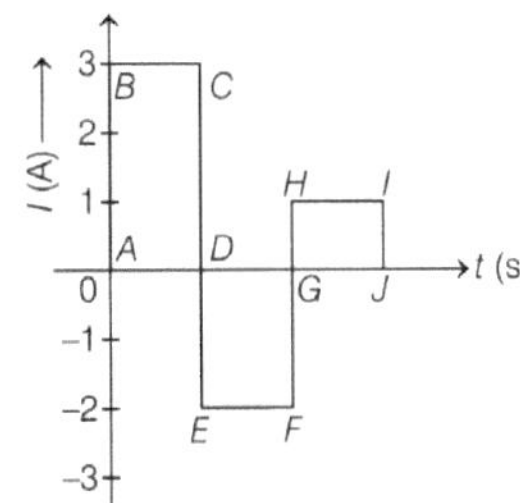

(a) 2 J   (b) 18 J
(c) 28 J   (d) 10 J

12. The rate at which energy is delivered by a current is determined by
(a) heat   (b) electric power
(c) potential difference   (d) work

13. In an electrical circuit three incandescent bulbs A, B and C of rating 40 W, 60 W and 100 W, respectively are connected in parallel to an electric source. Which of the following is likely to happen regarding their brightness?
(a) Brightness of all the bulbs will be the same
(b) Brightness of bulb A will be the maximum
(c) Brightness of bulb B will be more than that of A
(d) Brightness of bulb C will be less than that of B

14. An electric kettle consumes 1 kW of electric power when operated at 220 V. A fuse wire of what rating must be used for it?   **(NCERT Exemplar)**
(a) 1 A   (b) 2 A   (c) 4 A   (d) 5 A

15. LED indicator of a TV in your house operates at 0.75 V and 100 mA. Then its power is
(a) 75 mW   (b) 1.00 mW
(c) 0.75 mW   (d) 7.5 mW

• Assertion-Reasoning MCQs

Direction (Q. Nos. 16-20) Each of these questions contains two statements Assertion (A) and Reason (R). Each of these questions also has four alternative choices, any one of which is the correct answer. You have to select one of the codes (a), (b), (c) and (d) given below.
(a) Both A and R are true and R is the correct explanation of A.
(b) Both A and R are true, but R is not the correct explanation of A.
(c) A is true, but R is false.
(d) A is false, but R is true.

16. Assertion Longer wires have greater resistance and the smaller wires have lesser resistance.

Reason Resistance is inversely proportional to the length of the wire.

17. Assertion The connecting wires are made of copper.

Reason The electrical conductivity of copper is high.

18. Assertion When the resistances are connected end-to-end consecutively, they are said to be in series.

Reason In case the total resistance is to be decreased, then the individual resistances are connected in parallel.

19. Assertion The fuse is placed in series with the device.

Reason Fuse consists of a piece of wire made of a metal or an alloy of appropriate melting point.

20. Assertion The 200 W bulbs glow with more brightness than 100 W bulbs.

Reason A 100 W bulb has more resistance than 200 W bulb.

• Case Based MCQs

21. Read the following and answer questions from (i) to (v) given below

The relationship between potential difference and current was first established by George Simon Ohm called Ohm's law. An electric circuit is shown below to verify Ohm's law.

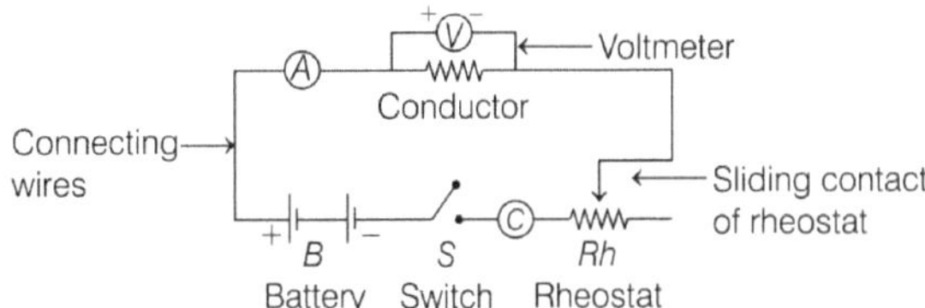

Although Ohm's law has been found valid over a large class of materials, there do exist metals and devices used in electric circuits where the proportionality of V and I does not hold.

(i) Materials which follow Ohm's law are
    (a) ohmic conductors   (b) non-ohmic conductors
    (c) insulators   (d) superconductors
(ii) For insulator at room temperature, the graph between V and I is given. Which one is correct?

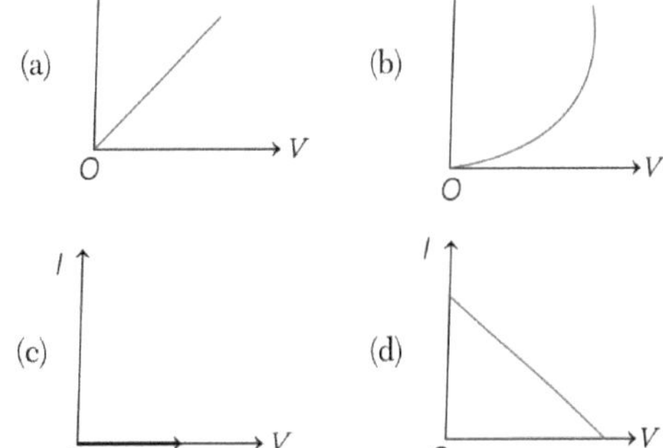

(iii) The slope of V - I graph (V on x-axis and I on y-axis) gives
  (a) charge
  (b) reciprocal of resistance
  (c) resistance
  (d) reciprocal of charge

(iv) By increasing the voltage across a conductor, the
  (a) current will decrease
  (b) resistance will increase
  (c) resistance will decrease
  (d) current will increase

(v) When a 9 V battery is connected across a conductor and the current flows is 0.1 A, the resistance is
  (a) $90\,\Omega$ (b) $9\,\Omega$
  (c) $0.9\,\Omega$ (d) $900\,\Omega$

22. Read the following and answer the questions from (i) to (v) given below

The electrical energy consumed by an electrical appliance is given by the product of its power rating and the time for which it is used. The SI unit of electrical energy is Joule (as shown in figure).

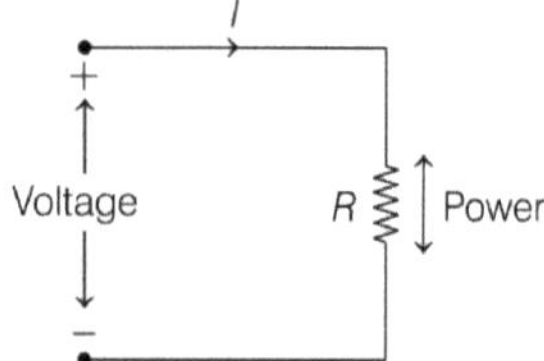

Actually, Joule represents a very small quantity of energy and therefore it is inconvenient to use where a large quantity of energy is involved.

(i) The SI unit of electric energy per unit time is
  (a) joule   (b) joule-second
  (c) watt   (d) watt-second

(ii) Kilowatt-hour is equal to
  (a) 3.6×10^4 J   (b) 3.6×10^6 J
  (c) 36×10^6 J   (d) 36×10^4 J

(iii) The energy dissipated by the heater is E. When the time of operating the heater is doubled, the energy dissipated is
  (a) doubled   (b) half
  (c) remains same   (d) four times

(iv) The power of a lamp is 60 W. The energy consumed in 1 minute is
  (a) 360 J   (b) 36 J
  (c) 3600 J   (d) 3.6 J

(v) Calculate the energy transformed by a 5 A current flowing through a resistor of $2\,\Omega$ for 30 minutes.
  (a) 40 kJ   (b) 60 kJ
  (c) 10 kJ   (d) 90 kJ

Subjective Questions

• Short Answer Type Questions

1. State the law which gives the relationship between current and potential difference. Define the unit of resistance.

2. Define resistance. Give its SI unit.   **(CBSE 2019)**

3. The values of current I flowing in a given resistor for the corresponding values of potential difference V across the resistor are as given below

V (volts)	0.5	1.0	1.5	2.0	2.5	3.0	4.0	5.0
I (amperes)	0.1	0.2	0.3	0.4	0.5	0.6	0.8	1.0

Plot a graph between V and I and also calculate the resistance of that resistor.   **(CBSE 2018)**

4. Why are coils of electric toasters and electric irons made of alloy rather than a pure metal?   **(NCERT)**

5. (i) List the factors on which the resistance of a conductor in the shape of a wire depends.

  (ii) Why are metals good conductors of electricity, whereas glass is a bad conductor of electricity? Give reason.

  (iii) What type of material is used in electrical heating devices? Give reason.   **(CBSE 2018)**

6.
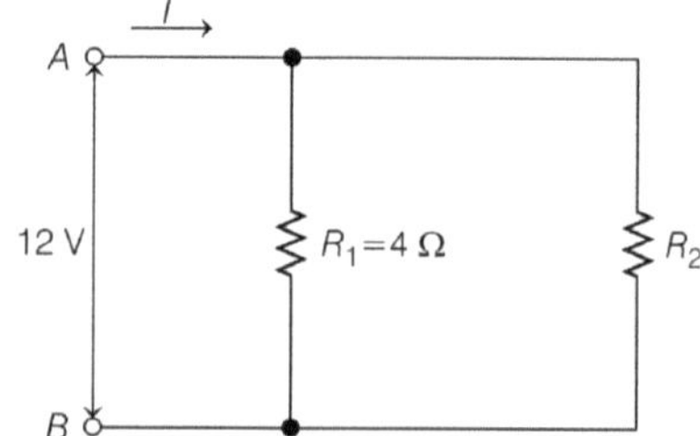

A student has two resistors $2\,\Omega$ and $3\,\Omega$. She has to put one of them in place of R_2 as shown in the circuit. The current that she needs in the entire circuit is exactly 9 A.

Show by calculation which of the two resistors she should choose.

7. A metal wire has diameter of 0.25 mm and electrical resistivity of $0.8 \times 10^{-8}\,\Omega$-m.

  (i) What will be the length of this wire to make a resistance $5\,\Omega$?

  (ii) How much will the resistance change, if the diameter of the wire is doubled?

8. Redraw the given circuit, putting in an ammeter to measure the current through the resistors and a voltmeter to measure the potential difference across $12\,\Omega$ resistor. What would be the readings in ammeter and voltmeter? **(NCERT)**

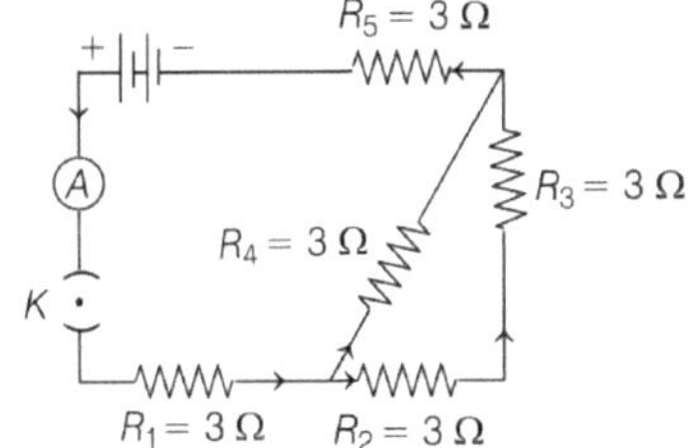

9. What is the reason of connecting electrical appliances in parallel combination in household circuit?

10. What is (i) the highest and (ii) the lowest total resistance which can be secured by combinations of four coils of resistances $4\,\Omega$, $8\,\Omega$, $12\,\Omega$ and $24\,\Omega$? **(NCERT)**

11. Consider the circuit diagram as given below

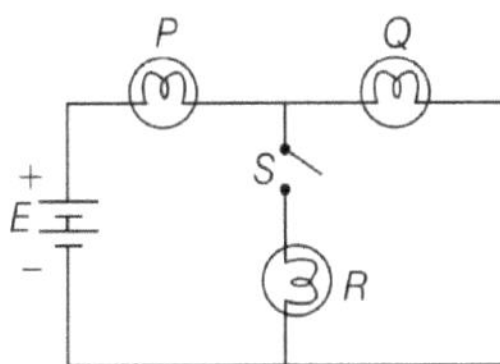

If $R_1 = R_2 = R_3 = R_4 = R_5 = 3\,\Omega$, then find the equivalent resistance of the circuit.

12. With the help of suitable circuit diagram prove that the reciprocal of the equivalent resistance of a group of resistances joined in parallel is equal to the sum of the reciprocals of the individual resistances. **(CBSE 2019)**

13. A battery E is connected to three identical lamps P, Q and R as shown in figure. Initially, the switch S is kept open and the lamp P and Q are observed to glow with same brightness. Then, switch S is closed.

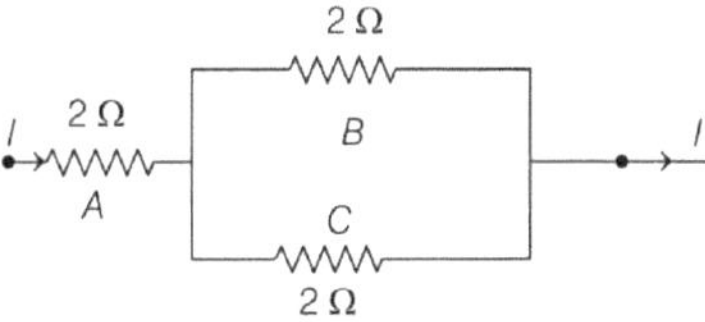

How will the brightness of glow of bulbs P and Q change? Justify your answer.

14. (i) Write Joule's law of heating.
(ii) Two lamps, one rated 100 W, 220 V and the other 60 W, 220 V are connected in parallel to electric main supply.
Find the current drawn by two bulbs from the line, if the supply voltage is 220 V. **(CBSE 2018)**

15. In an electrical circuit, two resistors of $2\,\Omega$ and $4\,\Omega$ are connected in series to a 6 V battery. Find the heat dissipated by the $4\,\Omega$ resistor in 5 s. **(NCERT Exemplar)**

16. Why does the cord of an electric heater not glow while heating element does? **(NCERT)**

17. Why fuse are used in electrical circuits?

18. Define the SI unit of electric power. What is the commercial unit of electrical energy?

19. The electric power consumed by a device may be calculated by using either of the two expressions $P = I^2 R$ or $P = V^2/R$.

The first expression indicates that the power is directly proportional to R, whereas the second expression indicates inverse proportionality. How can seemingly different dependence of P on R in these expressions be explained?

20. Three $2\,\Omega$ resistors, A, B and C are connected as shown in figure. Each of them dissipates energy and can withstand a maximum power of 18 W without melting. Find the maximum current that can flow through the three resistors? **(NCERT Exemplar)**

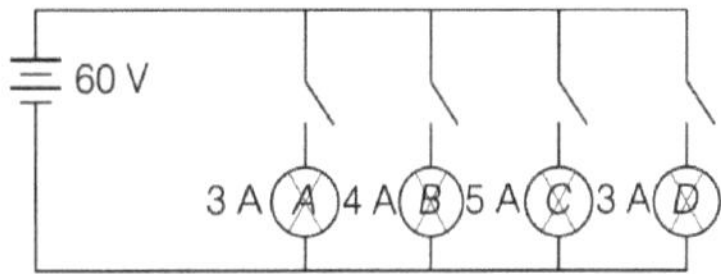

21. An electric geyser rated 1500 W, 250 V is connected to a 250 V line mains. Solve
(i) the electric current drawn by it.
(ii) energy consumed by it in 50 h.
(iii) cost of energy consumed, if each unit costs ₹ 6.

• Long Answer Type Questions

22. In the given circuit, A, B, C and D are four lamps connected with a battery of 60 V.

Analyse the circuit to answer the following questions.
(i) What kind of combination are the lamps arranged in (series or parallel)?
(ii) Explain with reference to your above answer, what are the advantages (any two) of this combination of lamps?
(iii) Explain with proper calculations which lamp glows the brightest.
(iv) Find out the total resistance of the circuit.

23. Find the equivalent resistance of the following circuit. Also, find the current and potential at each resistor.

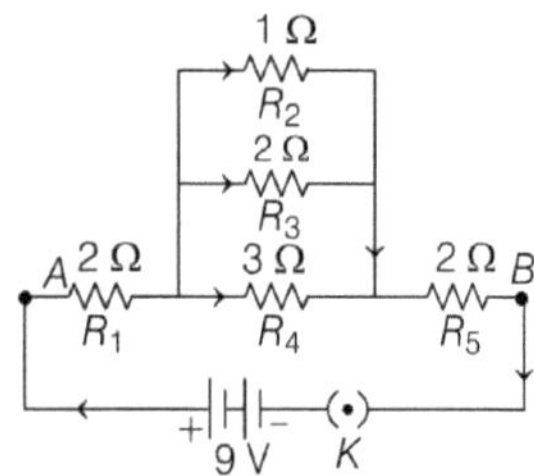

24. (i) State Ohm's law.
(ii) How is an ammeter connected in an electric circuit?
(iii) The power of a lamp is 100 W. Find the energy consumed by it in 1 min.
(iv) A wire of resistance $5\,\Omega$ is bent in the form of a closed circle. Find the resistance between two points at the ends of any diameter of the circle.

25. An electric lamp of resistance $20\,\Omega$ and a conductor of resistance $4\,\Omega$ are connected to a 6 V battery as shown in the circuit given below.

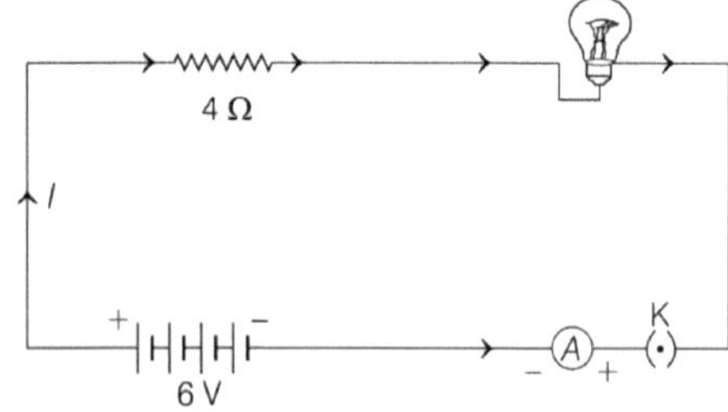

Calculate
(i) the total resistance of the circuit.
(ii) the current through the circuit.
(iii) the potential difference across the (a) electric lamp and (b) conductor.
(iv) the power of the lamp. (CBSE 2019)

26. (i) How should two resistors, with resistances $R_1(\Omega)$ and $R_2(\Omega)$ be connected to a battery of e.m.f. V volts so that the electrical power consumed is minimum?
(ii) In a house, 3 bulbs of 100 watt each are lighted for 5 hours daily, 2 fans of 50 watt each are used for 10 hours daily and an electric heater of 1.00 kWh is used for half an hour daily. Calculate the total energy consumed in a month of 31 days and its cost at the rate of ₹ 3.60 per kWh.

27. (a) Define power and state its SI unit.
(b) A torch bulb is rated 5V and 500 mA. Calculate its
(i) power
(ii) resistances
(iii) energy consumed when it is lighted for $2\dfrac{1}{2}$ hours.

• Case Based Questions

28. Read the following and answer the questions from (i) to (v) given below

Several resistors may be combined to form a network. The combination should have two end points to connect it with a battery or other circuit elements. When the resistors are connected in series, the current in each resistor is same but the potential difference is different in each resistor.

When the resistors are connected in parallel, the voltage drop across each resistor is same but the current is different in each resistor.

(i) What do you mean by complex circuit?
(ii) In the graph, it shows the resistance in series and parallel for two identical wires. Which of the following denotes series combination and parallel combination, individually?

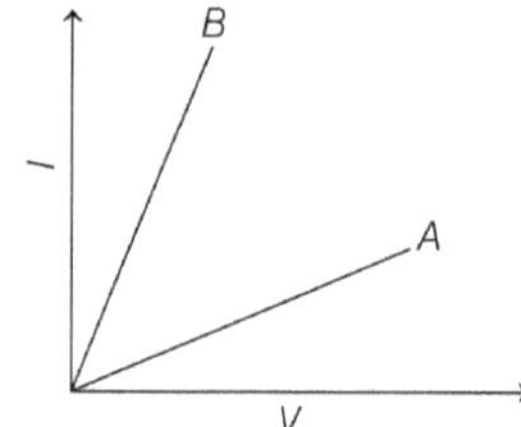

(iii) What is the equivalent resistance of the circuit given below?

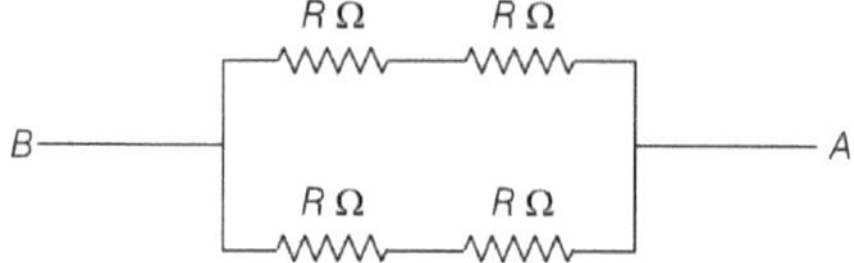

(iv) What is minimum effective resistance?
(v) When three resistors of resistances R, $2R$ and $3R$ are connected in series then, how will be the value of current gets affected in each resistor by applying a voltage V across the circuit?

29. Read the following and answer the questions from (i) to (v) given below

A cell or a battery is the source of electrical energy. Due to the chemical reactions inside them a potential difference is setup which is responsible for the flow of current through any electrical circuit.

So, to maintain this flow, the source continuously has to provide the energy. But only a part of this energy helps in maintaining the current consumed into useful work.

Rest of it may be consumed in the form of heat by raising the temperature of the appliances.

(i) How heat produced in a resistor is related to current flowing in that resistor?

(ii) Give two practical application of heating effect of current.

(iii) Which type of energy is transformed into heat energy?

(iv) An electric iron of resistance 25 Ω takes a current of 7 A. Calculate the heat developed in 0.5 min.

(v) 200 J of heat is produced in 10 s in a 5 Ω resistance. Find the potential difference across the resistor.

30. Read the following and answer questions from (i) to (v) given below

In resistance for a system of the resistor, there are two methods of joining the resistors together as shown below

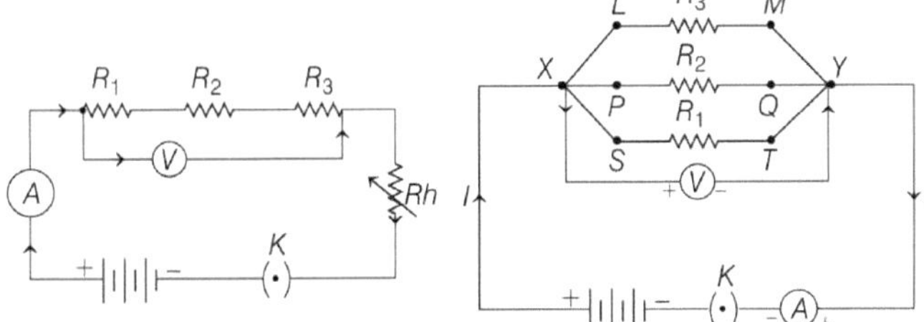

It showed an electric circuit in which 3 resistors having resistor R_1, R_2 and R_3 respectively are joined end to end i.e in series.

While the combination of the resistors in which 3 resistors connected together which point X and Y are said to be parallel.

(i) Calculate the potential difference across a series combination of resistors.

(ii) What is the value of current in a series combination?

(iii) Write the formula of electrical energy dissipated in the resistor.

(iv) If 200 resistors, each of value 0.2 Ω are connected in series, what will be the resultant resistance?

(v) What will be the effective resistance shown in figure below?

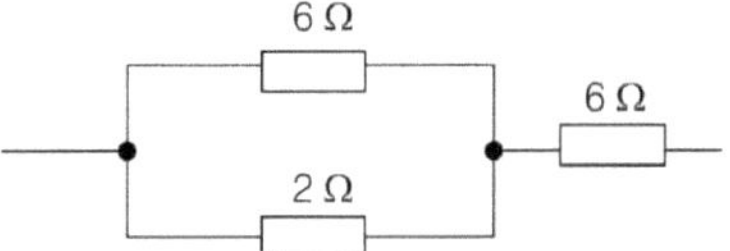

EXPLANATIONS

Objective Questions

1. (c) Option (c) represents correct set-up for studying the dependence of the current on the potential difference across a resistor because ammeter A is connected in series while voltmeter V is connected across parallel of resistor R.

2. (c) At given voltage, current I is inversely proportional to resistance, i.e. $I \propto \dfrac{1}{R}$. At given voltage I is maximum for R_1, therefore, R_1 is minimum.

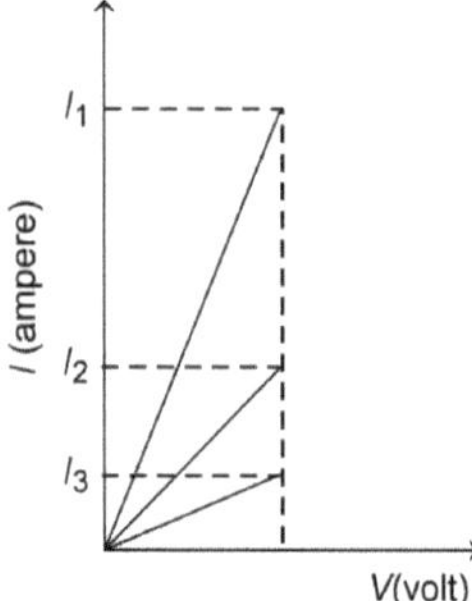

At given voltage, $\qquad I_1 > I_2 > I_3$

$\therefore \qquad\qquad R_1 < R_2 < R_3$

or $\qquad\qquad R_3 > R_2 > R_1$

3. (c) Resistivity depends on the nature of material and the temperature but does not depend on the shape of the resistor.

4. (a) True; Specific resistance of a conductor increases on increasing its temperature.

5. (c) In first case,

Resistivity of the conductor, $\rho = \dfrac{RA'}{l}$ ...(i)

In second case,

Resistivity of the conductor, $\rho = \dfrac{RA'}{2l}$ ...(ii)

$\because$ For same material, resistivity of the conductor will be same.

So, on substituting the value of ρ in Eq. (ii), we have

$$\frac{RA}{l} = \frac{RA'}{2l} \Rightarrow A' = 2A$$

6. (b) A material that offers higher resistance as compared to conductors to the flow of electron, so has small number of free electrons is called a poor conductor.

7. (a) The maximum resistance is obtained when resistors are connected in series combination.

Thus equivalent resistance

$$R_{eq} = R_1 + R_2 + R_3 + R_4$$
$$= \frac{1}{2} + \frac{1}{2} + \frac{1}{2} + \frac{1}{2} = 2\,\Omega$$

8. (d) Resistance between terminals A and B

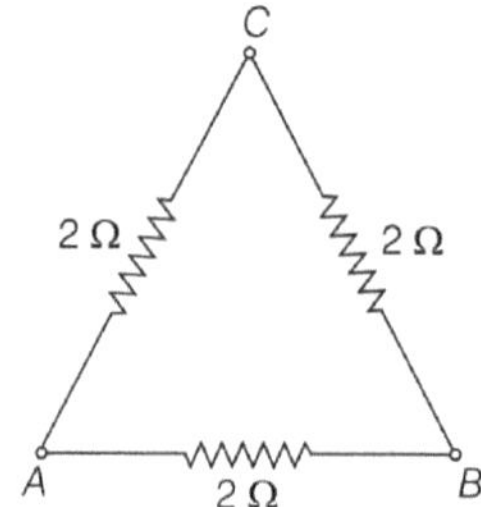

$= (2\,\Omega,\ 2\,\Omega \text{ in series}) \text{ parallel to } 2\,\Omega$

$= (2+2) \| 2\,\Omega = 4\,\Omega \| 2\,\Omega = \dfrac{4 \times 2}{6} = \dfrac{4}{3}\,\Omega$

9. (a) As, R_{eq}

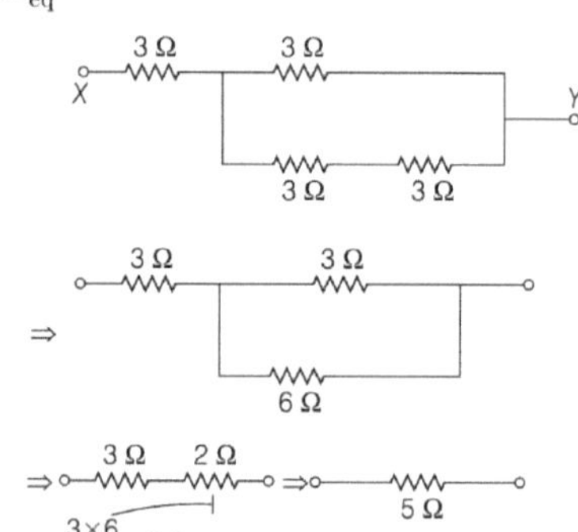

10. (b) The filament of electric bulb is made up of tungsten because it has a very high resistance.

11. (c), As heat produced, $H = I^2 Rt$

Here, $R = 2\,\Omega$

For AD, $H_1 = 3^2 \times 2 \times 1 = 18\,\text{J}$

For DG, $H_2 = (-2)^2 \times 2 \times 1 = 8\,\text{J}$

For GJ, $H_3 = (1)^2 \times 2 \times 1 = 2\,\text{J}$

$\therefore$ Total amount of heat produced in 3 s is,

$$H = H_1 + H_2 + H_3$$
$$\Rightarrow \qquad H = 18 + 8 + 2 = 28\,\text{J}$$

12. (b) Electric power determines the rate at which energy is delivered by a current.

13. (c) Bulbs are rated presuming that they all are connected with the same voltage supply. In parallel combination, voltage across each bulb is same, so greater the watt, greater the brightness.

$\therefore$ Brightness (B) of 3 bulbs are as follows

$$B_{100} > B_{60} > B_{40}$$
$$\Rightarrow \qquad B_C > B_B > B_A$$

14. (*d*) Given, power, $P = 1\,\text{kW} = 1000\,\text{W}$

Voltage, $\quad V = 220\,\text{V}$

Current, $\quad I = ?$

$$I = \frac{P}{V} = \frac{1000}{220} = 4.5\,\text{A}$$

Thus, the rating of fuse-wire is 5 A which is greater than 4.5 A.

15. (*a*) Given, $V = 0.75\,\text{V}, I = 100\,\text{mA} = 100 \times 10^{-3}\text{A} = 0.1\,\text{A}$

∴ Power, $\quad P = VI = 0.75 \times 0.1$

$\Rightarrow \qquad P = 75\,\text{mW}$

16. (*c*) As we know, resistance of conductor depends on the length of conductor as $R \propto l$

As the length of wire is more, resistance of conductor is more.

∴ A is true but R is false.

17. (*a*) Copper conducts the current without offering much resistance due to high electrical conductivity. Hence, conducting wires are made of copper.
∴ Both A and R are true and R is the correct explanation of A.

18. (*b*) Resistors are connected in series, when they join end-to-end consecutively with each other. In parallel combination, the total resistance is always less than the least resistance in combination.
∴ Both A and R are true but R is not the correct explanation of A.

19. (*b*) Fuse is a safety device that is used in household circuits. It is connected in series with the main supply.

Fuse consists of an alloy of lead and tin which has appropriate melting point.

∴ Both A and R are true but R is not the correct explanation of A.

20. (*a*) The resistance, $R = \dfrac{V^2}{P}$

$$R \propto \frac{1}{P}$$

i.e. Higher the wattage of a bulb, lesser is the resistance and so it will glow brighter.

∴ Both A and R are true and R is the correct explanation of A.

21. (i) (*a*) Materials that follow Ohm's law are called ohmic conductor. *V* - *I* graph is a straight line passing from origin for ohmic conductors.

(ii) (*c*) *V* - *I* curve for insulator is straight line that lies on voltage axis at room temperature.

(iii) (*b*) Slope of *V* - *I* graph $= \dfrac{I}{V} = \dfrac{1}{R}$.

(iv) (*d*) On increasing the voltage, the resistance remains same but current increases.

(v) (*a*) Given, $V = 9\,\text{V}, I = 0.1\,\text{A}$

∴ $\qquad R = \dfrac{V}{I} = \dfrac{9}{0.1} = 90\,\Omega$

22. (i) (*c*) The SI unit of electric energy per unit time is watt.

∵ $\qquad P = \dfrac{\text{electric energy}}{\text{time}} = \dfrac{\text{J}}{\text{s}} = \text{Js}^{-1} = \text{W}$

(ii) (*b*) 1 kilowatt-hour is equal to 3.6×10^6 joule.

(iii) (*a*) As $E \propto t$

∴ When the time of operating the heater is doubled, the energy dissipated is doubled.

(iv) (*c*) Given, $\quad P = 60\,\text{W}, t = 1\,\text{min} = 1 \times 60\,\text{s}$

∴ $\qquad E = P \times t = 60 \times 60$

$\Rightarrow \qquad E = 3600\,\text{J}$

(v) (*d*) Given, $I = 5\,\text{A}, R = 2\,\Omega, t = 30\,\text{min} = 1800\,\text{s}$

∴ $\qquad E = I^2 Rt = 5 \times 5 \times 2 \times 1800$

$\Rightarrow \qquad E = 90000 = 90\,\text{kJ}$

Subjective Questions

1. Ohm's law gives the relationship between current *I* flowing in a metallic wire and potential difference *V*, across its terminals. According to this law, the electric current flowing through a conductor is directly proportional to the potential difference applied across its ends, providing physical conditions remains unchanged.

i.e. $\qquad V \propto I$ or $V = IR$

where *R* is constant of proportionality called resistance of conductor at a given temperature.

Unit of resistance is ohm. It is said to be 1 ohm, if potential difference of 1 volt across the ends of the conductor makes a current of 1 A to flow through it.

i.e. $\qquad 1\,\text{ohm}\,(\Omega) = \dfrac{1\,\text{V}}{1\,\text{A}} = \text{VA}^{-1}$

2. Resistance is the property of a conductor by virtue of which it opposes/resists the flow of charges/flow of current through it. Its SI unit is **ohm** and is represented by the Greek letter Ω (ohm). **Resistance of a conductor is given by** $R = \dfrac{V}{I}$.

3. Scale : At *x*-axis, 1 div (1 cm) = 0.1 A

At *y*-axis, 1 div (1 cm) = 0.5 V
The graph between current and potential difference is shown below.

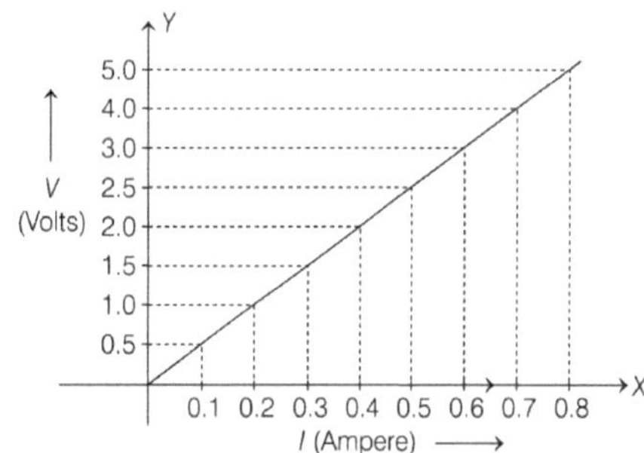

Resistance (*R*) of the resistor is determined by the slope of *V*-*I* graph.

$\therefore$ Resistance $= R = $ Slope of graph $= \dfrac{V}{I}$

$\therefore \qquad R = \dfrac{y_2 - y_1}{x_2 - x_1} = \dfrac{1.5 - 1.0}{0.3 - 0.2}$

$\qquad\qquad = \dfrac{0.5}{0.1} = 5\,\Omega$

4. Alloys have a higher resistivity than their constituent metals. They do not oxidise or burn at higher temperatures as they have high melting point. Thus, they are used to make coils of electrical toasters and electric irons rather than pure metals.

5. (i) Following factors on which resistance of a wire depends
(a) length of wire : $R \propto l$

(b) area of cross-section of wire : $R \propto \dfrac{1}{A}$

(c) resistivity of material of wire : $R \propto \rho$

$\therefore \qquad R = \rho\,\dfrac{l}{A}$

(ii) Metals are good conductors as their resistivity is very low whereas glass is a bad conductor having high resistivity.

(iii) Alloys are used as heating elements as their resistivity and melting points both are very high.

6. The given circuit is shown below

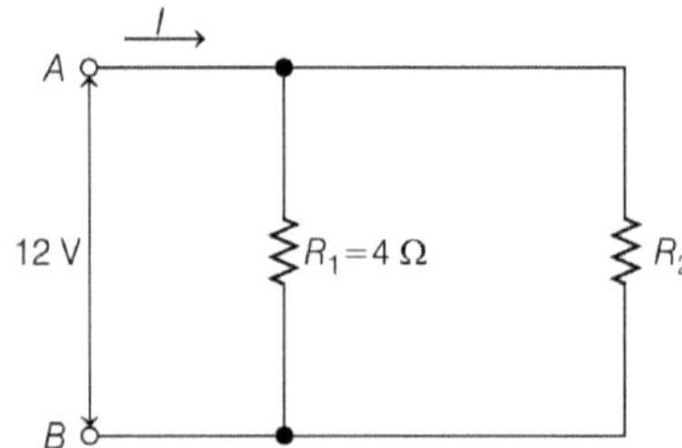

Let R be the resistance of the entire circuit.

Given, overall current needed, $I = 9\,\text{A}$

Voltage, $\qquad V = 12\,\text{V}$

Using Ohm's law, $V = IR$

$\Rightarrow \qquad R = \dfrac{V}{I} = \dfrac{12}{9} = \dfrac{4}{3}\,\Omega$

Now, the resistors R_1 and R_2 are in parallel combination.

$\therefore \qquad \dfrac{1}{R} = \dfrac{1}{R_1} + \dfrac{1}{R_2} \Rightarrow \dfrac{1}{R} = \dfrac{1}{4} + \dfrac{1}{R_2}$

$\Rightarrow \qquad \dfrac{3}{4} = \dfrac{1}{4} + \dfrac{1}{R_2} \qquad \left[\because R = \dfrac{4}{3}\,\Omega\right]$

$\Rightarrow \qquad \dfrac{1}{R_2} = \dfrac{3}{4} - \dfrac{1}{4} = \dfrac{2}{4} = \dfrac{1}{2}$

$\Rightarrow \qquad R_2 = 2\,\Omega$

So, the student should choose $2\,\Omega$ resistor.

7. Given, diameter $= 0.25\,\text{mm}$

Resistivity, $\rho = 0.8 \times 10^{-8}\,\Omega\text{-m}$

(i) Resistance, $R = 5\,\Omega$

We know that, $R = \dfrac{\rho l}{A}$

$\Rightarrow \qquad l = \dfrac{RA}{\rho} = \dfrac{5 \times \pi \times \left[\dfrac{0.25}{2} \times 10^{-3}\right]^2}{0.8 \times 10^{-8}}$

$\left[\because A = \pi r^2 \text{ and } r = \dfrac{D}{2}\right]$

$\qquad = \dfrac{5 \times \pi \times 1.56 \times 10^{-8}}{0.8 \times 10^{-8}} = 30.62\,\text{m}$

(ii) $\therefore$ Resistance, $R = \dfrac{\rho l}{A}$

$\qquad = \dfrac{\rho l}{\pi\left(\dfrac{D}{2}\right)^2} = \dfrac{\rho l}{\pi} \times \dfrac{4}{D^2}$

$\left[\because A = \pi r^2 \text{ and } r = \dfrac{D}{2}\right]$

$R' = \dfrac{\rho l}{A} = \dfrac{\rho l}{\pi\left(\dfrac{2D}{2}\right)^2} \qquad [\because D \text{ has become } 2D]$

$\qquad = \dfrac{\rho l}{\pi D^2}$

Now, $\qquad \dfrac{R'}{R} = \dfrac{\rho l}{\pi D^2} \div \dfrac{\rho l \times 4}{\pi D^2}$

$\qquad = \dfrac{\rho l}{\pi D^2} \times \dfrac{\pi D^2}{\rho l \times 4} = \dfrac{1}{4}$

$\therefore \qquad R' = \dfrac{R}{4}$

Thus, resistance will decrease by 4 times.

8.

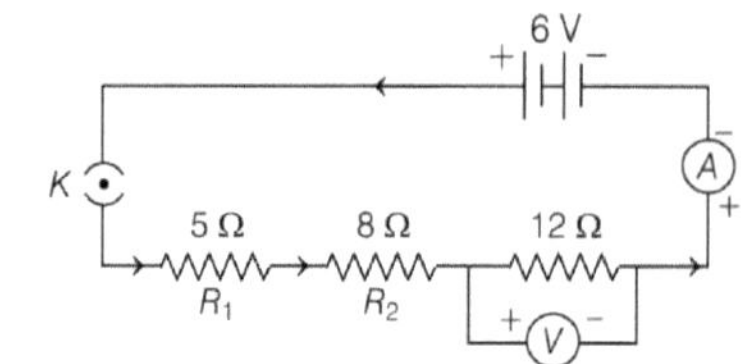

Equivalent resistance of the circuit,

$R = R_1 + R_2 + R_3 = 5 + 8 + 12 = 25\,\Omega$

$[\because R_1, R_2 \text{ and } R_3 \text{ are connected in series}]$

In series combination, current flowing through all the resistances is same and equal to the total current flowing through the circuit.

$\therefore$ Current in the resistors,

$\qquad I = \dfrac{V}{R} = \dfrac{6}{25} = 0.24\,\text{A}$

$\therefore$ Ammeter reading $= 0.24\,\text{A}$

Potential across $12\,\Omega$ resistance,

$\qquad V = IR = 0.24 \times 12 = 2.88\,\text{V}$

$\therefore$ Voltmeter reading is $2.88\,\text{V}$.

9. Parallel combination of resistances is highly useful in circuits used in daily life, as the circuits used have components of different resistances requiring different amounts of current.

This type of combination in a circuit divides the current among the components (electrical gadgets), so that they can have necessary amount of current to operate properly. This is the reason of connecting electrical appliances in parallel combination in household circuit.

10. (i) Resistance is maximum when resistors are connected in series.

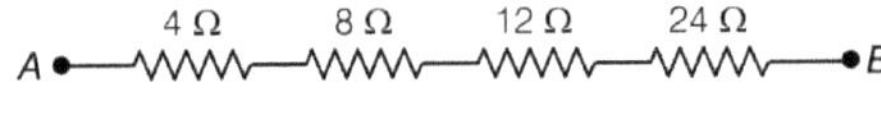

$$R_{max} = 4 + 8 + 12 + 24 = 48\,\Omega$$

(ii) Resistance is minimum when resistors are connected in parallel.

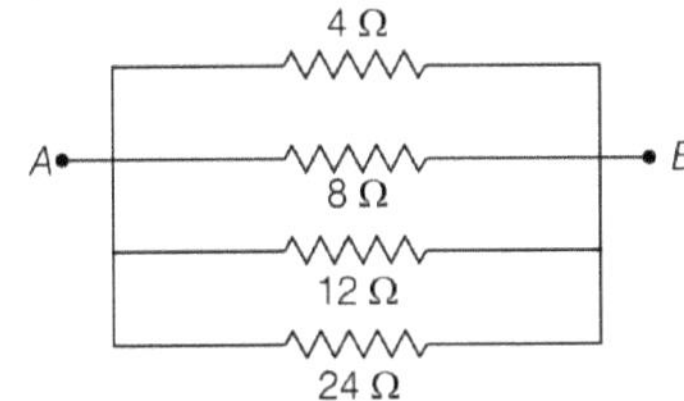

$$R_{min.} = 1 / \left[\frac{1}{4} + \frac{1}{8} + \frac{1}{12} + \frac{1}{24} \right] = \frac{24}{12}\,\Omega = 2\,\Omega$$

11. From the combination, it can be observed that R_2 and R_3 are in series order.

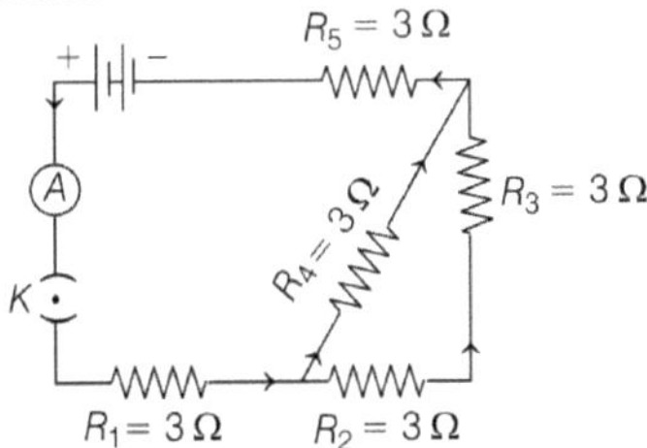

As current through R_2 and R_3 is same. So, their equivalent resistance is $R' = R_2 + R_3 = 3\,\Omega + 3\,\Omega = 6\,\Omega$

Now, the given circuit can be redrawn as shown below

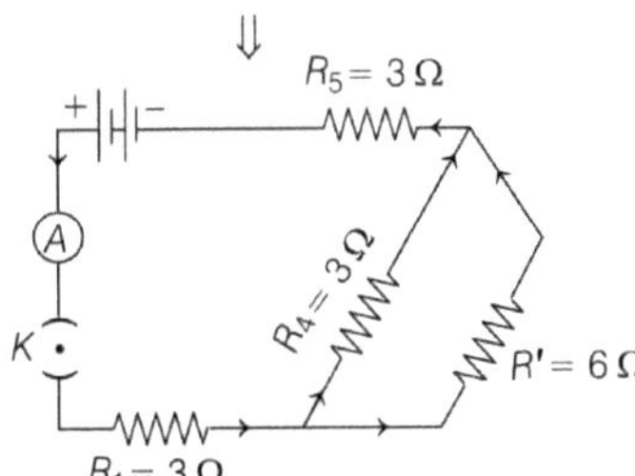

Now, it can be seen that R_4 and R' are in parallel combination. As, currents through R_4 and R' are different. So, their equivalent resistance can be calculated as below

$$\frac{1}{R''} = \frac{1}{R'} + \frac{1}{R_4} = \frac{1}{6} + \frac{1}{3} = \frac{1+2}{6} = \frac{3}{6} = \frac{1}{2}$$

$$\therefore \qquad R'' = 2\,\Omega$$

Now, the given circuit can be redrawn as shown below

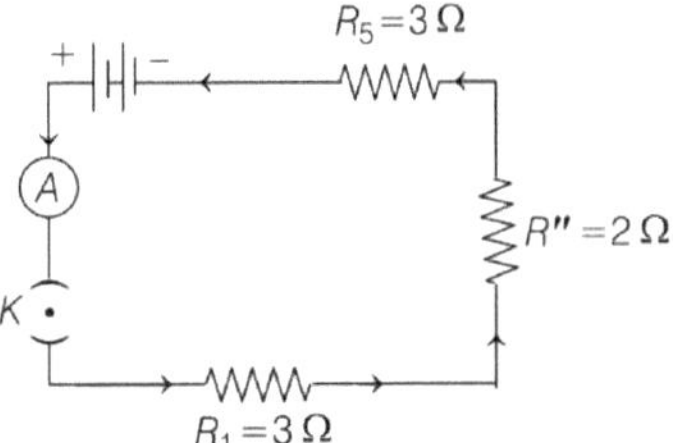

Now, it is clear from the above circuit that all the resistances R_5, R'' and R_1 are in series combination.

As, current through R_1, R'' and R_5 is same.

∴ Equivalent resistance of the circuit is

$$R = R_5 + R'' + R_1 = 3\,\Omega + 2\,\Omega + 3\,\Omega = 8\,\Omega$$

12. The following figure shows the connection of resistors in parallel

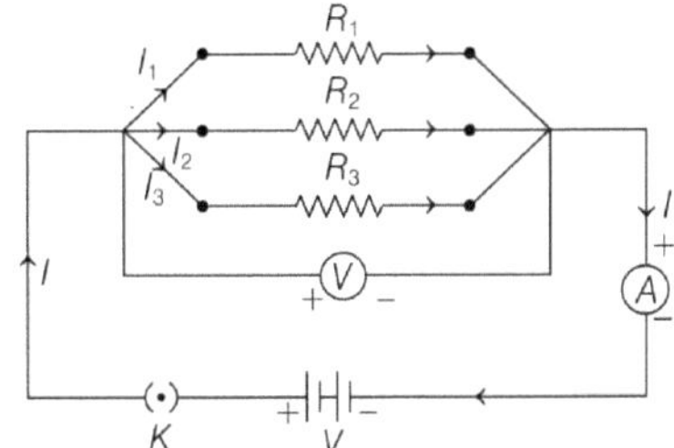

An applied potential difference V produces current I_1 in R_1, I_2 in R_2 and I_3 in R_3.

Total current, $I = I_1 + I_2 + I_3$ ...(i)

By Ohm's law, $I_1 = \dfrac{V}{R_1}$, $I_2 = \dfrac{V}{R_2}$ and $I_3 = \dfrac{V}{R_3}$

If R is the equivalent resistance, then $I = \dfrac{V}{R}$

Thus, $\dfrac{V}{R} = \dfrac{V}{R_1} + \dfrac{V}{R_2} + \dfrac{V}{R_3}$ [from Eq. (i)]

$\Rightarrow \qquad \dfrac{V}{R} = V\left(\dfrac{1}{R_1} + \dfrac{1}{R_2} + \dfrac{1}{R_3} \right)$

$\Rightarrow \qquad \dfrac{1}{R} = \dfrac{1}{R_1} + \dfrac{1}{R_2} + \dfrac{1}{R_3}$

13. The brightness of glow of bulb P will increase and brightness of glow of bulb Q will decrease.

This is because, on closing S, bulbs Q and R will be in parallel and the combination will be in series with bulb P. Hence, the total resistance of the circuit will decrease and the current flowing in the circuit will increase. Therefore, the glow of bulb P will increase.

Also, bulbs Q and R will be in parallel in this case. So, the current gets divided and lesser current flows through Q and hence the glow of bulb Q decreases.

14. (i) According to Joule's law of heating, amount of heat produced in a resistor is

(a) directly proportional to square of current flowing through the resistor.

$$\therefore \qquad H \propto I^2$$

(b) directly proportional to resistance of the resistor.

$$\therefore \qquad H \propto R$$

(c) directly proportional to time for which the current flows through the resistor.

$$\therefore \qquad H \propto t$$

Hence, $\qquad H = I^2 Rt$

(ii)

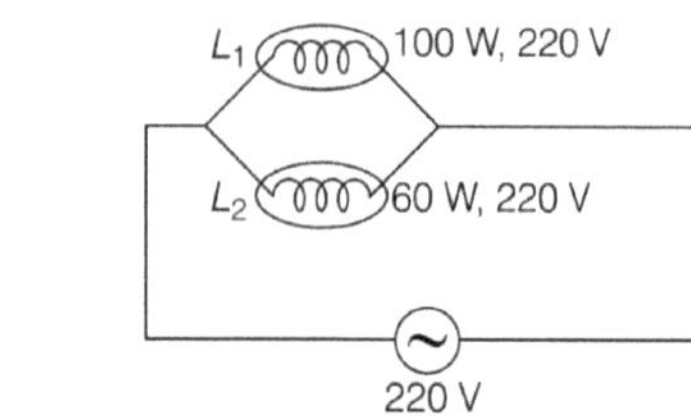

Here, potential, $V = 220\,V$

Power, $P_1 = 100\,W, P_2 = 60\,W$

As, current drawn is given by

$$I = \frac{\text{Power } (P)}{\text{Voltage } (V)} \qquad [\text{From } P = VI]$$

So, $\qquad I_1 = \dfrac{100}{220} = 0.45\,A$ and $I_2 = \dfrac{60}{220} = 0.27\,A$

15. Given, $R_1 = 2\,\Omega, R_2 = 4\,\Omega, t = 5s, V = 6\,V$

$\therefore$ Net resistance, $R = R_1 + R_2 = 2\,\Omega + 4\,\Omega = 6\,\Omega$

$\therefore$ Current, $I = \dfrac{V}{R} = \dfrac{6V}{6\Omega} = 1\,A$

In series, same 1 A current passes through both resistors.

$\therefore$ Heat dissipated, $H = I^2 R_1 \times t = (1)^2 \times 4 \times 5 = 20\,J$

16. The heating element of heater is made up of an alloy that has very high resistance. So when the current flows through it, it becomes very hot and glows red. But the resistance of cord is less because it is made up of copper or aluminium, so it does not glow.

17. Electric fuse is used to protect the electrical circuit from overloading and short circuit. When the current flowing through a circuit exceeds the safe limit, the temperature of fuse wire increases and due to heating effect, it gets melt and breaks the circuit.

18. The SI unit of electric power is watt (W). It is the power consumed by a device that carries 1 A of current when operated at a potential difference of 1 V. Thus,

$1\,W = 1\,volt \times 1\,ampere = 1\,VA$

The commercial unit of electrical energy is kilowatt hour (kWh), commonly known as 'unit'.

$$1\,kWh = 3.6 \times 10^6\,J$$

19. $P = I^2 R$ is used when current flowing in every component of the circuit is constant. This is the case of series combination of the devices in the circuit.

$P = V^2/R$ is used when potential difference (V) across every component of the circuit is constant. This expression is used in case of parallel combination in the circuit. In series combination, R is greater than the value of R in parallel combination.

20. Resistance, $R = 2\,\Omega$

Maximum power, $P_{max} = 18\,W$

Maximum current, $I_{max} = ?$

$$P = I^2 R$$

$$\Rightarrow \qquad I = \sqrt{\frac{P}{R}} = \sqrt{\frac{18}{2}} = 3\,A = I_{max}$$

Maximum current that can flow through $2\,\Omega$ resistor is 3 A. This current divides along B and C because they are in parallel combination. Voltage across B and C remains same and hence $I \propto \dfrac{1}{R}$. Since, B and C have same resistance $2\,\Omega$ each, and has same current. i.e. $I = \dfrac{3}{2} = 1.5\,A$ flowing through B and C.

21. Given, power, $P = 1500\,W$,

Voltage, $V = 250\,V$

(i) Electric current drawn,

$$I = \frac{P}{V} = \frac{1500}{250} = 6\,A$$

(ii) Energy consumed, $E = \text{Power} \times \text{Time}$

$\qquad = 1500 \times 50 \qquad [\because t = 50\,h]$

$\qquad = 75000\,Wh = 75\,kWh$

$\qquad\qquad\qquad\qquad [\because 1\,kW = 1000\,W]$

$\qquad = 75\,unit \qquad [\because 1\,unit = 1\,kWh]$

(iii) $\because$ Cost of energy consumed $= 75 \times 6 = ₹\,450$

22. The given circuit is shown below

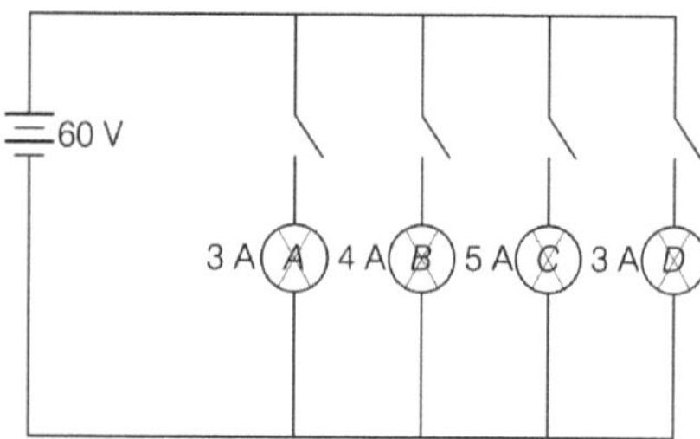

(i) In the circuit, all the lamps have same voltage, i.e. 60 V but each lamp is having different current. So, the lamps are arranged in parallel combination.

(ii) The two advantages of lamps in parallel combination are

(a) if one lamp gets faulty, it will not affect the working of other lamps.

(b) in parallel combination of lamps, each lamp will use the full potential of the battery.

(iii) The lamp with the highest power will glow the brightest.

As, power = Voltage × Current

In this case, all the lamps have same voltage i.e., 60 V.

For lamp A, current $= 3$ A

$\therefore$ Power $= 60 \times 3 = 180$ W

For lamp B, current $= 4$ A

$\therefore$ Power $= 60 \times 4 = 240$ W

For lamp C, current $= 5$ A

$\therefore$ Power $= 60 \times 5 = 300$ W

For lamp D, current $= 3$ A

$\therefore$ Power $= 60 \times 3 = 180$ W

As, the lamp C is having the maximum power, so it will glow the brightest.

(iv) Let R be the total resistance of the circuit.

Total current in the circuit, $I = 3 + 4 + 5 + 3 = 15$ A

Voltage, $V = 60$ V

Using Ohm's law, $V = IR$

$\Rightarrow$ $R = \dfrac{V}{I} = \dfrac{60}{15} = 4\,\Omega$

23. In the given circuit, R_2, R_3 and R_4 are in parallel combination. As, currents through R_2, R_3 and R_4 are different. So, their equivalent resistance R is

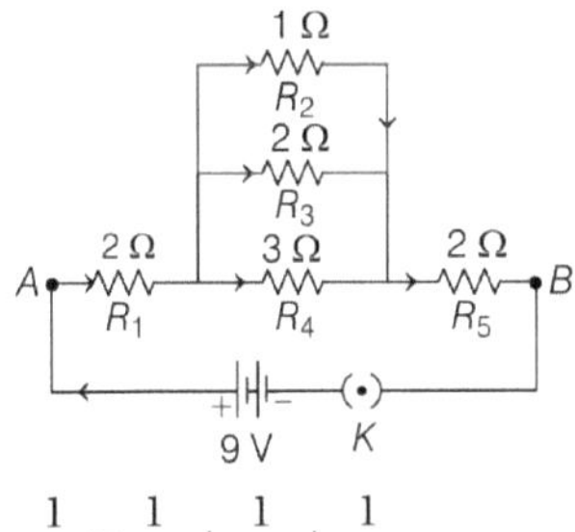

$$\dfrac{1}{R'} = \dfrac{1}{R_2} + \dfrac{1}{R_3} + \dfrac{1}{R_4}$$

$$= \dfrac{1}{1} + \dfrac{1}{2} + \dfrac{1}{3} = \dfrac{6 + 3 + 2}{6} = \dfrac{11}{6}$$

$\Rightarrow$ $R' = \dfrac{6}{11}\,\Omega$

Now, the given circuit can be redrawn as shown below

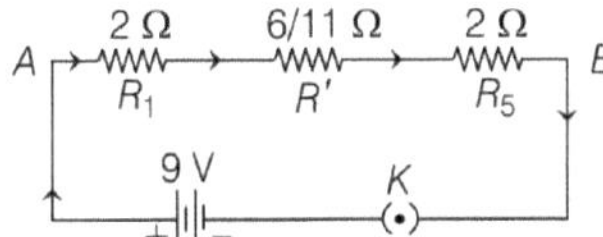

Now, R_1, R' and R_5 are in series combination. As, current through R_1, R' and R_5 is same.

So, equivalent resistance of the whole circuit is

$$R = R_1 + R' + R_5$$

$$= 2 + \dfrac{6}{11} + 2 = \dfrac{22 + 6 + 22}{11} = \dfrac{50}{11}\,\Omega$$

Now, total current flowing through the circuit,

$$I = \dfrac{V}{R} = \dfrac{9}{\dfrac{50}{11}} = \dfrac{99}{50} \approx 2\,\text{A}$$

Current through R_1 and R_5 will be same as these are in series combination and will be equal to the total current flowing through the circuit.

$\therefore$ $I = I_1 = I_5 = 2$ A

Potential drop at R_1,

$$V_1 = I_1 R_1 = 2 \times 2 = 4\,\text{V}$$

Potential drop at R_5,

$$V_5 = I_5 R_5 = 2 \times 2 = 4\,\text{V}$$

Now, potential drop at R', V' can be calculated as

$$V = V_1 + V_5 + V'$$

$\Rightarrow$ $9 = 4 + 4 + V'$

$\Rightarrow$ $V' = 1$ V

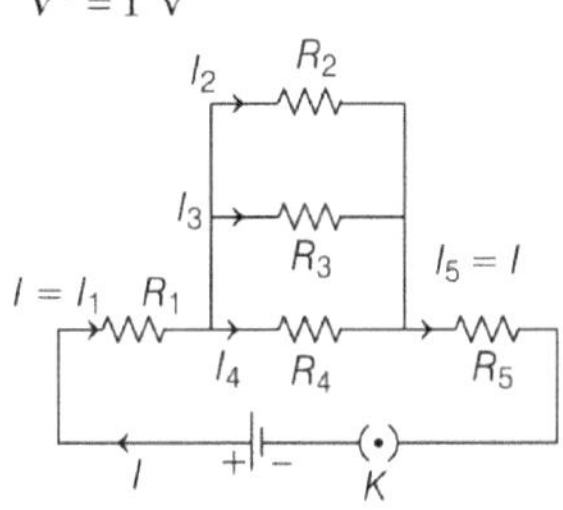

As R_2, R_3 and R_4 are in parallel combination, so potential drop at all resistances will be same as 1 V.

$$V_2 = V_3 = V_4 = V' = 1\,\text{V}$$

Current through R_2,

$$I_2 = \dfrac{V_2}{R_2} = \dfrac{V'}{R_2} = \dfrac{1}{1} = 1\,\text{A}$$

Similarly, $I_3 = \dfrac{V_3}{R_3} = \dfrac{V'}{R_3} = \dfrac{1}{2} = 0.5\,\text{A}$

and $I_4 = \dfrac{V_4}{R_4} = \dfrac{V'}{R_4} = \dfrac{1}{3} = 0.33\,\text{A}$

24. (i) A states that the electric current flowing through a conductor directly proportional to the potential difference applied across its ends provided the physical conditions such as temperature remains unchanged.

(ii) An ammeter is connected in series in a circuit.

(iii) Given, $P = 100$ W and time $t = 1$ min $= 60$ s.

As, energy $E = Pt = 100 \times 60 = 6000$ J

(iv) Given, a wire with resistance $5\,\Omega$.

Now, wire is converted into a ring as shown below

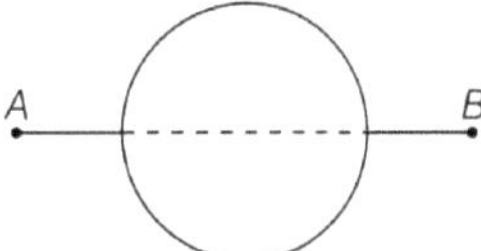

The equivalent circuit,

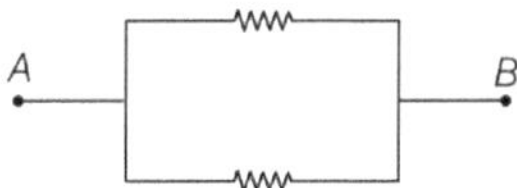

Hence, $R_{eq} = R_{AB} = \dfrac{2.5 \times 2.5}{2.5 + 2.5} = 1.25$ W

25. Given, resistance of lamp $(R_1) = 20\,\Omega$

Resistance of conductor $(R_2) = 4\,\Omega$

Potential difference of battery $(V) = 6$ V

(i) Total resistance,

$$R = R_1 + R_2 = 20 + 4 = 24\,\Omega$$

(ii) Current through the circuit
$$I = \frac{V}{R} = \frac{6}{24} = 0.25 \text{ A}$$

(iii) (a) Potential difference across electric lamp $= IR_1$
$$= 0.25 \times 20 = 5 \text{ V}$$

(b) Potential difference across conductor
$$= IR_2 = 0.25 \times 4 = 1 \text{ V}$$

(iv) Power of lamp $= I^2 R_1$
$$= (0.25)^2 \times 20$$
$$= 0.0625 \times 20 = 1.25 \text{ W}$$

26. (i) Power is given as, $P = VI$ where V is the voltage and I is the current. Power consumed is minimum when the current passing is minimum. So, the resistors should be connected in series.

(ii) Power of each bulb $= 100$ W

Total power of 3 bulbs
$$P_B = 3 \times 100 = 300 \text{ W}$$

Energy consumed by 3 bulbs in a day,
$$E_B = P_B \times t_B$$
$$= 300 \text{W} \times 5 \text{ h} = 1.5 \text{ kWh} \qquad [\because t_B = 5 \text{ h}]$$

Similarly, power of 2 fans, $P_F = 2 \times 50 \text{ W} = 100 \text{ W}$

Energy consumed by 2 fans, $E_F = P_F \times t_F$
$$= 100 \text{ W} \times 10 \text{ h} \qquad [\because t_F = 10 \text{ h}]$$
$$= 1 \text{ kWh}$$

Now, energy consumed by heater in a day
$$E_H = P_H \times t_H$$
$$= 1 \text{kWh} \times \frac{1}{2} \text{h} \quad \left[\because P_H = 1 \text{ kWh}, t_H = \frac{1}{2} \text{ h}\right]$$
$$= 0.5 \text{ kWh}$$

Total energy consumed in a day
$$E = E_B + E_F + E_H$$
$$= (1.5 + 1 + 0.5) \text{ kWh} = 3 \text{ kWh}$$

Energy consumed in a month of 31 days
$$= E \times 31 = 93 \text{ kWh}$$

$\therefore$ The cost of energy consumed
$$= (₹ 3.60/\text{kWh}) \times (93 \text{ kWh})$$
$$= ₹ 334.80$$

27. (a) Power is defined as the rate at which electric energy is dissipated or consumed in an electric circuit.
$$P = VI = I^2 R = V^2/R$$

The SI unit of electric power is watt (W).

It is the power consumed by a device that carries 1 A of current when operated at a potential difference of 1 V.
$$1 \text{ W} = 1 \text{ volt} \times 1 \text{ ampere} = 1 \text{ VA}$$

(b) Given, voltage rating, $V = 5$ V and current rating $I = 500$ mA

(i) As, we know power of bulb
$$P = VI = 5 \times 500 \times 10^{-3} \qquad [\because \text{A } 1\text{mA} = 10^{-3}\text{A}]$$
$$= 2.5 \text{ W}$$
$$= 2.5 \times 10^{-3} \text{ kW}$$

(ii) Resistance of bulb,
$$R = \frac{V}{I} \qquad \text{(Ohm's law)}$$
$$\Rightarrow \quad R = \frac{5}{500 \times 10^{-3}} = 10 \Omega$$

(iii) Energy consumed in $2\frac{1}{2}$ hour
$$E = \text{P.t.} = \frac{2.5 \times 2.5}{1000} \qquad \left[2\frac{1}{2} \text{ hour} = 2.5 \text{ hour}\right]$$
$$= \frac{6.25}{1000} = 0.00625 \text{ kWh}$$

28. (i) The electrical circuit in which some resistances are connected in series combination and some in parallel combination, this type of combination is called complex circuit.

(ii) Resistance in series is always greater than resistance in parallel. The slope of V-I graph gives resistance.

Hence, line B denotes resistance in series combination and line A denotes resistance in parallel combination.

(iii) Equivalent circuit diagram is

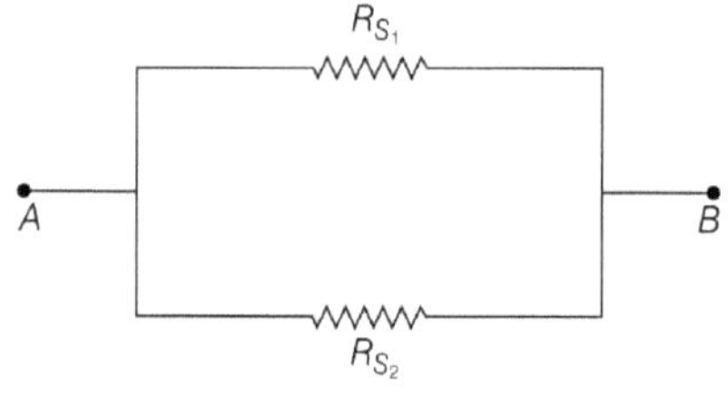

$$R_{S_1} = R + R = 2R$$
$$R_{S_2} = 2R + 2R = 4R$$

Both of them are in parallel.

$\therefore \qquad R_{eq} = \dfrac{R_{S_2} \times R_{S_1}}{R_{S_1} + R_{S_2}} = \dfrac{4}{3} R$

(iv) When the equivalent resistance is less than the resistance of least resistor. This is known as minimum effective resistance.

(v) In series combination, the value of current is same through each resistor.

So, it will not be affected at all.

29. (i) According to Joule's law of heating, the heat produced in a resistor is directly proportional to the square of current flowing through that resistor.

(ii) Practical application of heating effect of current is electric heater, electric iron etc.

(iii) Electrical energy is transformed into heat energy.

(iv) Given, resistance $R = 25 \ \Omega$; current $I = 7$ A; Time $t = 0.5$ min $= 0.5 \times 60 = 30$ s. Heat $H = ?$

We know that, Heat $H = I^2 Rt$
$$H = (7)^2 \times 25 \times 30 = 36750 \text{ J}$$
$$= 3.68 \times 10^4 \text{ J}$$

So, the heat developed is 3.68×10^4 J.

(v) Given, Heat $H = 200\,J$, Resistance, $R = 5\,\Omega$

Time $t = 10\,s$, Potential difference $V = ?$

We know that,

Heat, $H = I^2 Rt$

$$\Rightarrow \text{Current, } I = \sqrt{\frac{H}{Rt}}$$

$$7 = \sqrt{\frac{200}{5 \times 10}} = 2\,A$$

So, the potential difference across the resistor is

$$V = IR \qquad\qquad \text{[by Ohm's law]}$$

$$= 2 \times 5 = 10\,V$$

30. (i) (a) An applied potential V produces current I in the resistors and R_1, R_2 and R_3 causing a potential drop V_1, V_2 and V_3 respectively, through each resistor.

Total potential, $V = V_1 + V_2 + V_3$

(ii) (a) In series combination of resistors, the current is same at every point of the circuit, i.e. the current through each resistor is same.

(iii) (c) Electrical energy = Power × Time

$$\Rightarrow \qquad W = P \times T = VIT$$

(iv) (b) Resistance of each resistor $= 0.2\,\Omega$

Total resistance in series $R_S = n \times R = 200 \times 0.2$

$$\Rightarrow \qquad R_S = 40\,\Omega$$

(v) (d) Resistor of $6\,\Omega$ and $2\,\Omega$ are in parallel.

$$\therefore \qquad R_P = \frac{R_1 \times R_2}{R_1 + R_2}$$

$$= \frac{6 \times 2}{6 + 2}$$

$$R_P = \frac{3}{2}\,\Omega$$

Equivalent circuit is shown below,

3/2 Ω   6 Ω

Both of them are in series

$$\therefore \qquad R_{eq} = \left(\frac{3}{2} + 6\right)\Omega$$

$$\Rightarrow \qquad R_{eq} = \frac{15}{2}\,\Omega$$

Chapter Test

Multiple Choice Questions

1. Which of the following obeys Ohm's law?
   (a) Filament of a bulb
   (b) LED
   (c) Nichrome
   (d) Transistor

2. What is the minimum resistance which can be made using five resistors each of $1/5\ \Omega$?
   (a) $1/5\ \Omega$
   (b) $1/25\ \Omega$
   (c) $1/10\ \Omega$
   (d) $25\ \Omega$

3. Two resistors of resistance $2\ \Omega$ and $4\ \Omega$ when connected to a battery will have
   (a) same current flowing through them when connected in parallel
   (b) same current flowing through them when connected in series
   (c) same potential difference across them when connected in series
   (d) different potential difference across them when connected in parallel

4. Two bulbs have the following ratings
   (i) 40 W, 220 V
   (ii) 20 W, 110 V
   The ratio of their resistances is
   (a) 1 : 2
   (b) 2 : 1
   (c) 1 : 1
   (d) 1 : 3

5. At the time of short circuit, the electric current in the circuit
   (a) varies continuously
   (b) reduces substantially
   (c) does not change
   (d) increases heavily

Assertion-Reasoning MCQs

Direction (Q. Nos. 6-8) Each of these questions contains two statements Assertion (A) and Reason (R). Each of these questions also has four alternative choices, any one of which is the correct answer. You have to select one of the codes (a), (b), (c) and (d) given below.

   (a) Both A and R are true and R is the correct explanation of A.
   (b) Both A and R are true, but R is not the correct explanation of A.
   (c) A is true, but R is false.
   (d) A is false, but R is true.

6. **Assertion** At high temperatures, metal wires have a greater chance of short circuiting

   Reason Both resistance and resistivity of a material vary with temperature.

7. **Assertion** Incandescent bulb passes an electric current through a metal filament to produce heat.

   Reason The higher the wattage, the more energy is consumed.

8. **Assertion** Heater wire must have high resistance and high melting point.

   Reason If resistance is high, the electric conductivity will be less.

Short Answer Type Questions

9. Draw the V-I graph for ohmic and non-ohmic conductors.

10. A wire of resistance $5\ \Omega$ is bent in the form of a closed circle. Find the resistance between two points at the ends of any diameter of the circle.

11. Give two characteristics properties of copper wire which makes it suitable for use as fuse wire.

12. A copper wire has diameter 0.5 mm and resistivity $\rho = 1.6 \times 10^{-8}\ \Omega$-m. What will be the length of its wire to make its resistance $10\ \Omega$? How much does the resistance change, if diameter is doubled?

13. Two conducting wires of same material and of equal lengths and equal diameters are first connected in series and then parallel in a circuit across the same potential difference, what is the ratio of heat produced in series and parallel combinations?

14. Compare the power used in $2\ \Omega$ resistor in each of the following circuits (i) a 6 V battery in series with 1 Ω and resistors, (ii) a 4 V battery in parallel with $12\ \Omega$ and $2\ \Omega$ resistors.

Long Answer Type Questions

15. Two metallic wires A and B are of same material where length of wire A is l and wire B is $2l$ and radius of wire A is r and wire B is $2r$.

   (i) When both of them are connected in series, find the ratio of total resistance in series combination with wire A.

   (ii) When both of them are connected in parallel, Find the ratio of total resistance in parallel combination with wire A.

16. (i) Two lamps rated 100 W, 220 V and 10 W, 220 V are connected in parallel to 220 V supply. Calculate the total current through the circuit.

   (ii) Two resistors X and Y of resistances $2\ \Omega$ and $3\ \Omega$ respectively are first joined in parallel and then in series. In each case, the supplied voltage is 5 V.

   (a) Draw circuit diagrams to show the combination of resistors in each case.

   (b) Calculate the voltage across the $3\ \Omega$ resistor in the series combination of resistors.

Answers

Multiple Choice Questions
   1. (c)   2. (b)   3. (b)   4. (b)   5. (d)

Assertion-Reasoning MCQs
   6. (a)   7. (b)   8. (d)

For Detailed Solutions
Scan the code

CHAPTER 6

Magnetic Effects of Electric Current

In this Chapter...

- Magnetic Field
- Electric Motor
- Electromagnetic Induction

In 1820, Christian Oersted discovered that a compass needle get deflected when a current carrying metallic conductor is placed nearby it. He concluded that the deflection of compass needle was due to the magnetic field produced by the electric current.

Hence, it was deduced that electricity and magnetism are related to each other.

Magnetic Field

It is the space around a magnet in which its effect can be experienced i.e. its force can be detected. It is a **vector** quantity. The SI unit of magnetic field is **Tesla**.

Magnetic Lines of Force

They are the imaginary lines representing magnetic field around a magnet. When iron fillings are kept near a magnet, they get arranged in a pattern which represents the magnetic field lines.

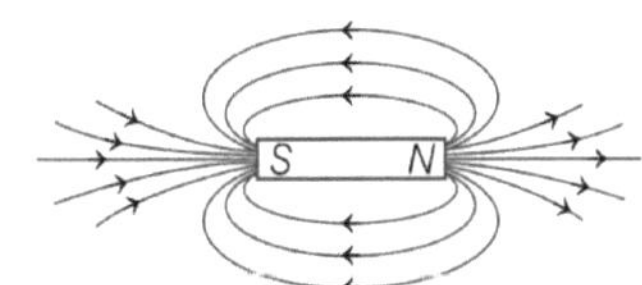

Magnetic field lines around a bar magnet

A compass needle behaves as a small bar magnet whose one end points towards North and other end towards South.

Properties of Magnetic Field Lines

The magnetic field lines have the following properties

- They originate from North pole of a magnet and end at its South pole, by convention.
- These lines are closed and continuous curves.
- They are crowded near the poles, where the magnetic field is strong and separated far from the poles, where the magnetic field is weak.
- Field lines never intersect with each other. If they do, that would mean that there are two directions of the magnetic field at the point of intersection, which is impossible.

Magnetic Field due to a Current Carrying Conductor

When electric current flows through a metallic conductor, a magnetic field is produced around it.

Different magnetic field patterns are produced by current carrying conductors of different shapes.

Magnetic Field due to a Current through a Straight Conductor

The magnetic field lines around a current carrying straight conductor are concentric circles whose centres lie on the wire.

The magnitude of magnetic field B produced by a straight current carrying wire at a given point is

(i) **Directly proportional** to the current I passing through the wire,

i.e. $\quad\quad\quad\quad B \propto I \quad\quad\quad\quad\quad$ ...(i)

(ii) **Inversely proportional** to the distance r from the current carrying conductor,

i.e. $\quad\quad\quad\quad B \propto \dfrac{1}{r} \quad\quad\quad\quad\quad$ ...(ii)

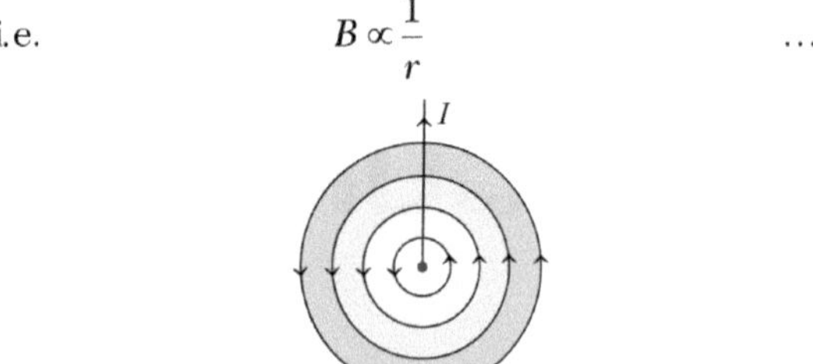
Concentric field lines around a straight conductor

By using Eqs. (i) and (ii), we get, $\quad B \propto \dfrac{I}{r}$

If the direction of current in a straight wire is known, then the direction of magnetic field produced by it is obtained by Maxwell's right hand thumb rule.

Maxwell's Right Hand Thumb Rule

It states that, if you hold the current carrying straight wire in the grip of your right hand in such a way that the stretched thumb points in the direction of current, then the direction of the curl of the fingers will give the direction of the magnetic field. This rule is also called **Maxwell's corkscrew rule.**

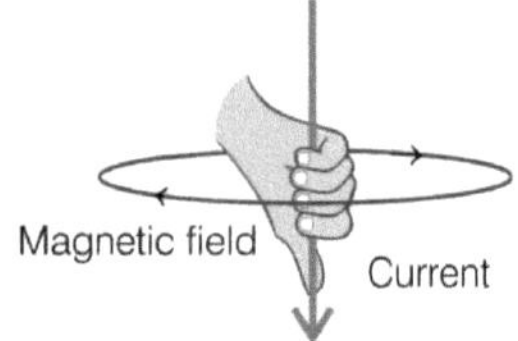

Maxwell's right hand thumb rule

Magnetic Field due to a Current through a Circular Loop

The magnetic field lines due to a circular coil are shown in the given figure.

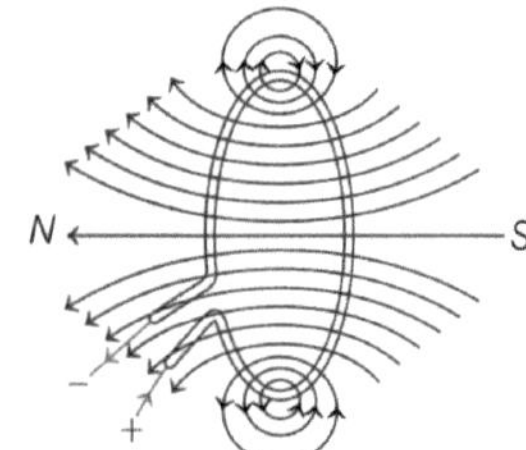

Magnetic field lines due to a
current through a circular loop

At every point on a current carrying circular loop, the magnetic field is in the form of concentric circles around it. As we move away from it, the circles would become larger and larger.

When we reach the centre of loop, the field appears to be a straight line. The magnetic field produced by current carrying circular wire at a given point is

(i) **Directly proportional** to the amount of current (I) passing through it,

i.e. $\quad\quad\quad\quad B \propto I \quad\quad\quad\quad\quad$ ...(i)

(ii) **Directly proportional** to the number of turns (N) of the wire,
i.e. $\quad\quad\quad\quad B \propto N \quad\quad\quad\quad\quad$ ...(ii)

This is because the current in each turn is in the same direction. Therefore, the field due to these turns get added up.

Thus, the strength of magnetic field produced by a current carrying circular coil can be increased by

- increasing the number of turns of the coil.
- increasing the current flowing through the coil.

Magnetic Field due to a Current in a Solenoid

A solenoid is defined as a coil consisting of a large number of circular turns of insulated copper wire. These turns are wrapped closely to form a cylinder.

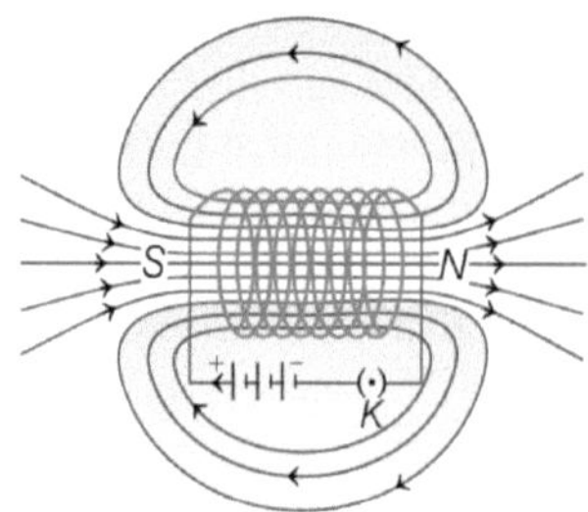

Magnetic field lines of force due to a current
carrying solenoid

The field lines around a current carrying solenoid are similar to that produced by a bar magnet. This means that a current carrying solenoid behaves as if it has North pole and South pole. The field lines inside the solenoid are parallel to each other.

Thus, the strength of magnetic field is the same, i.e. uniform at all points inside a solenoid.

Electromagnet

The strong magnetic field produced inside a solenoid can be used to magnetise a piece of magnetic material like soft iron when placed inside the coil. The magnet so formed is called electromagnet.

The magnetic effect remains only till the current is flowing through the solenoid.

An electromagnet is used in electric bells, electric motors, telephone diaphragms, loudspeakers and for sorting scrap metal.

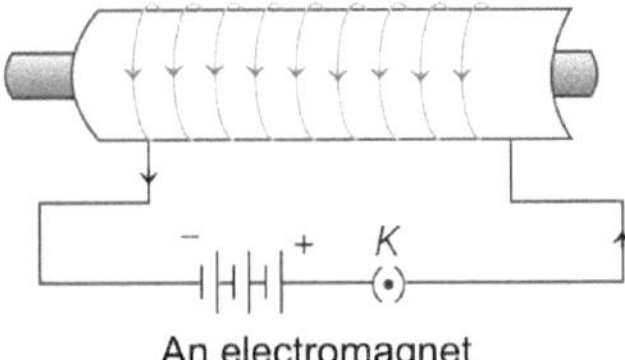

An electromagnet

Force on a Current Carrying Conductor in a Magnetic Field

When a current carrying conductor is placed in a magnetic field, it experiences a force. The force acting is due to interaction between magnetic field produced by the current carrying conductor and external magnetic field in which the conductor is placed.

The direction of force on the conductor depends on the following factors

(i) **Direction of current** The direction of force on the conductor can be reversed by reversing the direction of current.

(ii) **Direction of magnetic field** The direction of force on the conductor can be reversed by reversing the direction of magnetic field by interchanging the position of poles.

Force on the conductor is maximum when the direction of current is at right angles to the direction of magnetic field.

Fleming's Left Hand Rule

The direction of force which acts on a current carrying conductor placed in a magnetic field is given by Fleming's left hand rule.

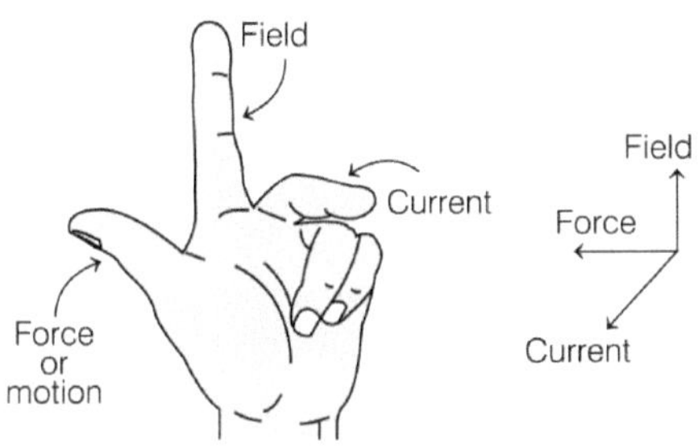

Fleming's left hand rule

It states that, if the forefinger, thumb and middle finger of left hand are stretched mutually perpendicular to each other, such that the forefinger points along the direction of external magnetic field, middle finger indicates the direction of current, then the thumb points towards the direction of force acting on the conductor.

Electric Motor

It is a rotating device used for converting electric energy into mechanical energy.

Principle

It is based on the principle that when a rectangular coil is placed in a magnetic field and current is passed through it, two equal and opposite forces act on the coil which rotate it continuously.

Construction

It consists of a rectangular coil, connected to a source of current and a switch.

The **commutators** R_1 and R_2 are fixed to the coil and pressed tightly against the brushes X and Y.

The function of commutator is to reverse the direction of current flowing through the coil, after every half rotation. In an electric motor, split rings act as commutator.

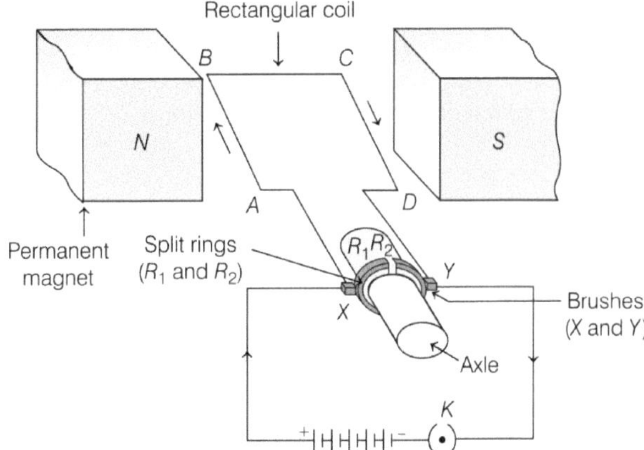

A simple electric motor

Working

- Let coil $ABCD$ be in horizontal position. When the key is closed, the current flows in the coil $ABCD$ through brush X and flows back to the battery through the brush Y via ring R_2.
- No force acts on arms BC and AD as they are parallel to magnetic field. Arm AB experiences a force in downward direction and arm CD experiences an equal force in upward direction.
- The direction of force is obtained by applying Fleming's left hand rule. This causes the coil to rotate in the anti-clockwise direction.
- When the rotating coil is in the vertical position, the brushes lose contact with the rings and current stops flowing. But the coil does not stop due to inertia of motion.
- When the coil rotates, the rings change their positions and come in contact with opposite brushes.
- This reverses the direction of current through the coil but the direction of current on right hand side of the coil remains the same.
- So, the force on right hand side is always upwards and a force on left hand side is always in downward direction. Thus, the coil continues to rotate in anti-clockwise direction.

The speed of rotation of the motor can be increased by
- increasing the strength of the current in the coil.
- increasing the number of turns in the coil.
- increasing the area of the coil.
- increasing the strength of magnetic field.

Commercial Electric Motor

It has the following components
- An electromagnet in the place of permanent magnet.
- A large number of turns of conducting wire in the current carrying coil.
- A soft iron core on which the coil is wound. The combination of soft iron core and coil is called **armature**. It enhances the power of motor.
- Electric motor is used in electric fans, refrigerators, mixers, washing machines, computers, MP3 players, etc.

Electromagnetic Induction

Production of an electric current in a closed circuit by a changing magnetic field is called an **induced current.** This phenomenon is called **electromagnetic induction.**

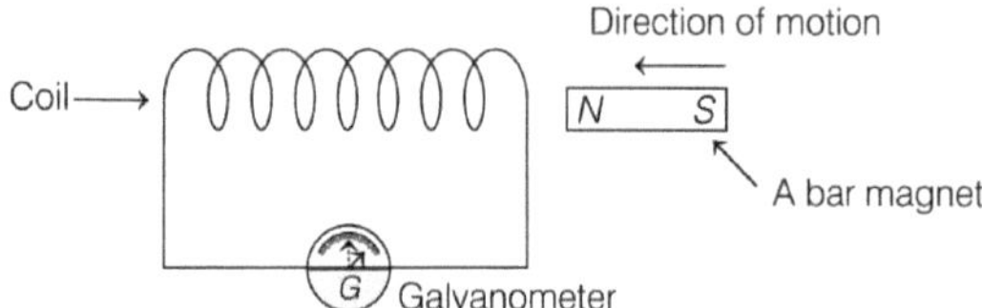

A bar magnet is pushed inside a fixed current carrying coil

Fleming's Right Hand Rule

The direction of induced current is given by Fleming's right hand rule. It states that, if the forefinger, middle finger and thumb of the right hand are stretched at right angles to each other, with the forefinger in the direction of the magnetic field and the thumb in the direction of the motion of the wire, then the induced current in the wire is in the direction of the middle finger.

> ### Galvanometer
> It is an instrument that can detect the presence of current in a circuit. The pointer remains at zero (the centre of the scale) for zero current flowing through it.
> Depending upon the direction of current, it deflects either to the left or to the right of the zero mark.

Ways to Induce Current in a Circuit

There are different methods by which current can be induced in a circuit

(i) **By Moving a Coil in a Magnetic Field** Current can be induced in coil either by moving it in a magnetic field or by changing the magnetic field around it as indicated by deflection in galvanometer needle.

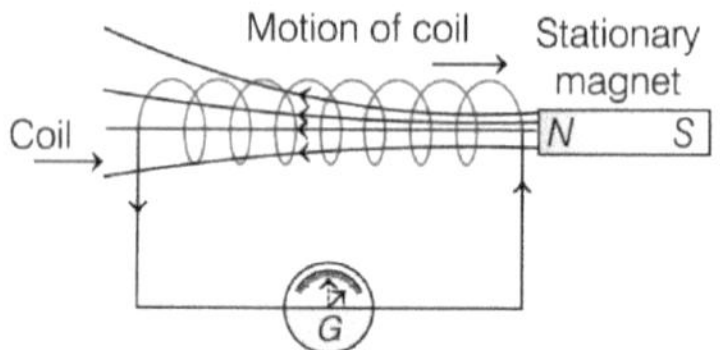

Moving coil towards stationary magnet

The induced current is found to be maximum when the direction of motion of the coil is at right angle to the magnetic field.

The direction of induced current can be reversed by reversing the direction of magnetic field. If the coil as well as the magnet are stationary, then no current is induced in the coil.

(ii) **By Changing the Magnetic Field Around a Nearby Coil** Consider two coils, where coil 1 is called as primary coil and coil 2 as secondary coil. Primary coil is connected to a battery.

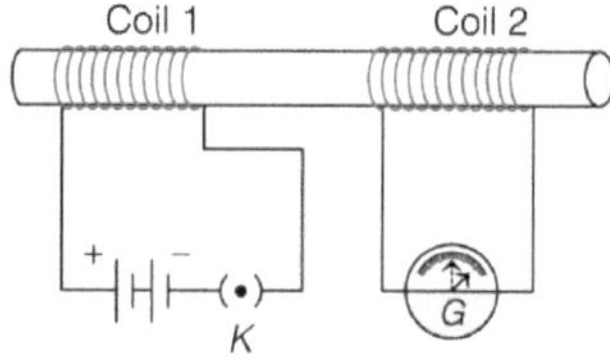

Set up of two stationary coils, where current is induced in coil 2 when current in coil 1 is changed

When the key (K) is closed, the current in primary coil takes a little time to rise from zero to a maximum value. This causes a momentary change in the magnetic field around this coil. This induces a momentary current in the secondary coil.

The same happens in the reverse direction when the key (K) is opened. Current is induced in coil 2 when current in coil 1 is changed which is indicated by the deflection in galvanometer needle.

Chapter Practice

Objective Questions

• Multiple Choice Questions

1. Which of the following is the property of magnetic field lines ?
  (a) Magnetic field lines are closed and continuous curves
  (b) Magnetic field lines never intersect with each other
  (c) Magnetic field lines are crowded near the poles
  (d) All of the above

2. Which of the following is the correct representation of uniform magnetic field?

(a) 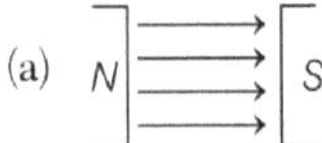   (b) 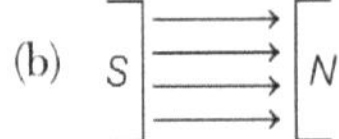

(c)    (d)

3. Which of the following correctly describes the magnetic field near a long straight wire?   **(NCERT)**
  (a) The field consists of straight lines perpendicular to the wire
  (b) The field consists of straight lines parallel to the wire
  (c) The field consists of radial lines originating from the wire
  (d) The field consists of concentric circles centred on the wire

4. A constant current flows in a horizontal wire in the plane of the paper from East to West as shown in figure. The direction of the magnetic field at a point will be North to South

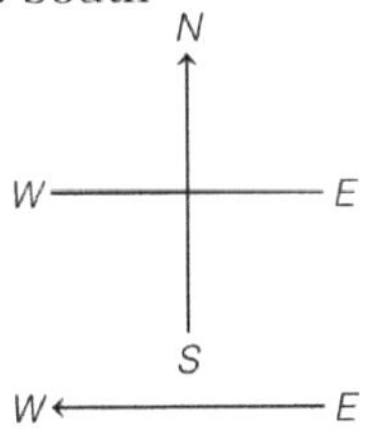

                                          (NCERT)

(a) directly above the wire
(b) directly below the wire
(c) at a point located in the plane of the paper, on the North side of the wire
(d) at a point located in the plane of the paper, on the South side of the wire

5. Four students A, B, C and D plotted the sketch of the patterns of magnetic field lines representing the magnetic field around a current carrying straight wire as shown. Whose sketch is correctly represented?

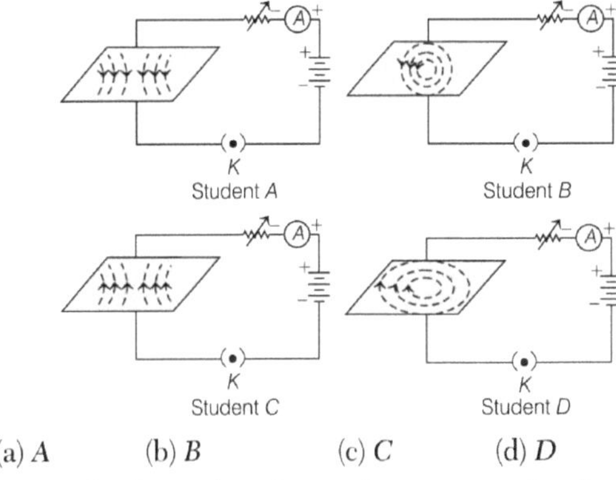

(a) A (b) B (c) C (d) D

6. A circular loop placed in a plane perpendicular to the plane of paper carries a current when the key is ON. The current as seen from points A and B (in the plane of paper and on the axis of the coil) is anti-clockwise and clockwise, respectively.

The magnetic field lines point from B to A. The N-pole of the resultant magnet is on the face close to   **(NCERT Exemplar)**

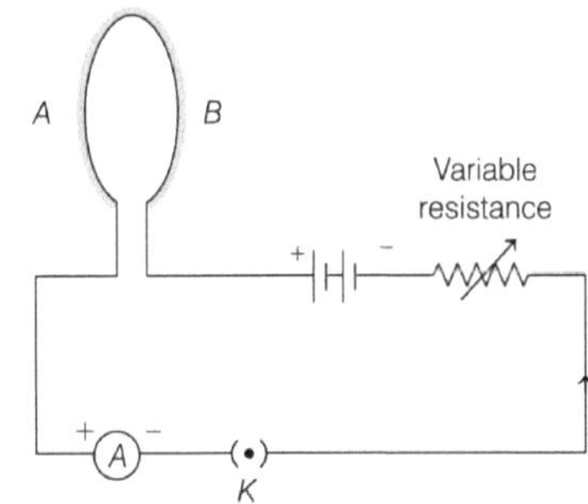

(a) *B*

(b) *A*

(c) *A*, if the current is small and *B*, if the current is large

(d) *B*, if the current is small and *A*, if the current is large

7. Which of the following properties of a proton can change when it moves freely in a magnetic field?

(a) Mass   (b) Speed   **(NCERT)**

(c) Velocity   (d) Momentum

8. A positively charged particle (α-particle) projected towards West is deflected towards North by a magnetic field. The direction of magnetic field is

(NCERT)

(a) towards South   (b) towards East

(c) downwards   (d) upwards

9. The strength of magnetic field inside a long current carrying straight solenoid is

(a) more at the ends than at the centre

(b) minimum in the middle

(c) same at all point

(d) found to increase from one end to the other

10. Match the items in Column I with the items in Column II and choose the correct codes given below.

Column I	Column II
A. SI unit of magnetic field	(i) Small bar magnet that rotates
B. Magnetic field inside solenoid	(ii) Tesla
C. Compass needle	(iii) Temporary magnet
D. Solenoid	(iv) Uniform value

Codes

	A	B	C	D
(a)	(ii)	(iv)	(i)	(iii)
(b)	(iii)	(ii)	(iv)	(i)
(c)	(i)	(iii)	(ii)	(iv)
(d)	(iv)	(i)	(iii)	(ii)

11. A uniform magnetic field exists in the plane of paper pointing from left to right as shown in the figure. In the field, an electron and a proton move as shown in the figure. The electron and the proton experience   **(NCERT Exemplar)**

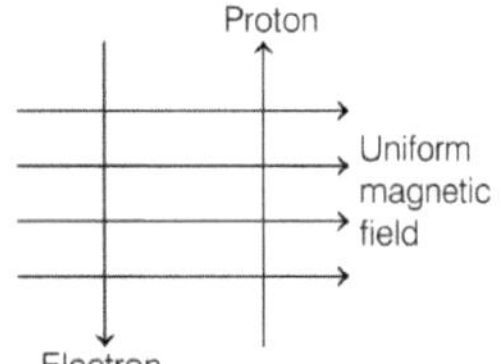

(a) forces both pointing into the plane of paper

(b) forces both pointing out of the plane of paper

(c) forces pointing into the plane of paper and out of the plane of paper, respectively

(d) force pointing opposite and along the direction of the uniform magnetic field, respectively

12. A rectangular loop carrying a current *i* is situated near a long straight wire such that the wire is parallel to one of the sides of the loop and is in the plane of the loop. If a steady current *i* is created in wire as shown in figure below, then the loop will

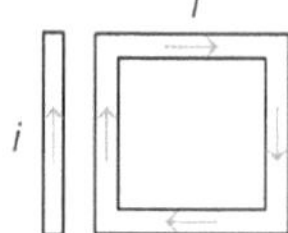

(a) rotate about an axis parallel to the wire

(b) move towards the wire

(c) move away from the wire or towards right

(d) remain stationary

13. The direction of the induced electric current in a conductor, when placed in a varying magnetic field can be assessed by   **(CBSE 2020)**

(a) Maxwell's right hand-thumb rule

(b) Ohm's law

(c) Fleming's left hand rule

(d) Fleming's right hand rule

14. In the arrangement shown in figure below, there are two coils wound on a non-conducting cylindrical rod. Initially, the key is not inserted. Then, the key is inserted and later removed. Then,   **(NCERT Exemplar)**

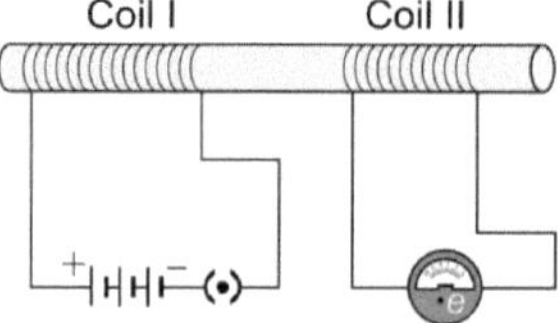

(a) The deflection in the galvanometer remains zero throughout.

(b) There is a momentary deflection in the galvanometer only when the key is removed.

(c) There are momentary galvanometer deflections that die out shortly; the deflections are in the same direction.

(d) The galvanometer shows momentary deflections in opposite directions.

15. Match the terms of Column I with Column II and choose the correct option from the codes given below.

	Column I		Column II
A.	Direction of force	(i)	Direction of magnetic force on a North pole
B.	Direction of induced current	(ii)	Fleming's left hand rule
C.	Direction of magnetic field produced by straight current carrying conductor	(iii)	Maxwell's right hand thumb rule
D.	Direction of magnetic field lines at a point in a magnet	(iv)	Fleming's right hand rule

Codes

	A	B	C	D
(a)	(ii)	(iv)	(iii)	(i)
(b)	(i)	(ii)	(iii)	(iv)
(c)	(ii)	(iii)	(i)	(iv)
(d)	(i)	(iii)	(ii)	(iv)

• Assertion-Reasoning MCQs

Direction (Q. Nos. 16-20) For given questions two statements are given-one labelled Assertion (A) and the other labelled Reason (R). Select the correct answer to these questions from the codes (a), (b), (c) and (d) as given below.

    (a) Both A and R are true and R is the correct explanation of A.

    (b) Both A and R are true, but R is not the correct explanation of A.

    (c) A is true, but R is false.

    (d) A is false, but R is true.

16. Assertion The magnetic field is stronger at a point which is nearer to the conductor and goes on decreasing on moving away from the conductor.

    Reason The magnetic field B produced by a straight current carrying wire is inversely proportional to the distance from the wire.

17. Assertion A current carrying conductor experiences a force in a magnetic field.

    Reason The force acting on a current carrying conductor in a magnetic field is due to interaction between magnetic field produced by the conductor and external magnetic field.

18. Assertion If an electron, moving vertically from outer space, enters the earth's magnetic field, then it gets deflected towards West.

    Reason Electron has negative charge.

19. Assertion The magnetic field produced by a current carrying solenoid is independent of its length and cross-sectional area.

    Reason The magnetic field inside the solenoid has variable value.

20. Assertion Production of an electric current in a closed circuit by a changing electric field is called an induced current.

    Reason The direction of induced current is given by Fleming's right hand rule.

• Case Based MCQs

21. Read the following and answer the questions from (i) to (v) given below

A solenoid is a long helical coil of wire through which a current is running in order to create a magnetic field.

The magnetic field of a solenoid is the superposition of the fields due to the current through each coil. It is nearly uniform inside the solenoid and close to zero outside and is similar to the field of a bar magnet.

The following graph is obtained by a researcher, while doing an experiment to see the variation of the magnetic field with respect to the current in the solenoid. The unit of magnetic field as given in the graph attached is in (mT) and the current is given in (A).

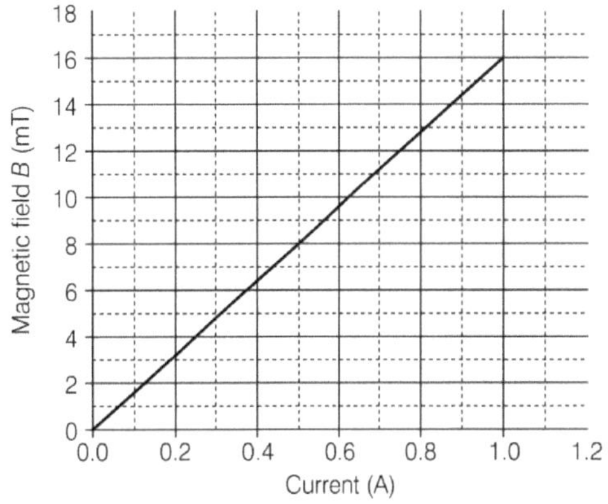

(CBSE Sample Paper)

    (i) What type of energy conversion is observed in a linear solenoid?

        (a) Mechanical to magnetic

        (b) Electrical to magnetic

        (c) Electrical to mechanical

        (d) Magnetic to mechanical

(ii) What will happen, if a soft iron bar is placed inside the solenoid?

   (a) A high amount of electric charge flows in the bar resulting in short-circuit.

   (b) The bar will be magnetised as long as there is current in the circuit

   (c) The bar will be magnetised permanently

   (d) The bar will not be affected by any means

(iii) The magnetic field lines produced inside the solenoid are similar to that of

   (a) a bar magnet

   (b) a straight current carrying conductor

   (c) a circular current carrying loop

   (d) electromagnet of any shape

(iv) After analysing the graph, a student writes the following statements.

   I. The magnetic field produced by the solenoid is inversely proportional to the current.

   II. The magnetic field produced by the solenoid is directly proportional to the current.

   III. The magnetic field produced by the solenoid is directly proportional to square of the current.

   IV. The magnetic field produced by the solenoid is independent of the current.

   Which of the following would be the correct statement(s).

   (a) Only IV   (b) I, III and IV

   (c) Both I and II   (d) Only II

(v) From the graph, deduce which of the following statements is correct?

   (a) For a current of 0.8 A, the magnetic field is 13 mT.

   (b) For larger currents, the magnetic field increases non-linearly.

   (c) For a current of 0.8 A, the magnetic field is 1.3 mT.

   (d) There is not enough information to find the magnetic field corresponding to 0.8 A current.

22. Read the following and answer the questions from (i) to (v) given below

A student wants to study the working of electric motor. He used a model of DC motor for electromagnetism as shown in figure.

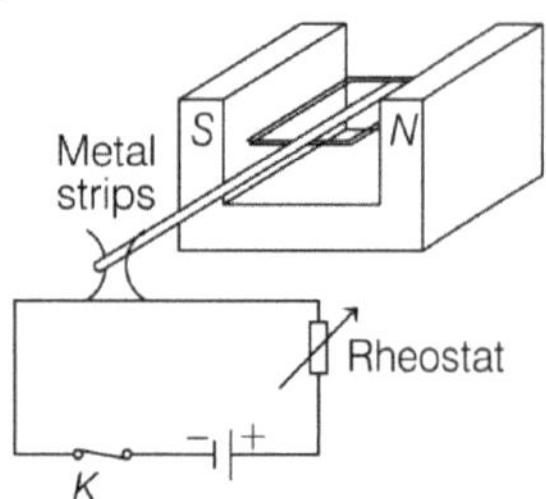

He fixed the two ends of the coil to a pair of curved elastic metal strips. The metal strips are connected to the power supply with a rheostat.

(i) The direction of rotation of the coil, when viewed from the front by the student is

   (a) clockwise

   (b) anti clockwise

   (c) First half clockwise and other half anti-clockwise

   (d) First half anti-clockwise and other half clockwise

(ii) The student is still testing on the feasibility of using metal strips in the model. His observations are given below.

   I. As the current reverses in the coil for every half turn, the coil rotates in one direction.

   II. The speed of rotation of the motor is increased, if the value of current is increased.

   III. The direction of force, acting on the coil is given by Fleming's left hand rule.

   IV. The coil continues its rotation in magnetic field even if there is no current in circuit.

   The correct observations made by him are

   (a) I, II and IV   (b) II, III and IV

   (c) I, II and III   (d) II and III

(iii) Commercial electric motors do not use

   (a) an electromagnet to rotate the armature.

   (b) effectively large number of turns of conducing wire in the current carrying coil

   (c) a permanent magnet to rotate the armature

   (d) a soft iron core on which the coil is wound

(iv) Which one of the following is true about electric motor?

   (a) It converts electrical energy into mechanical energy

   (b) It converts mechanical energy into electrical energy

   (c) It converts magnetic energy into electric energy

   (d) It converts electric energy into magnetic energy

(v) The direction of magnetic field at a place is coming out of the paper. A wire whose direction of current flow is as shown in the figure is placed there. In which direction is the force due to the magnetic field experienced by the wire?

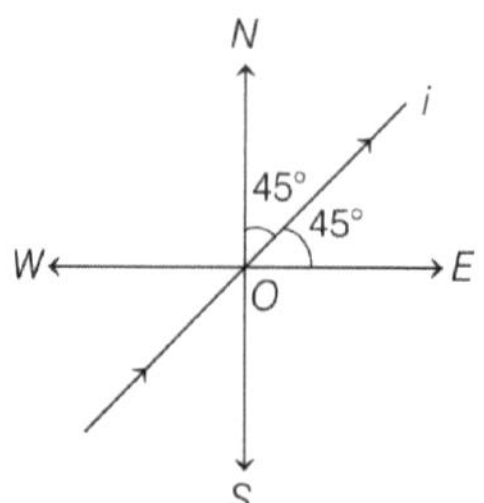

   (a) North-West direction

   (b) North direction

   (c) South-West direction

   (d) South-East direction

Subjective Questions

• Short Answer Type Questions

1. List the properties of magnetic lines of force. Why do two magnetic lines of force not intersect with each other? **(NCERT)**

2. The adjoining diagram shows two parallel straight conductors carrying same current. Copy the diagram and draw the pattern of the magnetic field lines around them showing their directions. What is the magnitude of magnetic field at a point X which is equidistant from the conductors? Give justification for your answer. **(CBSE 2019)**

3. How will the strength of the magnetic field change when the point where magnetic field is to be determined is moved away from the straight wire carrying constant current? Justify your answer. **(CBSE 2019)**

4. AB is a current carrying conductor in the plane of the paper as shown in figure. What are the directions of magnetic fields produced by it at points P and Q?

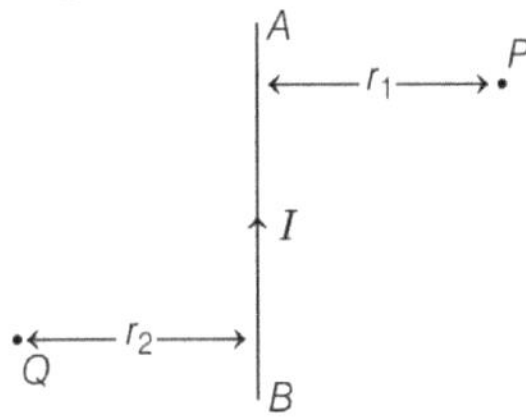

Given $r_1 > r_2$, where will the strength of the magnetic field be larger? **(NCERT Exemplar)**

5. A horizontal power line carries a current from East to West direction. What is the direction of the magnetic field due to the current in the power line at a point above and at a point below the power line?

6. A circular loop carrying a current is placed on a horizontal surface (current is in the clockwise direction).

What is the direction of its magnetic field at the centre? What is the direction of the magnetic field at a point outside the surface of the loop?

7. Find the direction of magnetic field due to a current carrying circular coil held

(i) Vertically in North-South plane and an observer looking it from East sees the current to flow in anti-clockwise direction.

(ii) Vertically in East-West plane and an observer looking it from South sees the current to flow in anti-clockwise direction.

(iii) Horizontally and an observer looking at it from below sees current to flow in clockwise direction.

8. How does a solenoid behave like a magnet? Can you determine the North and South poles of a current carrying solenoid using a bar magnet? Explain. **(NCERT)**

9. Give reasons for the following

(i) There is either a convergence or a divergence of magnetic field lines near the ends of a current carrying straight solenoid.

(ii) The current carrying solenoid when suspended freely rests along a particular direction.

(iii) The strength of magnetic field is uniform inside a solenoid. **(CBSE 2020)**

10. When is the force experienced by a current carrying conductor placed in a magnetic field largest? Which rule determines the direction of force on current carrying conductor?

11. A magnetic field is non-uniform but its direction is constant (East to West) is set-up in a chamber. A charged particle enters the chamber and travels undeflected along a straight path with constant speed.

What do you say about the initial velocity of the particle?

12. An α-particle (positive charge) enters, a uniform magnetic field at right angles to it as shown below.

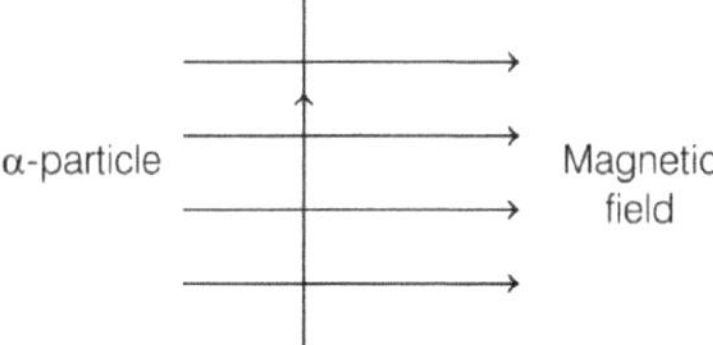

In which direction α-particle moves, if the direction of magnetic field gets reversed?

13. State whether an α-particle will experience any force in a magnetic field, if (α-particles are positively charged particles).

(i) It is placed in the field at rest.

(ii) It moves in the magnetic field parallel to field lines.

(iii) It moves in the magnetic field perpendicular to field lines.

Justify your answer in each case.

14. The electron enters in uniform magnetic field with three different ways as shown below.

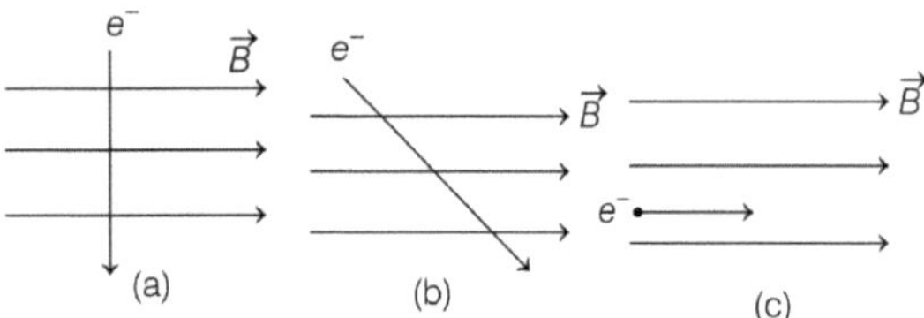

Identify the case in which the force on electron will be maximum and minimum, respectively. Give reasons for your answer. Find the direction of maximum force acting on electron.

15. The figure shows the split ring commutator and the two carbon brushes in their respective positions.

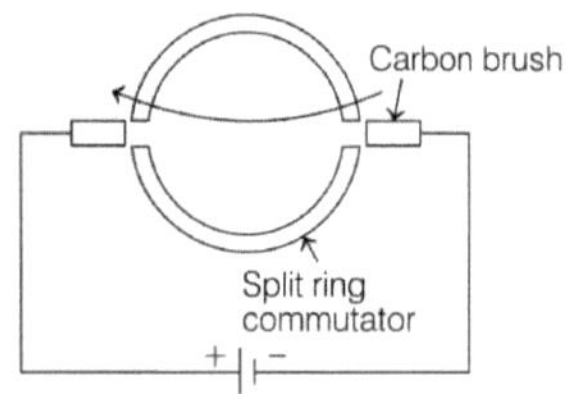

What can you say about carbon brush and split ring commutator?

16. Sketch the schematic diagram of electric motor. What is the role of split rings in an electric motor? **(NCERT)**

17. (i) In what ways the speed to rotation of an electric motor is increased?

(ii) Name some devices in which electric motors are used. **(NCERT)**

18. A circular metallic loop is kept above the wire AB as shown below.

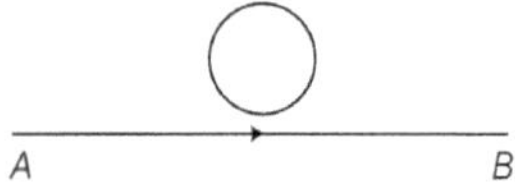

What is the direction of induced current produced in the loop, if the current flowing in the straight wire

(i) is steady, i.e. does not vary?

(ii) is increasing in magnitude?

Justify your answer in each case.

19. In the arrangement shown in figure there are two coils wound on a non-conducting cylindrical rod. Initially the key is not inserted in the circuit. Later the key is inserted and then removed shortly after.

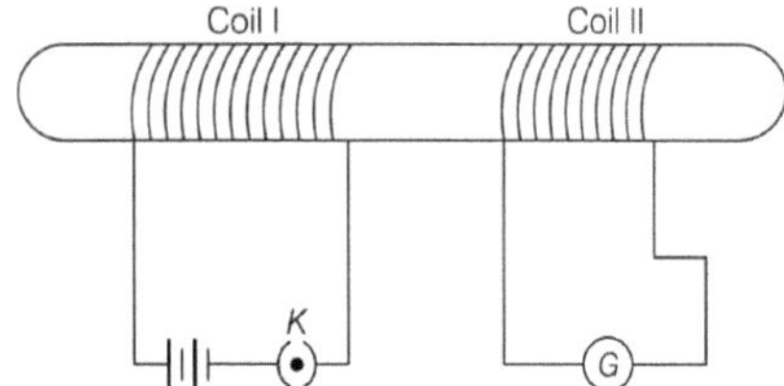

What are the two observations that can be noted from the galvanometer reading?

20. (i) A coil of insulated wire is connected to a galvanometer. What would be observed if a strong bar magnet with its south pole towards one face of the coil is

(a) moved quickly towards it?

(b) moved quickly away from it?

(c) held stationary near it?

(ii) Name the phenomenon involved.

(CBSE 2020, NCERT)

• Long Answer Type Questions

21. Why does a magnetic compass needle pointing North and South in the absence of a nearby magnet get deflected when a bar magnet or a current carrying loop is brought near it? Describe some salient features of magnetic lines of field concept. **(NCERT Exemplar)**

22. PQ is a current carrying conductor in the plane of the paper as shown in the figure below.

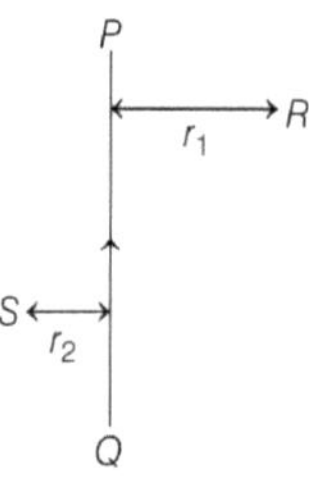

(i) Find the directions of the magnetic fields produced by it at points R and S.

(ii) Given $r_1 > r_2$, where will the strength of the magnetic field be larger? Give reasons.

(iii) If the polarity of the battery connected to the wire is reversed, how would the direction of the magnetic field be changed?

(iv) Explain the rule that is used to find the direction of the magnetic field for a straight current carrying conductor. **(CBSE Sample Paper)**

23. What is solenoid? Draw the pattern of magnetic field lines of (i) a current carrying solenoid and (ii) a bar magnet.

List two distinguishing features between the two fields. **(CBSE Delhi, 2019)**

24. (i) State Fleming's left hand rule.

(ii) Write the principle of working of an electric motor.

(iii) Explain the function of the following parts of an electric motor.

(a) Armature   (b) Brushes

(c) Split ring   **(CBSE 2018, NCERT)**

25. (i) What is meant by electromagnetic induction? Name one device which works on the principle of electromagnetic induction.

(ii) Describe three different ways to produce induced current in a coil of wire.

• Case Based Questions

26. Read the following and answer the questions from (i) to (v) given below

A bar magnet is moved in and out of a coil, i.e. connected to a sensitive centre zero meter as shown in the figure given below.

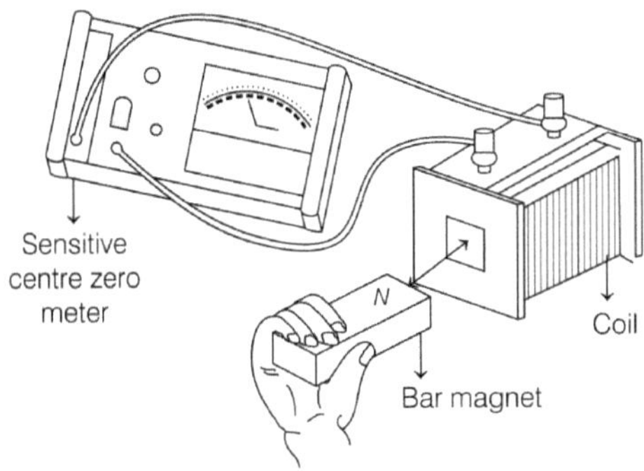

The meter needle swings to the left when the magnet is moving towards the coil.

(i) How the needle behaves when the bar magnet is at rest?

(ii) How the needle behaves when the bar magnet is at rest and the coil is moving away from the magnet?

(iii) In which condition, the meter needle swings to the left?

(iv) Which phenomenon is involved in this?

(v) Give two applications based on the given phenomenon.

27. Read the following and answer the questions from (i) to (v) given below

A child performs an activity with a special material. He fixes a sheet of white paper on a drawing board using some adhesive material and places that material in the centre of it.

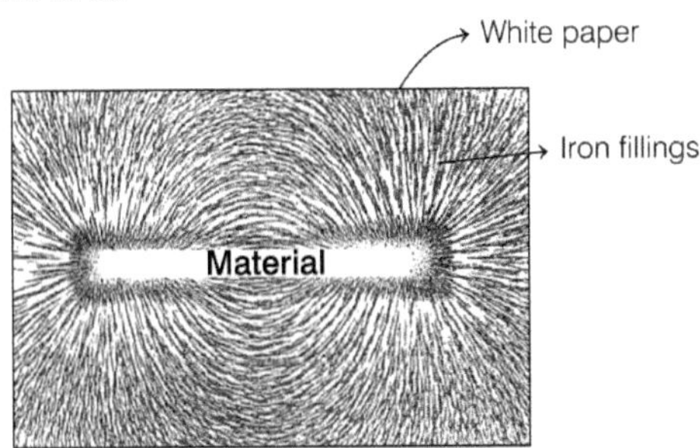

Then he sprinkles some iron fillings uniformly around it with a salt-sprinkler and taps the board gently.

(i) What type of material is placed on white paper?

(ii) Why do the iron fillings arrange in such a pattern?

(iii) What should we call to the region in which magnetic force can be detected?

(iv) What do the lines on pattern demonstrate?

(v) Does degree of closeness of the field lines relate something?

28. Read the following and answer the questions from (i) to (v) given below

Jay performs an experiment by using two different coils of copper wire having different number of turns.

He inserted them over a non conducting cylindrical roll as shown.

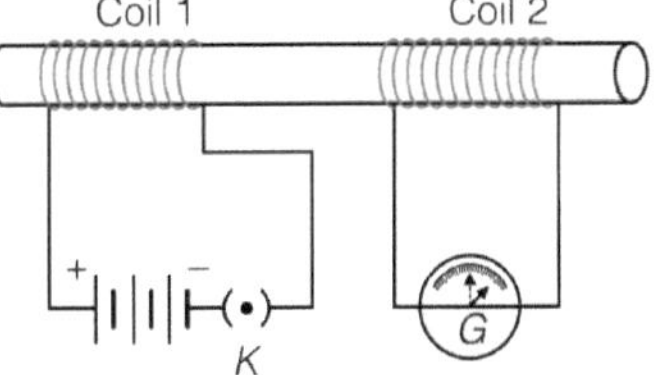

Setup of two stationary coils

Then he connects the coil-1, having large number of turns in series with a battery and plug key and other coil-2 with galvanometer. As, he plug the key, he observes some deflection in galvanometer.

(i) Why there is deflection in the galvanometer when a key is inserted in the circuit ?

(ii) When there is flow of induced current through a coil ?

(iii) Jay disconnected coil-1 from the battery and noted the following observation.

"The needle momentarily moves but to the opposite direction". Justify the statement.

(iv) When will the induced current is found to be highest?

(v)

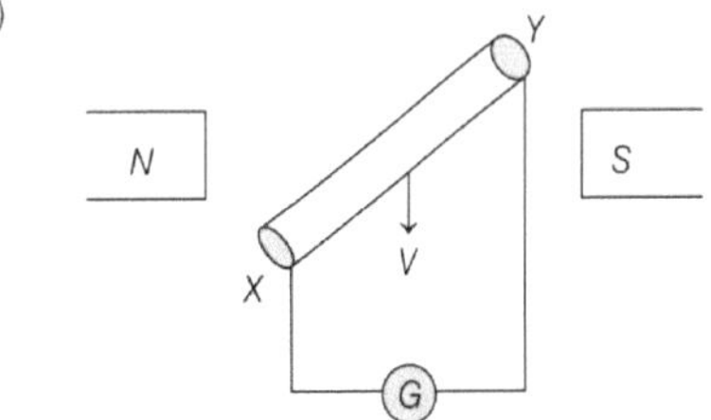

A conducting rod XY moves across two magnets as shown and the needle in galvanometer gets deflected momentarily. What is the name of this physical phenomenon?

EXPLANATIONS

Objective Questions

1. (d) Properties of magnetic field lines are as following

  (a) Magnetic field lines are closed and continuous curves.

  (b) Magnetic field lines never intersect with each other.

  (c) Magnetic field lines are crowded near the poles.

Hence, option (d) is correct.

2. (a) In a uniform magnetic field, the magnetic field lines of force are parallel and equidistant from each other.

The correct representation of uniform magnetic field is shown below.

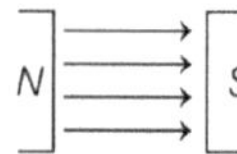

3. (d) The magnetic field lines due to a straight current carrying wire are concentric circles with centre on the wire.

4. (b) According to right hand thumb rule, when conductor is held in right hand, keeping thumb from East to West. The curve of the finger will be from North to South at a point lying directly below the wire.

5. (d) The magnetic field lines around a straight current carrying conductor are concentric circles and the direction of magnetic field is given by right hand thumb rule.

6. (b) The N-pole of the resultant magnet is on the face close to A, because the magnetic field lines enter in loop from B and come out from A.

Also, as a matter of fact magnetic lines come out of the N-pole of magnet. Therefore, face close to A represents N-pole. The currents in A and B are same.

7. (d) Proton is a charged particle. When it moves in a magnetic field, a magnetic force is applied due to its velocity and hence the momentum changes.

8. (d) The positively charged particle is moving towards West, i.e. the direction of current is towards West (current flows in the direction of the motion of positive charge).

The particle is deflected towards North, so the direction of force is towards North.

Thus, from Fleming's left hand rule, the direction of magnetic field is in upward direction.

9. (c) The strength of magnetic field inside a long current carrying straight solenoid is same at all points.

Therefore, correct option is (c).

10. The correct match for the given items is

A – (ii) The SI unit of magnetic field is Tesla (T).

B – (iv) The magnetic field inside solenoid has a uniform value.

C – (i) A compass needle is a small bar magnet that can rotate.

D – (iii), Solenoid is a temporary magnet.

11. (a) In the given figure, the proton and electron are moving in opposite direction to each other and in perpendicular to the direction of magnetic field. Now, we know that the direction of current is taken opposite to the direction of motion of electron.

So, both electron and proton has current in same direction. Therefore, the forces acting on it are given by Fleming's left hand rule and they are pointing into the plane of the paper.

12. (b) The force on the left side of loop is attractive because the direction of current in wire and loop is same, while on right side of loop, force is repulsive.

The force on perpendicular sides is zero. Hence, the attractive force is greater than repulsive force, so, the loop will move towards the wire.

13. (d) The direction of the induced electric current in a conductor, when placed in a varying magnetic field can be assessed by Fleming's right-hand rule.

14. (d) When key is inserted and removed, then the magnetic field lines pass through second coil increase and decrease in two cases respectively.

Therefore, the direction of current in two cases is in opposite directions and the galvanometer shows momentary deflections in opposite directions.

15. (a) The correct match for the given term is

(A)–(ii) The direction of force on a current carrying is given by Fleming's left hand rule.

(B)–(iv) The direction of induced current is given by Fleming's right hand rule.

(C)–(iii) The direction of magnetic field produced by a straight current carrying conductor is given by Maxwell's right hand thumb rule.

(D)–(i) The direction of magnetic field lines at a point in a magnet is the direction of magnetic force on a North pole.

16. (a) The magnitude of magnetic field is

  (i) directly proportional to the current I passing through the wire.

 (ii) inversely proportional to the distance r from the wire.

The magnetic field is stronger at a point which is nearer to the conductor and goes on decreasing on moving away from the conductor.

∴Both A and R are true and R is the correct explanation of A.

17. (b) When a current carrying conductor is placed in a magnetic field, it experiences a force except when it is placed parallel to the magnetic field. The force acting on a current carrying conductor depends on magnetic field produced by the current carrying conductor and external magnetic field.

∴Both A and R are true but R is not correct explanation of A.

18. (b) The Earth's magnetic field is towards North and velocity of electron is downwards. By applying, Fleming's left hand rule, the direction of force is towards West. Also, electron has a negative charge.

∴Both A and R are true but R is not correct explanation of A.

19. (c) The magnetic field is independent of length and area of solenoid, it only depends on the number of turns and current flowing through the solenoid. It is uniform inside the solenoid.

∴A is true but R is false.

20. (*d*) When a closed circuit is placed in a varying magnetic field, an electric current is produced in it which is known as induced current.

The direction of induced current is given by Fleming's right hand rule.

∴ A is false but R is true.

21. (i) (*c*) A linear solenoid is an electromagnetic device that converts electrical energy into mechanical energy.

(ii) (*b*) When a soft iron bar is placed inside the solenoid, it will magnetise the iron bar as long as there is current in the circuit. Hence, the strength of the magnetic field inside the solenoid will also increase.

(iii) (*a*) The magnetic field lines produced inside the solenoid are similar to that produced by a bar magnet. The field lines inside the solenoid are parallel to each other. The magnetic field lines due to a current carrying solenoid and bar magnet are shown below

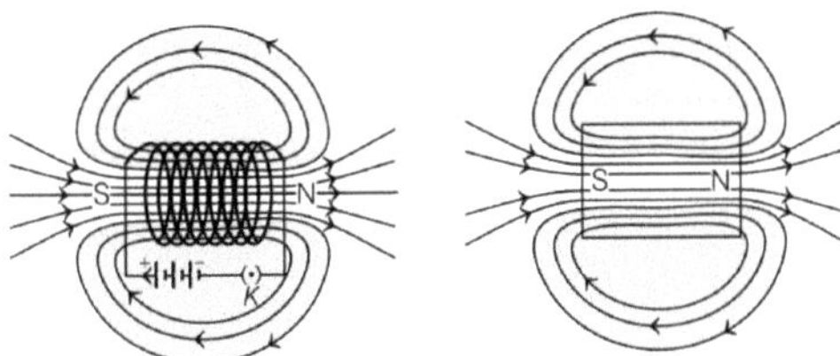

Field lines produced by a current carrying solenoid

Field lines produced by a bar magnet

(iv) (*d*) The given magnetic field *versus* current graph is linear. It is clear that magnetic field increases with increase in current. Hence, the magnetic field produced by the solenoid is directly proportional to the current.

(v) (*a*) From graph, when current = 0.8 A, the magnetic field is 13 mT.

Upto current of 1.0 mA, the magnetic field increases linearly with current.

For larger values of current (>1A), the graph does not depict any information.

22. (i) (*b*) The direction of rotation of the coil, when viewed from the front is anti-clockwise.

(ii) (*c*) Observations (I), (II) and (III) are correct while (IV) can be corrected as, when there is no current in the coil, it will stop rotating because force is produced only when there is flowing current in coil.

(iii) (*c*) Commercial electric motors do not use permanent magnet to rotate the armature because permanent magnets are weak and do not produce strong magnetic field in the region.

(iv) (*a*) Electric motor is a device which converts electrical energy into mechanical energy.

(v) (*d*) By applying, Fleming's left hand rule, the direction of force experienced by wire due to magnetic field is South-East direction.

Subjective Questions

1. The properties of magnetic field lines are

(i) They originate from North pole of a magnet and end at its South pole.

(ii) They form closed and continuous curves.

(iii) They never intersect each other.

(iv) They are uniform inside the magnet.

If two magnetic field lines intersect each other, then at the point of intersection, there will be two directions of magnetic field lines, which is not possible. Hence, the magnetic field lines never intersect with each other.

2. Magnetic field lines due to parallel current carrying conductors are shown in figure.

Magnetic field at X will be zero as both conductors are equal in magnitude and are opposite in direction.

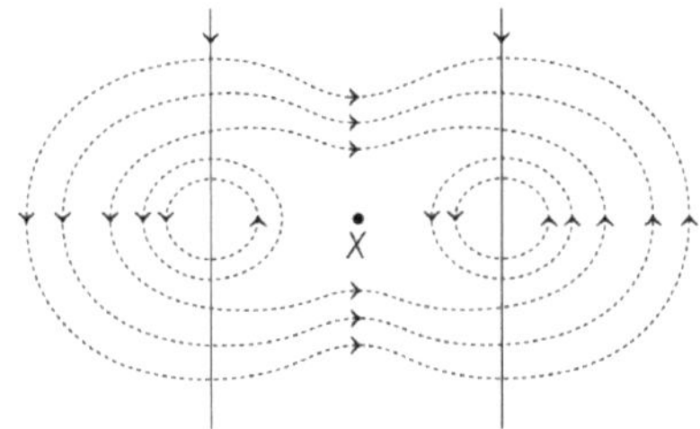

3. The strength of the magnetic field is inversely proportional to the distance i.e. $B \propto \dfrac{1}{r}$.

As, the point where magnetic field is to be determined is moved away from the straight wire carrying constant current, the magnetic field strength decreases.

4. According to the right hand thumb rule, magnetic field at P is directed into the plane of paper and at Q, it is out of the plane of paper. The strength of the magnetic field at Q will be larger as strength of the field $\propto \dfrac{1}{r \, (\text{distance})}$.

Here, $r_1 > r_2$

∴ $B_1 < B_2$ i.e. B_2 has larger field.

5. According to right hand thumb rule,

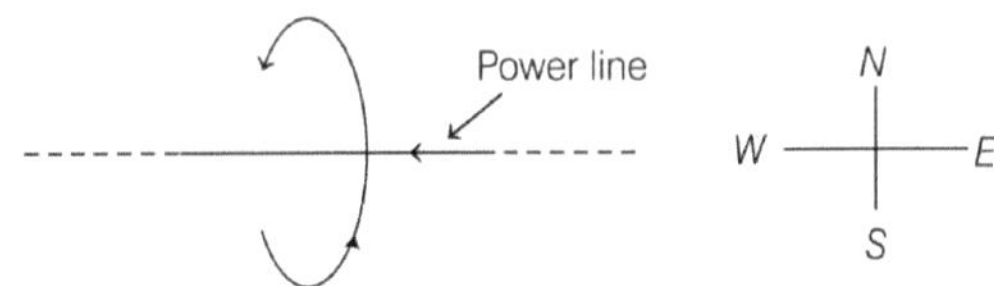

(i) The direction of magnetic field at a point above the power line is from South to North.

(ii) The direction of magnetic field at a point below the power line is from North to South.

6. The magnetic field lines are concentric circles at every point on a current carrying circular loop.

The direction of magnetic field is determined by right hand thumb rule. At the centre of the circular loop, the magnetic field lines are straight and points towards North.

The direction of magnetic field lines at the point outside the surface of the loop is shown below.

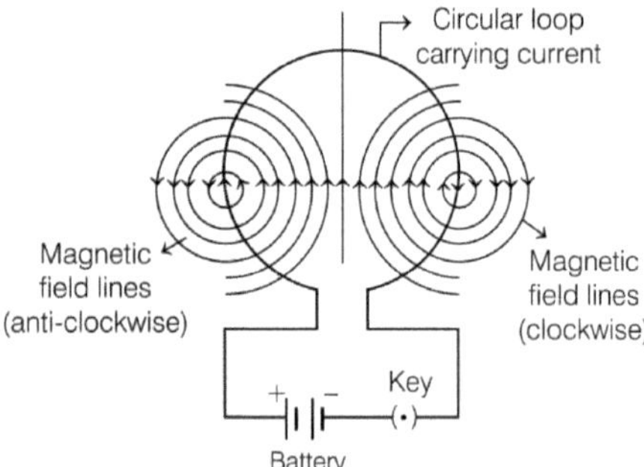

7. (i) When the coil is kept in the North-South plane and the current is flowing in the anti-clockwise through the loop, then the magnetic field is in the East to West direction.

   (ii) When the coil is in vertically East-West plane and current through the coil is in anti-clockwise direction, then the magnetic field is in the South to North direction.

   (iii) When a circular coil carrying current is placed horizontally and the direction of the current is clockwise, then the direction of the field for the observer positioned below the coil is in the downward direction.

8. A solenoid behaves like a magnet when electric current passes through it.

   One end of a solenoid behaves as a North pole and the other end behaves as a South pole. We can use a bar magnet to determine the North and South poles of a current carrying solenoid by using the property, i.e. like poles repel and unlike poles attract each other.

   The end of solenoid which attracts North pole of a bar magnet is magnetic South pole of the solenoid. The end of solenoid which repels the North pole of a bar magnet is the magnetic North pole of the solenoid.

9. (i) The magnetic field lines are crowded (convergent) near the poles of solenoid. Hence, the magnetic field is strong and divergent, where the magnetic field is weak.

   (ii) A freely suspended current carrying solenoid always points in the North-South direction even in the absence of any other magnet. Because the earth itself behaves as a magnet or solenoid to point always in a particular direction.

   (iii) The field lines around a current carrying solenoid are similar to field lines of a bar magnet. So, inside the solenoid field lines are parallel to each other and the strength of magnetic field is same i.e. uniform at all points inside a solenoid.

10. The force experienced by a current carrying conductor placed in a magnetic field is the largest, when conductor is kept perpendicular to the direction of the magnetic field.

    Fleming's left hand rule determines the direction of force on a current carrying conductor. It states that, if the forefinger (magnetic field), middle finger (current and thumb are stretched mutually, then the direction of force acting on conductor is given by thumb.

11. If a charged particle moves parallel or anti-parallel to the magnetic field, no magnetic force will act on it and remains undeflected. So, in the given condition either the charged particle enters East to West or West to East as shown below.

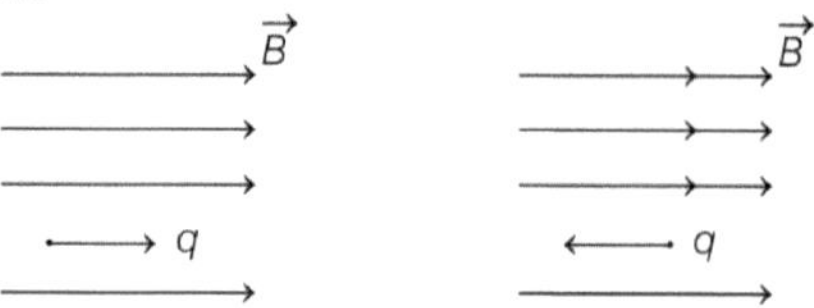

12. Here, the force acting on the α-particle is directed perpendicular to the plane of paper in inward direction by Fleming's left hand rule. If the direction of magnetic field gets reversed then the force will also act in opposite direction of α-particle i.e. the force experienced by α-particle is now in outward direction to the plane of paper.

13. (i) No, it will not experience any force. As, magnetic field exerts force on a moving charged particle only.

    (ii) No, it will not experience any force because magnetic field exerts a force in perpendicular direction to motion of the particle.

    (iii) Yes, it will experience a force in a direction perpendicular to the direction of its own motion and the direction of magnetic field can be determined by Fleming's left hand rule.

14. Force on electron is maximum in case (a), because here the direction of motion of electron is perpendicular to the direction of magnetic field **B**.

    Similarly, the force on electron is minimum in case (c) because, in this case the direction of motion of electron is along the direction of magnetic field **B**, as electron is moving along **B**.

    Hence, the direction of maximum force acting on electron is perpendicular to the plane of paper and directed into it.

15. When the gaps of the split ring commutator are aligned with the carbon brushes, then contacts are broken and the current is temporarily cut-off.

    However, the coil keeps on rotating in the same direction due to its inertia until the split ring commutator and the carbon brushes are in contact again.

16. The schematic diagram of electric motor is shown below,

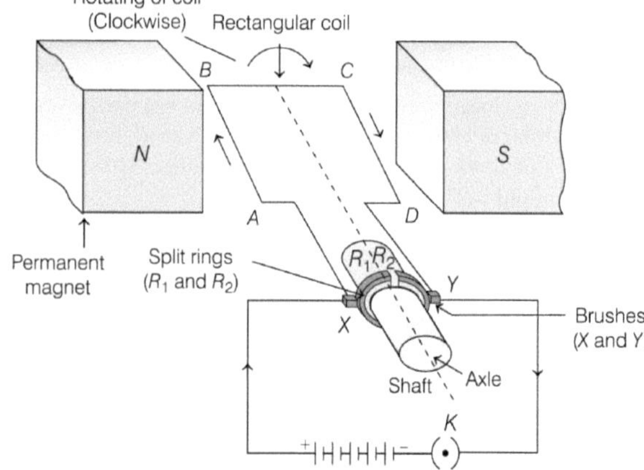

Split rings act as commutator and its function is to reverse the direction of current flowing through the coil.

17. (i) The speed of rotation of the motor can be increased by
- increasing the strength of the current in the coil.
- increasing the number of turns in the coil.
- increasing the area of the coil.
- increasing the strength of magnetic field.

(ii) Electric motor is used in electric fans, refrigerators, mixers, washing machine, computers, MP3 player, etc.

18. (i) No induced current will be produced in the loop as the constant current flowing in the straight wire produces a constant magnetic field. Hence, no induced current is produced in the loop.

(ii) Since, current in the straight wire is changing, hence induced current will be produced in it. According to Fleming's right hand rule, the current flowing in the loop will be in clockwise direction.

19. The observation that can be noted from the galvanometer reading are

(i) There are momentary galvanometer deflections that die out shortly.

(ii) The deflections are in opposite directions.

20. (i) (a) Galvanometer gets deflection in one direction.

(b) Galvanometer gets deflection in opposite direction of the first one.

(c) Galvanometer shows no deflection.

(ii) Phenomenon involved is electromagnetic induction.

21. When a magnetic compass needle pointing North and South in the absence of a nearly magnet or a current loop, it is acting upon by the earth's magnetic field only. But in the presence of a magnet or a current loop (which also has a magnetic field) the earth's magnetic field near the compass is modified and the needle is deflected from North and South directions.

The salient features of magnetic field lines are

(i) A magnetic field line is directed from North-pole to South-pole outside the magnet.

(ii) A magnetic field line is a closed and continuous curve.

(iii) The magnetic field lines never intersect each other, because if two lines meet, it means that force is acting in two directions at that point which is not possible.

(iv) Closer the field lines, stronger is the magnetic field and *vice-versa* is also true.

(v) Magnetic field lines are parallel and equidistant, those represent a uniform magnetic field.

22. (i) According to right hand thumb rule, the magnetic field produced by PQ at point R is into the plane of the paper and at point S is out of the plane of paper.

(ii) Here, $r_1 > r_2$

The magnetic field will be larger at point S as compared to that at point R.

This is because the magnetic field produced by a straight current-carrying conductor is inversely proportional to the distance from the wire. So, the magnetic field will be larger at the point which is nearer to the conductor.

As, point S is nearer to the conductor as compared to point R. So, field at S > field at R.

(iii) If the polarity of the battery is reversed, the current will be going from top to bottom in the wire and the magnetic field lines will now be in the clockwise direction on the plane, which is perpendicular to the wire carrying current.

(iv) Maxwell's right hand thumb rule is used to find the direction of the magnetic field for a straight current carrying conductor.

This law states that, if you hold the current carrying straight wire in the grip of your right hand in such a way that the stretched thumb points in the direction of current, then the direction of the curl of the fingers will give the direction of the magnetic field.

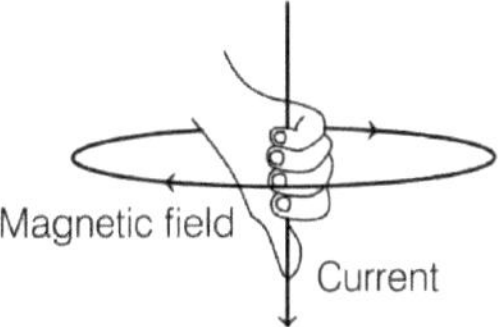

23. A solenoid is defined as a coil consisting of a large number of circular turns of insulated copper wire. These turns are wrapped closely to form a cylinder.

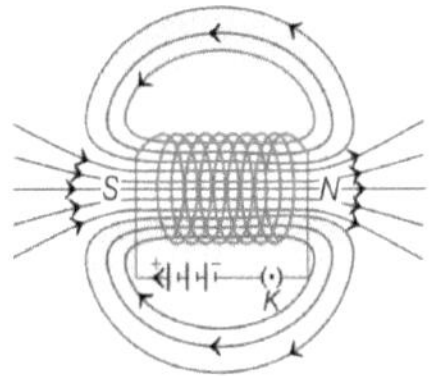

(i) Magnetic field lines of force due to a current carrying solenoid

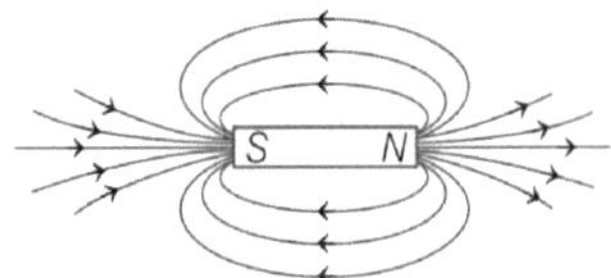

(ii) Field lines around a bar magnet

Distinguishing features are as follow
- Magnetic field outside the solenoid is negligible as compared to the bar magnet.
- Magnetic field of solenoid can be varied as per our requirement just by changing current or core of solenoid but in bar magnet it is fixed.

24. (i) Fleming's left hand rule states that, if the forefinger, thumb and middle finger of left hand are stretched mutually perpendicular to each other, such that the forefinger points along the direction of external magnetic field, middle finger indicates the direction of current, then the thumb points towards the direction of force acting on the conductor.

(ii) Electric motor is based on the principle that, when a rectangular coil is placed in a magnetic field and current is passed through it, two equal and opposite forces act on the coil which rotate it continuously.

 (iii) (a) **Armature** It is a coil wound over a soft iron core. It rotates in magnetic field, when a current flows through it.

    (b) **Brushes** They provide a sliding contact and facilitate current through armature while it rotates in field.

    (c) **Split ring** It ensures unidirectional current through armature as it rotates in field.

25. (i) An electric current produced in a closed circuit by a changing magnetic field is called an induced current. This phenomenon is called electromagnetic induction. An electric generator works on the basis of electromagnetic induction.

 (ii) Three different ways to produce induced current in a coil of wire are as following

    (a) If a magnetic field is changed around a coil, then an induced current is set up in it. It can be done by taking a bar magnet and bringing it closer to the coil or taking it away from the coil.

    (b) If a coil is moved in a magnetic field, then an induced current is set up in the coil.

    (c) By changing the magnitude of current flowing through another coil kept close to the coil.

26. (i) Since, the magnet is at rest, so no current is induced in the coil.

 (ii) Since, the bar magnet is at rest and the coil is moving away from the magnet, needle of the galvanometer coil swing towards right.

 (iii) When the magnet will move towards the coil, the meter needle swings to the left.

 (iv) The phenomenon involved in this is electromagnetic induction (EMI). In this phenomenon, current is induced in the circuit by changing the magnetic field.

 (v) Electric generators, transformers etc., are the applications of electromagnetic induction.

27. (i) Bar magnet is placed on white paper which attracts the sprinkled iron fillings.

 (ii) The bar magnet exerts its influence in the region surrounding it. Therefore, the iron fillings experience a force and this force makes iron fillings to arrange in a pattern.

 (iii) The region surrounding a magnet, in which the force of the magnet can be detected, is said to have a magnetic field.

 (iv) The iron fillings arrange themselves in a particular alignment that are called magnetic field lines. These field lines represent the region in which force of the magnet can be detected.

 (v) The relative strength of the magnetic field is shown by the degree of closeness of the field lines. The field is stronger, as the force acting on the pole of the magnet is greater, where the field lines are crowded.

28. (i) As the current in first coil changes, the magnetic field associated with it also changes. Hence, the current is induced in coil-2.

 (ii) By Faraday's law of electromagnetic induction, the induced current flows in a coil only when there is a change in the magnetic field within the coil.

 (iii) A current carrying coil has a magnetic field just like bar magnet. In experiment, if coil-1 is disconnected from battery, then the needle momentarily moves, but to the opposite side. It means the current flows in the opposite direction in coil-2.

 (iv) The induced current is found to be highest when the direction of motion of the coil is at right angles to the magnetic field.

 (v) The phenomenon associated with this is electromagnetic induction.

Chapter Test

Multiple Choice Questions

1. Which of the following is the correct representation of magnetic field lines due to a bar magnet?

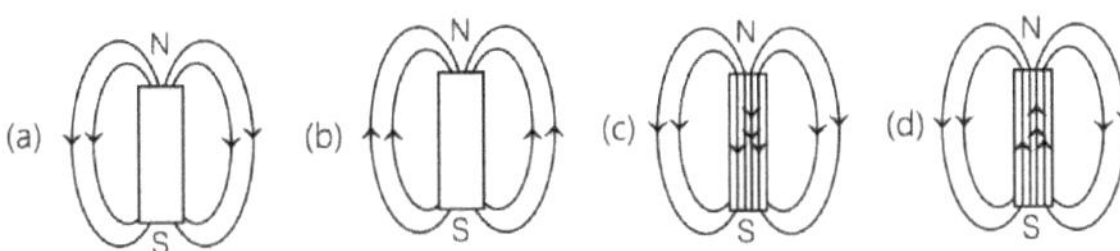

2. Choose the incorrect statement from the following regarding magnetic lines of field.
   (a) The direction of magnetic field at a point is taken to be the direction in which the North pole of a magnetic compass needle points.
   (b) Magnetic field lines are closed curves.
   (c) If magnetic field lines are parallel and equidistant, they represent zero field strength.
   (d) Relative strength of magnetic field is shown by the degree of closeness of the field lines.

3. The magnetic field at a distance r from a long wire carrying current I is 0.4 T. The value of magnetic field at a distance $2r$ is
   (a) 0.2 T   (b) 0.1 T   (c) 0.15 T   (d) 1 T

4. A coil, carrying a current is arranged within a magnetic field. The coil experiences forces that can make it move.

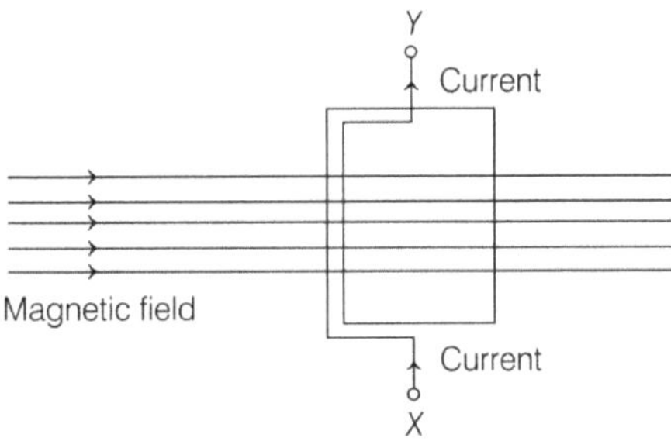

   In which direction does the coil move?
   (a) Along the magnetic field   (b) Turns about the axis XY
   (c) Out of the paper   (d) From Y to X

5. Which of the following is not the application of electric motor?
   (a) Washing machines   (b) Mixers and grinders
   (c) Electric drills   (d) Transformers

Assertion-Reasoning MCQs

Direction (Q. Nos. 6-8) Each of these questions contains two statements Assertion (A) and Reason (R). Each of these questions also has four alternative choices, any one of which is the correct answer. You have to select one of the codes (a), (b), (c) and (d) given below.

(a) Both A and R are true and R is the correct explanation of A.
(b) Both A and R are true, but R is not the correct explanation of A.
(c) A is true, but R is false.
(d) A is false, but R is true.

6. Assertion When current passes through a solenoid, then it tends to contract.

Reason The current flowing through two parallel wires in the same direction gives rise to force of attraction on each other.

7. Assertion Galvanometer is used to measure polarity.

Reason Galvanometer is an instrument which is used to detect current in any circuit.

8. Assertion A pump operated by electric motor starts pumping liquid.

Reason Motor converts mechanical energy to electrical energy.

Short Answer Type Questions

9. What are magnetic field lines? Justify the following statements.
   (i) Two magnetic field lines never intersect each other.
   (ii) Magnetic field lines are closed curves.

10. List some methods of producing magnetic fields.

11. It is established that an electric current through a conductor produces a magnetic field around it. Is there a similar magnetic field produced around a thin beam of moving (i) alpha particles, (ii) neutrons? Justify your answer in each case.

12. How can it be shown that a magnetic field exists around a wire through which a direct current is passing?

13. Meena draws magnetic field lines of field close to the axis of a current carrying circular loop. As she moves away from the centre of the circular loop, she observes that the lines keep on diverging. How will you explain her observation?

14. (i) Two circular coils P and Q are kept close to each other, of which coil P carries a current. If coil P is moved towards Q, then will some current be induced in coil Q? Give reason for your answer and name the phenomenon involved.
   (ii) What happens, if coil P is moved away from Q?
   (iii) State few methods of inducing current in a coil.

Long Answer Type Questions

15. With the help of a diagram of experimental set-up describe an activity to show that the force acting on a current carrying conductor placed in a magnetic field increases with increase in field strength.

16. How electric motor works?

Answers

Multiple Choice Questions

   1. (d)   *2. (c)*   *3. (a)*   *4. (b)*   *5. (d)*

Assertion-Reasoning MCQs

   6. (a)   *7. (b)*   *8. (c)*

For Detailed Solutions
Scan the code

CHAPTER 7

Our Environment

In this Chapter...

- Ecosystem
- Food Chain, Trophic Levels, Energy flow and Food Web
- Environmental Problems

All those things and set of conditions that influence the life of an organism like their growth, survival, development and reproduction, constitute the **environment**.

It is composed of physical surrounding (e.g. air, water), living beings (e.g. plants, animals) and climatic conditions (e.g. rainfall, temperature) of the region.

Ecosystem

It is the structural and functional unit of biosphere. It is a stable ecological unit where regular input of energy and circulation of matter takes place. The term ecosystem was coined by **AG Tansley** (in 1935).

All the interacting or living organisms (biotic components) in an area together with the non-living constituents (abiotic components) of the environment form an ecosystem, e.g. a lake, a field or a forest.

Types of Ecosystem

There are two types of ecosystem, i.e. natural and artificial ecosystem.

1. Natural Ecosystem

The naturally existing ecosystem without any human support is called as **natural ecosystem**. Depending upon the habitats, natural ecosystem may be terrestrial (desert, grassland and forest) and aquatic (ponds, lakes, estuaries and marine).

2. Artificial Ecosystem

An ecosystem which is created and maintained by humans is called as **artificial** or **man-made ecosystem**. It rely on human efforts to sustain. It does not possess a self-regulating mechanism.

e.g. Aquariums, botanical gardens, field crops, etc. Agro-ecosystem is the largest man-made ecosystem.

Components of Ecosystem

The ecosystem encompasses both living (biotic) and non-living (abiotic) components of the earth.

1. Biotic Components

These include all the living organisms present in the ecosystem, i.e. plants, animals and microorganisms.

On the basis of food, they consume the different living organisms can be categorised into three groups. These are as follows

(i) **Producers** All green plants and certain blue-green algae which can produce food by the process of photosynthesis are producers. These are also called **autotrophs**. These are the source of nutrition for rest of ecosystem.

(ii) **Consumers** These are dependent on producers for their nutritional requirement and consume food prepared by producers. These are also called **heterotrophs**.

Consumers can be further divided into the following three categories

- **Herbivores** These are **primary consumers** which feed directly on the producers, i.e. plants. e.g. Grazing animals.
- **Carnivores** The carnivores which feed on herbivores are called **secondary consumers**.
- Some are **predators** which attack and kill their prey and feed on their bodies. Some are **scavengers** that feed on dead animals that they find. These are called **tertiary consumers.**
- **Omnivores** These are animals that feed on both plants and animals, e.g. humans and bears.

(iii) **Decomposers** These are microorganisms which feed on decaying and dead organic matter. They breakdown the remains of dead animals and plants, to release simpler inorganic materials, making nutrients available to producers.

e.g. Bacteria and fungi.

2. Abiotic Components

The abiotic components of an ecosystem are the non-living components on which living organisms depends. These components are light, temperature, water, atmospheric gases, wind, etc.

Food Chain

It is a linear network of living organisms in a community through which energy is transferred in the form of food. It describes relationship of organisms about 'who eats whom'.

Food chain in nature; (a) in forest, (b) in grassland and (c) in a pond

On the basis of choice of habitat, food chains are of two types

(i) **Terrestrial food chain** It is the food chain present on land.

e.g. Grass $\rightarrow$ Insects $\rightarrow$ Snake $\rightarrow$ Hawk.

(ii) **Aquatic food chain** It is the food chain present in different water bodies.

e.g. Phytoplankton $\rightarrow$ Zooplankton $\rightarrow$ Fish $\rightarrow$ Shark

Trophic Levels

The transfer of food or energy takes place through various steps or levels in the food chain known as trophic levels.

The producers (autotrophs) are present at the **first trophic level**. They fix solar energy, making it available for consumers (heterotrophs). The herbivores or the primary consumers are found at the **second trophic level**.

Small carnivores or secondary consumers are present at the **third trophic level**. The large or the tertiary consumers form the **fourth trophic level**.

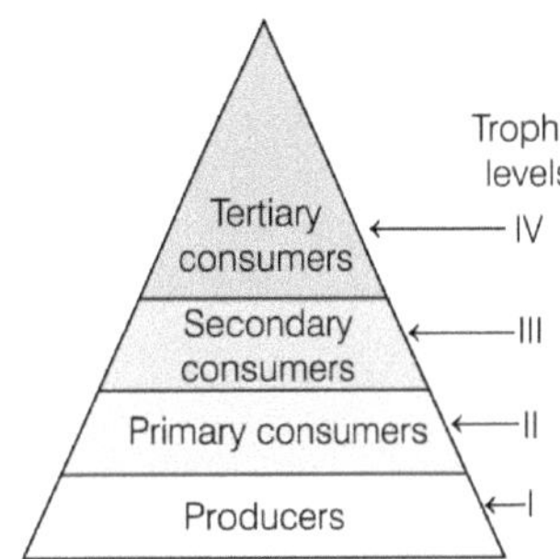

Trophic levels in an ecosystem

Energy Flow

- The green plants in a terrestrial ecosystem capture about 1% of the energy of sunlight (light energy). They convert it into food (chemical energy).
- When green plants are eaten by primary consumers, a great deal of energy is lost as heat and an average of 10% of the energy of food eaten by an organism is turned back into its own body and made available for the next level of consumers. This is known as the **10% law** (Lindemann in 1942).

Therefore, 10% can be taken as the average value for the amount of organic matter that is present at each step and reaches to the next trophic level.

- The loss of energy at each step is very large. Only a little energy is available for the next level of consumers, food chains generally consist of three or four steps.

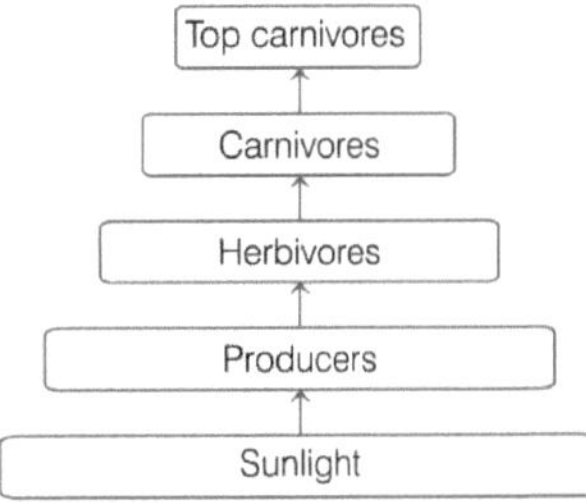

Flow of energy in an ecosystem

- The flow of energy is unidirectional, i.e. the energy which passes to the next trophic level, does not come back to the lower trophic level.

Food Web

It is the interconnection of different food chains, which correlate at various trophic levels operating in an ecosystem. Each organism is generally eaten by two or more other kinds of organisms. They in turn are eaten by several other organisms.

Food web consisting of many interlinked food chains

Environmental Problems

Human are an integral part of the environment. Various human activities pollute the environment in various ways and pose. Serious environmental problems such as biomagnification, ozone layer depletion, waste accumulation are as follows

Biological Magnification or Biomagnification

It is the phenomenon of progressive increase in the concentration of non-biodegradable toxicants in organisms at each successive trophic level. It is also called **bioconcentration**. These toxic chemicals enter the food chain through pesticides like DDT.

The maximum concentration of these chemicals gets accumulated in humans as they occupy the topmost place in any food chain.

Depletion of Ozone Layer

Ozone (O_3) is a molecule formed by three atoms of oxygen. It is found in the stratosphere. It shields the surface of the Earth from harmful ultraviolet (UV) radiations of the Sun.

Formation of Ozone Layer

Ozone is a product of UV radiations acting on oxygen (O_2) molecule. The high energy UV radiations split apart some molecular oxygen (O_2) into free oxygen (O) atoms. These atoms are very reactive and combine with the molecular oxygen to form ozone.

$$O_2 \xrightarrow{\text{UV}} O + O; O + O_2 \longrightarrow O_3 \text{ (Ozone)}$$

Ozone Depleting Substance

The increasing use of synthetic chemicals like **Chlorofluorocarbons** (CFCs) which are used in refrigerants as coolant and in fire extinguishers are responsible for ozone layer depletion.

In the atmosphere, UV radiations breakdown CFCs molecules and release chlorine atom. These atoms on reacting with ozone, dissociate ozone molecules into oxygen.

Thus, it leads to depletion of ozone layer.

Managing the Garbage We Produce

The household waste is called **garbage**. Every household produces a lot of garbage on daily basis. Improvements in our lifestyle have resulted in greater amounts of waste material generation. These waste substances can be divided into two main groups

(i) **Biodegradable substances** The substances which can be disposed off naturally by the action of microorganisms like bacteria, fungi, etc., are called biodegradable substances.
e.g. Tea leaves, waste paper, left over food, etc.

(ii) **Non-Biodegradable substances** The substances that cannot be converted into harmless simpler forms by the action of microorganisms are called non-biodegradable substances. These are toxic, harmful, may be inert and accumulate in the environment or food chain.
e.g. Plastics, insecticides, heavy metals, etc.

Methods of Waste Disposal

Various methods of waste disposal are as given below

(i) **Recycling** It is the processing of waste materials to form new products.

(ii) **Composting** Biodegradable domestic wastes can be buried in a pit, dug into ground and are converted into compost and used as manure.

(iii) **Incineration** It is burning of a substance at high temperature to form ash. It is commonly used to dispose hospital waste.

(iv) **Landfills** Solid waste is dumped into a low lying area and covered with soil.

(v) **Sewage treatment** Organic material in the sewage is allowed to settle down and decompose in large tanks. The water from these tanks is cleaned and is released into waterbodies.

(vi) **Biogas production** In some places, sewage is decomposed anaerobically to yield biogas and manure.

Note Disposable paper cups which are biodegradable in nature are now being used in trains instead of plastic cups and kulhads.

As the production of kulhads at a large scale resulted in the loss of top fertile layer of soil which leads to soil erosion, whereas, plastic cups are non-biodegradable in nature, therefore cause environmental problems.

Chapter Practice

Objective Questions

• Multiple Choice Questions

1. Which of the following is an incorrect pair?
(a) River—Natural ecosystem
(b) Air—Biotic component
(c) Crop field—Artificial ecosystem
(d) Water—Abiotic component

2. Which of the following is not a functional component of an ecosystem?
(a) Communities
(b) Decomposers
(c) Sunlight
(d) Energy flow

3. Flow of energy in an ecosystem is always
(a) unidirectional   **(NCERT Exemplar)**
(b) bidirectional
(c) multidirectional
(d) no specific direction

4. The diagram represents the flow of energy within a balanced ecosystem.

The boxes represents various trophic levels. Select the option which gives correct identification and main function or characteristic

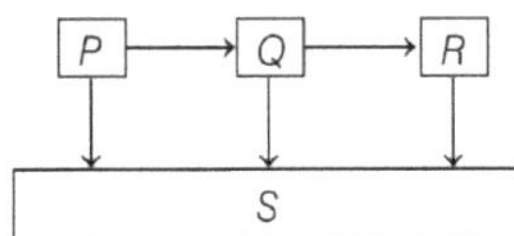

(a) P-Producers : They are heterotrophic in nature
(b) Q-Primary consumers : They eat only plants and their products
(c) R-Herbivores : They are secondary consumers
(d) S-Decomposers : They act as tertiary consumers in a food chain

5. In the given food chain, organisms are labelled as A to D. Match the labelling referred in Column I with their most suitable feature in Column II.

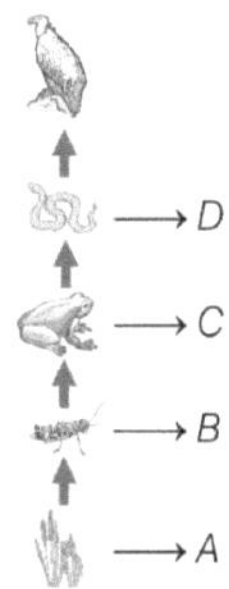

Column I		Column II
A	1.	Primary carnivore
B	2.	Secondary carnivore
C	3.	Autotrophs
D	4.	Primary consumer

Codes

	A	B	C	D			A	B	C	D
(a)	3	4	1	2		(b)	4	3	2	1
(c)	3	1	4	2		(d)	3	2	1	4

6. What will happen if deer is missing in the food chain given below?   **(NCERT Exemplar)**

$$Grass \rightarrow Deer \rightarrow Tiger$$

(a) The population of tiger increases
(b) The population of grass decreases
(c) Tiger will start eating grass
(d) The population of tiger decreases and the population of grass increases

7. The diagram shows the flow of energy through an ecosystem.

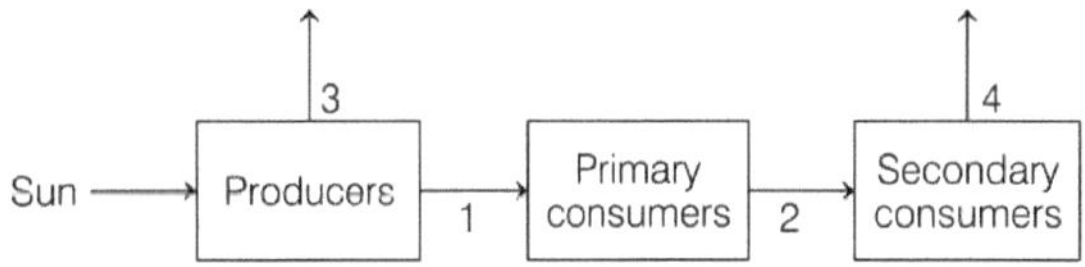

The smallest amount of energy transferred between organisms and the largest amount of energy lost to the ecosystem is represented by which arrows?

	Smallest energy transfer	Largest energy loss
(a)	4	3
(b)	2	1
(c)	2	3
(d)	1	4

8. Which of the following represents the labelled parts X and Y correctly?

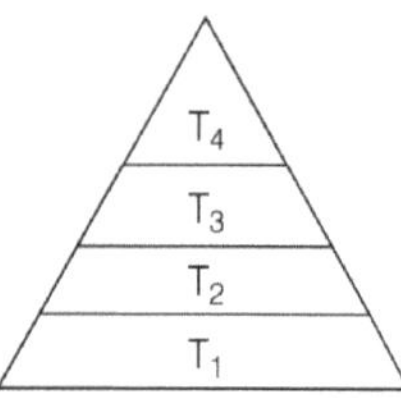

	X	Y
(a)	Primary consumer	Producer
(b)	Secondary consumer	Decomposer
(c)	Primary consumer	Secondary consumer
(d)	Carnivore	Herbivore

9. Carefully study the given pyramid of energy flow in an ecosystem. Select the option which gives correct identification and their examples.

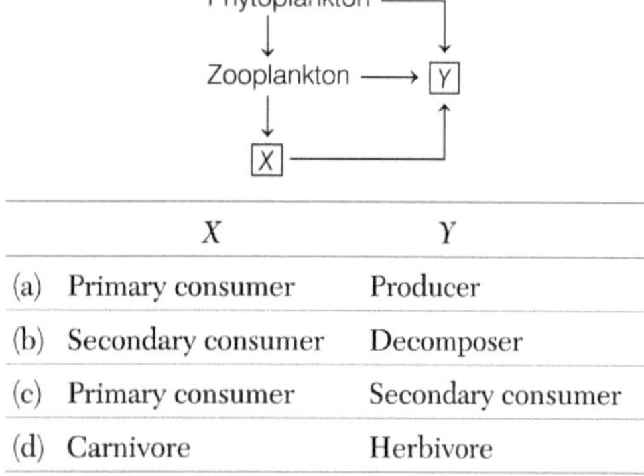

(a) T_1—Herbivores—Deer   (b) T_2—Producers—Fungi
(c) T_3—Omnivores—Bear   (d) T_4—Decomposers—Grass

10. Which of the following pyramid given below correctly represents the food chain?

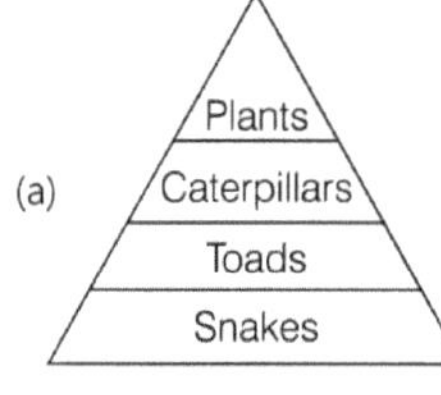

(a)

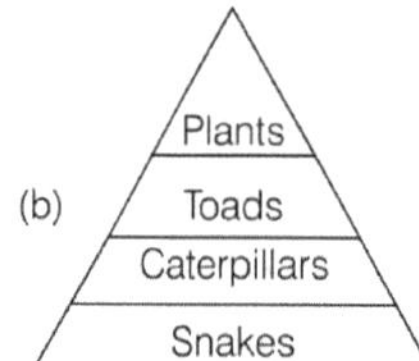

(b)

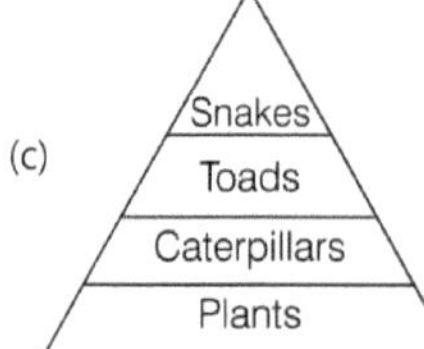

(c)

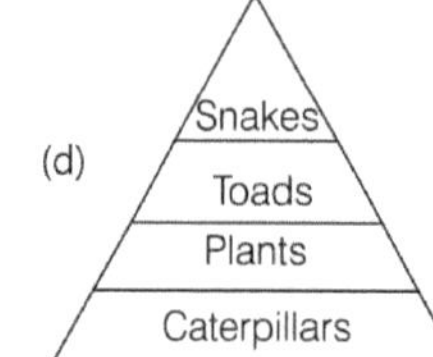

(d)

11. Identify the option that indicates the same trophic level of different organisms in the given food web.

(a) Goat, Snake, Owl   (b) Rabbit, Fox, Peacock
(c) Frog, Fish, Bird   (d) Tiger, Fox, Eagle

12. What happens in biological magnification?
(a) There is a progressive increase in the level of harmful substances through trophic levels
(b) There is a progressive increase in the body weight through trophic levels
(c) There is a progressive increase in number of organisms through trophic levels
(d) There is a progressive increase in biological activities through trophic levels

13. Which of the following chemicals cause the thinning of layer P?

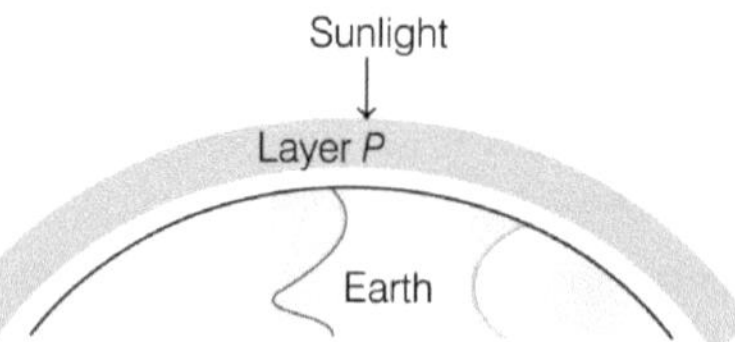

(a) Sulphur dioxide   (b) Nitrogen dioxide
(c) Chlorofluorocarbon   (d) Carbon dioxide

14. Which of the following is the correct reaction involved in formation of ozone layer?
(a) $O_2 \xrightarrow{UV} O + O; O + O_2 \longrightarrow O_3$
(b) $O + O \longrightarrow O_2; O_2 + O \longrightarrow O_3$
(c) $O_2 \xrightarrow{Infrared} O + O; O + O + O \longrightarrow O_3$
(d) $O_2 + O \longrightarrow O_3; O_3 \longrightarrow O_2 + O$

15. Burning of waste products at high temperature to form ash, reduces waste considerably. This method of waste disposal is called
(a) composting   (b) sewage treatment
(c) recycling   (d) incineration

Assertion-Reasoning MCQs

Direction (Q. Nos. 16-20) Each of these questions contains two statements, Assertion (A) and Reason (R). Each of these questions also has four alternative choices, any one of which is the correct answer. You have to select one of the codes (a), (b), (c) and (d) given below.

(a) Both A and R are true and R is the correct explanation of A
(b) Both A and R are true, but R is not the correct explanation of A
(c) A is true, but R is false
(d) A is false, but R is true

16. Assertion Biotic components of an ecosystem include all the living organisms present in that ecosystem.

Reason Biotic components also include wind, gases, light, etc.

17. Assertion Food chains generally consist of more than four trophic levels.

Reason There is loss of energy at each trophic level and very little usable energy remains after four trophic levels.

18. Assertion Producers are present at the first trophic level.

Reason Consumers or heterotrophs fix energy and make it available for autotrophs.

19. Assertion Certain pesticides and other chemicals used to protect our crops from diseases and pests are non-biodegradable.

Reason They do not get accumulated at various trophic levels.

20. Assertion Ozone layer shields the surface of Earth from UV radiations.

Reason The UV radiations are highly damaging to organisms.

Case Based MCQs

21. Read the following and answer the questions from (i) to (v) given below

A group of scientists analysed samples of four different animals from a river for possible accumulation of DDT in their body due to biomagnification. The result obtained is shown in the given graph.

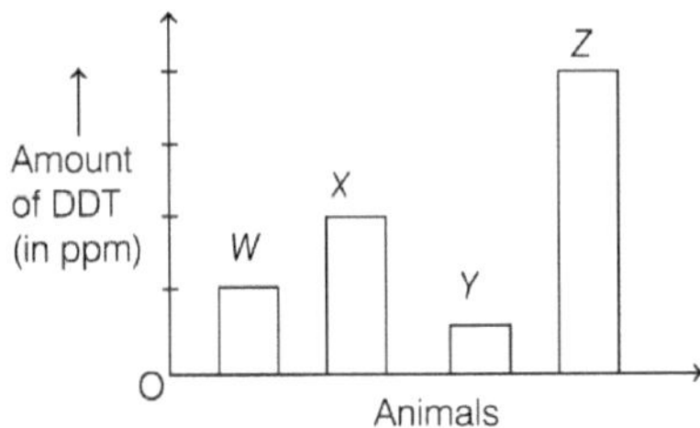

(i) The correct order of animals in food chain operating in a river is
(a) $W \to X \to Y \to Z$
(b) $Y \to W \to X \to Z$
(c) $Z \to X \to W \to Y$
(d) $X \to W \to Z \to Y$

(ii) If concentration of DDT in W is estimated to be 0.4 ppm, then amount of DDT in Y and Z would respectively be
(a) 0.02 ppm and 2 ppm
(b) 2 ppm and 0.02 ppm
(c) 0.3 ppm and 0.5 ppm
(d) 0.04 ppm and 0.02 ppm

(iii). Due to biomagnification, which of the following substances accumulate and go on concentrating at each trophic level?
(a) Biodegradable substances
(b) Non-biodegradable substances
(c) Biotic components
(d) Abiotic components

(iv) The decomposers are not included in the food chain. The correct reason for the same is because decomposers :
(a) act at every trophic level of the food chain
(b) do not breakdown organic compounds
(c) convert organic material to inorganic forms
(d) release enzymes outside their body to convert organic material to inorganic forms

(v) Which amongst the following are hazardous for the environment?
I. Pesticides   II. Fertilisers
III. Heavy metals   IV. Manures

Codes
(a) I, II and IV   (b) I and II
(c) I, II and III   (d) Only IV

22. Read the following and answer the questions from (i) to (v) given below

Sheenu took three different types of solid wastes R, S and T. She buried them under the soil in a pit, as she wanted to study their rate of decomposition. Her findings are shown in the given graph.

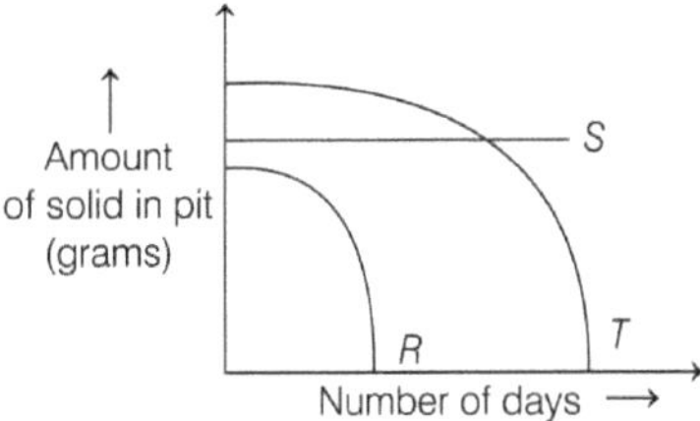

(i) Which of the following waste does not decompose at all?
(a) R (b) S
(c) T (d) Both (a) and (c)

(ii) Choose the correct statements regarding non-biodegradable wastes.
   I. Easily decomposed by fungi.
   II. Enter into food chain and get magnified.
   III. Biological in origin.
   IV. Cause soil pollution.
   Codes
   (a) I and II   (b) II and IV
   (c) I and IV   (d) II and III

(iii) Which of the following solid waste comes under the category of R?
   (a) Cow dung   (b) Leather shoes
   (c) Plastic bottles   (d) Electronic waste

(iv) Which of the following is the safe method of disposal of the non-biodegradable waste?
   (a) By recycling
   (b) By burning
   (c) By disposing them in water bodies
   (d) By mixing with biodegradable waste

(v) Incineration is another method of waste disposal which is used for
   (a) kitchen waste
   (b) electronic waste
   (c) biomedical waste
   (d) plastic waste

PART 2
Subjective Questions

• Short Answer Type Questions

1. Define an ecosystem. Draw a block diagram to show the flow of energy in an ecosystem. **(CBSE 2019)**

2. (i) What do you understand by the term ecosystem?
   (ii) Autotrophs are at the first level of food chain. Give reason.
   (iii) In a food chain of frogs, grass, insects and snakes, assign trophic level to frogs. To which category of consumers do they belong to? **(CBSE 2020)**

3. What is the role of decomposers in the ecosystem? **(NCERT)**

4. Natural water bodies are not regularly cleaned whereas an aquarium needs regular cleaning. Why? **(CBSE 2019)**

5. How does study of food chain in an area or habitat help us? Give an example of four steps of food chain operating in a large lake.

6. Based on their feeding habits, differentiate between parasites and decomposers.

7. What are trophic levels? Give an example of a food chain and state the different trophic levels in it. **(NCERT)**

8. Number of trophic levels is limited to 3-4 in a food chain. Give reason.

9. What will happen if we kill all the organisms in one trophic level?

10. State 10% law. Explain with an example how energy flows through different trophic levels.

11. Indicate the flow of energy in an ecosystem. Why it is unidirectional? **(NCERT Exemplar)**

12. What do you mean by biological magnification?

13. What is biological magnification? Will the levels of this magnification be different at different levels of the ecosystem? **(NCERT Exemplar)**

14. Write the major cause of ozone depletion. What steps should be taken to limit the damage to ozone layer?

15. Explain how ozone being a deadly poison can still perform an essential function for our environment. **(CBSE 2020)**

16. Give reason why a food chain cannot have more than four trophic levels? **(CBSE 2020)**

17. (i) Explain the role of UV radiation in producing ozone layer.
   (ii) Mention the reaction involved.
   (iii) Why is excessive use of CFCs a cause of concern?

18. How is ozone formed in the upper atmosphere? State its importance. What is responsible for its depletion? Write one harmful effect of ozone depletion. **(CBSE 2019)**

19. Give some methods that could be applied to reduce accumulation of pesticides in our body.

20. How can you help in reducing the problem of waste disposal? Give any two methods.

21. If all the waste we generate is biodegradable, will this have no impact on the environment?

22. Give any two ways in which non-biodegradable substances would affect the environment.

23. Why should biodegradable and non-biodegradable wastes be discarded in two separate dustbins?

24. 'Effective segregation of wastes at the point of generation is very important'. Justify this statement.

25. Sheenu went to a picnic where she saw a pond. Her teacher gives her an assignment to draw the pond ecosystem and show its different components. Help her to complete the assignment.

26. Name the wastes which are generated in your house daily. What measures would you take for their disposal? **(NCERT Exemplar)**

27. A modern insecticide has been introduced with certain new properties like, accumulation in the bodies of predators, broken down by soil bacteria, easily washed into lakes and rivers and taken up by plant roots.

Among all these properties, which one will help in reducing or keeping the level of environment pollution to lowest?

28. Mona eats curd and yogurt and follows vegetarian diet. For this food intake, what should be the trophic level occupied by her in a food chain ?

• Long Answer Type Questions

29. What are decomposers? What will be the consequence of their absence in an ecosystem? **(NCERT Exemplar)**

30. (i) What are consumers? What will be the consequence of the absence of primary consumers in an ecosystem?
(ii) What will be the direction of energy transfer in each of the following cases?
(a) Grasshopper eaten by a frog
(b) Deer feeds on grass
(c) Deer eaten by a lion

31. (i) Will the impact of removing all the organisms in a trophic level be different for different trophic levels?
(ii) Can the organisms of any trophic level be removed without causing any damage to the ecosystem? **(NCERT Exemplar)**

32. (i) 'Energy flow in a food chain is unidirectional'. Justify this statement.
(ii) Explain how the pesticides enter a food chain and subsequently get into our body. **(CBSE 2014)**

33. (i) How do food chains get shortened? How does the shortening of food chain affect the biosphere?
(ii) How will you justify that vegetarian food habits give us more calories?

34. Explain some harmful effects of agricultural practices on the environment. **(NCERT Exemplar)**

35. What is ozone and how does it affect any ecosystem? **(NCERT Exemplar)**

36. (i) What is 'environmental pollution'?
(ii) Distinguish between biodegradable and non-biodegradable pollutants.
(iii) Choose the non-biodegradable pollutants from the list given below
Paper, DDT, Radioactive waste, Plastic, Insecticides.

37. Suggest any five activities in daily life, which are eco-friendly. **(NCERT Exemplar)**

38. What are the reasons for the shift from plastic to kulhads and then finally to paper cups? **(CBSE 2020)**

• Case Based Questions

39. Read the following and answer the questions from (i) to (v) given below

Food web is the interconnection of different food chains, which correlate at various trohpic levels operating in an ecosystem.

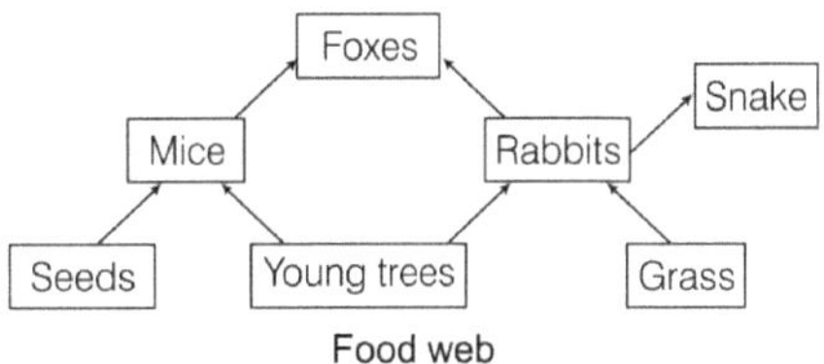

(i) How many food chains are present in the given food web?
(ii) Name the primary consumer in the given food web.
(iii) How much percentage of energy is less at each trophic level?
(iv) If all the foxes are killed due to a disease, what will be your observations about food web?
(v) Name the organism in which accumulation of toxic non-biodegradable substances is the lowest.

40. Read the following and answer the questions from (i) to (v) given below

Food chains are very important for the survival of most species. When only one element is removed from the food chain it can result in extinction of a species in some cases.

The foundation of the food chain consists of primary producers.Primary producers or autotrophs can use either solar energy or chemical energy to create complex organic compounds, whereas species at higher trophic levels cannot and so must consume producers or other life that itself consumes producers.

Because the Sun's light is necessary for photosynthesis, most life could not exist if the Sun disappeared.

Even so, it has recently been discovered that there are some forms of life, chemotrophs that appear to gain all their metabolic energy from chemosynthesis driven by hydrothermal vents, thus showing that some life may not require solar energy to thrive.

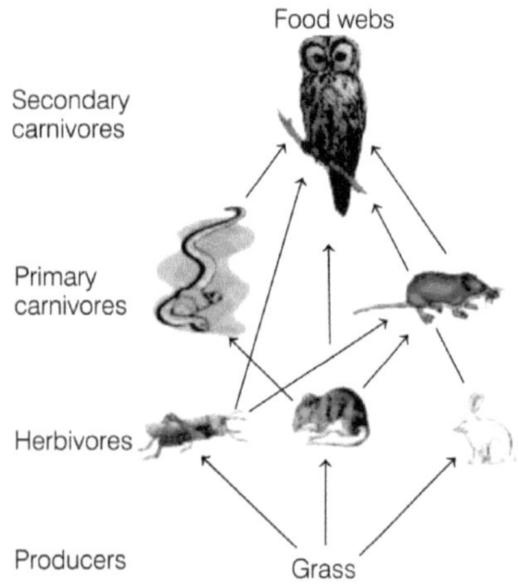

(i) If 10,000 J solar energy falls on green plants in a terrestrial ecosystem, what percentage of solar energy will be converted into food energy?

(ii) Why decomposers are not included in the food chain?

(iii) How primary consumers are different from primary carnivores?

(iv) State one reason that limits the number of trophic levels in a food chain.

(v) In the given food web, name the organism in which highest accumulation of toxic substance is found.

41. Read the following and answer the questions from (i) to (v) given below

Each organism is generally eaten by two or more other kinds of organisms. They in turn are eaten by several other organisms.

Study the figure which shows the similar relationship between various organisms of ecosystem through a food web.

Analyse the populations and their effects on each other.

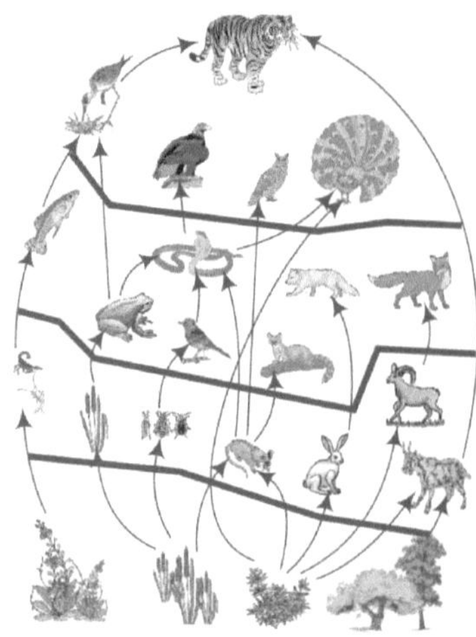

(i) How many trophic levels are there in the longest food chain?

(ii) What is the role of rabbit in the given food web?

(iii) Give the significance of food web.

(iv) Why do all food chain start with plants?

(v) What leads an organism to increase in number?

42. Read the following and answer the questions from (i) to (v) given below

To study the ozone layer depletion, Mrs. Sharma, a science teacher draw the given flow chart on the blackboard. She asked students to fill the bubbles labelled as 1-5 in the flow chart.

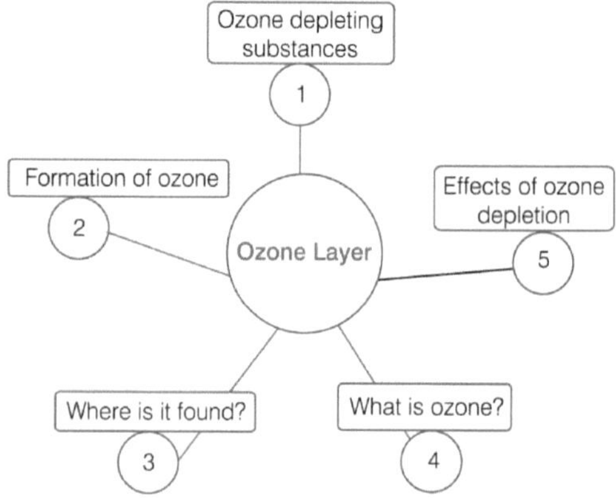

(i) What are ozone depleting substance?

(ii) How is ozone formed?

(iii) Ravi want to drawn a ozone layer in a diagram showing different layers of atmosphere, where he should label it?

(iv) What is the difference between good ozone and bad ozone?

(v) What could be the effect of ozone depletion?

EXPLANATIONS

Objective Questions

1. (*b*) Option (*b*) is incorrect pair and can be corrected as Air is abiotic (non-living) component of ecosystem.

2. (*d*) The flow of energy is not a functional component of an ecosystem.

3. (*a*) Flow of energy in an ecosystem is always unidirectional.

4. (*b*) In the given diagram, *P* represents producers as every food chain begins with plants which are autotrophic in nature. *Q* is primary consumer that depends on plants directly, i.e. they are herbivores.

R could be carnivores or omnivores and acts as secondary consumer in the food chain as it depends upon plant eating animals.

S are decomposers that help in cleaning our environment by acting on dead and decaying organic matter and decompose them into soil.

Thus, option (*b*) gives correct identification and main function or characteristic.

5. (*a*) The given food chain is as follows

Grass → Grasshopper → Frog → Snake → Hawk
  A   *B*   *C*   *D*   *E*

A. Grass acts as producer in the given food chain as it is autotrophic in nature and make its own food in the presence of sunlight. All living organisms depend upon plants directly or indirectly.

B. Grasshoppers are primary consumers as they feed on plants (grass) directly.

C. Frogs are primary carnivores as they feed on plant-eating animals (grasshoppers).

D. Snakes are secondary carnivores as they eat flesh of other animals and feed on primary carnivores majorly.

Thus, option (*a*) is correct.

6. (*d*) If deer is missing in the given food chain, there will not be sufficient food for the tigers. Some of the tigers will die because of starvation and hence, the population of tigers will decrease. Since grass is eaten by deers, the population of grass will also increase when deer is missing.

7. (*c*) In a food chain, only around 10 % of the available energy is passed on to the next trophic level. The rest of the energy is lost to the ecosystem in form of heat.

As the trophic level increases, the amount of energy transfer decreases.

Secondary consumers receive the smallest amount of energy from primary consumers.

Hence, arrow 2 shows smallest energy transfer, whereas arrow 3 shows largest energy loss as 90% of energy at producer level is lost to the ecosystem, whereas only 10% of energy is transferred to the primary consumers.

8. (*b*) In the given food chain, *X* could be small fish who feeds on zooplankton.

Hence, *X* is a secondary consumer. *Y* acts on every trophic level which means it is a decomposer who acts on dead remains of living organisms.

9. (*c*) In the given pyramid of energy, T_1, T_2, T_3 and T_4 represent the trophic levels. T_1 represents plants which are producers, e.g. grass, T_2 represents herbivores who are plant-eating animals, e.g. deer. T_3 represents both carnivores or omnivores who feeds on plant-eating animals, e.g. bear. T_4 represents tertiary consumers who feed on other animals, e.g. lion,

Hence, option (c) is correct.

10. (*c*) *C* represents the correct pyramid in a food chain. Population of producers (plants) are maximum in a food chain to support other animals. As the trophic level increases, the number of organisms decreases.

11. (*c*) The given food web contains various food chains interconnected with each other.

Frog, bird and fish act as secondary consumers in their respective food chains, therefore acquire same trophic level , i.e. third trophic level in their respective food chain.

12. (*a*) Biomagnification is the phenomenon of progressive increase in the concentration of non-biodegradable toxicants in organisms at each successive trophic level. It is also called bioconcentration.

13. (*c*) The layer *P* is ozone layer that protects us from harmful UV rays of Sun. Chlorofluorocarbon is responsible for depletion of ozone layer.

14. (*a*) High energy UV radiations split apart molecular oxygen (O_2) into free oxygen atoms (O) which are highly reactive and combine with molecular oxygen to form ozone layer.

15. (*d*) Incineration involve degradation of wastes by burning them at high temperature.

16. (*c*) A is true, but R is false.

All living organisms are biotic components of ecosystem whereas all non-living things such as wind, gases, light, water, etc., are abiotic components of ecosystem.

17. (*d*) A is false, but R is true.

Food chains generally consist up to three or four trophic levels because there is loss of energy at each trophic level and very little usable energy remains after three or four trophic levels.

18. (*c*) A is true, but R is false.

Autotrophs (producers) are present at the first trophic level because they fix solar energy, making it available for consumers or heterotrophs.

19. (*c*) A is true, but R is false.

Certain pesticides and other chemicals used to protect our crops from diseases and pests do not get degraded (i.e. non-biodegradable). So, they get accumulated progressively at each trophic level.

20. (*a*) Both A and R are true and R is the correct explanation of A. Ozone layer is present in the stratosphere region of our atmosphere. It shields the surface of Earth from harmful UV radiations of Sun which are highly damaging and can cause various health issues and diseases such as skin cancer, cataract, etc.

21. (i) (*b*) Due to biomagnification, the concentration of harmful chemicals such as DDT increases at each successive trophic level.
The maximum concentration of DDT gets accumulated in Z and least is found in Y.
Therefore, the correct order of animals in food chain is $Y \rightarrow W \rightarrow X \rightarrow Z$.

(ii) (*a*) The concentration of DDT is found to be less in organisms of lower trophic level and higher in organisms of higher trophic levels.
If the amount of DDT in W is estimated to be 0.4 ppm then in Y, it has to be less than 0.4 ppm, i.e. 0.02 ppm and in Z, it has to be more the 0.4 ppm, i.e 2 ppm.
Hence, option (*a*) is correct.

(iii) (*b*) The progressive increase in the concentration of non-biodegradable toxicants in organisms at each successive trophic level is known as biomagnification.

(iv) (*a*) Decomposers are microorganisms that breakdown dead and decayed organisms into simpler inorganic materials, making nutrients available to primary producers. They act at every trophic level of the food chain.
Hence, they do not have a fix position in the food chain.

(v) (*c*) Toxic chemicals and non-biodegradable substances such as pesticides, fertilisers and heavy metals are hazardous to the environment, whereas manures are organic substance made by decomposing dead and decayed living organisms buried under the soil.

22. (i) (*b*) S is the solid waste that does not decompose at all. According to the graph, there is no change in number of days for the amount of decomposition take place in S waste.
Hence, it is a non-biodegradable waste.

(ii) (*b*) Substances which do not decompose by the action of microorganisms present in the soil are known as non-biodegradable substances.
They enter into food chain through soil and get magnified into higher trophic levels. In soil, they also cause pollution which decreases the soil fertility.

(iii) (*a*) Solid waste R completely decomposes in very few days which means it is an easily decomposable biodegradable waste. e.g. Cow dung, fruit pulp, etc.

(iv) (*a*) Non-biodegradable waste can be decomposed by recycling or by dumping underground into landfills.

(v) (*c*) Incineration is a method of waste disposal in which burning of substances take place at high temperature to form ash. It is used to dispose off hospital or harmful wastes of biomedical industries.

Subjective Questions

1. Ecosystem is defined as the structural and functional unit of biosphere. It is a stable ecological unit where continuous input of energy and circulation of matter occurs.

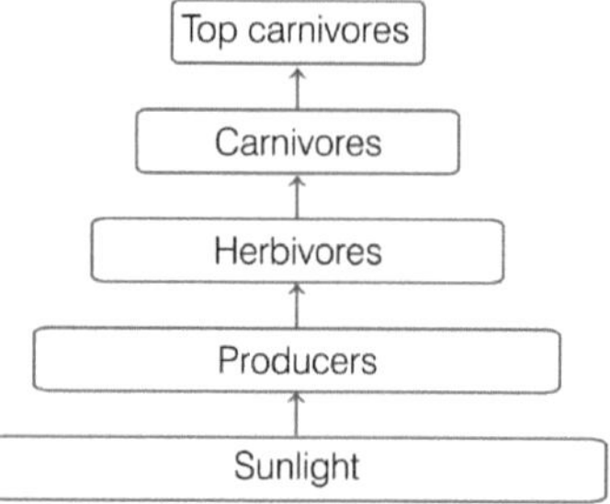

Flow of energy in an ecosystem

2. (i) Ecosystem is the structural and functional unit of biosphere and is a stable ecological unit where regular input of energy and circulation matter takes place.

(ii) Autotrophs can make their own food in the presence of sunlight. They are the ultimate source of energy for each and every organism of a food chain. Hence, every chain always starts with producers (autotrophs) that is why they are placed at the first trophic level of food chain.

(iii) In given food chain, Grass→ Insects→ Frogs→ Snakes

Frogs assign at third trophic level. They acts as secondary consumers who feeds of primary consumers (i.e. insects).

3. Organisms that feed on dead plants and animals are called decomposers, e.g. bacteria, fungi, etc. They breakdown the complex organic compounds present in the dead remains into simpler substances and obtain nutrition from them. These substances are released into the soil and to the atmosphere.

Thus, they play the following roles
(i) They help in recycling of materials, replenishment of the soil's nutrients, etc.
(ii) They clean our surroundings by decomposing dead organisms and organic wastes.

4. Natural water bodies are example of natural ecosystem. They exist naturally without any human support, whereas aquarium is an artificial ecosystem which is created and maintained by humans. It rely on human efforts to sustain. It does not possess a self-regulating mechanism.

5. The study of food chain in an area or habitat helps in
(i) understanding the energy transfer through organisms.
(ii) understanding the ecological balance in a habitat or ecosystem.

(iii) understanding harmful human activities and disruption of ecological balance, if any.

An example of four steps of food chain operating in a large lake is as follows

Algae → Protozoan → Small fish → Big fish.

6. Parasites are organisms (animals or plants) that live in or an other organism (host) and take benefits by deriving nutrients from it, i.e. they get food or protection from host organism, e.g. *Cuscuta*.

On other hands, decomposers are organisms that breakdown dead or decaying organisms into simple inorganic substances. e.g. Fungi.

7. The transfer of food or energy takes place through various levels in the food chain, which are known as trophic levels. e.g.

Trees	→	Rabbit	→	Snake	→	Hawk
(First trophic level)		(Second trophic level)		(Third trophic level)		(Fourth trophic level)
[Producers]		[I consumer]		[II consumer]		[III consumer]

8. In a food chain, about 80-90% of the energy available at a trophic level is lost during its transfer to next trophic level. Hence, amount of energy available goes on decreasing at each successive trophic level.

If a plant fixes 4000 J energy, then next three successive trophic levels will get 400 J, 40 J and 4 J, respectively (according to 10% law). If another level is added in a food chain then it will get only 0.4 J energy. Thus, usually food chains remain shorter and limited to 3-4 trophic levels only.

9. If we kill all the organisms in one trophic level, the lower trophic level will grow more in number and the higher trophic level will not survive.

Hence, flow of energy from one trophic level to other will not take place.

10. According to 10% law, only 10% of the energy entering a particular trophic level of organisms is available for transfer to the next higher trophic level.

The flow of energy through a food chain is unidirectional and it moves progressively through various trophic levels as follows

(i) Green plants capture 1% of energy of the sunlight that falls on their leaves and convert it into food energy.

(ii) When green plants are eaten by primary consumers, a great deal of energy is lost as heat to the environment. On an average only 10% of food eaten is turned into its own body and made available for the next level of consumers.

(iii) Thus, 10% can be taken as average value of the amount of organic matter present at each step and reaches the next level of consumers.

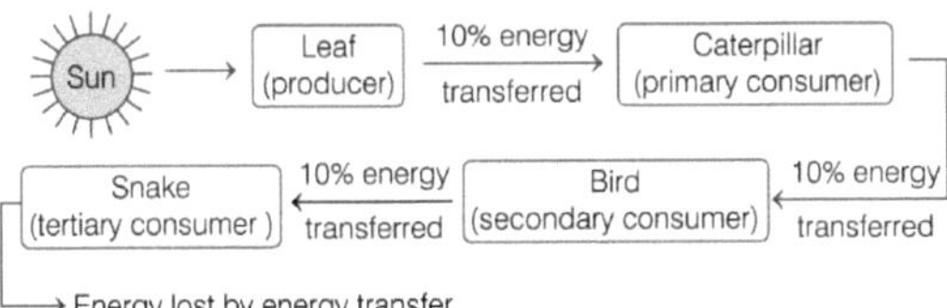

11. The flow of energy in an ecosystem occurs in the following sequence

Sun ⟶ Producer ⟶ Herbivore ⟶ Carnivore
(Primary consumer)   (Secondary consumer)

The flow of energy is unidirectional because of the reasons given below

(i) Energy flows progressively from one trophic level to another and cannot revert back. Energy given out as heat is lost to the environment and does not return to be used again.

(ii) The available energy decreases at higher trophic level. Out of the total energy available at a particular trophic level, only 10% is passed on to the next trophic level, making it impossible for energy to flow in the reverse direction.

12. Biological magnification also known as biomagnification is the phenomenon of progressive increase in the concentration of non-biodegradable toxicants in organisms at each successive trophic level.

13. Biological magnification refers to the increase in the concentration of certain toxicants at each successive trophic level.

No, the levels of magnification will not be same in all trophic levels. When the chemicals do not get degraded and get accumulated progressively at each trophic level, it leads to biomagnification. Biomagnification is more in organisms of higher trophic levels.

14. Depletion of ozone is mainly caused due to the excessive use of Chlorofluorocarbons (CFCs). These are synthetic chemicals which are used as refrigerants and in fire extinguishers.

Steps which should be taken to limit the damage to ozone layer include

(a) Minimising the use of aerosol spray propellants containing fluorocarbons and chlorofluorocarbons.

(b) Exercising control over large scale nuclear explosions and limited use of supersonic planes.

15. Ozone layer filter the Sun's ultraviolet radiation (UV-B), thereby protecting the environment from its harmful effects and also play key role in regulating the temperature.

16. The energy and biomass decrease from lower to higher trophic levels, so the length of food chain is restricted and cannot have more than four trophic levels.

17. (i) UV radiation acts on the O_2 molecule. Higher energy of UV split apart O_2.

(ii) $O_2 \xrightarrow{\text{UV}} O + O$

$O + O_2 \longrightarrow O_3$
(Ozone)

(iii) CFCs rise up in stratosphere where UV radiation splits them releasing molecular chlorine (Cl^-). It reacts with O_3 and releases oxygen, so O_3 gets depleted.

18. Ozone at the higher levels of the atmosphere is a product of UV radiations acting on oxygen (O_2) molecule. The high energy UV radiations split apart some molecular oxygen (O_2) into free oxygen (O) atoms. These atoms are very reactive and combine with the molecular oxygen to form ozone.

$$O_2 \xrightarrow{\text{UV}} O + O$$
$$O + O_2 \longrightarrow O_3$$
$$\text{(Ozone)}$$

It shields the surface of the Earth from harmful ultraviolet (UV) radiations of the Sun.

Due to environmental pollution, ozone layer has began to deplete in the 1980s.

This was mainly due to the increasing use synthetic chemicals like **Chlorofluorocarbons** (CFCs). These are used in refrigerants as coolant and in fire extinguishers.

Due to depletion of ozone layer harmful UV rays can penetrate or enter our atmosphere.These radiations are highly damaging to organisms. They can cause skin cancer in human beings, damage eyes (cause disease called **cataract**), decrease crop yield, disturb global rainfall, etc.

19. Following methods could be applied to reduce the accumulation of pesticides in our body.
 (i) Minimise the use of pesticides
 (ii) Consuming washed fruits and vegetables
 (iii) Developing vegetarian feeding habits
 (i.e. feed upon plants as plants belong to lower trophic level so, they have less accumulation of insecticides, whereas organisms of higher trophic level have higher concentration of insecticides and pesticides).

20. We can reduce the problem of waste disposal by the following methods
 - **Recycling** The solid wastes such as paper, plastics, glass and metals, etc., are recyclable. So, waste paper can be sent to paper mills for reprocessing to form newspaper. The plastic articles can be melted and remoulded again to make new articles.
 - **Biodegradable waste** The waste such as left over food, fruits, animal dung, peels of vegetables can be converted into compost by burying them in a pit dug in ground and can be used as manure.

21. If all the waste is biodegradable, then there will be no accumulation of waste on the Earth and it would be a cleaner place to live.

But if, this biodegradable waste is too large in amount then its slow degradation may lead to air pollution (due to release of gases) as well as water and land pollution.

22. The two ways in which non-biodegradable substances would affect the environment are
 (i) They make the environment poisonous and unfit for survival of living forms of life.
 (ii) They block the transfer of energy and minerals in the ecosystem.

23. Biodegradable materials are broken down by microorganisms present in nature into simple harmless substances. Non-biodegradable materials need a different treatment like heat and temperature for disposal and hence, both should be discarded in two different dustbins.

24. Effective segregation of waste as biodegradable and non-biodegradable is much easier to recycle. Biodegradable waste used to make manure can out of compost, whereas non-biodegradable waste could be recycled and reused for various purposes. Also effective segregation of wastes means that less waste goes to landfill, which makes it cheaper and better for people and environment.

25. A pond ecosystem refers to freshwater ecosystem where there are various organisms dependent on each other with the prevailing water environment for their nutrients and survival.

Phytoplankton $\rightarrow$ Zooplankton $\rightarrow$ Small fish $\rightarrow$ Big fish

There are two components of the pond ecosystem
 (i) **Abiotic** It includes water, dissolved minerals, oxygen and carbon dioxide. Sunlight is the main source of energy.
 (ii) **Biotic** It consists of phytoplanktons, zooplanktons, aquatic insects, fishes and other aquatic animals. These organisms are classified as producers, consumers and decomposers.

26. The waste generated in our house and measures for its disposal are given in the table below

Household wastes	Measures for disposal
Kitchen waste like bottles, plastics, food, etc.	Prepare a compost pit
Paper wastes like newspaper, envelopes, etc.	Should be recycled
Plastic bags	Should be safely dumped in garbage bins for non-biodegradable wastes
Vegetable/fruit peels/rind	Can be placed near trees/plants, so that on decomposition enrich the soil with nutrients
All other wastes	Segregation into biodegradable and non-biodegradable wastes

27. Insecticides are non-biodegradable chemicals added to crop fields to stop the growth of insects infecting the crops.

Modern insecticides are being developed keeping in mind, the harm they cause to the environment and its components.

Biodegradable insecticides can be decomposed into harmless substances, which will subsequently be dispersed in their specific pathways and cause no pollution.

Non-biodegradable insecticides build up in the fat tissues of the body and pass on to organisms that feed on them.

Hence, they accumulate along the food chain resulting in significant amounts in the tissues of consumers at the highest trophic level.

The property of newly developed insecticide includes that it can easily get decomposed into simpler components by soil bacteria.

28. As Mona follows vegetarian diet along with milk products. She should be considered as occupying third trophic level because the curd is prepared by the milk of cow/buffalo by the action of bacteria, but the energy of the milk is getting transferred from cow to Mona, so Mona is at the third trophic level.

$$\text{Grass} \longrightarrow \text{Cow (milk)} \longrightarrow \text{Human}$$
(First trophic level) (Second trophic level) (Third trophic level)

29. Organisms which breakdown the complex organic compounds present in dead and decaying matter into simpler inorganic materials are called **decomposers**, e.g. certain bacteria and fungi.

Decomposers act as cleaning agents of environment by decomposing dead bodies of plants and animals. They also help in recycling of materials, replenishment of soil's nutrients, etc.

The consequence of their absence in an ecosystem can be disastrous. The dead bodies would persist for long, leading to their accumulation and thus, polluting the environment. The biogenetic nutrients associated with these remains will not be returned back to the environment.

As a result, all the nutrients present in soil, air and water would soon be exhausted and the whole life cycle of organisms will be disrupted.

30. (i) Consumers are the organisms who derive energy by eating plants or other organisms as they cannot produce food on their own. Absence of primary consumers in nature would lead to enormous growth of plants and decline in the population of carnivore animals, who eat them. Hence, the whole food web will get distrupted.

(ii) The direction of energy transfer in following cases are as follows

    (a) Primary consumer (grasshopper) to secondary consumer (frog).

    (b) Producer (grass) to primary consumer (deer).

    (c) Primary consumer (deer) to secondary consumer (lion).

31. (i) Yes, the impact of removing all the organisms in a trophic level will be different for different trophic levels. The lower trophic level of an ecosystem has a greater number of individuals than the higher trophic levels. Removal of producers will affect all the organisms of successive trophic levels and it will threat their survival.

The removal of higher trophic level will lead to increase in organisms of lower trophic level and the organisms of higher trophic level will die due to the shortage of food.

(ii) No, removal of all organisms of a trophic level will disturb the ecosystem. Killing of higher trophic level organisms will cause explosion in the population of lower trophic level organisms. This will adversely affect the ecosystem and thus environment.

32. (i) The producers convert solar energy into chemical energy in the form of organic compounds. The primary consumers (herbivores) derive their nutrition from the producers. According to the energy transfer law, only 10% of energy is transferred from one trophic level to the other.

So, the energy that is captured by the producers does not revert back to the Sun and the energy transferred to the herbivores does not come back to the producers. It just keeps on moving to the next trophic level in one direction. That is why the flow of energy in the food chain is always unidirectional.

(ii) A large number of pesticides and chemicals are used to protect our crops from pests and diseases. Some of these chemicals are washed down from the soil, while some enter the water bodies. From the soil, they are absorbed by plants along with water and minerals and from the water bodies, they are taken up by aquatic plants and animals. This is how these chemicals enter the food chain.

As these chemicals cannot decompose, they accumulate progressively at each trophic level. This increase in the concentration of harmful chemicals with each step of the food chain is called biomagnification. As human beings occupy the top level in any food chain, these chemicals get accumulated in our bodies in considerably high amount causing diseases.

33. (i) Undesirable activities of man eliminate growth of organisms belonging to one or more trophic levels in a food chain. Thus, the food chain gets shortened, e.g. hunting tigers for their skin, etc.

It causes imbalance in the functioning of ecosystem and biosphere. If organisms of one trophic level are eliminated, the organisms prior to that trophic level will flourish and increase in number. Also, the organisms of the subsequent trophic level will sharply decrease, thereby creating an imbalance.

(ii) Vegetarian food chain is advantageous in terms of energy because it has less number of trophic levels. As we know, only 10% of the energy is transferred to the next trophic level in a food chain, so if a person is vegetarian then, he would have maximum amount of energy by consuming producers or plants in a food chain.

34. Some harmful effects of agricultural practices on the environment are as follows

(i) **Soil degradation** Extensive cropping causes loss of soil fertility. Also, over the time it can lead to soil erosion and finally to desertification.

(ii) **Pollution** Use of synthetic chemical fertilisers and pesticides leads to soil, water and air pollution.

(iii) **Water shortage** Excess use of groundwater for agriculture lowers the water level. This results in acute water shortage at many places.

(iv) **Biomagnification** The chemical pesticides, being non-biodegradable accumulate in organisms in increasing amounts at each trophic level.

(v) **Deforestation** Indiscriminate cutting of trees for agriculture has resulted in loss of habitat for wildlife. Thus, it also causes damage to natural ecosystem.

35. Ozone is a triatomic molecule, i.e. made up of three atoms of oxygen joined together. Its molecular formula is O_3. It can affect any ecosystem in the following ways

(i) It protects against ultraviolet rays if, present in stratosphere.

(ii) Ozone dissipates the energy of UV rays by undergoing dissociation followed by reassociation.

$$O_2 \xrightarrow{\text{UV}} O + O \; ; \; O + O_2 \longrightarrow \underset{\text{(Ozone)}}{O_3}$$

(iii) In atmosphere, it is highly toxic and causes injury to mucous membranes, eye irritation and internal haemorrhages in animals and humans.

36. (i) Environmental pollution is an undesirable change in the physical, chemical or biological characteristics of the natural environment, brought about by man's activities. This pollution may affect the soil, water or air.

(ii) Differences between biodegradable and non-biodegradable pollutants are as follows

Biodegradable pollutants	Non-biodegradable pollutants
These pollutants can be broken down into non-toxic substances in nature by the action of microorganisms.	These pollutants cannot be broken down into non-toxic substances by microorganisms.
They get recycled thus, do not need any dumping sites.	They cannot be recycled thus, require dumping sites.
They cause minimum environmental pollution.	They cause maximum environmental pollution.

(iii) Non-biodegradable pollutants include DDT, radioactive waste, plastic, insecticides.

37. Some daily life eco-friendly activities are

(i) **Save a tree, use less paper** You can buy 'tree-free' 100% post-consumer recycled paper for everything from greeting cards to toilet paper. Paper with a high post-consumer waste content uses less pulp and keeps more waste paper out of landfills.

(ii) **Opt bamboo for hardwood floors** Bamboo is considered as an environmental-friendly flooring material due to its high yield and the relatively fast rate at which it replenishes itself. It takes just 4-6 years for bamboo to mature, compared to 50-100 years for typical hardwoods. Also look for sources that use formaldehyde-free glues.

(iii) **Reduce plastics, reduce global warming** Unfortunately, plastics are made from petroleum, the processing and burning of which is considered one of the main contributors to global warming, according to the EPA. In addition, sending plastics to the landfill also increases greenhouse gases. Reduce, reuse and recycle our plastics are one of the best ways to combat global warming.

(iv) **Use healthier paints** Conventional paints contain solvents, toxic metals and Volatile Organic Compounds (VOCs) that can cause smog, ozone pollution and indoor air quality problems with negative health effects, according to the EPA. These unhealthy ingredients are released into the air, while we are painting, drying of paint and even after the paints are completely dry.

(v) **Use compost** Instead of using synthetic fertilisers, compost provides a full complement of soil organisms and the balance of nutrients needed to maintain the soil's health. Healthy soil minimises the population of weeds.

38. Materials that remain for a long time in the environment, without getting decomposed by any natural agents, also causing harm to the environment are called non-biodegradable. Plastic cups are non-biodegradable and raised the concern towards hygiene, thus they were replaced by kulhads.

Kulhads are made up of clay on a large scale resulted in the loss of top fertile soil. It is replaced by disposable paper cups because the paper can be recycled, it is biodegradable and is eco-friendly material which does not cause environment pollution.

39. (i) There are 6 food chains that constitute to form the given food web. These are as follows
  1. Seeds → Mice → Foxes
  2. Young trees → Mice → Foxes
  3. Young trees → Rabbits → Foxes
  4. Grass → Rabbits → Foxes
  5. Grass → Rabbits → Snake
  6. Young trees → Rabbits → Snake

(ii) The primary consumers are the organisms who directly feed on the producers. In the given food web, rabbits and mice are the primary consumers, whereas foxes and snake are the secondary consumers.

(iii) About 90% of energy is loss at each trophic level.

(iv) The foxes feed on the rabbits and mice. If all the foxes are killed then there will be no direct predator of rabbits and mice, hence the number of rabbits and mice (i.e. both are primary consumers) will increase in the given ecosystem, which will disturb its balance.

(v) Accumulation of toxic non-biodegradable substances increases at each trophic level. It is least in organisms of first trophic level (i.e. seeds), young trees and grass and highest in organisms of third trophic level (i.e. foxes and snake).

40. (i) The green plants in a terrestrial ecosystem capture about 1% of the energy of sunlight (light energy). They convert it into food energy (chemical energy). Therefore, if 10,000 J solar energy falls on green plants in a terrestrial ecosystem, only 1% of solar energy, i.e. 100 J will be converted into food energy.

(ii) Decomposers are not included in the food chain as they act at every trophic level of the food chain.

(iii) Primary consumers are those organisms who directly feed on plants, e.g. herbivores.
Primary carnivores are those organisms who feeds on plant-eating animals, e.g. snake.

(iv) Decrease in energy at higher trophic levels (according to 10% law) is one of the main reason that limits the number of trophic levels in a food chain.

(v) Owl is placed at highest trophic level in the given food web, therefore the accumulation of non-biodegradable toxic materials are found to be highest in them due to biomagnification.

41. (i) The longest food chain consist of maximum five trophic levels.

(ii) Rabbit is a herbivore as it feeds on plants directly. Its role in the given food web is to transfer the energy from producers to carnivores.

(iii) The significance of food web is as follows

(a) Food chain provides pathways for availability of food.

(b) It allows endangered populations to grow in size.

(iv) Sun or solar energy is the ultimate source of energy for the Earth. Only plants can utilise this energy to make their on food.

(v) When predator for a particular organism decreases in number, the organisms start increasing in number.

As the animals which used to feed on them decrease in number, therefore, the population of those organisms increases.

42. (i) Substances that are responsible for depletion ozone layer or breakdown of ozone molecules are known as ozone depleting substances.

e.g. CFCs, halogens, nitrous oxide, CCl_4 and CH_4 are ozone depleting substances responsible for ozone layer depletion.

(ii) Atomic oxygen is highly reactive. It combines with molecular oxygen to form ozone.

$$O_2 \xrightarrow{\text{UV}} [O] + [O]$$
$$2O_2 + 2[O] \longrightarrow 2O_3 \text{(Ozone)}$$

(iii) Ozone layer is found in the stratosphere around 15-30 km above the Earth's surface.

(iv) Ozone is a triatomic molecule made up of three atoms of oxygen (O_3). It is present in atmosphere as an ozone layer shield that protects us from high energy UV radiations. So, it is known as good ozone whereas near the surface of earth ozone act as a highly poisonous gas. Hence, known bad ozone.

(v) Cancers, mutations, effect on eyesight, global warming, weakening of immune system, etc., are some adverse effects of ozone depletion.

Chapter Test

Multiple Choice Questions

1. Which of the following option correctly represents the biotic and abiotic components of ecosystem?

	Biotic components	Abiotic components
(a)	Soil	Water
(b)	Plants	Animals
(c)	Animals	Decomposers
(d)	Decomposers	Water

2. Biomagnification is highest in
(a) producer
(b) primary consumer
(c) secondary consumer
(d) decomposer

3. Organisms which synthesise carbohydrates from inorganic compounds using radiant energy are called
(a) decomposers   (b) producers
(c) herbivores   (d) carnivores

4. In a food chain, the snake an predates as rabbit which fed on fresh green bushes. What percentage of the energy accumulated by rabbit, would be acquired by snakes?
(a) 90%   (b) 10%
(c) 50%   (d) 25%

5. Bad ozone is formed in
(a) atmosphere
(b) ionosphere
(c) stratosphere
(d) troposphere

Assertion-Reasoning MCQs

Direction (Q. Nos. 6-8) Each of these questions contains two statements, Assertion (A) and Reason (R). Each of these questions also has four alternative choices, any one of which is the correct answer. You have to select one of the codes (a), (b), (c) and (d) given below.

(a) Both A and R are true and R is the correct explanation of A
(b) Both A and R are true, but R is not the correct explanation of A
(c) A is true, but R is false
(d) A is false, but R is true

6. Assertion (A) The autotrophs are at the first trophic level.

Reason (R) Autotrophs fix up the solar energy and make it available for consumers.

7. Assertion (A) The green plants capture about 10% of the energy of sunlight that falls on their leaves.

Reason (R) When green plants are eaten by primary consumers, a great deal of energy is lost as heat to the environment.

8. Assertion (A) Biodegradable domestic wastes can be buried in a pit, dug into ground.

Reason (R) They are converted into compost and used as manure.

Short Answer Type Questions

9. Suggest one word for each of the following statements.
  I. The physical and biological world where we live.
  II. The physical factors like rainfall, wind, soil are termed as.
  III. Trophic level of plant-eating animals.
  IV. Each level of food chain where transfer of energy takes place.

10. What percentage of solar energy is trapped and utilised in terrestrial and aquatic ecosystem?

11. Which chemical is used in fire extinguishers? How is it harmful?

12. Among all four types of animals, i.e. carnivores, decomposers, herbivores and producers, how does energy flow in an ecosystem, occur through these organisms? Explain with the help of example.

13. How are water bodies affected by sewage disposal?

Long Answer Type Questions

14. 'Number of vultures are decreasing remarkably now-a-days, which is a matter of concern'.

Answer the following questions related to the above given statement.
(i) Vultures belong to which category of animals?
(ii) What is their role in nature to maintain ecological balance?
(iii) At which trophic level, will you place vultures in a food chain?
(iv) How much energy is passed on at each trophic level in a food chain? Give the energy flow diagram of an ecosystem.
(v) Mention one of the main cause for this decline in the number of vultures.

15. Salman wants to volunteer for Swachh Bharat Abhiyan intership. He got a responsibility to device various methods for garbage management. Help him to write various ways to control and manage garbage.

Answers

Multiple Choice Questions

1. (d)   2. (c)   3. (b)   4. (b)   5. (d)

Assertion-Reasoning MCQs

6. (a)   7. (d)   8. (a)

For Detailed Solutions
Scan the code

Practice Paper 1[*]

(Solved)

General Instructions

■ Time : 2 Hours
■ Max. Marks : 40

1. There are 11 questions in the question paper. All questions are compulsory.
2. **Section A**, Question no. 1 to 3 is a Case Based Questions, which has four MCQs/Questions. Each question carries one mark.
3. **Section B**, Question no. 4 to 8 are Short Answer Type Questions. Each question carries 2/3 marks.
4. **Section C**, Question no. 9-11 are Long Answer Type Questions. Each question carries 5 marks.
5. There is no overall choice. However, internal choices have been provided in some questions. Students have to attempt only one of the alternatives in such questions.

As exact Blue-print and Pattern for CBSE Term II exams is not released yet. So the pattern of this paper is designed by the author on the basis of trend of past CBSE Papers. Students are advised not to consider the pattern of this paper as official, it is just for practice purpose.

Section A

1. Read the following and answer the questions from (i) to (iv) given below

A student wants to study the dependence of potential difference (V) on current (I) flowing across a resistor. He plotted a graph by taking I along X-axis and V along Y-axis of all his observations.

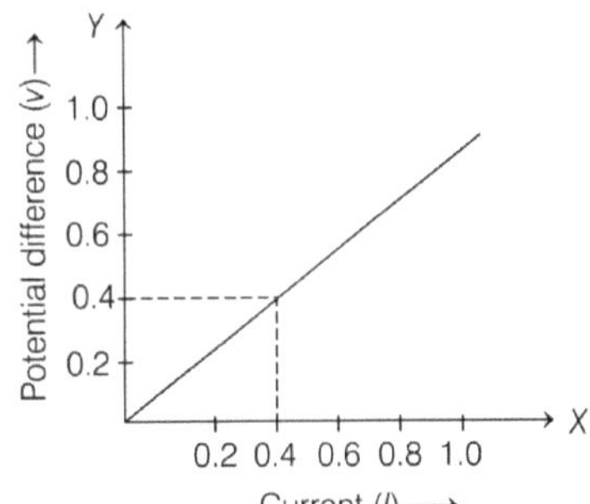

(i) The value of resistance used in the circuit is
    (a) $1\,\Omega$ (b) $2\,\Omega$ (c) $4\,\Omega$ (d) $0.5\,\Omega$

(ii) The inverse of the slope of V-I curve gives
    (a) resistance   (b) conductance   (c) reactance   (d) resistivity

(iii) The correct representation of Ohm's law is
    (a) $V \propto \dfrac{1}{I}$ (b) $I \propto \dfrac{1}{V}$ (c) $V \propto I$ (d) $I \propto V$

(iv) His friend noticed some observations from this demonstration as follows
    1. The slope of the line gives the resistance of a conductor.
    2. Motion of electrons through a conductor is retarded by its resistance.
    3. All conductors do not obey Ohm's law.
    Which of the following observation(s) is/are correct?
    (a) 1 and 2   (b) 2 and 3   (c) 1 and 3   (d) 1, 2 and 3

Or

What is the use of the variable resistor in the circuit in the Ohm's law experiment shown below?

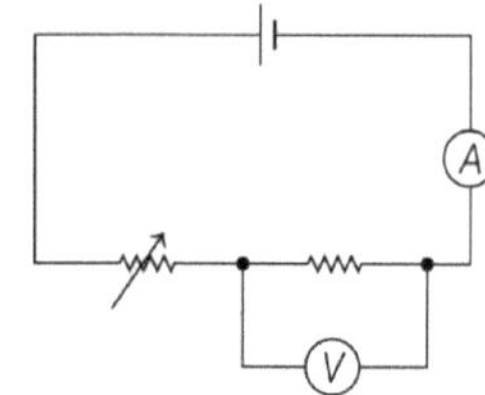

I. To change the voltage across the fixed resistor.

II. To change the resistance across the fixed resistor.

III. To change the current flowing through the fixed resistor.

(a) Only I
(b) Only III
(c) I and III only
(d) I, II and III

2. Read the following and answer the questions from (i) to (iv) given below

In modern periodic table, some properties show a regular trend when we move along a period from left to right or in a group from top to bottom.

Atomic size refers to the radius of an atom. It may be visualised as the distance between the centre of the nucleus and the outermost shell of an isolated atom. It is measured in picometres.

About 75% of all elements in one periodic table are metals. The most common metal found in the Earth's crust is aluminium. The non-metals also are some of the most abundant elements in the universe including the Earth's crust, the atmosphere and the human body.

The position of three elements A, B and C in the periodic table are shown below

Group 16	Group 17
—	—
—	A
—	—
B	C

(i) State whether A is a metal or non-metal.

(ii) State whether C is more reactive or less reactive than A.

(iii) Will C be larger or smaller in size than B?

(iv) Which type of ion- cation or anion, will be formed by A?

Or

What are metalloids? Give examples.

3. Read the following and answer the questions from (i) to (iv) given below

Sex-determination is the method by which distinction between males and females is established in a species. The sex of an individual is determined by specific chromosomes. In human beings, it is determined as follows

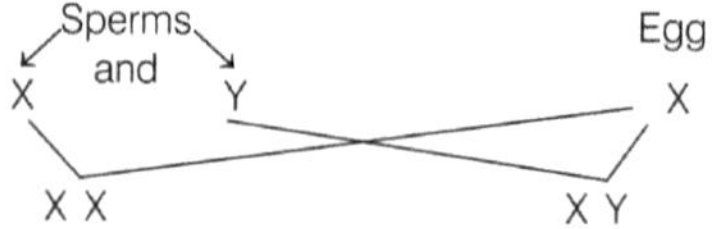

(i) In XX-XY type of sex-determination,
(a) females produce two different types of gametes
(b) males produce two different types of gametes
(c) female produces gametes with Y-chromosome
(d) male produces gametes with X-chromosome only

(ii) A couple has six daughters. What is the possibility of them having a girl child next time?
(a) 10%
(b) 90%
(c) 100%
(d) 50%

(iii) Number of chromosome present in the egg cell of a human female is
(a) 23 pairs
(b) 23
(c) 22
(d) 22 pairs

(iv) Choose the incorrect statement from the following set of statements.

I. XX-XY type of sex-determination is the example of male heterogamety.

II. XX-XY type of sex-determination is the example of female heterogamety.

III. There are always 50% chances of having a baby girl child.

IV. Changes in the non-reproductive tissues can be passed on to the DNA of the germ cells.

Codes
(a) I and III
(b) II and IV
(c) III and IV
(d) I and III

Or

Sex of human child is determined by
(a) size of the egg
(b) size of the sperm
(c) type of the sperm
(d) type of the egg

Section B

4. Choose the kind of chemical bonding (ionic bond, covalent bond, both ionic and covalent bonds) present in the following compounds. Potassium chloride, magnesium oxide, sulphuric acid, ammonium hydroxide, zinc sulphide, phosphorus trichloride (PCl_3). **[2 M]**

Or

Write the name and structure of a saturated compound in which the carbon atoms are arranged in a ring. Give the number of single bonds present in this compound. **[2 M]**

5. Differentiate between pollen tube and style. **[2 M]**

6. For the current carrying solenoid as shown below, draw magnetic field lines and give reason to explain that out of the three points A, B and C at which point, the field strength is maximum and at which point, it is minimum.

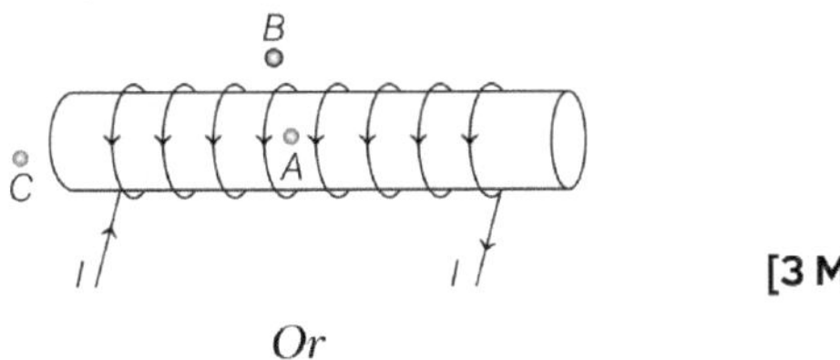

[3 M]

Or

Diagram shows the lengthwise section of a current carrying solenoid.

⊗ Indicates current entering into the page,

⊙ Indicates current emerging out of the page.

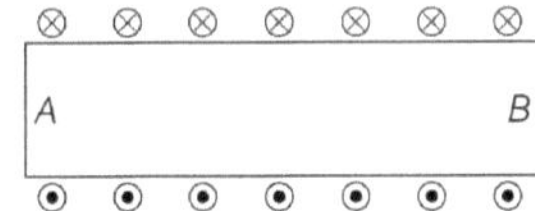

Decide which end of the solenoid A or B, will behave as North pole. Give reason for your answer. Also, draw field lines inside the solenoid. **[3 M]**

7. Give an example of each of the following
(i) A carbon compound containing two double bonds.
(ii) A molecule in which central atom is linked to three other atoms.
(iii) A compound containing both ionic and covalent bonds. **[3 M]**

Or

Define homologous series. Examine it with an example. Will there be any change in their physical properties? Give reason for your answer. **[3 M]**

8. Give any three points of differentiation between acquired and inherited characters with one example each. **[3 M]**

Section C

9. (i) Which is the better way to connect lights and other appliances in domestic circuit, series connection or parallel connection? Justify your answer.

(ii) An electrician has made electric circuit of a house in such a way that, if a lamp gets fused in a room of the house, then all the lamps in other rooms of the house stop working. What is the defect in this type of circuit wiring? Give reason.

Or

Three incandescent bulbs of 100 W each are connected in series in an electric circuit. In another set of three bulbs of the same wattage are connected in parallel to the source.

(i) Will the bulb in the two circuits glow with the same brightness? Justify your answer.

(ii) Now, let one bulb in both the circuits get fused. Will the rest of the bulbs continue to glow in each circuit? Give reason.

10. Differentiate between monohybrid and dihybrid crosses with the help of an example.

Or

Explain the term 'regeneration' as used in relation to reproduction of organisms. Describe briefly how regeneration is carried out in multicellular organisms like *Hydra*?

11. (i) How can pregnancy be prevented surgically?
(ii) Study the diagram given below

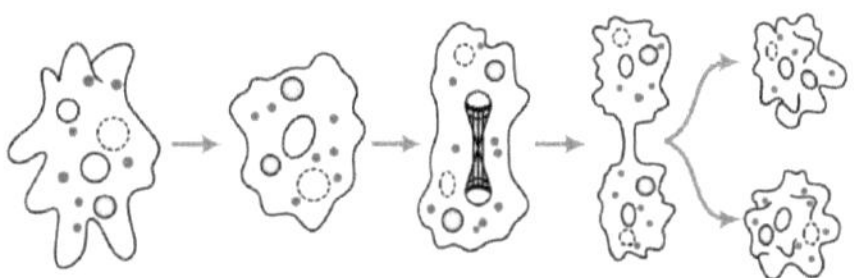

(a) Identify the process.
(b) Which organism uses the above method for reproduction?
(c) How is the above method different from the process of fragmentation?

Or (i) Why should biodegradable and non-biodegradable wastes be discarded in two separate dustbins?

(ii) Why do we exemplify crop fields as artificial ecosystem?

Explanations

1. (i) (*a*) The slope of *V-I* graph gives resistance.

$$\therefore \quad \text{Resistance} = \frac{0.4 - 0}{0.4 - 0} = \frac{0.4}{0.4} = 1\Omega$$

(ii) (*b*) The inverse of the slope of *V-I* curve gives conductance. i.e.

$$\frac{1}{\text{Slope}} = \frac{1}{\text{Resistance}(R)} = \text{Conductance}(\sigma)$$

(iii) (*d*) The correct representation of Ohm's law is $I \propto V$. It states that current flowing through the conductor is directly proportional to the potential difference applied across the conductor.

(iv) (*d*) All the observations are correct. The slope of the line in *V-I* graph gives the resistance of a conductor whereas motion of electrons through a conductor is retarded by its resistance.

All conductors do not obey Ohm's law i.e., Ohm's law is not universal.

Or (*c*) Ohm's law states that the resistance (ratio of the voltage across the fixed resistor to the current flowing through it) is constant. The aim of Ohm's law experiment is to find the resistance of a fixed resistor. By adjusting the variable resistor.
- the voltage across the variable resistor and fixed resistor will change.
- the total resistance in the circuit will change leading to a change in current flowing through the fixed resistor.

2. (i) Since, *A* belongs to group 17 and has 7 valence electrons so it is a non-metal because it will gain one electron to complete its octet.

(ii) *C* lies below *A* and belong to the same group. As we move down a group, the size increases and electronegative character decreases. With the decrease in electronegative character, the electron accepting tendency and hence the reactivity of non-metals decreases, so *C* is less reactive than *A*.

(iii) *C* and *B* both belongs to the same period therefore, *C* is smaller than *B* in size because as we move left to right in a period, atomic size decreases due to increased effective nuclear charge.

(iv) As discussed in that element *A* has a tendency to gain electron to complete its octet. It needs to take up one electron, so it will form anion (A^-).

Or These are some elements which exhibit the properties of both metals and non-metals. These are called metalloids. In modern periodic table, a *zig-zag* line separates metals from non-metals.
The border line elements—boron, silicon, antimony are intermediate in properties, so they are called mtalloids or semi-metals.

3. (i) (*b*) In XX-XY type of sex-determination (human's sex-determination), the males produce two different types of gametes, one contains X-chromosome whereas the other contains Y-chromosome.

(ii) (*d*) When a sperm having an X-chromosome fuses with the egg, the zygote formed will develop into a female baby whereas when a sperm having Y-chromosome fuses with the egg, the zygote formed will develop into a male baby. Thus, there are always 50% chances of having a girl child by the couple.

(iii) (*d*) Gametes are haploid in nature, i.e they contain half the number of chromosomes as compared to other somatic cells. Human beings have 23 pairs of chromosomes. Therefore, the egg cell (gamete) contains 23 chromosomes only.

(iv) (*b*) Statements II and IV are incorrect and can be corrected as
- XX-XY type of sex-determination shows male heterogamety and female homogamety.
- Changes in the non-reproductive tissues cannot be passed on to the DNA of the germ cells.

Or (*c*) Sex of a human child is determined by the type of sperm (X or Y) that fuses with egg during fertilisation.

A sperm with an X-chromosome will produce a baby girl and that with Y-chromosome will produce a baby boy on fertilisation.

4.

Ionic bond	Covalent bond	Both ionic and covalent bond
(i) Potassium chloride	Phosphorus trichloride	Sulphuric acid
(ii) Magnesium oxide		Ammonium hydroxide
(iii) Zinc sulphide		

Or Cyclopropane

$$\triangle \; \equiv \;$$

Cyclopropane contains three C—C single bond and six C—H single bond.

Total 9 single bonds are present in cyclopropane.

5. Differences between pollen tube and style are as follows

Pollen Tube	Style
A tube growing out of pollen grain when it reaches stigma.	The middle elongated part of the carpel, i.e. female part of a flower.
It transports male gametes from pollen grains to ovules.	The attachment of stigma to the ovary.

6. Magnetic field lines due to a solenoid

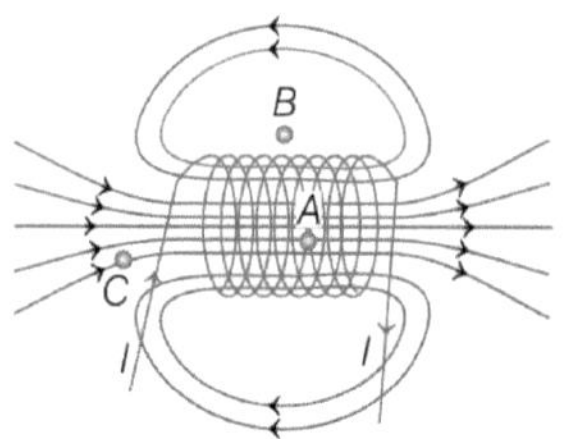

In case of an ideal solenoid, magnetic field strength is maximum at point A and is minimum or zero at point B. This is because the magnetic field is strong, where magnetic field lines are crowded and is weak, where magnetic field lines are far apart. At the point C, the density of the field lines is less than that of point A but greater than that of point B. So, the order of magnetic field at points A, B and C is

$$B_B < B_C < B_A$$

Or From diagram, we can see that current is entering from A and emerging out from B.

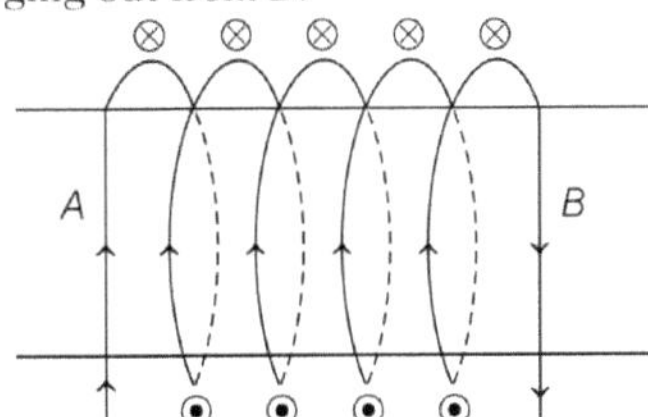

Thus, using right hand thumb rule, direction of magnetic field lines is from B to A. We know that, magnetic field lines move from North to South direction. Thus, B represents North pole or A represents South pole.

7. (i) Carbon dioxide (CO_2)

(ii) Ammonia molecule (NH_3) $H \!-\! \overset{\bullet\bullet}{N} \!-\! H$
$\quad\quad\quad\quad\quad\quad\quad\quad\quad\quad\quad |$
$\quad\quad\quad\quad\quad\quad\quad\quad\quad\quad\quad H$

(iii) Ammonium chloride (NH_4Cl) contains both ionic and covalent bonds.

$$\left[\begin{array}{c} H \\ | \\ H\!-\!N\!-\!H \\ | \\ H \end{array} \right]^{+} Cl^{-}$$

Or A series of similarly constituted compounds in which the members present have the same functional group and similar chemical properties and any two successive members in a particular series differ in their molecular formula by $(-\,CH_2)$ unit, is called a homologous series, e.g. alkane series C_nH_{2n+2}.

CH_4	Methane	C_2H_6	Ethane
C_3H_8	Propane	C_4H_{10}	Butane
C_5H_{12}	Pentane		

With increase in the molecular mass, a gradual change in their physical properties is seen. e.g. The melting and boiling points increase with increasing molecular mass.

8. Differences between acquired and inherited traits are as follows

Acquired Characters	Inherited Characters
They develop in the organism during their lifetime.	They are received by the organisms from their parents.
They do not bring any change in the genes of organisms.	They bring about certain changes in the genes of the organisms.
They are lost with the death of the individual, e.g. intelligence.	They are transferred to the next generation, e.g. free and fused earlobes.

9. (i) Parallel connection is a better way to connect lights and other appliances in domestic circuit.

It is because

(a) when we connect a number of devices in parallel combination, each device gets the same potential as provided by the battery and it keeps on working even, if other devices stop working.

(b) parallel connection is helpful when each device has different resistances and requires different current for its operation as in this case the current divides itself through different devices unlike series connection.

(ii) Electrician has made series connection of all the lamps in electric circuit of house because of which, if one lamp gets fused, all the other lamps stop working.

This is due to the fact that when devices are connected in series, then if one device fails, the circuit gets broken and all the devices in that circuit stop working.

Or (i) Let us assume that the resistance of each bulb be R. The circuit diagram in two cases may be drawn as given below

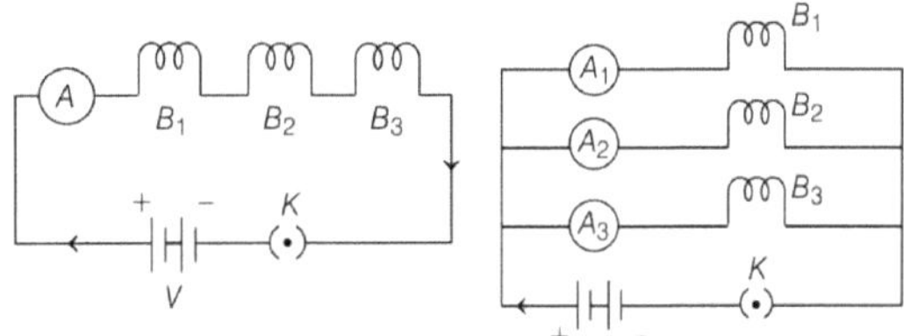

Equivalent resistance in series combination

$$R_S = R + R + R = 3R, \text{ voltage} = V$$

Let current through each bulb in series combination be I_1.

By Ohm's law, $V = I_1 \times 3R \Rightarrow I_1 = \dfrac{V}{3R}$

$\therefore$ Power consumption of each bulb in series combination,

$$P_1 = I_1^2(3R) = \left(\frac{V}{3R}\right)^2 \times 3R = \frac{V^2}{9R^2} \times 3R = \frac{V^2}{3R} \qquad ...(i)$$

For parallel circuit, the resistance of each bulb $= R$

Voltage across each bulb $= V$

$\qquad\qquad\qquad$ [$\because$ same voltage in parallel combination]

$\therefore$ Power consumption of each bulb in parallel combination is given by

$$P_2 = \frac{V^2}{R} \qquad ...(ii)$$

From Eqs. (i) and (ii), we get

$$\frac{P_2}{P_1} = \frac{(V^2/R)}{(V^2/3R)}$$

$$\Rightarrow \quad \frac{V^2}{R} \times \frac{3R}{V^2} = 3 \quad \Rightarrow \quad P_2 = 3P_1$$

Therefore, each bulb in parallel combination glows 3 times brighter than that of each bulb in series combination.

(ii) When one bulb gets fused then in series combination, the circuit gets broken and current stops flowing, whereas in parallel combination, same voltage continues to act on the remaining bulbs and hence other bulbs continues to glow with same brightness.

10. Differences between monohybrid and dihybrid crosses are as follows

Monohybrid cross between homozygous tall plant and homozygous short plant is shown below

Monohybrid cross	A hybridisation cross in which inheritance of only one pair of contrasting characters is studied.
Dihybrid cross	A cross in which inheritance of two pairs of contrasting characters is simultaneously studied.

Dihybrid cross between pure breed of plants having Round and Green seed and Wrinkled and Yellow seeds is shown below

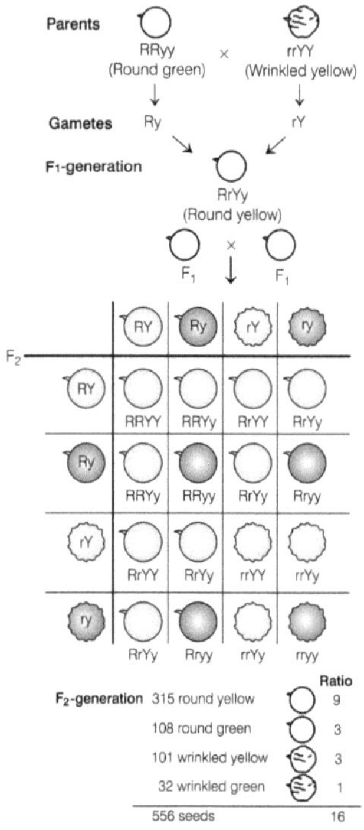

Or

Regeneration is used in relation to reproduction because reproduction is the process by which a living organism is able to produce new individuals of its own kind likewise regeneration is the ability of some organisms to give rise to new organisms when the individual is cut or broken up into many pieces.

It is seen in *Hydra* and *Planaria*.

Regeneration in Multicellular Organism like *Hydra*

(i) It is carried out by specialised cells.

(ii) When *Hydra* is cut or broken up into many pieces, these specialised cells proliferate and make large number of cells.

(iii) From this mass of cells, different cells undergo changes to become various cell types and tissues.

(iv) These changes take place in an organised sequence referred to as development thereby making each piece to grow into a separate individual.

11. (i) When vas deferens in males are blocked surgically, sperm transfer is be prevented. Similarly, when Fallopian tubes are blocked in females the egg will not be able to reach the uterus therby preventing pregnancy.

(ii) (a) The process in the figure depicts binary fission in *Amoeba*, a method of asexual reproduction.

(b) Binary fission also occurs in *Euglena* and *Paramecium*, etc.

(c) Differences between fission and fragmentation are as follows

Fission	Fragmentation
It is the division of parent body into two identical daughter cells.	It is the division of parent body into two or more small fragments.
It occurs in unicellular organisms or multicellular organisms with simple body organisation.	It occurs only in multicellular organisms with complex cellular organisations.
e.g. *Amoeba, Plasmodium* (protozoan)	e.g. *Spirogyra* (algae)

Or (i) Biodegradable materials are broken down by microorganisms in nature into simple harmless substances. Non-biodegradable materials need a different treatment like heat and temperature for disposal and hence, both should be discarded in two different dustbins.

(ii) Artificial ecosystems are those ecosystems which are modified and managed by human beings.

Crop fields are man-made. Here plants do not grow naturally rather most of the plants are grown by humans according to the season, type of soil, etc.

In crop fields, the land is managed, soil is prepared for sowing seeds, then irrigated and further progress is also kept under observation for getting good yield.

This is why, crop fields are known as artificial ecosystem.

Practice Paper 2[*]

(UnSolved)

General Instructions

- Time : 2 Hours
- Max. Marks : 40

1. There are 11 questions in the question paper. All questions are compulsory.
2. **Section A**, Question no. 1 to 3 is a Case Based Questions, which has four MCQs/Questions. Each question carries one mark.
3. **Section B**, Question no. 4 to 8 are Short Answer Type Questions. Each question carries 2/3 marks.
4. **Section C**, Question no. 9-11 are Long Answer Type Questions. Each question carries 5 marks.
5. There is no overall choice. However, internal choices have been provided in some questions. Students have to attempt only one of the alternatives in such questions.

** As exact Blue-print and Pattern for CBSE Term II exams is not released yet. So the pattern of this paper is designed by the author on the basis of trend of past CBSE Papers. Students are advised not to consider the pattern of this paper as official, it is just for practice purpose.*

Section A

1. Read the following and answer the questions from (i) to (iv) given below.

   After the discovery of large number of elements it became necessary to classify them and arrange them in a regular manner in order of their periodic properties. In order to study the properties of all these elements separately, scientists felt the necessity to group elements having similar characteristics together. So, all the elements have been divided into few groups in such a way that elements in the same group have similar properties of elements.

   In 1817, Johann Wolfgang Dobereiner' triad to arrange the elements with similar properties into groups. He identified some groups fo three elements having similar physical and chemical properties, known as Dobereiner's triads.

   In 1865, John Newlands arranged all known elements in the order of increasing atomic masses and found that the properties of every eighth element are similar to the properties of the first element.

   (i) If Cl, Br, I is a Dobereiner's triad and the atomic masses of Cl and I are 35.5 and 127 respectively, then the atomic mass of Br is

   (a) 162.5   (b) 91.5   (c) 81.25   (d) 45.625

   (ii) Example of Dobereiner's triad is

   (a) Li, Al, Ca   (b) Li, Na, K   (c) Li, K, Na   (d) K, Al, Ca

   (iii) A and B are two elements having similar properties which obey Newlands' law of octaves. How many elements are there in between A and B ?

   (a) 7   (b) 8   (c) 5   (d) 6

   (iv) According to the Newland's law of octaves, the properties of magnesium are similar to those of

   (a) beryllium   (b) lithium   (c) sodium   (d) potassium

   Or

   On what basis the elements are arranged in Dobereiner's triad?

   (a) Atomic number   (b) Atomic mass

   (c) Number of neutrons   (d) Number of electrons

2. Read the following and answer the questions from (i) to (iv) given below.

Devices in series and parallel.

You must have seen tiny bulbs strung together for decorating buildings during festivals like Diwali, and occasions like marriages, etc. These bulbs are connected in series and the mains voltage is applied to the combination. (as shown in figure)

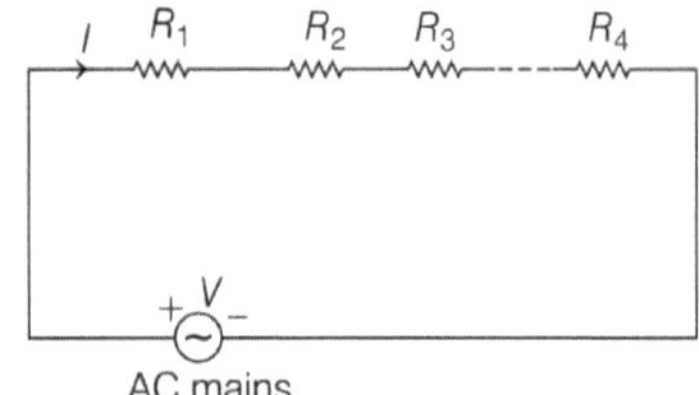

The potential difference (V) of the mains gets divided across the bulbs ($V = V_1 + V_2 + V_3 + \dots$)

So, a small potential difference exists across each bulb, close to that required to make the bulb work.

(i) The equivalent resistor of series combination of four equal resistors is S. If they are joined in parallel, the total resistance is P. The relation between S and P is given by $S = nP$, then the minimum possible value of n is (as shown in figure)

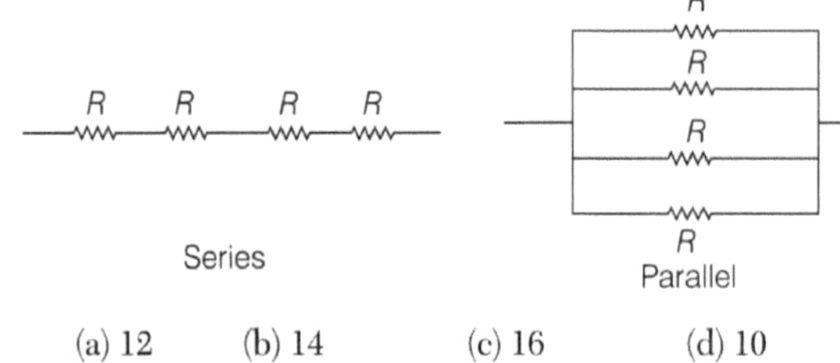

  (a) 12   (b) 14   (c) 16   (d) 10

(ii) In a series combination when high resistors are connected with each other then, the value of current for the potential difference V will be
(a) increased
(b) decreased
(c) increased first then decreased
(d) None of the above

(iii) In the circuit shows below, the value of current I flowing will be

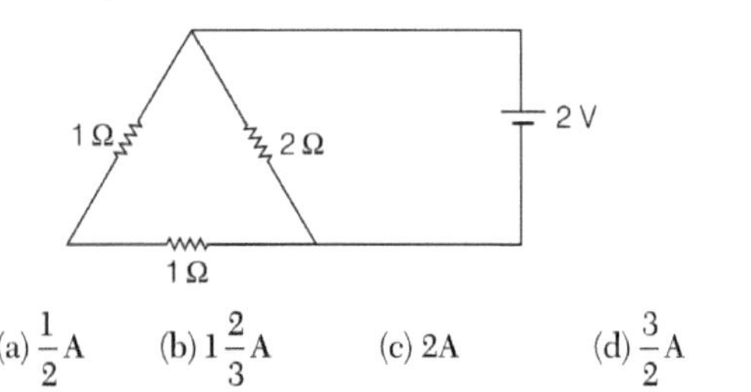

  (a) $\dfrac{1}{2}$A   (b) $1\dfrac{2}{3}$A   (c) 2A   (d) $\dfrac{3}{2}$A

(iv) Which arrangement of 3Ω resistors will give a total resistance of 7Ω?

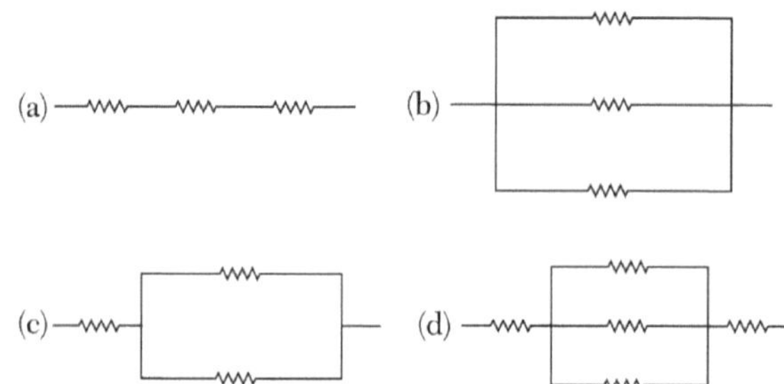

Or Which of the following option(s) is/are correct for the given statements about series combination?

(i) Current flowing in series combination is same in all the resistors of the circuit.

(ii) Potential difference across each resistor in the circuit is same.

(iii) Equivalent resistance of the circuit is the product of all the resistances.

  (a) Only (i)   (b) Only (ii)
  (c) Only (i) and (ii)   (d) Only (i), (ii) and (iii)

3. Read the following and answer the questions from (i) to (iv) given below.

The amount of ozone in the atmosphere began to drop sharply in the 1980s. This decrease has been linked to synthetic chemicals which are used as refrigerants and in fire extinguishers.

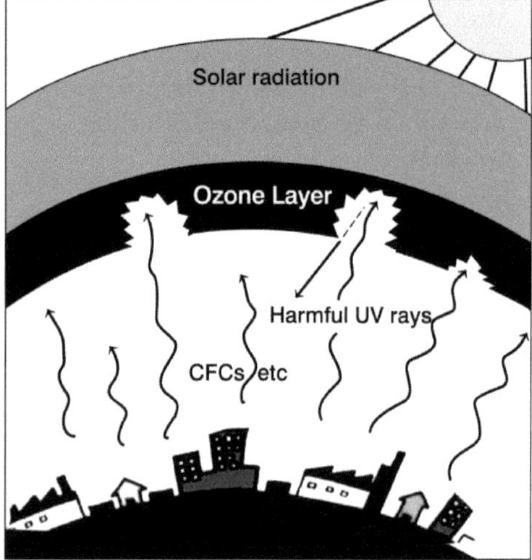

(i) Which layer of the atmosphere consists of ozone layer?

(ii) Why ozone is important for us?

(iii) Give one reason for damaging ozone layer.

(iv) What are the effects due to depletion of ozone layer?

Or

Where was the first ozone hole discovered?

Section B

4. 'Males are heterogametic' Explain. **[2 M]**

5. What are the advantages of connecting electrical appliances in parallel with the battery instead of connecting them in series? **[2 M]**

Or

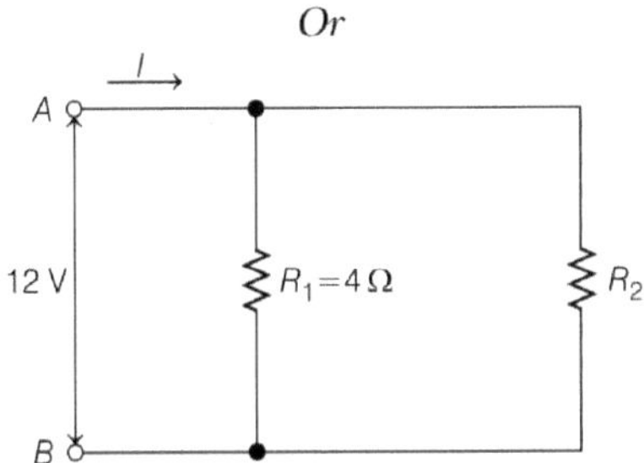

A student has two resistors $2\,\Omega$ and $3\,\Omega$. She has to put one of them in place of R_2 as shown in the circuit. The current that she needs in the entire circuit is exactly 9 A. Show by calculation which of the two resistors she should choose. **[2 M]**

6. An element X belongs to 3rd period and group 16 of the modern periodic table.

(i) Determine the number of valence electrons and the valency of X.

(ii) Molecular formula of the compound when X reacts with hydrogen and write its electron dot structure.

(iii) Name the element X and state whether it is metallic or non-metallic. **[3 M]**

Or Consider the part of periodic table given below and answer the following questions.

Group → Period↓	1	2	13	14	15	16	17	18
1	a							j
2	b	e				g	h	k
3	c			f			i	l
4	d							

(i) The atom of which element is smaller in size e or h?

(ii) Which element is the most electropositive in nature?

(iii) Which element has only one proton in its atom?

(iv) What is the valency of g?

(v) How many valence electrons does g have?

(vi) Name the element which is a metalloid. **[3 M]**

7. It is the responsibility of the government to arrange for the management and disposal of waste. As an individual you have no role to play. Do you agree. Support your answers with two reasons. **[3 M]**

Or "The chromosome number of the sexually producing parents and their offsprings is the same". Justify this statement. **[3 M]**

8. A magnetic compass needle is placed in the plane of paper near point A as shown in the figure. In which plane should a straight current carrying conductor be placed, so that it passes through A and there is no change in the deflection of the compass? Under what condition is the deflection maximum and why? **[3 M]**

Section C

9. Define all the events in correct sequence that lead to pregnancy in a female.

Or

What is meant by the word contraception? Discuss the types of surgical method of contraception.

10. (i) Describe an activity to obtain magnetic field line around current carrying straight conductor.

(ii) State the rule used to find the direction of this magnetic field.

(iii) How does magnitude of magnetic field depend on current through a conductor?

Or (i) Prachi draws magnetic field lines of field close to the axis of a current carrying circular loop. As she moves away from the centre of the circular loop. As she moves away from centre of the circular loop, she observes that the lines keep on diverging. How will you explain her observation?

(ii) How will you use a solenoid to magnetise a steel bar?

11. (i) What are hydrocarbons? Give examples.

(ii) Give the structural differences between saturated and unsaturated hydrocarbons with two examples each.

(iii) What is functional group? Give examples of four different functional groups.

Or Define structural isomer and draw the isomeric structures of butane. Compare the structure of benzene and cyclohexane by drawing them.

Answers

1. *(i) - (c); (ii) - (b); (iii) - (d); (iv) - (a, b)*

2. *(i) - (c); (ii) - (b); (iii) - (c); (iv) - (d, a)*

Practice Paper 3*

(UnSolved)

General Instructions

- Time : 2 Hours
- Max. Marks : 40

1. There are 11 questions in the question paper. All questions are compulsory.
2. **Section A**, Question no. 1 to 3 is a Case Based Questions, which has four MCQs/Questions. Each question carries one mark.
3. **Section B**, Question no. 4 to 8 are Short Answer Type Questions. Each question carries 2/3 marks.
4. **Section C**, Question no. 9-11 are Long Answer Type Questions. Each question carries 5 marks.
5. There is no overall choice. However, internal choices have been provided in some questions. Students have to attempt only one of the alternatives in such questions.

As exact Blue-print and Pattern for CBSE Term II exams is not released yet. So the pattern of this paper is designed by the author on the basis of trend of past CBSE Papers. Students are advised not to consider the pattern of this paper as official, it is just for practice purpose.

Section A

1. Read the following and answer the questions from (i) to (iv) given below

Menstrual cycle is the cycle of events taking place in female reproductive organs, under the control of sex hormones, in every 28 days.

Diagrammatic representation of various events occurring during menstrual cycle is shown below

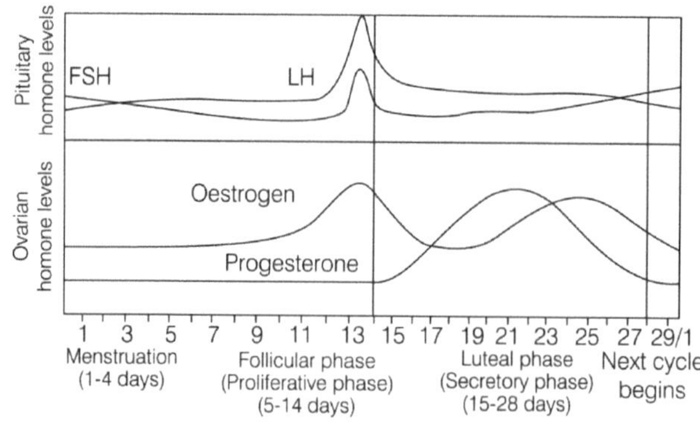

(i) What changes take place in the uterus of a menstruating female?
   (a) Release of egg into uterus
   (b) Fusion of male and female gametes
   (c) Breakdown of uterine lining
   (d) Building up of uterine lining\

(ii) Zygote differs from embryo in a manner that
   (a) it is larger in size
   (b) it is single-celled
   (c) it is multicellular
   (d) it is obtained as a result of fusion

(iii) The average duration of human pregnancy is
   (a) 7 months
   (b) 6 months
   (c) 12 months
   (d) 9 months

(iv) The release of eggs from the ovary of a human female is called

(a) ovulation   (b) menstruation
(c) pregnancy   (d) fertilisation

Or Uterus is also called

(a) ureter   (b) fallopian tube
(c) womb   (d) ovary

2. Read the following and answer the questions from (i) to (iv) given below

Food, clothes, medicines, books, or many of the things are all based on this versatile element carbon. In addition, all living structures are carbon based. The earth's crust has only 0.02% carbon in the form of minerals. The element carbon occurs in different forms in nature will widely varying physical properties. Both diamond and graphite are formed by carbon atoms, the difference lies in the manner in which the carbon atoms are bonded to one another. Carbon has the unique ability to form bonds with other atoms of carbon, giving rise to large molecules. This property is called catenation.

(i) The various layers of carbon atoms in graphite are held together by .... force?

(a) H-bonding   (b) weak van der Waals'
(c) London   (d) electrostatic

(ii) Which of the following statements is not correct?

(a) Graphite is much less dense than diamond
(b) Graphite is black and soft
(c) Graphite has low melting point
(d) Graphite feels smooth and slippery

(iii) Which of the following are isomers?

(a) Butane and isobutene   (b) Ethane and ethene
(c) Propane and propyne   (d) Butane and isobutane

(iv) Which one of the following is not an allotrope of carbon?

(a) Soot   (b) Graphite
(c) Diamond   (d) Carborundum

Or

Propane has the molecular formula C_3H_8. It has

(a) 10 covalent bonds   (b) 12 covalent bonds
(c) 8 covalent bonds   (d) 3 covalent bonds

3. Read the following and answer the questions from (i) to (iv) given below

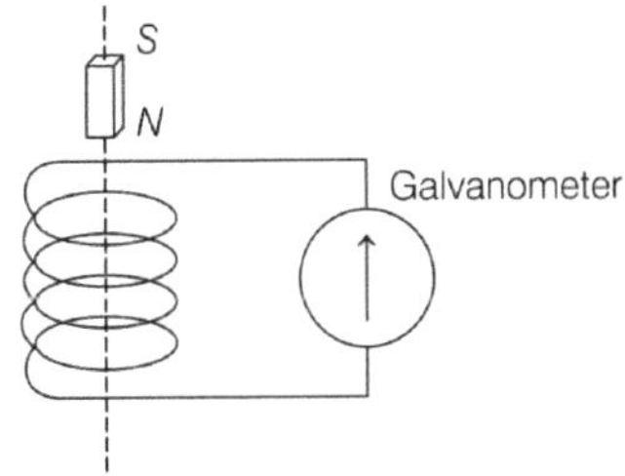

A galvanometer pointer gives a momentary deflection to the right of the zero position when it is connected to a small coil and a magnet is allowed to fall towards the coil.

(i) Where will the galvanometer pointer move, if the magnet moves through the coil and it falls away from the coil?

(ii) Predict the direction of induced current using Fleming's right hand rule.

(iii) What is the magnitude of the induced current in the circular loop KLMN of radius r, if the straight wire PQ carries a steady current of magnitude 1 ampere?

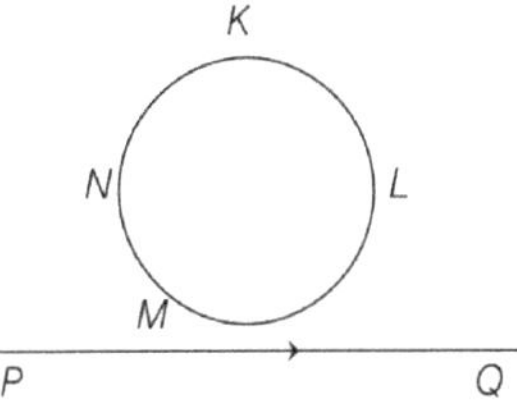

(iv) How can you show that the magnetic field produced by a given electric current in the wire decreases as the distance from the wire increases?

Or

State the phenomenon of "electromagnetic induction".

Section B

4. A plant is heterozygous for a pair of alleles. This plant is self-pollinated and the resulting seeds are germinated and allow to grow.

Write the ratios of phenotypes and genotypes of expected offsprings. **[2 M]**

5. Draw the electron dot structure of

(a) H_2S molecule
(b) Ethene **[2 M]**

Or

Write any two difference between covalent and ionic compounds. **[2 M]**

6. What is meant by pollination? Differentiate between the two modes of pollination in flowering plants. **[3 M]**

7. What is meant by non-biodegradable waste? Why is the government stressing more on the use of jute/paper bags instead of plastic bags? **[3 M]**

Or

The sperms are tiny bodies that consist of mainly genetic material and a long tail

(i) Where are the sperms produced?

(ii) What is the role of the long tail?

(iii) How are the sperms delivered from the site of their production?   **[3 M]**

8. An electric iron consumes energy at a rate of 840 W when heating is at the maximum rate and 360 W when the heating is at the minimum rate. The applied voltage is 220 V.

What is the value of current and the resistance in each case?   **[3 M]**

Or

Derive an expression for equivalent resistance in the following case

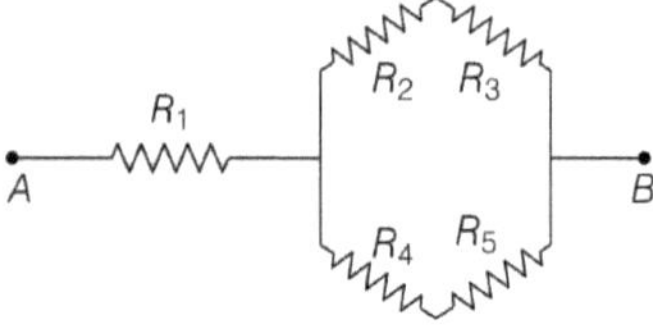

Decide which resistances are in series and parallel. Solve for series and then for parallel.

Combine both the results to get the equivalent resistance.   **[3 M]**

Section C

9. (i) State any three characteristics of sexual reproduction.

(ii) Explain what happens to the egg, once it gets fertilised in human female.

Or

What harmful effects do agricultural practices have on the environment?

10. A small valued resistance XY is connected across the ends of a coil. Predict the direction of induced current in the resistance XY, when

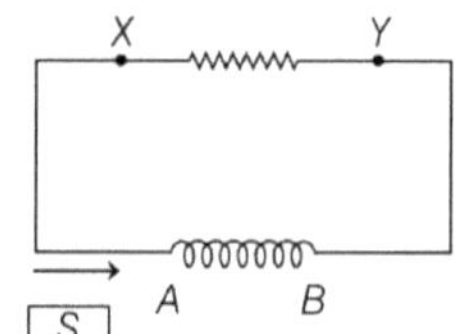

(i) South pole of a magnet moves towards end A of coil.

(ii) South pole of magnet moves away from end A of the coil.

Or A coil made of insulated copper wire is connected to a galvanometer. What will happen to the deflection of the galvanometer if this coil is moved towards a stationary bar magnet and then moved away from it? Give reason for your answer and name the phenomenon involved.

11. Consider two elements A (atomic number = 17) and B (atomic number = 19).

(i) Write the positions of these elements in the modern periodic table giving justification.

(ii) Write the formula of the compound formed when A combines with B.

(iii) Draw the electron dot structure of the compound and state the nature of the bond formed between the two elements.

Or (i) How is the valency of an element determine if its electronic configuration is known? Determine the valency of an element of atomic number 9.

(ii) Which one of the above elements belonging to the fourth period has bigger atomic radius and why?

Answers

1. (i) - (c); (ii) - (b); (iii) - (d); (iv) - (a, c)

2. (i) - (b); (ii) - (c); (iii) - (d); (iv) - (d, a)

Printed by Libri Plureos GmbH in Hamburg,
Germany